CONDUCT AND CHARACTER

Readings in Moral Theory

FIFTH EDITION

Mark Timmons
University of Arizona

THOMSON
™
WADSWORTH

Australia • Canada • Mexico • Singapore • Spain
United Kingdom • United States

THOMSON

WADSWORTH

Publisher: Holly J. Allen
Philosophy Editor: Steve Wainwright
Assistant Editors: Lee McCracken, Barbara Hillaker
Editorial Assistant: John Gahbauer
Technology Project Manager: Julie Aguilar
Marketing Manager: Worth Hawes
Marketing Assistant: Andrew Keay
Marketing Communications Manager: Laurel Anderson
Executive Art Director: Maria Epes

Print Buyer: Judy Inouye
Permissions Editor: Joohee Lee
Production Service: Matrix Productions Inc.
Copy Editor: Ann Whetstone
Cover Designer: Yvo Riezebos
Cover Image: Rafeket Kenaan/Marlena Agency
Compositor: International Typesetting
    and Composition
Cover and Text Printer: Malloy, Inc.

For more information about our products,
contact us at:
Thomson Learning Academic Resource Center
1-800-423-0563

For permission to use material from this text
or product, submit a request online at
http://www.thomsonrights.com.
Any additional questions about permissions
can be submitted by email to
thomsonrights@thomson.com.

Library of Congress Control Number: 2005921990

ISBN 0-534-58909-X

Thomson Higher Education
10 Davis Drive
Belmont, CA 94002-3098
USA

Asia (including India)
Thomson Learning
5 Shenton Way
#01-01 UIC Building
Singapore 068808

Australia/New Zealand
Thomson Learning Australia
102 Dodds Street
Southbank, Victoria 3006
Australia

Canada
Thomson Nelson
1120 Birchmount Road
Toronto, Ontario M1K 5G4
Canada

UK/Europe/Middle East/Africa
Thomson Learning
High Holborn House
50–51 Bedford Row
London WC1R 4LR
United Kingdom

Latin America
Thomson Learning
Seneca, 53
Colonia Polanco
11560 Mexico
D.F. Mexico

Spain (including Portugal)
Thomson Paraninfo
Calle Magallanes, 25
28015 Madrid, Spain

To my brothers
John, Bryan, and Andy

About the Author

Mark Timmons is professor of philosophy at the University of Arizona. He is author of Morality without Foundations (1999) and Moral Theory: An Introduction (2002). He is editor of Kant's Metaphysics of Morals: Interpretative Essays (2002) and co-editor of Moral Knowledge? (1996) and of Metaethics after Moore (2005).

Contents

Preface

This fifth edition of *Conduct and Character* includes a balance of classical and contemporary writings on moral theory designed to introduce students to the study of ethics. This book is organized according to type of moral theory and is preceded by an introductory essay, which provides students with the needed conceptual framework for understanding this field of inquiry.

This collection is suitable for ethics courses that focus on theory, and it can serve as a supplementary text for "applied" ethics courses. It can also serve as reading for an ethics component in introductory philosophy courses.

The changes I have made for this new edition are partly responsive to the valuable input I have received from those instructors who have used this book in their courses. But I have also made changes that I hope will "freshen up" this book's coverage of work in contemporary moral theory. I have added papers by David Shoemaker, "Egoisms," and Joshua Glasgow, "Kant's Principle of Universal Law," which were written for the chapters on egoism and Kantian ethical theory, respectively. I have also slightly expanded the selection from Kant by including some of his remarks about the casuistry of suicide, lying, development of one's talents, and beneficence that are from his final work in moral theory, *The Metaphysics of Morals*. I've done this to help combat the false impression that Kant's moral theory is committed to some sort of rigorism that allows no room for moral judgment in arriving at moral decisions and is therefore insensitive to morally relevant details of particular cases.

Because the term "consequentialism" has become the preferred generic term for the kind of moral theory of which utilitarianism is one species, I have changed the title of Chapter 5. And to that chapter, I have added a discussion of Mill's view by Stephen Darwall, "Utilitarianism: Act or Rule?" and Brad Hooker's article "Rule-Consequentialism." Virtue ethics and ethics of care continue to flourish in contemporary moral theory. In order to reflect some of the most interesting recent work in these areas, I have added Christine Swanton's "A Virtue Ethical Account of Right Action" and Robert N. Johnson's "Virtue and Right" to the chapter on virtue ethics and Raja Halwani's "Care Ethics and Virtue Ethics" to the chapter on the ethics of care.

Because the chapters are self-contained, they can be taught in most any order. The order I have chosen reflects the fact that in my years of teaching ethics, students often begin with questions like: "Why not just do whatever you think will benefit yourself?" "Isn't morality just a matter of what some authority like God or society says it is?" So the readings begin with chapters on egoism (Chapter 2) and on the divine command theory and ethical relativism (Chapter 3) in which such questions are considered. The chapters that follow on the natural law theory (Chapter 4), Consequentialism (Chapter 5), and Kantian moral theory (Chapter 6) represent what are now taken to be "standard" moral theories. Chapters 7 and 8 feature, respectively, readings in virtue ethics and the ethics of care, which are considered to be reactions to the more standard theories and, as I mentioned, are currently receiving much philosophical attention. Moral pluralism (not to be confused with ethical relativism) is represented in Chapter 9 along with moral particularism, which is best understood in contrast to pluralism. Particularism is often taken to represent an "anti-theory" position in ethics and is another topic of much recent debate and discussion.

I would like to thank the following reviewers, who made helpful suggestions for this new edition of *Conduct and Character*: Bryan Baird, University of Georgia; Andrew Eshleman, University of Arkansas, Little Rock; Joseph Osei, Auburn University; David W. Shoemaker, Bowling Green State University; and Brad Elliott Stone, Loyola Marymount University.

Finally, I wish to thank Steve Wainwright, my editor at Wadsworth, who prompted me to do this new edition.

M. T.

CHAPTER 1

Introduction to Moral Theory

THE NATURE AND EVALUATION OF MORAL THEORIES

> The two main concepts of ethics are those of the right and the good;... The structure of an ethical theory is, then, largely determined by how it defines and connects these two basic notions.
>
> —JOHN RAWLS

In 1997, a research team headed by Ian Wilmut at the Roslin Institute near Edinburgh, Scotland, successfully cloned a lamb who became known as "Dolly"—the first mammal ever cloned. The process of cloning involves what is called somatic cell nuclear transfer in which the nucleus from the cell of an adult is implanted in an egg cell from which the nucleus has been removed. Because successful cloning of a lamb means that it is very likely that humans can be cloned, the news of Dolly sparked a moral (and legal) controversy over cloning humans—over *reproductive cloning*. Is reproductive cloning morally wrong as its critics claim, or is it (at least sometimes) morally right as its advocates insist?

Another kind of cloning, *therapeutic cloning*, is also ethically controversial and at the heart of debates over the morality of stem cell research. A stem cell, extracted from a human embryo, can presumably grow into any of the body's cell types. Many scientists hope to be able to use stem cells to treat many diseases including diabetes and Parkinson's disease. The idea would be to create human embryos that are specifically fashioned to match patients' tissue. However, the process of extracting stem cells from human embryos inevitably destroys those embryos. Because many people find the destruction of human embryos morally problematic, stem cell research is controversial.[1] Again, is therapeutic cloning morally wrong or is it (at least sometimes) morally right?

1

The ethics of human cloning is but one of a large number of morally controversial actions and practices. Readers are no doubt familiar with some of the moral controversy that surrounds abortion, the death penalty, euthanasia, homosexuality, discrimination, the treatment of animals, and the environment. And, as in the case of cloning, each of these issues raises general moral questions—basic questions about the rightness and wrongness of various actions and practices.

In addition to questions about the morality of actions, we also judge the goodness and badness of persons. What makes someone a morally good or morally bad person? Ethics is the branch of philosophy that addresses basic philosophical questions about the right and the good, and philosophers who attempt to answer such questions in a systematic way offer theories—*moral theories*—about the right and the good. Because philosophers offer competing answers to such questions, there are competing moral theories that are the focus of debate in ethics.

This anthology contains writings that explore some of the major theories in ethics—moral theories that are both historically influential and of current philosophical interest. But what is a moral theory? And how can competing moral theories be evaluated? This introduction addresses these and related questions so that the beginning student will have a framework for understanding the writings that follow.

In order to have a basic understanding of moral theory, there are five main tasks to accomplish. First, we need to clarify the basic *concepts* featured in a moral theory— the concepts of the right and the good (as well as those of the wrong and the bad). Second, we need to explain the *guiding aims* of a moral theory—what such a theory sets out to accomplish. Third, we need to explain the importance of moral principles in a moral theory. Fourth, the structure of a moral theory is determined by how it *connects* the concepts of the right and the good, and so we need to indicate some of the ways different theories connect these concepts and thus differ in structure. Finally, we need to explain some of the main *standards* that are used in evaluating a moral theory. In what follows, let us take up these tasks in order.

Basic Moral Concepts

As the opening quote from John Rawls indicates, the basic concepts in ethics are the concepts of the right and the good. They are often referred to respectively as the deontic and value concepts.

DEONTIC CONCEPTS

When we evaluate the morality of an action, we are primarily interested in whether the action is right or wrong. More precisely, we are interested in whether an action is *obligatory*, *wrong*, or *optional*. These are often called *deontic* concepts or categories (from the Greek word "deon" that means duty) because they concern what we ought to do (and hence have a duty to perform) or ought not to do (and hence have a duty not to perform). Here is a brief description of each of these categories.

Obligatory actions. An obligatory action is one that a person morally ought to perform. Typically, we refer to such actions as *duties*. Other terms used for this category include *required* and *right*. (Use of the term "right" requires special comment. See below.)

Wrong actions. An action is wrong when it is one that a person ought not to perform. Other terms used for this category include *forbidden, impermissible,* and *contrary to duty.*

Optional actions. An action is optional when it is neither obligatory nor wrong—one is morally permitted to perform the action, but is not required to. Sometimes actions in this category are referred to as *merely permissible* ("merely" because, although both optional actions and obligatory actions are permissible, actions of the former type are not required).

Obviously, these brief characterizations are not intended as illuminating definitions of these basic deontic concepts. To be told that an *obligatory* action is one that a person *ought* to perform is hardly illuminating. However, I hope these descriptions convey an intuitive sense of how these basic categories are understood in ethics.

What about the concept of the *right*? Talk of right action in ethics has both a narrow and a broad meaning. When it is used narrowly, to say that an action is right is to say that it is obligatory. We are using it this way when we say of someone that she did *the* right thing (she did what she morally ought to have done). But sometimes the term is used broadly to mean simply that an act is not wrong. Sometimes, for instance, when we say that what someone did was right, we mean that what he did was morally in the clear—that it was all right for him to do, that it was not wrong. Talk of right action in the broad sense covers both obligatory and optional actions. So when someone claims that an action is morally right, it is important to make clear whether she is using the term "right" narrowly or broadly. Figure 1.1 summarizes where "right" is used in the broad sense to mean "not wrong."

VALUE CONCEPTS

In addition to morally evaluating actions, we also evaluate people and other things as being good or bad. The concepts of the good and the bad are the basic value concepts. To say that something is good is to say that it has positive value, whereas to say that something is bad is to say that it has negative value. To understand more clearly the philosophical investigation into the nature of value, we

FIGURE 1.1   Deontic Concepts.

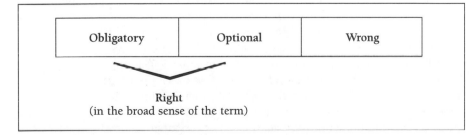

must begin by distinguishing between things with intrinsic value and things with extrinsic value.

To say that something has intrinsic positive value—that it is *intrinsically good*—is to say that there is something about *it* that makes it good in itself. In other words, its goodness is based on something that is inherent to the thing in question. (Intrinsic negative value or badness is understood in an analogous way.) By contrast, to say that something is merely *extrinsically good* is to say that it possesses its goodness because of how it is related to something that is intrinsically good. Here is an example.

Many people would agree that money is a good thing to possess. But in virtue of what is it good? Clearly, it is not something about the bits of paper and metal that compose money that make it good. Rather, the goodness of money is explained by the fact that it is useful *as a means* for obtaining things and services that are either intrinsically good or contribute to what has intrinsic value. Thus, assuming that money has positive value of some sort, it is merely extrinsically good.

Because the idea of extrinsic value is explained in terms of intrinsic value, the latter notion is the more basic of the two. Hence, in giving a theory of value, philosophers focus on intrinsic value. In doing so, they are concerned with the question of what makes something intrinsically good or intrinsically bad *in itself*. Things that are neither intrinsically good nor bad are intrinsically value-neutral.[2]

MORAL AND NONMORAL VALUE

Philosophers often distinguish between *moral value* and *nonmoral value*. Both types of value are important in ethics and require a brief explanation. Only responsible agents who can be praised or blamed, that is, *persons*, are capable of possessing (positive or negative) moral value or worth. In describing someone as morally good (or bad), we are saying something about that person's character. A morally good person is a person who has a virtuous character—who has certain positive character traits—whereas a morally bad person is one who has a vicious character—who has certain negative character traits. Some of the virtuous character traits include *honesty*, *beneficence*, *courage*, and *justice*, whereas the traits of *dishonesty*, *indifference to others*, *cowardice*, and *injustice* are among the vices. So a theory of moral value addresses the question of what makes someone a morally good or bad person.

Other items that have value—things, experiences, and states of affairs—possess nonmoral value. The term "nonmoral" only means that items possessing this sort of value are not responsible agents who can be praised or blamed. For example, some philosophers hold that experiences of pleasure are intrinsically good and that experiences of pain are intrinsically bad. Of course, pleasure and pain are experiences of persons, but such experiences—as experiences—are not agents who can be praised or blamed for anything. If an experience of pleasure is intrinsically good, then we say that it possesses positive nonmoral value.

Why is nonmoral value of any interest in ethics? The answer is that some philosophers have defended moral theories that make the rightness and wrongness of actions depend on how they promote what has intrinsic nonmoral value. One example would be a theory that accepts the following two claims: (1) the deontic status of an action (its rightness or wrongness) depends entirely upon how much intrinsic goodness or badness it would produce if performed and (2) pleasure alone is intrinsically good and pain alone is intrinsically bad.[3]

The Aims of a Moral Theory

Now that we have clarified the main concepts involved in moral evaluation, let us proceed to consider the guiding aims of a moral theory. Like any theory, a moral theory is supposed to satisfy certain aims that motivate and guide its development. There are two primary aims of moral theory prompted by what we have already identified as some of the main questions in ethics: a *theoretical* aim and a *practical* aim. Let us consider these in order.

First, there are questions about the *underlying nature* of right and wrong, good and bad—of duty and value. What makes an action right or wrong? What makes something good or bad?

The idea is that an action's being right or wrong depends on certain features of the action. One main aim of a moral theory is to reveal those features of actions that explain *why* they are right or wrong. Revealing such features would provide us with a theoretical understanding of the nature of right and wrong (similarly for good and bad) and serve as *criteria* of the right and the good. Thus, we can express the theoretical aim of a moral theory this way:

> *Theoretical Aim.* The theoretical aim of a moral theory is to reveal those underlying features of actions, persons, and other items of moral evaluation that make them right or wrong, good or bad. The underlying features that explain what makes an action right or wrong serve as moral criteria of rightness. The underlying features of persons and other items of evaluation that explain what makes them good or bad serve as criteria of value.

In addition to theoretical questions about the underlying nature of duty and value, philosophers are also interested in practical questions about what sort of method we might follow in figuring out what is dutiful or valuable in specific contexts of decision making. What method or procedure should we follow in trying to reach correct moral verdicts about the rightness and wrongness of actions and the goodness and badness of persons and other items of evaluation?

Just a scientists employ scientific methodology in coming to conclusions about matters of scientific dispute, moral philosophers hope to discover a proper methodology—a *decision procedure*—that could be used to arrive at correct or justified conclusions about matters of moral inquiry. Thus, the practical aim of moral theory can be expressed this way:

> *Practical aim.* The practical aim of moral theory is to discover a decision procedure that can be used to guide correct moral reasoning and decision making about matters of moral concern.

The theoretical and practical aims of moral theory are often thought to be related in that if we have theoretical knowledge about morality and thus know what makes an action right or wrong, then we might expect that a proper moral decision procedure would make use of such knowledge. In order to understand this point more clearly, let us consider the role of moral principles in a moral theory.

The Role of Moral Principles in a Moral Theory

A moral principle is a very general moral statement that purports to set forth conditions under which an action is right or wrong, or something is good or bad. Here is an example of a moral principle:

An action is wrong if and only if it would involve treating others as mere means to one's own ends.

Putting aside the question of whether this moral principle is correct, the main thing to notice is that it states a connection between an action's being morally wrong and its involving treatment of others as mere means to one's own ends. Moral principles have traditionally played a central role in attempts by moral philosophers to accomplish the theoretical and practical aims of moral theory.

Suppose we discover that what makes any action wrong is the fact that it would involve treating someone as a mere means to one's own ends. We could then conveniently express this theoretical knowledge by using the above moral principle. A moral principle, understood this way, would thus serve to satisfy the theoretical aim of a moral theory by providing a moral criterion.

Furthermore, with this moral principle in hand, we would presumably also have the basis of a proper decision procedure in ethics. The idea is that we apply the principle to a case under consideration in order to arrive at a correct or justified moral verdict about some specific action. A sample application of the moral principle in question is provided in Figure 1.2.

FIGURE 1.2   Sample Application of a Moral Principle.

Argument Component	Argument Scheme	Example Argument
Premise	1. Moral principle	1´. An action is wrong if and only if it would involve treating some person merely as a means to one's own ends.
Premise	2. Relevant factual information	2´. James's act of lying to Brenda involved treating Brenda merely as a means to James's own ends.
Conclusion	3. Conclusion about the morality of an action	3´. James's act of lying to Brenda was wrong.

A moral theory, then, is typically understood as composed of moral principles cast in a dual role. First, moral principles are intended to satisfy the theoretical aim of moral theory by stating those basic underlying features that make an action right or wrong, or make something good or bad. Second, such principles are also supposed to provide the basis of a decision procedure for coming to correct moral verdicts in specific situations.[4]

The Structure of a Moral Theory

In the quote at the beginning of this chapter, Rawls claims that the main concepts in ethics are the concepts of the right and the good. From what we have learned, we now know that ethics is concerned with the moral evaluation of conduct (rightness and wrongness) and with character (goodness and badness of persons). In addition, we have learned that ethics is also concerned with the nonmoral value (goodness and badness) of things, experiences, and states of affairs.

Let us say that an account of the nature of right and wrong action represents a *theory of right conduct*. Let us call an account of the nature of value a *theory of value*, and because we distinguish between moral and nonmoral value, a theory of value has two branches: a *theory of moral value* and a *theory of nonmoral value*. Figure 1.3 shows the various main branches of moral theory.

One question addressed by a moral theory is how these branches are related. Again, Rawls claims that the *structure* of a moral theory is determined by how a theory connects the concepts of the right and the good. For example, according to what we may call *value-based* theories, the concept of the good is more basic than the concept of the right. By contrast, according to *deontic-based* theories—often called *deontological* moral theories—the concept of the good is not more basic than the concept of the right.[5]

Among value-based theories, some take the concepts of nonmoral value to be most basic. Such theories define or characterize right action in terms of how actions and character traits are related to what has intrinsic nonmoral value. The natural law theory, featured in Chapter 4, and consequentialism, featured in

FIGURE 1.3   Main Branches of Moral Theory.

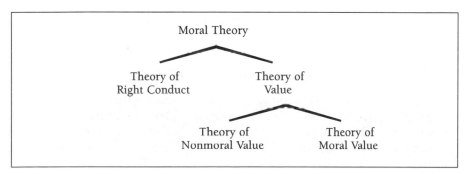

Chapter 5, are representatives of this kind of theory. By contrast, other value-based moral theories—versions of virtue ethics, represented in Chapter 7—take the category of moral value to be more basic than the category of right action. Such theories define or characterize right action in terms of some relation between actions and the notion of a virtuous person.

A deontological theory characterizes the rightness and wrongness of actions independently of considerations of value. Kant's ethics (Chapter 6) and the version of moral pluralism defended by W. D. Ross (Chapter 9) are representatives of this type of theory.

Brief Summary

Before turning to the question of how we are to evaluate a moral theory, let us sum up the main points from the previous sections.

Main concepts of moral theory. The two main concepts featured in moral theory are the concepts of the right (and wrong) and the good (and bad). The concepts of right and wrong are called "deontic" concepts and are used primarily to evaluate the morality of actions. The concepts of good and bad are the main concepts of value and are used in the moral evaluation of persons (their character) as well as in the evaluation of things, experiences, and states of affairs.

Two aims of moral theory. There are two main aims characteristic of moral theory. The theoretical aim is to explain the underlying nature of the right and the good by specifying criteria of the right and the good. The practical aim is to discover a decision procedure that can guide us in making correct decisions about matters of morality.

The role of moral principles. A moral theory is typically composed of moral principles that are intended to serve as criteria of the right and the good (thus satisfying the theoretical aim) and as the basis for a decision procedure (thus satisfying the practical aim).

The structure of moral theory. Considerations of structure concern how a theory connects the right and the good. Value-based theories make the good (value) more basic than the right and define or characterize the right in terms of the good. Deontological theories, by contrast, characterize the right independently of considerations of value.

How to Evaluate a Moral Theory

In this section, I will describe some of the main standards that are used to evaluate competing moral theories. But before doing so, let me recommend that readers who are studying moral theory for the first time return to this section when reading those articles that raise objections to the various theories featured in each chapter.

As we have seen, a moral theory has both a theoretical and practical aim. So it makes sense to evaluate such a theory by considering how well it satisfies these aims. How do we do this? There are various standards or criteria that philosophers have developed for determining how well a moral theory does in relation to the main theoretical and practical aims. Here, then, is a list of some criteria for evaluating a moral theory.

CONSISTENCY

One expects a moral theory to be consistent in its moral verdicts about what is right or wrong, or good or bad. One obvious way in which a moral theory might fail to be consistent is when its principles, together with relevant factual information, yield a conclusion that some specific concrete action is both right and wrong. We can express the *consistency criterion* as follows:

A moral theory should be consistent in the sense that its principles, together with relevant factual information, yield consistent moral verdicts about the morality of actions, persons, and other items of moral evaluation.

We should be careful here. If a theory leads to the conclusion that some concrete action, performed by a specific individual on a specific occasion, both is and it not obligatory (for example), then it is guilty of inconsistency. Similarly, if a theory leads to the conclusion that some general *type* of action both is and is not wrong (for example), then, again, it is inconsistent. But it is not inconsistent for a theory to yield the result that in *general* lying is wrong and at the same time yield the result that in *some specific case* a concrete act of telling a lie is not wrong. There need be no inconsistency here, because from the outset the claim that lying is wrong has been limited by the implicit modifier in *general*, implying that the normal rule may, in special circumstances, have exceptions.

It should be fairly obvious why this criterion is important for satisfying both aims of a moral theory. If a theory yields inconsistent moral verdicts about the morality of an action, then it simply fails to be useful as a decision procedure. Furthermore, if a moral theory yields inconsistent verdicts about items of moral evaluation, then presumably it fails to provide a correct moral criterion that explains the underlying nature of morality. So, consistency is a hallmark of a correct moral theory.

DETERMINACY

To say that a moral theory is determinate is to say that, at least in a large range of cases, its principles yield definite moral verdicts about whatever is being evaluated. When the principles of a moral theory (together with any relevant factual information) fail to yield a definite verdict about the morality of an action, then with respect to that action, the theory is indeterminate. Suppose, for instance, that a moral theory features a principle according to which an action is right if and only if it is respectful of persons. Unless the theory goes on to specify in a fairly specific way what counts as being respectful of persons, this principle (and hence the theory in question) will fail to yield determinate moral verdicts about a large range of actions. For example, is the death penalty respectful of persons? What about euthanasia? What about telling a lie in order to spare someone's feelings? So according to the *determinacy criterion*:

A moral theory should feature principles that, together with relevant factual information, yield determinate moral verdicts about the morality of actions, persons, and other items of moral evaluation in a wide range of cases.

A moral theory that is too indeterminate will fail to provide a useful decision procedure and thus fail to satisfy the practical aim of moral theory. Furthermore, if a theory features moral principles that are indeterminate, this may indicate that the theory fails to pinpoint those underlying features of actions, persons, and other items of moral evaluation that explain why they have the moral qualities they have. In this way, an indeterminate moral theory fails to satisfy the theoretical aim of moral theory.

APPLICABILITY

A moral principle might satisfy the consistency and determinacy standards yet still fail to be very useful as a decision procedure. Suppose a moral theory makes the rightness of an action depend on how much happiness it would bring about for all of those who will ever be affected by the action. Presumably, this principle, together with relevant factual information, logically implies consistent moral verdicts and verdicts that are determinate. Unfortunately, as human beings, we often are incapable of obtaining reliable information about the affects of our actions. In such cases, a principle like the one in question cannot be used as the basis of a useful decision procedure owing to limits on human knowledge about morally relevant facts. In such cases, we say that a principle lacks applicability. Thus, according to the *applicability criterion*:

The principles of a moral theory should be applicable in the sense that they specify relevant information about actions and other items of evaluation that human beings can typically obtain and use to arrive at moral verdicts on the basis of those principles.

Obviously, the rationale behind the applicability standard is the practical aim of a moral theory. The next three standards concern the theoretical aim of providing correct moral criteria.

INTERNAL SUPPORT

Although there is moral disagreement and uncertainty over moral issues such as abortion, euthanasia, the death penalty, homosexuality, and other controversial issues, there is widespread moral agreement about other issues of moral concern. For instance, we agree that rape is wrong, that killing innocent persons is wrong, that torture is wrong, that helping others is by and large right, and so forth.

In addition to being widely shared and deeply held, such moral beliefs are ones we would continue to hold were we to reflect carefully on their correctness. Let us call these moral beliefs our *considered moral beliefs*.

In determining whether the principles of a moral theory are correct, we test them by seeing whether they cohere with our considered moral beliefs. The idea is that when a moral principle, together with relevant factual information, logically implies one of our considered moral beliefs, then this counts in favor of the correctness of the principle. Thus, having correct moral implications tends to confirm a moral principle and the theory that includes it. On the other hand, when a moral principle, together with relevant factual information, implies moral verdicts that conflict with our considered moral beliefs, this counts against the correctness of the principle. Because this way of testing a moral principle is based on appealing to our considered *moral* beliefs—beliefs *internal* to morality—let us call it the *criterion of internal support*:

A moral theory whose principles, together with relevant factual information, imply our considered moral beliefs receives support—internal support—from those beliefs. On the other hand, if the principles of a theory have implications that conflict with our considered moral beliefs, this is evidence against the correctness of the theory.

Obviously, the rationale behind this standard is the theoretical aim of finding correct moral criteria.

EXTERNAL SUPPORT

Although the standard of internal support has to do with how well a moral theory coheres with beliefs internal to morality, the standard of external support has to do with how well a moral theory coheres with beliefs and assumptions from other fields of inquiry—fields of inquiry *external* to morality. The philosopher J. L. Mackie (1912–82) expressed the idea behind this standard when he wrote that "Moral principles and ethical theories do not stand alone: they affect and are affected by beliefs and assumptions which belong to other fields, and not the least to psychology, metaphysics, and religion."[6] Thus, a moral theory is more likely to be correct when its principles are corroborated by well-established beliefs and theories from other areas of nonmoral inquiry.

Thus, according to the *criterion of external support*:

The fact that the principles of a moral theory are supported by well-established nonmoral beliefs and assumptions (especially those from areas of nonmoral inquiry) is some evidence in favor of the theory. On the other hand, the fact that the principles of some moral theory conflict with established nonmoral beliefs and assumptions is some evidence against the theory.

As readers will discover in the chapters to follow, moral philosophers often appeal to beliefs and assumptions from areas of nonmoral inquiry in seeking support for their favored theory. For instance, advocates of the divine command theory often attempt to support the principles of that theory by appealing to theological premises. One argument for moral relativism appeals to considerations from cultural anthropology.

EXPLANATORY POWER

However, in order for a moral theory to satisfy the theoretical aim, it is not enough that its principles satisfy the standards of internal and external support. We are in search of principles that *explain* what makes an action right or wrong and what *makes* something good or bad. Thus, according to the *criterion of explanatory power*:

A moral theory should feature principles that explain why actions, persons, and other items of evaluation are right or wrong, good or bad.

In order to understand the importance of this standard, suppose there were an omnipotent moral sage who has great moral insight and for every action knows its deontic status—that is, knows whether it is right or wrong. We could then formulate a moral principle that said that an action is right if and only if the sage believes that it is right. Given that the sage really does have knowledge of the morality of every action, this principle (together with information about what the sage believes) would logically imply all of our considered moral beliefs (assuming that such beliefs are correct). In short, this principle would perfectly satisfy the criterion of internal support. But we would not want to say that this principle *explains why* an action is right or wrong. It is not the fact that the sage believes that a certain action is wrong that makes it wrong! Thus, the principle in question does not satisfy the standard of explanatory power.

Clearly, only when a moral theory satisfies the standard of explanatory power can we conclude that the theory satisfies the theoretical aim of moral theory. We may think of the standards of internal support and external support as being at the service of this more basic standard. Satisfying the standards of internal support and external support is a good indication (though not ironclad proof) that the theory also satisfies the standard of explanatory power.

To sum up, the criteria for evaluating a moral theory are represented by the standards of *consistency*, *determinacy*, *applicability*, *internal support*, *external support*, and *explanatory power*. The first three standards are particularly important for determining how well a theory satisfies the practical aim of moral theorizing, whereas the latter three are particularly important for determining how well a theory satisfies the theoretical aim of such theorizing.

In using these standards to evaluate a moral theory, here are two points to keep in mind. First, satisfying these standards is a matter of degree. For instance, the moral principles of a theory can be more or less determinate, and so forth for the other standards on our list.

Second, evaluating a moral theory is a comparative matter. That is, in order to judge the overall plausibility of any one moral theory, one needs to consider its competitors and how well they satisfy the various standards of evaluation. We are looking for a moral theory that is best overall—one that beats out the competition.

But exactly how are we to judge the *overall* adequacy of moral theory? Because there is a plurality of standards, we may find that one theory does better than its competitors in satisfying some, but not all, of the evaluative standards. Obviously, if one moral theory outperforms a competitor with regard to each of the six standards, then it is the more satisfactory of the two. But in other cases, where some of the standards favor one theory and others favor a competing theory, judging the overall superiority is not an easy matter. Although this may be disconcerting to someone just beginning the study of moral theory, it might be of some comfort to know that the same sort of difficulty arises in connection with evaluating scientific theories. There is a plurality of standards used for evaluating the overall plausibility of scientific theories, and sometimes one such theory will be favored by some of the relevant standards whereas another, competing theory, will be favored by some of the other standards. But such disputes do not undermine the validity or worth of scientific theorizing, and neither should analogous disputes among moral philosophers be taken to undermine the validity or worth of moral theorizing.

Preview

We have now completed our overview of some of the main ingredients of and standards for evaluating a moral theory. In the chapters to follow, readers will become acquainted with some varieties of the following moral theories:

Ethical egoism (Chapter 2)
Divine command theory (Chapter 3)
Moral relativism (Chapter 3)
Natural law theory (Chapter 4)
Consequentialism (Chapter 5)
Kant's moral theory (Chapter 6)
Virtue ethics (Chapter 7)
Ethics of care (Chapter 8)
Moral pluralism (Chapter 9)
Moral particularism (Chapter 9)

Many of these theories build on ideas that will be familiar to the reader. To see this, let us briefly revisit the ethical controversy surrounding human cloning—specifically, therapeutic cloning—with which we began.

If one examines letters to editors of newspapers and magazines, online discussions, and published articles on the topic, a variety of moral reasons are used in debating the issue of therapeutic human cloning. For instance, some argue that therapeutic cloning is morally wrong because (they claim) it is forbidden by God. The familiar idea that an action's rightness or wrongness is to be explained by facts about what God does and does not forbid is central to the *divine command theory* of morality.

By contrast, others argue that because cloning does not (in their opinion) violate any of the basic moral norms of our society it is not morally wrong. Their idea is that the rightness and wrongness of an action depends on the norms of one's culture or society. In essence, this is the main idea behind *moral relativism*.

Again, some opponents of cloning have argued that this kind of action is unnatural and thus morally wrong. The idea that an action's rightness or wrongness has essentially to do with whether or not the action is natural is certainly familiar (think of one of the often heard moral arguments against homosexuality) and represents the *natural law* tradition in moral theory.

Much of the controversy over the morality of therapeutic cloning focuses on the expected consequences of such a practice. Some argue that the practice of cloning will lead to grave social harms such as the cloning of "human" monsters. Others argue that at least some therapeutic cloning will have overall beneficial social consequences including advances in the treatment of various diseases. The guiding assumption in this particular dispute about the overall social consequences of cloning is that the morality of an action or practice is determined by the value of its consequences, a familiar and guiding idea of the moral theory known as *consequentialism*.

Other moral considerations that are brought to bear on the moral issue of cloning are similarly related to other moral theories featured in this book. So although readers may be studying ethics for the first time, many of the core ideas featured in these theories are familiar. In fact, one may think of the various theories featured in the readings to follow as attempts to develop such familiar ideas in a rigorous philosophical manner. This anthology, then, is an invitation to explore these ideas that are often taken for granted but only vaguely understood.[7]

Notes

1. The ethical controversy over therapeutic cloning prompted debates over government-sponsored financial support for stem cell research. On August 9, 2001, U.S. President George W. Bush announced that the government would approve and financially support research on colonies of stem cell lines already in existence (at the time of his announcement) but that it would not support the therapeutic cloning of new stem cell lines.

2. Notice that it is possible for something to be both intrinsically good and also extrinsically good at the same time. For example, some philosophers claim that possessing knowledge is one of the things that is intrinsically good. But these philosophers also recognize that having knowledge can also be good as a means and hence extrinsically good as well. If, for example, happiness is also something that is intrinsically good, then because having knowledge can be a means to happiness, knowledge is extrinsically good.

3. For an illuminating and slightly more detailed discussion of the various senses of "good" (including the distinction between moral and nonmoral value), see William Frankena, *Ethics*, 2nd ed. (Englewood Cliffs, NJ: Prentice-Hall, 1973), 62 and 79–83.

4. However, it should be noted that some moral theories feature principles that are intended to provide moral criteria and thus satisfy the theoretical aim of moral theory but are not intended to provide a useful decision procedure. Still, a complete moral theory will address both the theoretical and practical aims, even if the principles it features do not serve as both criteria and decision procedure.

5. One finds various labels that are used to classify moral theories in terms of structure. For instance, "teleological" and "consequentialist" are often used (sometimes interchangeably, sometimes not) in connection with certain varieties of what I am calling value-based theories. Moreover, the label "deontological" is often used to characterize those theories (some of them value-based) according to which morality sometimes requires that we not maximize good consequences. (The natural law theory featured in Chapter 4 is an example of such a theory.) Finally, among those theories typically classified as deontological, some of them are really a hybrid. Like a value-based theory, they make the rightness of certain types of actions dependent on considerations of value; but like a pure deontological theory, they make the rightness of other types of action independent of considerations of value. The moral theory of W. D. Ross (featured in Chapter 9) is an example of such a hybrid theory.

6. J. L. Mackie, *Ethics: Inventing Right and Wrong* (Harmondsworth, Middlesex, England: Penguin Books, 1977), 203.

7. This essay is a substantially revised version of the introductory essay featured in previous editions of this anthology. Much of it is based on Chapter 1 of my book *Moral Theory: An Introduction* (Lanham, MD: Rowman and Littlefield, 2002).

CHAPTER 2

Egoism

THE MYTH OF GYGES
Plato

Plato (428–348 B.C.E.) was a student of Socrates and a teacher of Aristotle. In a famous passage from The Republic, *Glaucon (one of the characters in the dialogue) argues to Socrates that, by nature, human beings are egoists strongly inclined to pursue their own self-interest. Thus "those who practice justice do so against their will because they lack the power to do wrong." To illustrate his point, Glaucon recounts the story of Gyges.*

So, if you agree, I will do the following: I will renew the argument of Thrasymachus; I will first state what people consider the nature and origin of justice; secondly, that all who practise it do so unwillingly as being something necessary but not good; thirdly, that they have good reason to do so, for, according to what people say, the life of the unjust man is much better than that of the just....

Splendid, he said, then listen while I deal with the first subject I mentioned: the nature and origin of justice.

They say that to do wrong is naturally good, to be wronged is bad, but the suffering of injury so far exceeds in badness the good of inflicting it that when men have done wrong to each other and suffered it, and have had a taste of both, those who are unable to avoid the latter and practise the former decide that it is profitable to come to an agreement with each other neither to inflict injury nor to suffer it. As a result they begin to make laws and covenants, and the law's command they call lawful and just. This, they say, is the origin and essence of justice; it stands between the best and the worst, the best being to do wrong without paying the penalty and the worst to be wronged without the power of revenge. The just then is a mean between two extremes; it is welcomed and honoured because of men's lack of the power to do wrong. The man who has that power, the real

From G. M. A. Grube, trans., *Plato's Republic*, copyright © 1974, revised 1992. Reprinted by permission of Hacket Publishing Co., Inc.

man, would not make a compact with anyone not to inflict injury or suffer it. For him that would be madness. This then, Socrates, is, according to their argument, the nature and origin of justice.

Even those who practise justice do so against their will because they lack the power to do wrong. This we could realize very clearly if we imagined ourselves granting to both the just and the unjust the freedom to do whatever they liked. We could then follow both of them and observe where their desires led them, and we would catch the just man redhanded travelling the same road as the unjust. The reason is the desire for undue gain which every organism by nature pursues as a good, but the law forcibly sidetracks him to honour equality. The freedom I just mentioned would most easily occur if these men had the power which they say the ancestor of the Lydian Gyges possessed. The story is that he was a shepherd in the service of the ruler of Lydia. There was a violent rainstorm and an earthquake which broke open the ground and created a chasm at the place where he was tending sheep. Seeing this and marvelling, he went down into it. He saw, besides many other wonders of which we are told, a hollow bronze horse. There were window-like openings in it; he climbed through them and caught sight of a corpse which seemed of more than human stature, wearing nothing but a ring of gold on its finger. This ring the shepherd put on and came out. He arrived at the usual monthly meeting which reported to the king on the state of the flocks, wearing the ring. As he was sitting among the others he happened to twist the hoop of the ring towards himself, to the inside of his hand, and as he did this he became invisible to those sitting near him and they went on talking as if he had gone. He marvelled at this and, fingering the ring, he turned the hoop outward again and became visible. Perceiving this he tested whether the ring had this power and so it happened: if he turned the hoop inwards he became invisible, but was visible when he turned it outwards. When he realized this, he at once arranged to become one of the messengers to the king. He went, committed adultery with the king's wife, attacked the king with her help, killed him, and took over the kingdom.

Now if there were two such rings, one worn by the just man, the other by the unjust, no one, as these people think, would be so incorruptible that he would stay on the path of justice or bring himself to keep away from other people's property and not touch it, when he could with impunity take whatever he wanted from the market, go into houses and have sexual relations with anyone he wanted, kill anyone, free all those he wished from prison, and do the other things which would make him like a god among men. His actions would be in no way different from those of the other and they would both follow the same path. This, some would say, is a great proof that no one is just willingly but under compulsion, so that justice is not one's private good, since wherever either thought he could do wrong with impunity he would do so. Every man believes that injustice is much more profitable to himself than justice, and any exponent of this argument will say that he is right. The man who did not wish to do wrong with that opportunity, and did not touch other people's property, would be thought by those who knew it to be very foolish and miserable. They would praise him in public, thus deceiving one another, for fear of being wronged. So much for my second topic.

As for the choice between the lives we are discussing, we shall be able to make a correct judgment about it only if we put the most just man and the most unjust man face to face; otherwise we cannot do so. By face to face I mean this: let us grant to the unjust the fullest degree of injustice and to the just the fullest justice, each being perfect in his own pursuit. First, the unjust man will act as clever craftsmen do—a top navigator for example or physician distinguishes what his craft can do and what it cannot; the former he will undertake, the latter he will pass by, and when he slips he can put things right. So the unjust man's correct attempts at wrongdoing must remain secret; the one who is caught must be considered a poor performer, for the extreme of injustice is to have a reputation for justice, and our perfectly unjust man must be granted perfection in injustice. We must not take this from him, but we must allow that, while committing the greatest crimes, he has provided himself with the greatest reputation for justice; if he makes a slip he must be able to put it right; he must be a sufficiently persuasive speaker if some wrongdoing of his is made public; he must be able to use force, where force is needed, with the help of his courage, his strength, and the friends and wealth with which he has provided himself.

Having described such a man, let us now in our argument put beside him the just man, simple as he is and noble, who, as Aeschylus put it, does not wish to appear just but to be so. We must take away his reputation, for a reputation for justice would bring him honour and rewards, and it would then not be clear whether he is what he is for justice's sake or for the sake of rewards and honour. We must strip him of everything except justice and make him the complete opposite of the other. Though he does no wrong, he must have the greatest reputation for wrongdoing so that he may be tested for justice by not weakening under ill repute and its consequences. Let him go his incorruptible way until death with a reputation for injustice throughout his life, just though he is, so that our two men reach the extremes, one of justice, the other of injustice, and let them be judged as to which of the two is the happier....

EGOISMS
David W. Shoemaker

David W. Shoemaker is assistant professor of philosophy at Bowling Green State University and author of many articles in ethics. *Ethical egoism makes the rightness or wrongness of actions depend on facts about one's self-interest. Thus, for instance, according to a very familiar version of this view, the right action for you to perform on some occasion is whichever alternative action (open to you on that occasion) will maximize your well-being. Some thinkers are led to this view because they believe psychological egoism—a thesis about human motivation according to which all human actions are ultimately done for the sake of the actor's self-interest. Shoemaker explains why the inference from psychological egoism to ethical egoism is fallacious (which, of course, does not refute either thesis) and then proceeds to critically examine both types of egoism. He concludes that all forms of psychological egoism are false, but he is more optimistic about the prospects for defending ethical egoism. Shoemaker distinguishes act from rule versions of ethical egoism and (using the set of evaluative criteria discussed in the introduction), he explains how a version of rule ethical egoism can seemingly satisfy these criteria. His cautious conclusion about ethical egoism is that, although it can withstand many standard objections that are thought to easily "refute" the view, there are some lingering worries that any of its defenders must face. (Readers should compare Shoemaker's distinction between act ethical egoism and rule ethical egoism with a similar distinction that comes up in Chapter 5 between act and rule consequentialism.)*

In a famous episode of the TV show *Friends*, Joey flummoxes Phoebe with his claim that "selfless good deeds don't exist." In other words, nothing you ever do is done solely for the sake of someone else's benefit, for there's always a benefit to yourself involved. Phoebe sets out to prove him wrong, but every time she seems to find a case that does so, she's thwarted. She first sneaks over to rake the leaves off the porch of her senior citizen neighbor, but he catches her, "force feeds" her cider and cookies, and "then I felt wonderful—that old jackass!" Phoebe eventually donates $200 to PBS during a telethon at which Joey is a telephone operator, and she claims that it will help support *Sesame Street*, which will bring happiness to children whose mothers *didn't* kill themselves, but she feels awful about doing so because she'd been saving up that money to buy a (really amazing) hamster. Nevertheless, her donation is the one that pushes the total amount over the top of the previous year's total, which puts Joey on TV as the operator who took the call, an event that all the friends were hoping for, and this makes Phoebe feel, once again, wonderful, much to her chagrin and Joey's smug delight.

So why do people do what they do? Once we think about Joey's ways of refuting Phoebe's attempts to prove him wrong, it starts to become difficult to think of any way of denying his "theory," which is a version of the view known as *psychological egoism,* according to which *all actions are done either solely or ultimately for the sake of self-interest*. This is a purely descriptive theory of all human motivation, a claim about the way people *are*. Now the first thing to do when hearing a claim of the form "All Xs are Ys," is to look for a counterexample, an example of an X that isn't a Y. But that's precisely what Phoebe attempted to do, with no success. No matter what she did for others, she wound up garnering some benefit for herself, usually in the form of pleasure at her good deed. We will, however, return to the search for counterexamples later.

Because the view seems at first glance to be right, some people might take it to provide an argument for *ethical egoism*, a normative theory according to which *all actions ought to be done solely/ultimately for the sake of self-interest*, that is, that one should always act so as to maximize one's own best, long-term interests. Now as a matter of logic, this argument simply fails, for it commits what is known as the *is/ought fallacy,* deriving a statement about what *ought to be* from a statement mere-ly about what *is.* But just because things are a certain way, that fact in and of itself doesn't at all provide a *justification* for their being the way they are. For example, consider the following analogous argument occasionally offered in Mississippi in the 1950s: "Our schools are and always have been segregated, so that's the way it ought to stay." The latter clause simply doesn't follow logically from the former.

Nevertheless, the failure of this particular "argument" does not imply that either psychological egoism or ethical egoism is false, nor does it imply that there aren't *other* ways of supporting ethical egoism. It is worth, then, exploring the two views in some more detail, analyzing what precisely they mean and seeing whether or not there are any plausible arguments in their favor.

The most famous argument in support of psychological egoism comes from Plato's *Republic,* a dialogue primarily between Socrates, Glaucon, and Adeimantus about the nature of justice. Socrates' view is that the life of the just (or *moral*) man is the best life possible, but in Book II, Glaucon presents Socrates with a particu-larly powerful challenge to that view by recounting the story of a Lydian shepherd who discovered a ring that, when twisted, made its bearer invisible. So what does he do with this powerful band of gold? He seduces the queen, attacks the king with her help, and takes over the kingdom.

Setting aside the more puzzling omissions of the story (e.g., how does being invis-ible help someone seduce a queen?), the question Glaucon is really posing is to all of us: what would *you* do if you had such a ring? If you are honest with yourself, you may find yourself imagining all sorts of "interesting" possibilities, some of which would likely be illegal, and some of which would surely be deemed "immoral." This suggests one of the two points of the story, namely, that the only reason people act justly (morally) in the first place is that it is in their self-interest to do so. Glaucon argues for this point by means of a straightforward speculative claim: Give this ring to both a just man and an unjust man, and what will happen? They'll both behave in precisely the same ways: they'll both steal lots of money, spy on people's private conversations to get information to increase their power, harm their enemies, and so forth. What this means for morality, then, is that the only reason people behave morally is *fear of getting caught.* It's just not in one's interest to be thrown in jail. But once that possibility is removed (with the Ring of Gyges), people could do all the stuff they really wanted to do and, indeed, they *would* do all that stuff, simply because being moral would no longer benefit them as much as being immoral.

The thought of Glaucon, then, is that justice—morality—is merely an *instrumen-tal* good. It is worthwhile to be moral only because it typically serves your interests: its benefits (to you) usually outweigh the possible punishment that might come your way for being immoral. But when the possibility of punishment is removed, it is no longer in your best interest to be moral and so the claims of morality will have no more hold over you. According to Glaucon, then, you *always* do what is in your own best interest (i.e., psychological egoism is true), and while doing so usually conforms with the demands of morality (because of the benefits being moral brings you), when it doesn't, you do and will shrug those demands aside.

Indeed, says Glaucon, this is what you *should* do, and this brings us to the sec-ond main point of the story, for he claims that the best life—the happiest life—will be that of the ethical egoist. To see why, Glaucon has us compare the life of the person who is cleverly "immoral"—someone whom people think follows the "moral" rules of society but who really just does whatever's in his self-interest—with the life of the person who adheres to "morality" but whom people think is actually immoral. Without all the usual benefits of adhering to society's "moral" rules, Glaucon asks, why would anyone ever want to do so? The "good" man, the man everyone thinks is actually immoral, will be shunned, hated, and eventually imprisoned. The "bad" man, the ethical egoist whom everyone thinks is actually adhering to society's moral code, will have lots of friends, make lots of deals, and eventually be rich and influential in his community. Obviously the "bad" man will have the better life by far. So if there are no benefits to me for adhering to society's "moral" code, then I have no reason to do so. Instead, I should focus solely on doing what's in my own best interest, for doing *that*, and not following society's "moral" rules, is the key to the best, happiest life.

What we have, then, are two views, psychological egoism and ethical egoism, each of which seems to have some support. What we need to do now is figure out whether either of them can withstand some critical scrutiny.

Psychological Egoism

Consider first psychological egoism, which, remember, makes a universal claim about human motivation: all actions are done solely/ultimately for the sake of self-interest. What precisely does this mean? As it turns out, the view is quite ambiguous, and once we articulate its various possible senses, it becomes less and less plausible.

Let's return once more to the attempts to provide counterexamples to psychological egoism. Many people would offer Mother Teresa as a paradigm case of clear-cut altruistic behavior: she devoted her life to working with and helping the poorest of the poor in India. Now surely she's not motivated by considerations of self-interest, is she?

The psychological egoist might offer two responses to this case. On the one hand, in helping the poor Mother Teresa surely *wants* to help the poor. But in doing what *she* most wants to do, she's behaving egoistically. On the other hand, we might take the Joey route: Mother Teresa's helping the poor because she gets satisfaction, even pleasure, either in this life or the next, for doing so. But that's surely a prime example of doing something for the sake of a benefit to oneself. Now each of these responses offers a different way of specifying what the phrase "acting from self-interest" means, so let's consider them each in turn.

1. *"Acting from self-interest" means "voluntarily doing what you (most) want to do"*? On this reading of the phrase, because Mother Teresa is voluntarily helping the poor, which is what she most wants to do, she's acting egoistically. But once we have articulated this version of psychological egoism, it just seems straightforwardly false, simply because I can obviously want to do what's not in my own self-interest. Consider the familiar case when a cashier in a store mistakenly gives you change for a twenty-dollar bill when you actually gave him a ten-dollar bill.

Suppose you're also a typical college student, which means you're broke, so you really need that money, and you also realize you could walk out of store with the money and get away with it. Nevertheless, you inform the cashier of the mistake, simply because you know it's the right thing to do. Now you clearly did what you wanted to do here. Nevertheless, what you wanted to do was not at all in your own best interests. So it seems that sometimes you act exclusively to fulfill a moral obligation, and conforming to demands of morality conflicts with what's in your own best interests.

Of course, the psychological egoist may simply react to this example as follows: "Don't you see that in admitting you returned the extra change because you wanted to that you were still acting egoistically? After all, you were still acting to satisfy *your own* desires! In this case, it was your desire to do the right thing, but that's still your *own* desire, and so that means you were still moved by self-interested considerations."

Responding in this way reveals this version of egoism is what we ought to call *Empty Psychological Egoism,* according to which *people always act to satisfy their own desires.* This version of the view is called "empty" insofar as it is now devoid of any real content. The psychological egoist on this version is simply saying that whenever you're moved to action, you are moved by your desires. Furthermore, because they are your desires, you are always moved self-interestedly. But if one construes "desires" as "whatever moves you," then *of course* you will always be motivated by *your* desires—such a claim is trivially true. Psychological egoism, however, if it is to avoid being an utterly empty claim, must say something more, namely, that all acts originate in a certain *type* of desire, namely self-interested desire. But even if all acts originate in desires *of* the self (your desires are, of course, *yours*) that doesn't at all mean that all acts originate in desires *for* the self, that is, self-interested desires.[1] So we can safely set this version of the view aside.

2. *"Acting from self-interest" means "acting so as to bring about a pleasant state of consciousness for oneself"?* Call this *Experiential Psychological Egoism.* This is Joey's view, and it is also the view many people have in mind when denying the possibility of genuinely altruistic actions. On this version, Mother Teresa helps the poor ultimately because it gives her pleasure or satisfaction. This version is importantly different from Empty Psychological Egoism because it specifies the right type of desire—a desire *for* the self—as being motivationally effective. Nevertheless, this version is problematic as well.

Our discussion of Empty Psychological Egoism above brought out the importance of figuring out just what the *target* of the motivational desire is precisely. If the desire is to produce some benefit to you, then it is self-interested; if the target is something else, then the desire is not self-interested. Now it is indeed often the case that the satisfaction of our desires—whatever their targets—produces some pleasure in us. But just because pleasurable feelings often *accompany* our satisfied desires, that doesn't at all mean that they are the *explanation* for our doing what we did. A desire's being self-interested, then, depends on the target of that desire and *not* on any of its associated experiences. But once we note this distinction, we can see that Experiential Psychological Egoism is indeed subject to counter-examples.

Suppose I want to buy some life insurance so my family will be financially secure upon my death. This seems an obviously non-egoistic act. Nevertheless, the Experiential Psychological Egoist might reply that what I really desire is peace of mind for *myself*, which will come from knowing my family is taken care of. To test this claim, we can try to prize apart the pleasant feeling associated with the satisfaction of the desire from the apparent object of the desire and see what I would really choose. So suppose that I were presented with the following choice: (a) my family's being taken care of *without my knowing it* (and thus no peace of mind for me), or (b) my family's not being taken care of while I peacefully (and falsely) think it is.[2] Suppose further that my memory of having made such a choice will immediately be erased afterwards. Would I (or anyone) always choose (b)? Surely not. For many, their family's well being is what truly matters, and if they were given such a choice, they would without hesitation choose (a). But (a) is non-egoistic, and so this provides a counterexample to Experiential Psychological Egoism: it is just not the case that all actions are performed for the sake of producing some pleasant state of consciousness for oneself.

Furthermore, there are some cases that just seem impossible to account for on *any* version of psychological egoism. David Hume gives us a rather famous one:

Let us suppose such a person ever so selfish; let private interest have engrossed ever so much his attention; yet in instances, where that is not concerned, he must unavoidably feel *some* propensity to the good of mankind, and make it an object of choice, if everything else be equal. Would any man, who is walking along, tread as willingly on another's gouty toes, whom he has no quarrel with, as on the hard flint and pavement? There is here surely a difference in the case. We surely take into consideration the happiness and misery of others, in weighing the several motives of action, and incline to the former, where no private regards draw us to seek our own promotion or advantage by the injury of our fellow-creatures.[3]

So it seems that sometimes, *at least when our own interests aren't at stake*, even the most selfish person will act from benevolence, and not from self-interest. When it's a choice between treading on someone's gouty toes by maintaining a straight path or swerving slightly at some inconvenience to ourselves, most of us, including the most selfish, will swerve. But on what grounds may this swerving be explained egoistically?

Now the hard-core egoist may still try to resist this case as a counterexample to his theory (however specified), by simply admitting as much: "Fine, when your interests aren't at stake, you might act benevolently. But whenever they *are* at stake, when it's a choice between your own interests and someone else's, you'll always act for the sake of your own interests." But to this reply there is yet another sort of case: revenge. Suppose your spouse is cheating on you with your best friend. You then decide to go on the *Jerry Springer Show* to inform the world that both your spouse and your friend, right alongside *you*, regularly hang out by schoolyards peddling drugs in the nude to elementary school kids. Now you know when you decide to go on the show that you're going to be nailed for revealing this information—you'll go to prison too. You are consciously and deliberately, then, acting against your own interests. Your intent is simply to exact revenge on your spouse and your friend, to make them suffer worse than you have. Now I suppose someone might still try to account for this case by saying you would be motivated by the pleasure you would get at seeing their faces, so against this last-ditch effort we may consider the ultimate act of revenge, what was purportedly the original final scene in the movie *Fatal Attraction*, in which the spurned Glenn Close character kills herself in order to frame the Michael Douglas character for the crime. And while this is the sort of case that occurs extremely rarely (if at all), we can at least *understand the motivation* involved, which cannot be one of self-interest.

Psychological egoism, in all its variants, is false. And we have already found that the argument from psychological egoism to ethical egoism is itself fallacious. But perhaps Glaucon's second challenge to Socrates, the claim that the life of the ethical egoist is the best life of all, still holds up. In other words, even if we *don't* act egoistically all the time, perhaps we *should*. It is to this view that we now turn.

Ethical Egoism

Ethical egoism is the view that you should always act so as to bring about the best consequences for yourself. But what does this mean, precisely? One caricature of the view is that you should do whatever you want whenever you want it, breaking all "moral" rules that stand in your way. This simply isn't accurate, though. What matters is your own *long-term* interest, and it may often be best for you in the long run to stick to the "moral" rules. After all, you're more likely to get greater benefits in the end if you don't alienate people and endanger yourself by committing "immoralities" left and right. Killing someone for pleasure, say, would not be very good for you in the long run, given that you could easily get caught and spend a lot of your precious time in prison.

But it is important to note as well that the "moral" rules are also not inviolable, if you are an ethical egoist. As Glaucon would insist, the *only* reason you should conform to the societal moral code would be in cases where it is in your own (long-term) interest. But where it isn't, you should definitely violate such a code. So when the cashier mistakenly gives you that extra change and you can get away with it, keep the money. On ethical egoism, you should be "kind" when it serves you and be a "scoundrel" when it serves you.

In order to evaluate such a claim, however, we need to articulate it a bit more precisely. Insofar as it is taken to be a normative ethical theory, the view must yield a criterion of what makes right acts right and wrong acts wrong. We will put this criterion in terms of rightness:

On ethical egoism, an act is right if and only if it produces a state of affairs whose consequences for the agent are no worse than the consequences of alternative states of affairs producible by any other action the agent could have performed.

Now there a few aspects to the criterion we need to examine. First, what counts as a "*good* consequence"? The ethical egoist's typical theory of value here is perhaps the easiest theory to articulate and understand of all normative ethical theories, for what counts as valuable is simply *whatever the agent deems valuable.*[4] So if you really like pleasurable states of consciousness, then you should try to produce states of affairs that bring you as much pleasure as possible. Or if you think knowledge is valuable, then you should try to produce states of affairs that bring you as much knowledge as possible. And so forth. Ethical egoism typically offers a purely subjective theory of value: if it's valuable to you, then it's what you ought to maximize.

A second aspect to notice is the comparative requirement. The way for you as an ethical egoist to deliberate is to consider one state of affairs you could produce through one action, and compare its consequences (in terms of what you deem valuable) to the consequences of a different state of affairs you could produce through another action. Whichever state of affairs includes the most long-term good for you is the state of affairs you should try to bring about.

A third aspect to notice is that you should maximize your own *long-term* good. While we will discuss this point in greater detail below, for now it should suffice to note that the view requires you to look beyond merely short-term benefits to include in your deliberations possible greater benefits that may accrue to you much later. For example, it is surely in your short-term interest to avoid undergoing the pain of a dentist's visit anytime soon, but you will be avoiding that short-term pain at the likely cost of undergoing a much greater pain down the road by failing to take care of your teeth. Short-term sacrifices, therefore, may be required to bring yourself greater benefits in the long run.

There have been a number of attempts to find fault with ethical egoism, but the view is surprisingly resistant to them. We can best develop the view and see how its advocates might respond to criticisms by deploying each of the evaluative criteria offered by Mark Timmons (see introduction).

1. *Consistency*. A theory yielding inconsistent moral verdicts, such that a specific action, or type of action, is both obligatory and wrong, would be useless, and some people have thought that ethical egoism does indeed yield such contradictory prescriptions. To see why, consider the following case. Suppose that it is in Marcia's overall self-interest to rig the election for student body president in her favor (she really needs to win because it will increase the likelihood that she'll get into her favored college, say). Suppose further that it is in Jan's overall self-interest to expose her older sister Marcia's plans (because doing so would finally bring Jan the attention that goes with being thought of as the "honorable" sister for once). Finally, consider the generally accepted moral principle that it is wrong to prevent someone else from doing what he/she ought (morally) to do. Given these considerations, it seems Jan both (a) ought to expose Marcia (given that it's in her own best interests), and (b) ought *not* to expose Marcia (given that in doing so she would prevent Marcia from doing what *she* ought to do). This is a blatant contradiction, however, and if this sort of case is implied by ethical egoism, then ethical egoism is false.[5]

The problem, though, is that the "generally accepted" moral principle simply isn't a necessary principle of *ethical egoism*. Notice that the principle seems to imply that it is wrong *for anyone* to prevent someone else from doing what he/she ought to do. But ethical egoism is specifically and singularly about maximizing benefits for the agent who performs the act in question: the question I am to ask is whether or not the act in question will produce the best consequences *for me*. That is my sole consideration as an ethical egoist, and any other so-called "moral principles," if they are in conflict with that prime directive, are irrelevant. So yes, if doing so is in my best overall self-interest, I should not prevent someone else from doing what he/she ought to do. But if it *isn't* in my best interests, then failing to prevent someone from doing what he/she ought to do would be *wrong*. In this case, then, Jan ought to prevent Marcia from doing what Marcia ought to do.

Put this way, we can see that ethical egoism can *never* issue inconsistent directives *for a specific agent*. It prescribes maximizing valuable consequences for you, and it is simply logically impossible for there to be a situation in which some act will both maximize and not maximize such valuable consequences, that is, for there to be some state of affairs you could produce that would both be best, and yet *not* be best, for you. Now there will certainly be cases in which I should do X in a set of circumstances and you should do not-X in those same circumstances (varying according to our individual set of interests), but that is not inconsistent in any objectionable sense. After all, most ethical theories will prescribe different actions for people with different interests and relationships in the same circumstances without drawing the charge of inconsistency at issue here. That charge is reserved for a theory that implies *you* ought to do both X and not-X in the same set of circumstances, and ethical egoism easily avoids such a charge.

2. *Determinacy*. If a theory yields indeterminate moral verdicts about specific cases, then it may fail to be very useful in helping its adherents decide what to do. And it looks like ethical egoism may very well succumb to the charge of indeterminacy insofar as it emphasizes doing what is in your own best *long-term* self-interest. How, it might be wondered, could I possibly know what it is in my best long-term interest? While one act may *seem* as if it will produce the best consequences overall for me, it may turn out not to do so, due to various unforeseen events: Certain acts I perform may have numerous ripple effects that wind up severely *undermining* my interests, but how could I determine that in advance?

This worry rests on a mistake, however, namely that being unable to foresee all possible consequences renders ethical egoism *indeterminate*. This mistake is brought to light, and easily addressed, though, by distinguishing between ethical egoism's *criterion of rightness* and its *decision procedure*. The criterion of rightness is perfectly determinate: the right action is always the one that brings about the best consequences for you, after all the dust has settled and the consequence-ripples have calmed down. But given that we can rarely, if ever, foresee what all those consequences will be, and given that we must act, the ethical egoist can say that the procedure for deciding what to do can simply be based on your evaluation of what you *expect* the best consequences to be, after a reasonable amount of deliberation spent sorting through the various circumstances and facts available to you. And corresponding to this distinction could be one in terms of assessment: We might evaluate the *moral rightness* of your action in terms of whether or not it in fact produced the best consequences for you, but we could assess your *moral responsibility* for the action—the appropriateness of blaming or praising you for it—in terms of what you *expected* the consequences to be. So in the case above, I did the wrong thing, but because I couldn't have reasonably expected things to turn out as they did, I shouldn't be blamed for doing what I did.

3. *Applicability*. The evaluative criterion of applicability has to do with whether or not the theory includes an adequate decision procedure, a reliable way of applying the theory to produce consistent and determinate moral verdicts. I have dealt with this issue a bit in the previous section. Once (if) we can work out the details of what the precise target of maximization is supposed to be, ethical egoism should be easily applicable, providing consistent and determinate moral verdicts about what to do. As long as one focuses on the *expected* consequences of one's action, after due deliberation and consideration, moral verdicts may be cranked out at a furious pace.

Along these lines, however, one might object that the theory cranks out *too many* moral verdicts, that it is *overly* applicable in virtue of being too demanding. Ethical egoism requires maximization of my self-interest, after all, and this seems to mean that I'm obligated to strive, in every action I perform, to do what's best for me, and this dictate applies even to the most trivial of actions. But if I'm required to deliberate about every action I perform, to consider, for example, whether it will benefit me most to sit in this chair or that, or put on my right sock before my left, I would be intellectually exhausted and miserable, never really getting anything done. But this result would surely render ethical egoism inapplicable to the living of anything remotely like a decent human life.

Such a result would indeed be a problem for ethical egoism, but there's no reason to think that it is required by the view. After all, there would be enormous costs to my self-interest if I engaged in this kind of constant calculation, so it would surely be better for me in the long run if I weren't required to do so. But according to ethical egoism, if it *wouldn't* be better for me to do so, *then I shouldn't*, that is, it's *not* a requirement of the theory that I engage in such constant calculation. What I should do instead is reserve such calculations for the decisions that really matter to me, where what I'm about to do is what I expect to have a real impact on my interests. In all other trivial matters, it will most likely be best overall for me if I live by a rule of thumb that allows room for spontaneity in the making of such decisions.

1. *Internal Support*. The idea here is that an ethical theory gains in plausibility the more it coheres with our considered moral beliefs, so if an ethical principle, together with relevant non-moral information, implies one of our antecedent moral beliefs, it is rendered more plausible; if this procedure, however, yields a conflict with one of our considered moral beliefs, it becomes less plausible.

This is the evaluative criterion on which ethical egoism seems to fare the worst, for it looks like it would easily produce obligations at one time or another to perform actions that directly contradict many, if not all, of our considered moral beliefs. For instance, if it is in my best long-term interest to murder someone I intensely dislike (and I can get away with it), then ethical egoism counsels that I murder him. But this obviously will conflict with our considered moral belief that murder is always wrong. Or to take a less dramatic example, it may be in my best interest to commit adultery, despite the fact that we believe such an action to be wrong. And the same will go for a variety of other considered moral beliefs, for when it serves my best interests, ethical egoism will counsel that I lie, break promises, steal, torture, and kill. It is for this reason that many philosophers have concluded that ethical egoism isn't an *ethical* theory at all; rather, it is best construed as a *challenge* to all ethical theories: why adhere to the demands of morality when it is not in my best interests?[6]

Such worries may be too hasty, however, for there are a variety of possible responses. Hobbes, for example, who advocated a kind of ethical egoism, was indeed concerned about the nefarious character he called the fool, someone who "hath said in his heart: 'there is no such thing as justice.'"[7] The fool alleges that "'every man's conservation and contentment being committed to his own care, there could be no reason why every man might not do what he thought conduced thereunto, and therefore also to make or not make, keep or not keep, covenants was not against reason, when it conduced to one's benefit.'"[8] This fool

does not therein deny that there be covenants, and that they are sometimes broken, some-times kept, and that such breach of them may be called injustice, and the observance of them justice, but he questioneth whether injustice ... may not sometimes stand with that reason which dictateth to every man his own good; and particularly then, when it con-duceth to such a benefit as shall put a man in a condition to neglect, not only the dispraise and revilings, but also the power of other men.[9]

Hobbes explicitly accepts the principle that reason dictates that one ought to maximize one's own good. The problem, though, is that he is using this principle to justify to citizens their obedience to the law of the sovereign (it is in their best interests), but if the principle *actually* allows for a bunch of fools to break the laws willy-nilly, the government would be a joke and Hobbes's entire project would be undermined. Hobbes's answer to the fool is fairly straightforward, though: anyone who reasons that it is in her best interests to commit "injustice" actually *fails to reason correctly*. In other words, Hobbes maintains that it is *not* in the best long-term interest of anyone to commit injustice, for the fool will always, eventually, be found out and punished, either by the state or by one's fellow citi-zens. Or, if he isn't found out, he will always either be on the run or be *worried* about being found out, and such costs to the fool will always outweigh the bene-fits of the considered injustice.[10]

This is a problematic empirical response, however, for two reasons. First, it is incredibly optimistic—foolhardy, even—to think that the actual cost to all poten-tial "fools" will exceed the benefits of their considered injustices. Surely there have been plenty of people who have gotten away with injustice, to their great benefit, without also having dealt with any serious escape/worry costs.[11] The Mafia don who dies peacefully at a ripe old age, while more of a rarity these days, should still give us pause at Hobbes's reply to the fool.

Second, and more importantly, Hobbes's reply simply ignores the deepest part of the worry, which is that the foundational source of morality cannot be my own interests, because that always leaves it as a theoretical possibility that the torture and murder of innocents, for example, *could be* the right thing to do, and that simply cannot be an acceptable implication of *any* moral theory. What we object to about Hobbes's reply is that it really misses the point: According to our considered convictions, certain actions are simply wrong regardless of how much you might benefit from them, and a moral theory that doesn't account for such convictions is inadequate from the get-go.

Nevertheless, the ethical egoist may indeed account for such convictions by revising the criterion of rightness to focus on actions only indirectly, via their relation to a set of rules. According to *rule ethical egoism (REE)*, then, *an act is right if and only if it conforms to a set of rules whose adherence by the agent produces consequences for that agent which are no worse than the consequences producible by any other adhered-to set of rules*.[12] On this view, the rightness or wrongness of an action is to be evaluated according to the value of a set of rules that directs one to perform that action. Now there is a lot involved in this formulation that may be unspecified or controversial, but what matters for our purposes here is that a fully-formed version of the theory could easily meet the demands of internal support, for surely one would be better off *in the long run* living in a society such as ours if one lived by a set of rules that outlawed the torture and murder of innocents, say, rather than to a set of rules that allowed such actions. As Shelly Kagan puts it, "It seems fair to suggest that, on the whole, the best way to get along with others—earning their trust and cooperation, and avoiding their wrath—is to conform to the rules of commonsense morality. No doubt, from the point of view of the individual agent, conforming to these rules will sometimes have its costs; normally, however, these will be more than outweighed by the various benefits."[13]

Of course, one might object that this is precisely the view that we had been focusing on before, the one in which we were directly evaluating the consequences of our individual acts. This isn't quite true, however. On the earlier act-focused version of ethical egoism, conforming to the rules of commonsense morality was a *rule of thumb*, a "rule" one was required to break whenever one expected the consequences of doing so to be better for oneself than conforming to the rule. On REE, on the other hand, such rules are *absolute* rules, not to be broken even if one judges the consequences to be better for oneself in a specific case. And this move at least allows the egoist a way out of the Hobbesian problem of internal support by eliminating even the theoretical possibility of clearly heinous actions.[14]

5. External Support. This evaluative criterion looks to support external to morality for the ethical theory in question, that is, are there any non-moral premises or beliefs that prop up, or at least cohere with, the theory? We have already seen the attempt to provide support for ethical egoism via considerations of psychological egoism. But psychological egoism is false, and anyway its truth—as a descriptive claim—cannot provide any *logical* support for the prescriptive claim of ethical egoism.

Nevertheless, if we believe that the *point* of an ethical theory is to better enable its adherents to live a flourishing, happy life, then it looks as if ethical egoism might be our best bet. The entire point of the theory, after all, is to maximize one's self-interest, and if there is a close causal relation between such successful maximization and individual happiness (as seems obvious), then a successful ethical egoist should be at least as happy as an adherent of any other ethical theory, perhaps more so. And this is precisely Glaucon's point in *The Republic*: We should compare the person who maximizes his own good (and yet has a reputation for being "good") to the person who always conforms to the demands of "justice" (but has the opposite reputation), and then "we'll be able to judge which of them is happier."[15] And Glaucon thinks it obvious that the first man will have much the happier life.

Nevertheless, there is a serious worry that deserves mention here because, paradoxically enough, if *everyone* (or most everyone) became an ethical egoist, each individual's chances for happiness could actually be reduced. Consider, for instance, the significant tax burden each of us currently bears to create a system of law enforcement required to make it in people's self-interest to smog-check their cars and to refrain from murder, theft, cheating on their taxes, etc. If instead we could count on people to act in accordance with *non*-egoistic principles, we could let our guard down and stop having to pay for such a system.[16] We will come back to this point later in our discussion of publicity.

In addition, if we take as a basic premise about morality that its point is something *other* than individual happiness, such as producing the greatest good impartially considered, or as being the best means for social cooperation, or as embodying universal principles of rationality, or as yielding principles in conformity with God's will, then ethical egoism fares even less well on the criterion of external support. This is a matter of great controversy, however, and it is anyway far from obvious that individual happiness shouldn't at least be a serious contender.

6. Explanatory Power. More fundamental than the previous two evaluative criteria, perhaps, this criterion looks to see how adequate the theory is in explaining *why* an act is wrong (or right). Very briefly, in both its versions (the act-focused and the rule-focused versions), ethical egoism does indeed provide a fairly straightforward and powerful explanatory basis for the wrongness and rightness of actions. On the one hand (in the "act" version), what makes an act wrong is its failure to maximize good consequences (however defined) for oneself, period. In the rule version of the theory, what makes an act wrong is its being disallowed by a set of rules whose adherence by an agent maximizes good consequences for him or her. So in either case, when I demand of myself an explanation for why I shouldn't perform some action, I have a ready—and readily understandable— answer: it will, either directly or indirectly, fail to produce the best long term consequences for me. And so why (goes the Platonic challenge) would I ever want to do *that*?

In sum, then, ethical egoism fares better than it might have been thought on the six evaluative criteria discussed above, and it often fares no worse than most other ethical theories in key areas. There remains one last evaluative criterion that is quite relevant to this issue, however, so let us examine it.

7. Publicity. What has seemed crucial to many is that ethical theories must be easily teachable. That is, if the moral principles of an ethical theory are in place to guide people's behavior, then those principles must be taught to them during their moral training as children or young adults. But ethical egoism, at first blush, seems quite at odds with this demand for publicity. After all, if the theory counsels that you should do whatever is in *your own* best long-term interest, then it seems you shouldn't teach the theory to anyone else, for if someone else starts to adhere to the principles of this theory, then she will be acting to maximize good consequences only for herself, and so she won't be available or willing to provide help to you anymore in the achievement of *your* own good (unless it's in her interest to do so). Furthermore, being viewed by others as an ethical egoist may cause them to react negatively towards you (as some kind of selfish monster), so it may again be in your best interest to keep the view to yourself. So insofar as the theory would likely counsel that you not teach it to others, it is inadequate with respect to this evaluative criterion.

Let us deal with the latter point first. What may be relevant to ameliorating this concern are certain marketing possibilities. In other words, how the theory is sold to others may go a long way towards erasing the negative connotations associated with it. One thing that might be emphasized about it has to do with its service in best promoting a certain take on the very point of morality, discussed above. Ethical egoism's finest promotional tool seems to be its relation to individual happiness. If this is taken to be the highest good (as it is for many people), then what *better* ethical theory could there be than one whose sole aim is to promote a self-interest whose offshoot will likely be happiness? Furthermore, the negative reactions could also be dampened by emphasizing the rule-based version of the theory, which will likely (more or less) comport with the rules most people take to be constitutive of commonsense morality. One would then be publicizing rules (such as keep your promises, don't steal, lie, murder, etc.) with which people are already familiar and which don't have the ring of selfishness about them. And if these rules are furthermore causally related to individual happiness at their foundation, then it seems the ethical egoist has the best of both worlds.

The former concern, about publicity taking away potential contributors to my own good, is perhaps more worrisome. This concern is again a more serious problem for the "act" version of the theory, though: it would indeed be hard to envision a scenario in which I would be justified (on the basis of my self-interest) in acting to advocate the theory to everyone else. I *might* be justified in publicizing it to a limited number of people, those whose help I expect to need for the pursuit of certain self-interested projects (and who would be justified in helping me on the grounds of their own self-interest). But this is not the general sort of publicity demanded by the criterion.

There is a deeper worry here, though, one to which I already alluded above, and it is brought out by consideration of the famous Prisoner's Dilemma case. Suppose that you and your accomplice Fabio have managed to steal the Queen's crown jewels from Buckingham Palace. You disabled the internal security cameras, but an external surveillance camera captured you both on the grounds, so you were both arrested and locked up in separate interrogation rooms. All the police have you on now is criminal trespassing, which carries a sentence of a year, but the detective in charge wants to nail you both for the more serious charge of grand theft. A trial will be expensive, though, and you may manage to get off altogether because you'll probably hire Johnny Cochran as your defense attorney, so the detective wants to get a confession out of both of you to save time and money and ensure a conviction. He thus offers you the following deal (which he'll also offer to Fabio): If you confess and incriminate Fabio, you'll be released on probation, and Fabio will serve ten years in prison. If you don't confess, and Fabio instead confesses and incriminates you, he'll be released and you'll serve ten years in prison. If you both confess, then you'll each get five years (cooperation reduces the charge). And if neither of you confesses, you'll each get one year for criminal trespassing. What should you do?

Suppose you're both ethical egoists, each wanting to do what's in your own best interest. You realize that the sentence you get will depend on what Fabio does, and Fabio will either keep his mouth shut or confess. If he keeps his mouth shut, then you're faced with either one year in prison (if you shut up too) or the opportunity to walk away scot-free (if you confess). If Fabio confesses, then you're faced with either ten years in prison (if you keep your mouth shut) or five years in prison (if you confess as well). So no matter what Fabio does, you should confess, given that you want what's best for yourself. But of course, if Fabio's an ethical egoist too, he'll reason in precisely the same way, so he'll confess. But now you both wind up with five years in prison (by doing exactly what the detective wanted).

The dilemma here is that, in doing what is in your individual best interests, you both wind up *worse off* than you would've been had you both done what was *not* in your individual best interests, namely, keeping your mouth shut. In other words, what is individually rational is collectively *irrational*. And even if you had made a deal beforehand to keep your mouths shut, when faced with the detective's offer it would still be in your individual self-interest to break the deal and confess (as it would be as well for Fabio), which would place you right back in the worse scenario.

Imagine, then, a world full of ethical egoists. Getting two or more of these folks to cooperate would seem to be impossible, for precisely the reasons illuminated in the Prisoner's Dilemma. If you and I have made a deal to exchange goods or services with one another, and I can get you to perform your part of that bargain first, it will always be in my individual best interest to skip my end of the deal—I'll get the goodies from you without having to do anything in return. But of course, if you're an ethical egoist as well, you'll realize that that's what I'll do, so you'll simply refuse to perform your end of the deal at all, which will leave us both *worse off* than we would have been if we'd simply stuck to our agreement. Furthermore, there are certain public goods it would be impossible to maintain if everyone were an ethical egoist. Pollution is bad for us all, and exhaust from cars without catalytic converters is a primary contributor, so the government has had to require all cars to get such equipment installed, even though doing so is rather expensive. But suppose the government merely *suggests* that people get this equipment. Surely my failure to do so won't affect the environment in any noticeable way, so if I want to maximize my self-interest, I shouldn't buy it. But then if everyone were to reason in this way, we'd have a horrible amount of pollution on our hands (and in our lungs), which is worse for everyone (including me). So it looks like the widespread individual maximization of self-interest would, in many respects, yield the paradoxical conclusion that self-interest would *not* be maximized. This result, then, would clearly seem to counsel against publicizing ethical egoism, which renders it fairly implausible as an ethical theory.

The standard way to respond to the Prisoner's Dilemma is to deploy an external enforcement mechanism, so that it becomes in one's self-interest to cooperate with others: if one fails to do so, one will be severely punished. But if the enforcement mechanism can somehow be *internalized* (via heavy guilt, say, at the thought of failing to do one's part), then the dilemma may be avoided, even though the pursuit of self-interest could still guide one's behavior. And this is one way we might think of REE. Because this version of ethical egoism evaluates actions only indirectly, via their relation to the set of rules whose internalization and adherence maximizes good consequences for the agent, a society of ethical egoists could perhaps avoid the Prisoner's Dilemma and collective action problems that beset the "act" version. As long as people associated a great cost with the breaking of the rules, then their self-interest would be more easily maximized, and this could allow for the maintenance of key public goods as well.

Furthermore (to return to the original problem), whether or not any specific act of *publicity* I perform maximizes good consequences for me would not be an issue on REE (given that it doesn't focus on direct evaluation of acts). There may, however, still be some question about whether or not such an action would be permitted by my optimal set of rules. This might be the case *if* it would be best for me to adhere to a set of rules that nearly everyone else adhered to as well. And it is possible to envision how this in fact might be the case: There may, after all, be significant vigilance and paranoia costs to keeping the theory to myself, or it may be that the level of deception I would have to maintain to keep the theory to myself could violate another rule against deception that would be part of my optimal set of rules. At any rate, though, while there are indeed some serious worries about publicity that the ethical egoist must deal with, they may not be entirely insurmountable on a fleshed-out version of REE.

Conclusion

All in all, then, some versions of ethical egoism can overcome many of the standard objections launched against it, and so there may be good reason to include it among the pantheon of the more "mainstream" ethical theories.[17] This is not to say, however, that the view escapes more sophisticated worries, or that it is just as plausible on every count as the other mainstream theories. There may remain, for instance, lingering doubts about the adequacy of ethical egoism when it comes to certain of the evaluative criteria, for example, internal support or publicity. What I have tried to maintain, though, is that the theory at least does have some powerful tools at its disposal to dislodge many of the common complaints about it, and this may be enough for people to (re)discover some of its more attractive elements.

Notes

1. This is a version of what Gregory S. Kavka calls "pseudo-egoism." See his *Hobbesian Moral and Political Theory* (Princeton, NJ: Princeton University Press, 1986), 35.
2. The example is Kavka's, ibid., 36–37.
3. David Hume, *An Enquiry Concerning the Principles of Morals*, (Indianapolis, IN: Hackett Publishing Co., 1983), §V, Part II (47).
4. I have put this subjective theory of value as being what constitutes the "typical" egoist theory, but it's perfectly possible for an ethical egoist to offer a more objective account, that is, to maintain that there are certain goods agents ought to pursue that are good for them *independently* of what they think. Indeed, this might be the theory of value advocated as part of Aristotle's brand of ethical egoism. Such a theory of value might be less attractive to budding ethical egoists, however, because it may be construed as smacking of paternalism: wouldn't *I* be the best judge of what's good for me? In addition, a subjective theory of value may help the egoist with certain worries about determinacy (see below). But at any rate, the criterion of rightness remains the same regardless of the theory of value included with it, so for our purposes this dispute is not terribly important.
5. This is a modified version of a case articulated by James P. Sterba in his "General Introduction" to James P. Sterba, *Morality in Practice*, 7th edition (Belmont, CA: Wadsworth/Thomson Learning, 2004), 7.
6. See, e.g., John Rawls, *A Theory of Justice* (Cambridge: Harvard University Press, 1971), 136. It might also be thought that this was precisely Glaucon's point as well, in Plato's *Republic*.
7. Thomas Hobbes, *Leviathan*, ed. by Edwin Curley (Indianapolis, IN: Hackett Publishing Company, 1994), 90.
8. Ibid.
9. Ibid.
10. Ibid., 91–92.
11. The Woody Allen movie, *Crimes and Misdemeanors*, is about precisely such a case.
12. See, for example, Kavka, pp. 357–368 for his interpretation of Hobbes as a rule egoist. See also Shelly Kagan, *Normative Ethics* (Boulder, CO: Westview Press, 1998), 199–204. Another helpful source is Brad Hooker's defense of rule *consequentialism* in "Rule-Consequentialism" (see this volume) and in *Ideal Code, Real World* (Oxford: Oxford University Press, 2000).
13. Kagan, 197.
14. Of course, this might depend on who you were. If you were extremely powerful and could torture with impunity, the rules for you might indeed require you to torture the innocent. REE may not, then, altogether eliminate the worry about the theoretical possibility of torture. What it might be construed as doing, however, is eliminating this as a theoretical possibility *for nearly all of us as we are or are likely to be*. I am grateful to Doug Portmore for pointing out this worry.
15. Plato, *The Republic*, trans. by G. M. A. Grube (revised by C. D. C. Reeve) (Indianapolis, IN: Hackett Publishing Company, 1992), 361d (p. 37).
16. I am grateful to Doug Portmore for putting the matter in this way.
17. Indeed, many have thought that Aristotle's brand of virtue ethics is in fact, at its core, a version of ethical egoism. See, e.g., Paula Gottlieb, "Aristotle's Ethical Egoism," *Pacific Philosophical Quarterly* 77 (1996): 1–18.

CHAPTER 3

Ethics by Authority

MORALITY IS BASED ON GOD'S COMMANDS
Robert C. Mortimer

Robert C. Mortimer wrote Christian Ethics *(1950). In the following selection taken from that book, Mortimer defends what is known as the divine command theory of ethics, according to which the rightness or wrongness of an action depends on God's commands. According to Mortimer, then, God's commands set forth a universally valid set of basic moral principles that are revealed to human beings in the Bible.*

T he Christian religion is essentially a revelation of the nature of God. It tells men that God has done certain things. And from the nature of these actions we can infer what God is like. In the second place the Christian religion tells men what is the will of God for them, how they must live if they would please God. This second message is clearly dependent on the first. The kind of conduct which will please God depends on the kind of person God is. This is what is meant by saying that belief influences conduct. The once popular view that it does not matter what a man believes so long as he acts decently is nonsense. Because what he considers decent depends on what he believes. If you are a Nazi you will behave as a Nazi, if you are a Communist you will behave as a Communist, and if you are a Christian you will behave as a Christian. At least, in general; for a man does not always do what he knows he ought to do, and he does not always recognize clearly the implications for conduct of his belief. But in general, our conduct, or at least our notions of what constitutes right conduct, are shaped by our beliefs. The man who knows about God—has a right faith—knows or may learn what conduct is pleasing to God and therefore right.

The Christian religion has a clear revelation of the nature of God, and by means of it instructs and enlightens the consciences of men. The first foundation is the doctrine of God the Creator. God made us and all the world. Because of that He has an absolute claim on our obedience. We do not exist in our own right, but

From Robert C. Mortimer, *Christian Ethics* (New York: Hutchinson's University Library, 1950).

only as His creatures, who ought therefore to do and be what He desires. We do not possess anything in the world, absolutely, not even our own bodies; we hold things in trust for God, who created them, and are bound, therefore, to use them only as He intends that they should be used. This is the doctrine contained in the first chapters of Genesis. God created man and placed him in the Garden of Eden with all the animals and the fruits of the earth at his disposal, subject to God's own law. "Of the fruit of the tree of the knowledge of good and evil thou shall not eat." Man's ownership and use of the material world is not absolute, but subject to the law of God.

From the doctrine of God as the Creator and source of all that is, it follows that a thing is not right simply because we think it is, still less because it seems to be expedient. It is right because God commands it. This means that there is a real distinction between right and wrong which is independent of what we happen to think. It is rooted in the nature and will of God. When a man's conscience tells him that a thing is right, which is in fact what God wills, his conscience is true and its judgment correct; when a man's conscience tells him a thing is right which is, in fact, contrary to God's will, his conscience is false and telling him a lie. It is a lamentably common experience for a man's conscience to play him false, so that in all good faith he does what is wrong, thinking it to be right. "Yea the time cometh that whoever killeth you will think that he doeth God service." But this does not mean that whatever you think is right is right. It means that even conscience can be wrong: that the light which is in you can be darkness....

The pattern of conduct which God has laid down for man is the same for all men. It is universally valid. When we speak of Christian ethics we do not mean that there is one law for Christians and another for non-Christians. We mean the Christian understanding and statement of the one common law for all men. Unbelievers also know or can be persuaded of that law or of part of it: Christians have a fuller and better knowledge. The reason for this is that Christians have by revelation a fuller and truer knowledge both of the nature of God Himself and of the nature of man.

The Revelation in the Bible plays a three-fold part. In the first place it recalls and restates in simple and even violent language fundamental moral judgments which men are always in danger of forgetting or explaining away. It thus provides a norm and standard of human behavior in the broadest and simplest outline. Man's duty to worship God and love the truth, to respect lawful authority, to refrain from violence and robbery, to live in chastity, to be fair and even merciful in his dealings with his neighbor—and all this as the declared will of God, the way man *must* live if he would achieve his end—this is the constant theme of the Bible. The effect of it is not to reveal something new which men could not have found out for themselves, but to recall them to what they have forgotten or with culpable blindness have failed to perceive....

And this leads to the second work of Revelation. The conduct which God demands of men, He demands out of His own Holiness and Righteousness. "Be ye perfect, as your Father in Heaven is perfect." Not the service of the lips but of the heart, not obedience in the letter but in the Spirit is commanded. The standard is too high: the Judge too all-seeing and just. The grandeur and majesty of the moral law proclaims the weakness and impotence of man. It shatters human pride and self-sufficiency: it overthrows that complacency with which the righteous regard the tattered robes of their partial virtues, and that satisfaction with which rogues rejoice to discover other men more evil than themselves. The revelation of the holiness of God and His Law, once struck home, drives men to confess their need of grace and brings them to Christ their Savior.

Lastly, revelation, by the light which it throws on the nature of God and man, suggests new emphases and new precepts, a new scale of values which could not at all, or could not easily, have been perceived.... Thus it comes about that Christian ethics is at once old and new. It covers the same ground of human conduct as the law of the Old Testament and the "law of the Gentiles written in their hearts." Many of its precepts are the same precepts. Yet all is seen in a different light and in a new perspective—the perspective of God's love manifested in Christ. It will be worth while to give one or two illustrations of this.

Revelation throws into sharp relief the supreme value of each individual human being. Every man is an immortal soul created by God and designed for an eternal inheritance. The love of God effected by the Incarnation the restoration and renewal of fallen human nature in order that all men alike might benefit thereby. The Son of God showed particular care and concern for the fallen, the outcast, the weak and the despised. He came, not to call the righteous, but sinners to repentance. Like a good shepherd, He sought especially for the sheep which was lost. Moreover, the divine drama of Calvary which was the cost of man's redemption, the price necessary to give him again a clear picture of what human nature was designed to be and to provide him with the inspiration to strive towards it and the assurance that he is not irrevocably tied and bound to his sinful, selfish past, makes it equally clear that in the eyes of the Creator His creature man is of infinite worth and value.

The lesson is plain and clear: all men equally are the children of God, all men equally are the object of His love. In consequence of this, Christian ethics has always asserted that every man is a person possessed of certain inalienable rights, that he is an end in himself, never to be used merely as a means to something else. And he is this in virtue of his being a man, no matter what his race or color, no matter how well or poorly endowed with talents, no matter how primitive or developed. And further, since man is an end in himself, and that end transcends this world of time and space, being fully attained only in heaven, it follows that the individual takes precedence over society, in the sense that society exists for the good of its individual members, not those members for society. However much the good of the whole is greater than the good of any one of its parts, and whatever the duties each man owes to society, individual persons constitute the supreme value, and society itself exists only to promote the good of those persons.

This principle of the infinite worth of the individual is explicit in Scripture, and in the light of it all totalitarian doctrines of the State stand condemned. However, the implications of this principle for human living and for the organization of society are not explicit, but need to be perceived and worked out by the human conscience. How obtuse that conscience can be, even when illumined by revelation, is startlingly illustrated by the long centuries in which Christianity tolerated the institution of slavery. In view of the constant tendency of man to exploit his fellow men and use them as the instruments of his greed and selfishness, two things are certain. First, that the Scriptural revelation of the innate inalienable dignity and value of the individual is an indispensable bulwark of human freedom and growth. And second, that our knowledge of the implication of this revelation is far indeed from being perfect; there is constant need for further refinement of our moral perceptions, a refinement which can only emerge as the fruit of a deeper penetration of the Gospel of God's love into human life and thought.

Another illustration of the effect of Scripture upon ethics is given by the surrender of the principle of exact retribution in favor of the principle of mercy. Natural justice would seem to require exact retributive punishment, an eye for an eye, a tooth for a tooth. The codes of primitive peoples, and the long history of blood feuds show how the human conscience has approved of this concept. The revelation of the divine love and the explicit teaching of the Son of God have demonstrated the superiority of mercy, and have pointed the proper role of punishment as correction and not vengeance. Because of the revelation that in God justice is never unaccompanied by mercy, in Christian ethics there has always been an emphasis on the patient endurance of wrongs in imitation of Calvary, and on the suppression of all emotions of vindictive anger. As a means to soften human relations, as a restraint of human anger and cruelty, so easily disguised under the cloak of justice, the history of the world has nothing to show comparable to this Christian emphasis on patience and mercy, this insistence that even the just satisfaction of our wrongs yields to the divine example of forebearance. We are to be content with the reform or at least the restraint of the evil-doer, never to seek or demand vengeance.

DOES MORALITY DEPEND ON GOD'S COMMANDS?
Mark Timmons

Mark Timmons is professor of philosophy at the University of Arizona and author of Morality without Foundations *(1999) and* Moral Theory: An Introduction *(2002). In this selection, Timmons first presents a version of the divine command theory and then, after evaluating various arguments in favor of the theory, he raises what has come to be called the Euthyphro Dilemma. This dilemma, which confronts theists, concerns the relationship between morality and God's commands. Either morality depends on God's commands or it does not. As Timmons explains, the dilemma for the theist is that both options involve having to sacrifice certain theistic claims about the nature of God. Timmons goes on to explain how the dilemma can be avoided, but its avoidance requires rejection of the divine command theory.*

According to the Christian, the commandment to love our neighbor is right not in virtue of the fact that God requires it; God requires it in virtue of the fact that it is naturally right.

—FRANZ BRENTANO[1]

In the minds of many people, there is a deep connection between morality and religion. Historically, of course, religious world-views contain a moral outlook as part of an overall vision of the place and purpose of human beings in the world. People brought up in a religious community thus come to associate morality with religion. In addition to the historical connection between morality and religion, there are other possible connections between them that are worthy of consideration but are often not distinguished.[2] In this chapter, we are primarily interested in a particular way in which morality has been thought to depend on religion, or more precisely, on the commands of God. The thought, central to the divine command moral theory, is that morality itself—what is right and wrong, good and bad—depends on God's commands. It is God's act of commanding that we avoid certain types of action that *makes* those actions wrong, and so forth for other moral concepts.[3]

The Theory

Let us focus for the time being on the theory of right action—that branch of moral theory that concerns the nature of right and wrong action. The main idea is that what makes an action right or wrong depends on (and thus can be expressed in terms of) God's commands. Theologian Robert C. Mortimer explains the view this way:

From the doctrine of God as Creator and source of all that is, it follows that a thing is not right simply because we think it is, still less because it seems to be expedient. It is right because God commands it. This means that there is a real distinction between right and wrong that is independent of what we happen to think. It is rooted in the nature and will of God (8/36).[4]

Mortimer mentions the rightness of actions being based on God's commands (by which he means an action's being obligatory), but all the other moral categories can be similarly characterized. In order to focus on the divine command theory, it will help if we express the essentials of the theory in terms of a set of basic principles.

Theory of Right Conduct

An action A is *obligatory* if and only if God commands that we A.
An action A is *forbidden (wrong)* if and only if God commands that we not A.

An action A is *optional* if and only if it is not the case that God commands that we A (thus, not obligatory), and it is not the case that God commands that we not A (thus, not forbidden). Less cumbersomely: if and only if God neither commands that we A nor that we not A.

Turning for a moment to the divine command theory's account of value—the goodness and badness of persons, things, experiences, and states of affairs—it is again facts about God's will that make certain things good and others bad (or evil). Typically, in presenting a theory of value, we are concerned with the nature of *intrinsic* goodness and badness. However, in connection with the divine command theory, it would be misleading at best to talk about what is intrinsically good—good in itself—since the very idea here is that nothing is intrinsically good or bad. Rather, on this theory it is something extrinsic to whatever is good or bad that confers upon it the value it has, namely, God's commands.[5] With this in mind, we can set forth the divine command theory of value.

Theory of Value

Something S is *good* if and only if God commands that we bring about or preserve S.[6]
Something S is *bad* if and only if God commands that we refrain from bringing about or preserving S.
Something S is *value-neutral* if and only if God neither commands that we bring about or preserve S nor that we refrain from bringing about or preserving S.

What is crucial for understanding the divine command theory is the idea that what makes an action right or wrong, or makes something good or bad, is nothing but brute facts about God's commands. The mere fact that he commands that we not kill, rape, torture, and so forth is what makes such actions wrong; their wrongness consists entirely in the fact that he commands that we not do such actions. Thus, the above principles represent an attempt to provide criteria of the right and the good. (You may recall the theoretical aim of a moral theory explained in the introductory chapter.)

How might the theory be used in leading us to correct moral verdicts about what is right or wrong, good or bad? One obvious way involves appealing to some source, such as the Bible, which purports to contain evidence of God's commands. According to Mortimer, for example, there are three principal ways in which the Bible provides moral guidance. First, "it recalls and restates in simple and even violent language fundamental moral judgments which men are always in danger of forgetting or explaining away. It thus provides a norm and standard of human behavior in the broadest and simplest outline" (15/36). For instance, the Ten Commandments of the Old Testament and Christ's teachings regarding love for fellow human beings in the New Testament provide general moral rules for all human beings.

Second, in addition to moral rules—which we might call the letter of the moral law as commanded by God—we find evidence of the proper spirit for following God's commands. Ideally, humans are to strive toward holiness by following God's commands not out of fear or self-interest but out of love for God. Because the moral goodness of persons has to do with their motives, this point about the spirit of morality presumably reveals the divine command theory's account of moral goodness: the moral goodness (and hence moral virtue) of individuals is measured by how closely they come to fulfilling God's commands out of the motive of love for God.

Finally, according to Mortimer, biblical revelation "suggests new emphases and new precepts, a new scale of human values which could not at all, or could not easily, have been [otherwise] perceived" (16/37). As an example, Mortimer notes that the Incarnation, signifying the restoration of fallen human nature, instructs us that God has equal concern for all human beings, including the outcast, downtrodden, and despised. This equal concern means that all human beings have a special dignity and that consequently all humans are to be treated as ends in themselves. The idea of human dignity is a moral idea that might otherwise be obscure to human beings except for revelation.

Thus, the divine command theory's principles of right conduct and value are intended as criteria—indicating what it is about an action or other item of evaluation that makes it right or wrong, good or bad. And, as we have just seen, these principles are the basis of a decision procedure, thus guiding our choices and actions.

Defending the Theory

Let us now consider why anyone might accept the divine command theory—or at least anyone who is already a theist. There are three types of arguments worth considering.

According to what I will call the *linguistic argument*, the divine command theory is true simply because "obligatory," when used in its moral sense, just means "commanded by God" (and so on for the other moral concepts). So consider someone who would deny the truth of any of the theory's moral principles. According to the linguistic argument, such a denial would be like denying the general claim that all bachelors are unmarried. If one denies this latter claim, while also intending to use the term "bachelor" as it is ordinarily used, then one shows a lack of understanding of the concept of a bachelor. Similarly, it might be claimed, if one denies the principles of the divine command theory, one thereby shows that one does not understand basic moral concepts like "obligatory," "good," and so on.

However, this appeal to meaning is implausible. Indeed, its implausibility is easily revealed by comparing the bachelor example with any of the divine command theory's principles. It certainly would show a lack of understanding on the part of someone to deny that all bachelors are unmarried, for it is manifestly clear that part of what we mean by the term "bachelor" is "someone who is unmarried." If we know that someone is a bachelor, the question of whether he is also unmarried is settled. Or to put it another way, if one claims that someone is a bachelor but then goes on to claim that he is married, one can be accused of contradicting oneself.

But similar points cannot be made about moral concepts. If one claims that some action is obligatory but that the action is not commanded by God (perhaps because the speaker does not believe there is a God), one has not thereby contradicted himself. So, the linguistic argument under consideration is not persuasive.[7]

Religious arguments for the theory appeal to theistic premises, for example, premises about the nature of God. We have already encountered one such argument in the first quote from Mortimer. He infers the truth of the divine command theory from the theistic claim that God is creator of all. We can elaborate Mortimer's line of thought as follows. God must be the creative source of morality and hence the divine command theory must be true, because if he were not the source of morality, then there would be some moral standards or principles independent of God. And if there are moral standards and principles independent of God, it follows that he would not be creator of all things. So, if God is creator of absolutely everything (except himself), then we are committed to the divine command theory. I will pass over this argument for now since we return to it in the next section where I will argue that the theist has good reason to question one of its basic assumptions.

We come finally to what I will call the *argument from moral objectivity*. This argument claims that the only moral theory that provides an objective basis for a single true morality is the divine command theory. According to monotheism, there is a single God who issues a set of commands to all human beings, regardless of culture and historical setting. This means that, unlike moral relativism, there is a single set of true moral principles, and hence the kinds of problems that infect relativism[8] do not apply to the divine command theory.

The problem with this argument is that it is premature. The other theories presented in this book (except for moral relativism) can each be understood as attempts to articulate and defend some single true morality and whose moral principles are thus put forth as objectively correct. Thus, in order for the argument from moral objectivity to have any real force, it would have to be true that the other various nonrelativist moral theories somehow fail. This remains to be seen; hence the argument is premature. Moreover, because there are serious problems with the divine command theory, we do have good reason to examine other theories. Let us now turn to a major criticism of the theory.

The Euthyphro Dilemma

Many thinkers (both theists and nontheists) have claimed that the divine command theory should be rejected owing to a dilemma that takes it name from the title of one of Plato's dialogs, the *Euthyphro*.[9] In this dialog, Euthyphro professes to know what piety is and Socrates questions him about it. After Euthyphro gives examples of what he takes to be pious actions, the dialog continues:

SOCR: Remember, then, that I did not ask you to tell me one or two of all the many pious actions that there are; I want to know what is characteristic of piety which makes all pious action pious. You said, I think, that there is one characteristic which makes all pious actions pious, and another characteristic which makes all impious actions impious. Do you remember? (7)

After some discussion, we get Euthyphro's answer:

EUTH: Well, I should say that piety is what all the gods love, and that impiety is what they all hate. (11)

Socrates then poses the crucial question:

SOCR: Now consider this question. Do the gods love piety because it is pious, or is it pious because they love it? (11)

Here, Socrates is asking about the relation between piety and the love of the gods. But the same question can be raised in connection with the relation between morality generally and the commands of God: Does God command that we do obligatory actions because they *are* obligatory, or is some action obligatory *because* God commands that we do it? To fully appreciate the force of the dilemma, it will be useful to pause for a moment and review a few of the key tenets of traditional theistic belief.

According to many versions of theism, there is a single personal God who is an all-perfect being, possessing every perfection to the highest degree. God's perfections include omniscience (all-knowing), omnipotence (all-powerful) as well as:

G1. *Creator*: God is creator of everything (other than himself). God's omnipotence ensures that he can bring about anything possible, and his being creator is a matter of his realizing his omnipotence in bringing about this particular world from among the possible worlds he might have created instead.

G2. *Full Rationality*: There is a sufficient reason for all of God's actions—everything he does, he does for a reason and with complete wisdom.

G3. *Perfect Moral Goodness*: God, as a being, is morally good in the fullest possible sense: He possesses every moral perfection to the highest possible degree. If we were to make a list of these perfections, we could begin by saying that he is all-just, omnibenevolent (all-loving), all-merciful, and so forth.

I won't pause to elaborate these tenets, hoping that my readers will find them clear enough for present purposes.

The Euthyphro Dilemma is a dilemma for the theist who accepts these claims about the nature of God. And, as noted above, it arises in connection with the question: How is morality related to God's commands? There are two possibilities. Either morality depends on God's commands or it doesn't. To be more precise, the two options are these. Either:

1. What is right and wrong depends on God's commands in the sense that his commands alone are what *make* actions right or wrong (similarly for goodness and badness),

or

2. God commands us to perform certain actions and refrain from performing others because certain actions *are* right and others *are* wrong and being fully rational he knows what is right and wrong and being completely good he issues commands to humanity that conform to his moral knowledge (similarly for goodness and badness).

The first option represents the divine command theory; the second option represents the rejection of the divine command theory because it presupposes that, independently of God's will, certain actions are right and others wrong.

The dilemma can now be easily explained. In response to the question about how God and morality are related, either the theist accepts the divine command theory (option 1) or not (option 2). Whichever option one takes, one runs afoul of one or more of the basic theistic tenets mentioned above. Let us see why.

First, if one embraces the divine command theory, then one is forced to give up G2—the claim that everything God does he does for a reason. To grasp this point is to grasp the very idea of the divine command theory. As I have been saying, according to the divine command theory, what makes an action obligatory is the mere fact that God commands that we do it. This means that God's commands are arbitrary—he has no reason for commanding that we keep our promises and avoid hurting others; he might just as well have commanded us to ignore our promises and ignore how our actions affect others.

We can perhaps bring out this point more clearly if we suppose that God does have reasons for his commands; for example, suppose he has some reason for commanding that we help others in need. But what sort of reason might that be? Apparently, it would be some fact about the action—some fact that makes that action an action we ought to do. But then if God is basing his commands on reasons of this sort, we are committed to saying that God commands what he does because certain actions are right or wrong and, given God's nature, he conforms his commands to what is (independently of his commands) right or wrong. So in supposing that God has reasons for his commands we are in effect rejecting the divine command theory. Thus, implied by the divine command theory is the idea that God's commands are arbitrary—that they are issued without reason.

Furthermore, if we accept the divine command theory, we cannot make good sense of God's goodness, which means that we are forced to abandon G3. Consider the claim that God is good. According to the divine command theory and, in particular, its principle about what makes something good, God is good if and only if God commands that we bring about or preserve him. Surely this is not correct, and not just because it is nonsense to talk about human beings bringing about or preserving an all-sufficient being. God is good in virtue of possessing certain characteristics, not as a result of commands he issues. For instance, the quality of being omnipotent is a good-making quality precisely because possession of knowledge is intrinsically good. The goodness of possessing knowledge, we might say, is an inherent property of such possession. God's goodness, then, is explained by the fact that he has various good-making qualities.

Since the divine command theory forces the theist to give up G2 and G3, the theist has reason to reject this theory.

What about the other option that involves rejecting the divine command theory? Notice first of all that it does not represent some alternative moral theory. Rather, all it says in effect is that God conforms his commands to what is right and wrong, but it does not tell us what it is that makes actions right or wrong. It leaves that open. However, this option also seems to be at odds with theism because it seems to conflict with G1—the idea that God is creator. After all, if we admit that right and wrong, good and bad are not a matter of God's will, aren't we saying that there exists a moral code or standard independent of God? Thus, he is not creator of everything, contrary to G1. Mortimer's religious argument, recall, was to the effect that we have to accept the divine command theory in light of the idea of God as creator.

Whether the theist accepts the divine command theory (option 1) or not (option 2), it looks as if she must give up an important tenet of theistic belief about God. Hence, the dilemma.

A Way Out

What are the theist's options at this point? It would be too much for the theist to give up the claims expressed in G2 and G3 to the effect that God is fully rational and is perfectly good. In particular, the theist cannot give up the claim about God's goodness since it is the basis for devotion and worship. If this is correct, the theist must reject the divine command theory.

But what about the other option? If we give up the divine command theory, must we compromise the idea of God as creator? Many philosophers and theologians do not think so. Let us see why.

The gist of the solution to the dilemma that I shall propose involves two claims. (1) There is an important sense in which what is right and wrong, good and bad, depend on God's creative choices, and so there is a sense in which morality depends on God. (2) However, the theist should accept the idea that there are basic facts about what is right and wrong, good and bad that are independent of God's commands. Maintaining both of these claims requires that we refine our understanding of God as creator; but (so I shall maintain) the theist need not give up anything essential to her theism in doing so. Let us take this one step at a time.

Given God's omnipotence, there are many possible worlds he might have created, much different from the actual world he did create. In particular, not only might he have created a planet in place of Earth with a very different environment, he might have created intelligent beings whose natures are importantly different from human nature. However, as a matter of fact (and for good reason) God created human beings—beings that are mortal, whose bodies are such that they can be harmed in various ways, who must work to develop certain talents and capacities, and so forth. Moreover, he placed humans in a certain kind of natural environment in which they must toil for food and shelter and that, because of limited resources, leads to competition among such beings. For a theist, all of this depends on God's will; it might have been different.

Now because humans are of a certain nature and find themselves in a certain environment, there are certain actions that, for example, it would be wrong to do owing to their effects on human well-being. Moral rules against murder and theft thus apply to human beings, but notice that part of the reason they apply has to do with the fact that God created humans with a certain nature and put them in a certain environment. Had he created another type of being who was, for instance, unharmable and where there was no need of property, rules against murder and theft would not apply. Thus, in a sense, God has control over what moral rules correctly apply to human beings. Hence, in a sense, God has control over morality, that is, over what is right and wrong for us to do.

Still, *given* that human beings are the way they are, there are certain moral principles or rules that are true or correct, and their truth or correctness is independent of God's commands. For creatures who can be harmed in all the ways humans can be harmed, certain actions are morally wrong perhaps because of how such actions adversely affect human well-being, or perhaps for some other reason. (It is the task of moral theory to discover what the reason is.) What God does in creating human beings is make it the case that a certain set of moral principles (those appropriate for humans) are the true or correct ones when it comes to questions of human morality.

At this point, an analogy might help. Suppose that I want to build a machine of some sort but that there are various ways in which I might design the machine's motor. I might construct it so that it runs on gasoline, or I might make it so that it runs on vegetable oil, or on beer, or whatever. The worth of the machine is its running well, and if I make the one that runs on gasoline, I should fill its tank with gas, but if I make the one that runs on vegetable oil, I should fill its tank accordingly. The idea is that whether I should fill the machine with one fluid or another depends on two factors: (1) facts about various sorts of motors and (2) my decision about what sort of motor to create. The suggestion, then, is that for various sorts of possible creatures subject to moral requirements, there are basic moral principles whose truth or correctness does not depend on God's will. (Just as facts about various motors and what they will run on is not up to me.) However, since God has control over the kind of creature he will create, he does exert control over which set of principles is to be followed. (Just as it is up to me to decide what kind of motor to build.)

Can a theist be happy with this solution? After all, although it grants that God has a kind of control over morality, it still maintains that basic moral principles are independent of God's will. It is not God's commanding that we refrain from murder that makes murder wrong, rather it is wrong because of how it affects the interests and lives of human beings. But should we understand the claim that God is creator to mean that, in addition to the physical universe that theists believe that he created, he also created moral standards and such abstract things as mathematical truths and the principles of logic?

Many philosophers hold that such standards, truths, and principles are not only true but are *necessarily* true. A truth is necessary when it is not possible for it to be false. Consider the mathematical proposition that $2 + 2 = 4$. This is not only true, but necessarily so: it is not possible for the equation to be otherwise. God couldn't make $2 + 2$ turn out to be 5 given the quantities designated by 2 and by 5 and given what we mean by '+' and '='. But so what? The fact that God cannot do or bring about what is impossible represents no genuine limit on God's omnipotence, as many theologians, including Aquinas, have argued. And so, if we understand basic moral principles to be necessarily true, we can likewise point out that it is no real limit on God's omnipotence that the truth of those principles does not depend on God's will. If we reconsider the claim about God (as creator as expressed in G1), we should reformulate it to say that as omnipotent God has power over everything that is not a matter of necessity. In particular, God is creator of the entire physical universe including human beings whose existence is certainly not a necessary fact.

Some theists might be reluctant to embrace this solution. But embracing the divine command theory is going to force the theist to reject or modify G2 and G3, and I've already mentioned why doing so is unattractive. Moreover, the reluctant theist should reflect on the fact that many theologians and philosophers embrace a solution like the one I have offered.[10]

Conclusion

The divine command theory is initially attractive for two reasons. First, it purports to set forth a single true morality for all human beings—a moral code that applies to all human beings regardless of their culture. Second, at least for theists, this theory comports with the sense that there is a deep-going connection between religion and morality.

However, we have found reason to reject the divine command theory. First, as we saw, the rightness or wrongness of actions cannot be properly explained simply in terms of their being commanded by God. It is not merely the fact that God commands that we perform some action that makes it obligatory. Thus, the principles of the divine command theory fail to specify a correct criterion of the right and the good; they fail to give us a proper explanation of what makes something right or wrong, good or bad. (You may recall the criterion of explanatory power that was explained in the introductory chapter.)

Second, we have found reason why, despite initial appearances, the theory is at odds with some basic tenets of theism and so the theist has reason to reject this theory. (Again, recall from the introductory chapter, the criterion of external support.) However, rejecting the divine command theory does not mean that religion generally and God's commands in particular are of no importance for morality. Indeed, we might even use the divine command theory's principles of right conduct and value as the basis of a decision procedure in ethics. Certainly, assuming there is a God of the sort believed in by many theists, one can look to revelation for some moral guidance. Moreover, one can look to revelation for some indication of what makes an action right or wrong, or some state of affairs good or bad.

Christ's teachings concerning love might be construed as advocating an ethic of universal benevolence—the idea behind the utilitarian moral theory (see Chapter 5). Mortimer, you may recall, claims that the Bible contains the idea that all humans possess a kind of dignity—an idea that is central in the moral philosophy of Immanuel Kant (see Chapter 6). The idea that human beings are created by God and designed to fulfill certain purposes is, of course, an idea to be found in the Bible and this idea is featured in Aquinas's version of the natural law moral theory that is the subject of the next chapter.

Notes

1. *The Origin of Our Knowledge of Right and Wrong* (1889).
2. For instance, it is sometimes claimed that acquiring moral *knowledge* requires appealing to religious authority or that being *motivated* to do what is right depends on accepting a religious outlook. These claims about knowledge and motivation are distinct from the divine command theory and will not be discussed in this essay.
3. Throughout this essay, and merely for convenience, I will use the masculine pronoun to refer to God.
4. All quotes from Mortimer are from *Christian Ethics* (New York: Hutchinson's University Library, 1950), and, for convenience, I will incorporate page references into the text, followed by page numbers from Mortimer's excerpt in this collection.
5. We might attempt to capture something of the contrast between things with intrinsic value and things having extrinsic value by distinguishing those things with regard to which God issues commands—things having what we might call *fundamental goodness or badness*—from those things which, because they are instrumental in bringing about what is fundamentally good or bad, can be said to have derivative value. But since this complication does not matter for our purposes, I will ignore it.
6. Strictly speaking, this characterization of nonmoral goodness makes everything that is nonmorally good something that human beings are in a position to do something about. But surely there could be things or states of affairs that are nonmorally good but that are beyond the range of what humans can either bring about or preserve (perhaps because they are in some remote corner of the universe that we will never experience). I thank Robert Audi for calling my attention to this problem. To fix this defect, either we can restrict these characterizations to only those things, experiences, and states of affairs that humans can do something about or we could replace reference to what God does and does not command with reference to what God does and does not *approve* of. (God may approve of all sorts of things that simply do not relate to human existence.) Since it is the divine command theory, I have chosen to express both the principles of right conduct and the principles of nonmoral value in terms of God's commands. So we are to understand the principles of nonmoral value as restricted in the manner just explained.
7. This does not mean that all possible versions of the linguistic argument are as easily refuted. Sophisticated linguistic arguments that cannot be considered here are to be found in, for example, Robert M. Adams, "A Modified Divine Command Theory of Ethical Wrongness," in Gene Outka and John P. Reeder (eds.), *Religion and Morality: A Collection of Essays* (New York: Doubleday and Company, Inc., 1973). Reprinted in Paul Helm (ed.), *Divine Commands and Morality* (Oxford: Oxford University Press, 1981).
8. Moral relativism is the subject of the following two selections.

9. Plato, Euthyphro, in *Euthyphro, Apology, Crito,* F. J. Church, trans. (Indianapolis, IN: The Bobbs-Merrill Company, Inc., 1976). All page references to this work are incorporated into the text.

10. See, for example, R. G. Swinburn, "Duty and the Will of God," *Canadian Journal of Philosophy* 4 (1974): 213–27. Reprinted in Paul Helm (ed.), *Divine Commands and Morality* (Oxford: Oxford University Press, 1981).

A DEFENSE OF ETHICAL RELATIVISM
Ruth Benedict

Ruth Benedict (1887–1948) was a pioneering American anthropologist and wrote Patterns of Culture (1935), an important work in comparative anthropology. Benedict argues that careful study of the cultural practices of different peoples supports the idea that what is and is not behaviorally normal is culturally determined. She argues for a similar point in connection with such moral distinctions as good and bad, and right and wrong. She suggests that phrases like "it is morally good" should be understood as being synonymous with "it is habitual."

Modern social anthropology has become more and more a study of the varieties and common elements of cultural environment and the consequences of these in human behavior. For such a study of diverse social orders primitive peoples fortunately provide a laboratory not yet entirely vitiated by the spread of a standardized worldwide civilization. Dyaks and Hopis, Fijians and Yakuts are significant for psychological and sociological study because only among these simpler peoples has there been sufficient isolation to give opportunity for the development of localized social forms. In the higher cultures the standardization of custom and belief over a couple of continents has given a false sense of the inevitability of the particular forms that have gained currency, and we need to turn to a wider survey in order to check the conclusions we hastily base upon this near-universality of familiar customs. Most of the simpler cultures did not gain the wide currency of the one which, out of our experience, we identify with human nature, but this was for various historical reasons, and certainly not for any that gives us as its carriers a monopoly of social good or of social sanity. Modern civilization, from this point of view, becomes not a necessary pinnacle of human achievement but one entry in a long series of possible adjustments.

These adjustments, whether they are in mannerisms like the ways of showing anger, or joy, or grief in any society, or in major human drives like those of sex, prove to be far more variable than experience in any one culture would suggest. In certain fields, such as that of religion or of formal marriage arrangements, these

From Ruth Benedict, "Anthropology and the Abnormal," *Journal of General Psychology* 10 (1934): 59–82. Reprinted by permission of Helen Dwight Reid Educational Foundation. Published by Heldref Publications, Washington, DC.

wide limits of variability are well known and can be fairly described. In others it is not yet possible to give a generalized account, but that does not absolve us of the task of indicating the significance of the work that has been done and of the problems that have arisen.

One of these problems relates to the customary modern normal-abnormal categories and our conclusions regarding them. In how far are such categories culturally determined, or in how far can we with assurance regard them as absolute? In how far can we regard inability to function socially as diagnostic of abnormality, or in how far is it necessary to regard this as a function of the culture?

As a matter of fact, one of the most striking facts that emerges from a study of widely varying cultures is the ease with which our abnormals function in other cultures. It does not matter what kind of "abnormality" we choose for illustration, those which indicate extreme instability, or those which are more in the nature of character traits like sadism or delusions of grandeur or of persecution, there are well-described cultures in which these abnormals function at ease and with honor, and apparently without danger or difficulty to the society.

The most notorious of these is trance and catalepsy. Even a very mild mystic is aberrant in our culture. But most peoples have regarded even extreme psychic manifestations not only as normal and desirable, but even as characteristic of highly valued and gifted individuals. This was true even in our own cultural background in that period when Catholicism made the ecstatic experience the mark of sainthood. It is hard for us, born and brought up in a culture that makes no use of the experience, to realize how important a role it may play and how many individuals are capable of it, once it has been given an honorable place in any society....

Cataleptic and trance phenomena are, of course, only one illustration of the fact that those whom we regard as abnormals may function adequately in other cultures. Many of our culturally discarded traits are selected for elaboration in different societies. Homosexuality is an excellent example, for in this case our attention is not constantly diverted, as in the consideration of trance, to the interruption of routine activity which it implies. Homosexuality poses the problem very simply. A tendency toward this trait in our culture exposes an individual to all the conflicts to which all aberrants are always exposed, and we tend to identify the consequences of this conflict with homosexuality. But these consequences are obviously local and cultural. Homosexuals in many societies are not incompetent, but they may be such if the culture asks adjustments of them that would strain any man's vitality. Wherever homosexuality has been given an honorable place in any society, those to whom it is congenial have filled adequately the honorable roles society assigns to them. Plato's *Republic* is, of course, the most convincing statement of such a reading of homosexuality. It is presented as one of the major means to the good life, and it was generally so regarded in Greece at that time.

The cultural attitude toward homosexuals has not always been on such a high ethical plane, but it has been very varied. Among many American Indian tribes there exists the institution of the berdache, as the French called them. These men-women were men who at puberty or thereafter took the dress and the occupations of women. Sometimes they married other men and lived with them. Sometimes they were men with no inversion, persons of weak sexual endowment who chose this role to avoid the jeers of the women. The berdaches were never regarded as of first-rate supernatural power, as similar men-women were in Siberia, but rather as leaders in women's occupations, good healers in certain diseases, or, among certain tribes, as the genial organizers of social affairs. In any case, they were socially placed. They were not left exposed to the conflicts that visit the deviant who is excluded from participation in the recognized pattern of his society.

The most spectacular illustrations of the extent to which normality may be culturally defined are those cultures where an abnormality of our culture is the cornerstone of their social structure. It is not possible to do justice to these possibilities in a short discussion. A recent study of an island of northwest Melanesia by Fortune describes a society built upon traits which we regard as beyond the border of paranoia. In this tribe the exogamic groups look upon each other as prime manipulators of black magic, so that one marries always into an enemy group which remains for life one's deadly and unappeasable foes. They look upon a good garden crop as a confession of theft, for everyone is engaged in making magic to induce into his garden the productiveness of his neighbors'; therefore no secrecy in the island is so rigidly insisted upon as the secrecy of a man's harvesting of his yams. Their polite phrase at the acceptance of a gift is, "And if you now poison me, how shall I repay you this present?" Their preoccupation with poisoning is constant; no woman ever leaves her cooking pot for a moment untended. Even the great affinal economic exchanges that are characteristic of this Melanesian culture area are quite altered in Dobu since they are incompatible with this fear and distrust that pervades the culture. They go farther and people the whole world outside their own quarters with such malignant spirits that all-night feasts and ceremonials simply do not occur here. They have even rigorous religiously enforced customs that forbid the sharing of seed even in one family group. Anyone else's food is deadly poison to you, so that communality of stores is out of the question. For some months before harvest the whole society is on the verge of starvation, but if one falls to the temptation and eats up one's seed yams, one is an outcast and a beachcomber for life. There is no coming back. It involves, as a matter of course, divorce and the breaking of all social ties.

Now in this society where no one may work with another and no one may share with another, Fortune describes the individual who was regarded by all his fellows as crazy. He was not one of those who periodically ran amok and, beside himself and frothing at the mouth, fell with a knife upon anyone he could reach. Such behavior they did not regard as putting anyone outside the pale. They did not even put the individuals who were known to be liable to these attacks under any kind of control. They merely fled when they saw the attack coming on and kept out of the way. "He would be all right tomorrow." But there was one man of sunny, kindly disposition who liked work and liked to be helpful. The compulsion was too strong for him to repress it in favor of the opposite tendencies of his culture. Men and women never spoke of him without laughing; he was silly and simple and definitely crazy. Nevertheless, to the ethnologist used to a culture that has, in Christianity, made his type the model of all virtue, he seemed a pleasant fellow....

. . . Among the Kwakiutl it did not matter whether a relative had died in bed of disease, or by the hand of an enemy, in either case death was an affront to be wiped out by the death of another person. The fact that one had been caused to mourn was proof that one had been put upon. A chief's sister and her daughter had gone up to Victoria, and either because they drank bad whiskey or because their boat capsized they never came back. The chief called together his warriors, "Now I ask you, tribes, who shall wail? Shall I do it or shall another?" The spokesman answered, of course, "Not you, Chief. Let some other of the tribes." Immediately they set up the war pole to announce their intention of wiping out the injury, and gathered a war party. They set out, and found seven men and two children asleep and killed them. "Then they felt good when they arrived at Sebaa in the evening."

The point which is of interest to us is that in our society those who on that occasion would feel good when they arrived at Sebaa that evening would be the definitely abnormal. There would be some, even in our society, but it is not a recognized and approved mood under the circumstances. On the Northwest Coast those are favored and fortunate to whom that mood under those circumstances is congenial, and those to whom it is repugnant are unlucky. This latter minority can register in their own culture only by doing violence to their congenial responses and acquiring others that are difficult for them. The person, for instance, who, like a Plains Indian whose wife has been taken from him, is too proud to fight, can deal with the Northwest Coast civilization only by ignoring its strongest bents. If he cannot achieve it, he is the deviant in that culture, their instance of abnormality.

This head-hunting that takes place on the Northwest Coast after a death is no matter of blood revenge or of organized vengeance. There is no effort to tie up the subsequent killing with any responsibility on the part of the victim for the death of the person who is being mourned. A chief whose son has died goes visiting wherever his fancy dictates, and he says to his host, "My prince has died today, and you go with him." Then he kills him. In this, according to their interpretation, he acts nobly because he has not been downed. He has thrust back in return. The whole procedure is meaningless without the fundamental paranoid reading of bereavement. Death, like all the other untoward accidents of existence, confounds man's pride and can only be handled in the category of insults.

Behavior honored upon the Northwest Coast is one which is recognized as abnormal in our civilization, and yet it is sufficiently close to the attitudes of our own culture to be intelligible to us and to have a definite vocabulary with which we may discuss it. The megalomaniac paranoid trend is a definite danger in our society. It is encouraged by some of our major preoccupations, and it confronts us with a choice of two possible attitudes. One is to brand it as abnormal and reprehensible, and is the attitude we have chosen in our civilization. The other is to make it an essential attribute of ideal man, and this is the solution in the culture of the Northwest Coast.

These illustrations, which it has been possible to indicate only in the briefest manner, force upon us the fact that normality is culturally defined. An adult shaped to the drives and standards of either of these cultures, if he were transported into our civilization, would fall into our categories of abnormality. He would be faced with the psychic dilemmas of the socially unavailable. In his own culture, however, he is the pillar of society, the end result of socially inculcated mores, and the problem of personal instability in his case simply does not arise.

No one civilization can possibly utilize in its mores the whole potential range of human behavior. Just as there are great numbers of possible phonetic articulations, and the possibility of language depends on a selection and standardization of a few of these in order that speech communication may be possible at all, so the possibility of organized behavior of every sort, from the fashions of local dress and houses to the dicta of a people's ethics and religion, depends upon a similar selection among the possible behavior traits. In the field of recognized economic obligations or sex tabus this selection is as nonrational and subconscious a process as it is in the field of phonetics. It is a process which goes on in the group for long periods of time and is historically conditioned by innumerable accidents of isolation or of contact of peoples. In any comprehensive study of psychology, the selection that different cultures have made in the course of history within the great circumference of potential behavior is of great significance.

Every society, beginning with some slight inclination in one direction or another, carries its preference farther and farther, integrating itself more and more completely upon its chosen basis, and discarding those types of behavior that are uncongenial. Most of those organizations of personality that seem to us most incontrovertibly abnormal have been used by different civilizations in the very foundations of their institutional life. Conversely the most valued traits of our normal individuals have been looked on in differently organized cultures as aberrant. Normality, in short, within a very wide range, is culturally defined. It is primarily a term for the socially elaborated segment of human behavior in any culture; and abnormality, a term for the segment that that particular civilization does not use. The very eyes with which we see the problem are conditioned by the long traditional habits of our own society.

It is a point that has been made more often in relation to ethics than in relation to psychiatry. We do not any longer make the mistake of deriving the morality of our locality and decade directly from the inevitable constitution of human nature. We do not elevate it to the dignity of a first principle. We recognize that morality differs in every society, and is a convenient term for socially approved habits. Mankind has always preferred to say, "It is morally good," rather than "It is habitual," and the fact of this preference is matter enough for a critical science of ethics. But historically the two phrases are synonymous.

The concept of the normal is properly a variant of the concept of the good. It is that which society has approved. A normal action is one which falls well within the limits of expected behavior for a particular society. Its variability among different peoples is essentially a function of the variability of the behavior patterns that different societies have created for themselves, and can never be wholly divorced from a consideration of culturally institutionalized types of behavior.

Each culture is a more or less elaborate working-out of the potentialities of the segment it has chosen. In so far as a civilization is well integrated and consistent within itself, it will tend to carry farther and farther, according to its nature, its initial impulse toward a particular type of action, and from the point of view of any other culture those elaborations will include more and more extreme and aberrant traits.

Each of these traits, in proportion as it reinforces the chosen behavior patterns of that culture, is for that culture normal. Those individuals to whom it is congenial either congenitally, or as the result of childhood sets, are accorded prestige in that culture, and are not visited with the social contempt or disapproval which their traits would call down upon them in a society that was differently organized. On the other hand, those individuals whose characteristics are not congenial to the selected type of human behavior in that community are the deviants, no matter how valued their personality traits may be in a contrasted civilization.

The Dobuan who is not easily susceptible to fear of treachery, who enjoys work and likes to be helpful, is their neurotic and regarded as silly. On the Northwest Coast the person who finds it difficult to read life in terms of an insult contest will be the person upon whom fall all the difficulties of the culturally unprovided for. The person who does not find it easy to humiliate a neighbor, nor to see humiliation in his own experience, who is genial and loving, may, of course, find some unstandardized way of achieving satisfactions in his society, but not in the major patterned responses that his culture requires of him. If he is born to play an important role in a family with many hereditary privileges, he can succeed only by doing violence to his whole personality. If he does not succeed, he has betrayed his culture; that is, he is abnormal.

I have spoken of individuals as having sets toward certain types of behavior, and of these sets as running sometimes counter to the types of behavior which are institutionalized in the culture to which they belong. From all that we know of contrasting cultures it seems clear that differences of temperament occur in every society. The matter has never been made the subject of investigation, but from the available material it would appear that these temperament types are very likely of universal recurrence. That is, there is an ascertainable range of human behavior that is found wherever a sufficiently large series of individuals is observed. But the proportion in which behavior types stand to one another in different societies is not universal. The vast majority of individuals in any group are shaped to the fashion of that culture. In other words, most individuals are plastic to the moulding force of the society into which they are born. In a society that values trance, as in India, they will have supernormal experience. In a society that institutionalizes homosexuality, they will be homosexual. In a society that sets the gathering of possessions as the chief human objective, they will amass property. The deviants, whatever the type of behavior the culture has institutionalized, will remain few in number, and there seems no more difficulty in moulding the vast malleable majority to the "normality" of what we consider an aberrant trait, such as delusions of reference, than to the normality of such accepted behavior patterns as acquisitiveness. The small proportion of the number of the deviants in any culture is not a function of the sure instinct with which the society has built itself upon the fundamental sanities, but of the universal fact that, happily, the majority of mankind quite readily take any shape that is presented to them....

THE CHALLENGE OF CULTURAL RELATIVISM
James Rachels

James Rachels (1941–2003) was professor of philosophy at the University of Alabama, Birmingham, from 1977 until his death. His books include Euthanasia and Morality *(1986),* The Elements of Moral Philosophy *(1986),* Created from Animals: The Moral Implications of Darwinism *(1991), and* Can Ethics Provide Answers? And Other Essays in Moral Philosophy *(1997). In the selection below, Rachels is critical of cultural relativism, according to which what is right or wrong, good or bad, is relative to the moral code of one's society or culture. After criticizing the cultural differences argument often used to support cultural relativism, Rachels argues that there are good reasons for rejecting this moral theory.*

> Morality differs in every society, and is a convenient term for socially approved habits.
>
> —RUTH BENEDICT, *PATTERNS OF CULTURE* (1934)

How Different Cultures Have Different Moral Codes

Darius, a king of ancient Persia, was intrigued by the variety of cultures he encountered in his travels. He had found, for example, that the Callatians (a tribe of Indians) customarily ate the bodies of their dead fathers. The Greeks, of course, did not do that—the Greeks practiced cremation and regarded the funeral pyre as the natural and fitting way to dispose of the dead. Darius thought that a sophisticated understanding of the world must include an appreciation of such differences between cultures. One day, to teach this lesson, he summoned some Greeks who happened to be present at his court and asked them what they would take to eat the bodies of their dead fathers. They were shocked, as Darius knew they would be, and replied that no amount of money could persuade them to do such a thing. Then Darius called in some Callatians, and while the Greeks listened asked them what they would take to burn their dead fathers' bodies. The Callatians were horrified and told Darius not even to mention such a dreadful thing.

This story, recounted by Herodotus in his *History*, illustrates a recurring theme in the literature of social science: different cultures have different moral codes. What is thought right within one group may be utterly abhorrent to the members of another group, and vice versa. Should we eat the bodies of the dead or burn them? If you were a Greek, one answer would seem obviously correct; but if you were a Callatian, the opposite would seem equally certain.

From James Rachels, *The Elements of Moral Philosophy* (New York: McGraw-Hill, 1986). Reprinted with permission of The McGraw-Hill Companies.

It is easy to give additional examples of the same kind. Consider the Eskimos. They are a remote and inaccessible people. Numbering only about 25,000, they live in small, isolated settlements scattered mostly along the northern fringes of North America and Greenland. Until the beginning of this century, the outside world knew little about them. Then explorers began to bring back strange tales.

Eskimo customs turned out to be very different from our own. The men often had more than one wife, and they would share their wives with guests, lending them for the night as a sign of hospitality. Moreover, within a community, a dominant male might demand—and get—regular sexual access to other men's wives. The women, however, were free to break these arrangements simply by leaving their husbands and taking up with new partners—free, that is, so long as their former husbands chose not to make trouble. All in all, the Eskimo practice was a volatile scheme that bore little resemblance to what we call marriage.

But it was not only their marriage and sexual practices that were different. The Eskimos also seemed to have less regard for human life. Infanticide, for example, was common. Knud Rasmussen, one of the most famous early explorers, reported that he met one woman who had borne twenty children but had killed ten of them at birth. Female babies, he found, were especially liable to be destroyed, and this was permitted simply at the parents' discretion, with no social stigma attached to it. Old people also, when they became too feeble to contribute to the family, were left out in the snow to die. So there seemed to be, in this society, remarkably little respect for life.

To the general public, these were disturbing revelations. Our own way of living seems so natural and right that for many of us it is hard to conceive of others living so differently. And when we do hear of such things, we tend immediately to categorize those other peoples as "backward" or "primitive." But to anthropologists and sociologists, there was nothing particularly surprising about the Eskimos. Since the time of Herodotus, enlightened observers have been accustomed to the idea that conceptions of right and wrong differ from culture to culture. If we assume that *our* ideas of right and wrong will be shared by all peoples at all times, we are merely naive.

Cultural Relativism

To many thinkers, this observation—"Different cultures have different moral codes"—has seemed to be the key to understanding morality. The idea of universal truth in ethics, they say, is a myth. The customs of different societies are all that exist. These customs cannot be said to be "correct" or "incorrect," for that implies we have an independent standard of right and wrong by which they may be judged. But there is no such independent standard; every standard is culture-bound. The great pioneering sociologist William Graham Sumner, writing in 1906, put the point like this:

The "right" way is the way which the ancestors used and which has been handed down. The tradition is its own warrant. It is not held subject to verification by experience. The notion of right is in the folkways. It is not outside of them, of independent origin, and

brought to test them. In the folkways, whatever is, is right. This is because they are traditional, and therefore contain in themselves the authority of the ancestral ghosts. When we
come to the folkways we are at the end of our analysis.

This line of thought has probably persuaded more people to be skeptical about
ethics than any other single thing. *Cultural Relativism,* as it has been called, challenges our ordinary belief in the objectivity and universality of moral truth. It
says, in effect, that there is no such thing as universal truth in ethics; there are
only the various cultural codes, and nothing more. Moreover, our own code has
no special status; it is merely one among many....

The Cultural Differences Argument

Cultural Relativism is a theory about the nature of morality. At first blush it seems
quite plausible. However, like all such theories, it may be evaluated by subjecting
it to rational analysis; and when we analyze Cultural Relativism we find that it is
not so plausible as it first appears to be.

The first thing we need to notice is that at the heart of Cultural Relativism
there is a certain *form of argument.* The strategy used by cultural relativists is to
argue from facts about the differences between cultural outlooks to a conclusion
about the status of morality. Thus we are invited to accept this reasoning:

1. The Greeks believed it was wrong to eat the dead, whereas the Callatians
   believed it was right to eat the dead.

2. Therefore, eating the dead is neither objectively right nor objectively wrong.
   It is merely a matter of opinion, which varies from culture to culture.

Or, alternatively:

1. The Eskimos see nothing wrong with infanticide, whereas Americans
   believe infanticide is immoral.

2. Therefore, infanticide is neither objectively right nor objectively wrong. It
   is merely a matter of opinion, which varies from culture to culture.

Clearly, these arguments are variations of one fundamental idea. They are both special cases of a more general argument, which says:

1. Different cultures have different moral codes.

2. Therefore, there is no objective "truth" in morality. Right and wrong are only
   matters of opinion, and opinions vary from culture to culture.

We may call this the *Cultural Differences Argument.* To many people, it is very persuasive. But from a logical point of view, is it a *sound* argument?

It is not sound. The trouble is that the conclusion does not really follow from the premise—that is, even if the premise is true, the conclusion still might be false. The premise concerns what people *believe*: in some societies, people believe one thing; in other societies, people believe differently. The conclusion, however, concerns *what really is the case*. The trouble is that this sort of conclusion does not follow logically from this sort of premise.

Consider again the example of the Greeks and Callatians. The Greeks believed it was wrong to eat the dead; the Callatians believed it was right. Does it follow, *from the mere fact that they disagreed,* that there is no objective truth in the matter? No, it does not follow; for it *could* be that the practice was objectively right (or wrong) and that one or the other of them was simply mistaken.

To make the point clearer, consider a very different matter. In some societies, people believe the earth is flat. In other societies, such as our own, people believe the earth is (roughly) spherical. Does it follow, *from the mere fact that they disagree,* that there is no "objective truth" in geography? Of course not; we would never draw such a conclusion because we realize that, in their beliefs about the world, the members of some societies might simply be wrong. There is no reason to think that if the world is round everyone must know it. Similarly, there is no reason to think that if there is moral truth everyone must know it. The fundamental mistake in the Cultural Differences Argument is that it attempts to derive a substantive conclusion about a subject (morality) from the mere fact that people disagree about it.

It is important to understand the nature of the point that is being made here. We are *not* saying (not yet, anyway) that the conclusion of the argument is false. Insofar as anything being said here is concerned, it is still an open question whether the conclusion is true. We *are* making a purely logical point and saying that the conclusion does not *follow from* the premise. This is important, because in order to determine whether the conclusion is true, we need arguments in its support. Cultural Relativism proposes this argument, but unfortunately the argument turns out to be fallacious. So it proves nothing.

The Consequences of Taking Cultural Relativism Seriously

Even if the Cultural Differences Argument is invalid, Cultural Relativism might still be true. What would it be like if it were true?

In the passage quoted above, William Graham Sumner summarizes the essence of Cultural Relativism. He says that there is no measure of right and wrong other than the standards of one's society: "The notion of right is in the folkways. It is not outside of them, of independent origin, and brought to test them. In the folkways, whatever is, is right."

Suppose we took this seriously. What would be some of the consequences?

1. *We could no longer say that the customs of other societies are morally inferior to our own.* This, of course, is one of the main points stressed by Cultural Relativism. We would have to stop condemning other societies merely because they are "different." So long as we concentrate on certain examples, such as the funerary practices of the Greeks and Callatians, this may seem to be a sophisticated, enlightened attitude.

However, we would also be stopped from criticizing other, less benign practices. Suppose a society waged war on its neighbors for the purpose of taking slaves. Or suppose a society was violently anti-Semitic and its leaders set out to destroy the Jews. Cultural Relativism would preclude us from saying that either of these practices was wrong. We would not even be able to say that a society tolerant of Jews is *better* than the anti-Semitic society, for that would imply some sort of transcultural standard of comparison. The failure to condemn *these* practices does not seem "enlightened"; on the contrary, slavery and anti-Semitism seem wrong *wherever* they occur. Nevertheless, if we took Cultural Relativism seriously, we would have to admit that these social practices also are immune from criticism.

2. *We could decide whether actions are right or wrong just by consulting the standards of our society.* Cultural Relativism suggests a simple test for determining what is right and what is wrong: all one has to do is ask whether the action is in accordance with the code of one's society. Suppose a resident of South Africa is wondering whether his country's policy of *apartheid*—rigid racial segregation—is morally correct. All he has to do is ask whether this policy conforms to his society's moral code. If it does, there is nothing to worry about, at least from a moral point of view.

This implication of Cultural Relativism is disturbing because few of us think that our society's code is perfect—we can think of ways it might be improved. Yet Cultural Relativism would not only forbid us from criticizing the codes of *other* societies; it would stop us from criticizing our *own*. After all, if right and wrong are relative to culture, this must be true for our own culture just as much as for others.

3. *The idea of moral progress is called into doubt.* Usually, we think that at least some changes in our society have been for the better. (Some, of course, may have been changes for the worse.) Consider this example: Throughout most of Western history the place of women in society was very narrowly circumscribed. They could not own property; they could not vote or hold political office; with a few exceptions, they were not permitted to have paying jobs; and generally they were under the almost absolute control of their husbands. Recently much of this has changed, and most people think of it as progress.

If Cultural Relativism is correct, can we legitimately think of this as progress? Progress means replacing a way of doing things with a *better* way. But by what standards do we judge the new ways as better? If the old ways were in accordance with the social standards of their time, then Cultural Relativism would say it is a mistake to judge them by the standards of a different time. Eighteenth-century society was, in effect, a different society from the one we have now. To say that we have made progress implies a judgment that present-day society is better, and that is just the sort of transcultural judgment that, according to Cultural Relativism, is impermissible.

Our idea of social *reform* will also have to be reconsidered. A reformer such as Martin Luther King, Jr., seeks to change his society for the better. Within the constraints imposed by Cultural Relativism, there is one way this might be done. If a society is not living up to its own ideals, the reformer may be regarded as acting for the best: the ideals of the society are the standard by which we judge his or her proposals as worthwhile. But the "reformer" may not challenge the ideals themselves, for those ideals are by definition correct. According to Cultural Relativism, then, the idea of social reform makes sense only in this very limited way.

These three consequences of Cultural Relativism have led many thinkers to reject it as implausible on its face. It does make sense, they say, to condemn some practices, such as slavery and anti-Semitism, wherever they occur. It makes sense to think that our own society has made some moral progress, while admitting that it is still imperfect and in need of reform. Because Cultural Relativism says that these judgments make no sense, the argument goes, it cannot be right.

CHAPTER 4

The Natural Law Theory

TREATISE ON LAW
St. Thomas Aquinas

Aquinas (1225–1274) is one of the most important figures in Western intellectual history. In the following passage from his Summa Theologiae *(Summary of Theology), he presents a classical version of the natural law theory of morality. Aquinas defines law as "an ordinance of reason for the common good, promulgated by him who has care of the community." Natural law is the part of God's eternal law that concerns how human beings ought to conduct themselves. The first precept of natural law is that "good is to be done and promoted, evil is to be avoided." Human beings have natural inclinations to seek their own good, including such things as self-preservation, continuance of the species, education, and living in society. Such ends, then, are basic values, and the first precept of natural law enjoins us to preserve and maintain them. Thus, for Aquinas, basic moral precepts reflect facts about human nature.*

Whether Law is Something Pertaining to Reason?

… It belongs to the law to command and to forbid. But it belongs to reason to command, as was stated above. Therefore law is something pertaining to reason…. Law is a rule and measure of acts, whereby man is induced to act or is restrained from acting; for *lex* (*law*) is derived from *ligare* (*to bind*), because it binds one to act. Now the rule and measure of human acts is the reason, which is the first principle of human acts, as is evident from what has been stated above. For it belongs to the reason to direct to the end, which is the first principle in all matters of action….

Whether Law is Always Directed to the Common Good?

… As we have stated above, law belongs to that which is a principle of human acts, because it is their rule and measure. Now as reason is a principle of human acts, so in reason itself there is something which is the principle in respect of all the rest. Hence to this principle chiefly and mainly law must needs be referred. Now the first principle in practical matters, which are the object of the practical reason, is the last end: and the last end of human life is happiness or beatitude, as we have stated above. Consequently, law must needs concern itself mainly with the order that is in beatitude. Moreover, since every part is ordained to the whole as the imperfect to the perfect, and since one man is a part of the perfect community, law must needs concern itself properly with the order directed to universal happiness.... Since law is chiefly ordained to the common good, any other precept in regard to some individual work must needs be devoid of the nature of a law, save in so far as it regards the common good. Therefore every law is ordained to the common good....

Whether Promulgation is Essential to Law?

... As was stated above, a law is imposed on others as a rule and measure. Now a rule or measure is imposed by being applied to those who are to be ruled and measured by it. Therefore, in order that a law obtain the binding force which is proper to a law, it must needs be applied to the men who have to be ruled by it. But such application is made by its being made known to them by promulgation. Therefore promulgation is necessary for law to obtain its force. . . . Law is nothing else than an ordinance of reason for the common good, promulgated by him who has the care of the community....

The natural law is promulgated by the very fact that God has instilled it into man's mind so as to be known by him naturally....

Whether There is an Eternal Law?

... As we have stated above, law is nothing else but a dictate of practical reason emanating from the ruler who governs a perfect community. Now it is evident, granted that the world is ruled by divine providence, as was stated in the First Part, that the whole community of the universe is governed by the divine reason. Therefore the very notion of the government of things in God, the ruler of the universe, has the nature of a law. And since the divine reason's conception of things is not subject to time, but is eternal, according to *Prov.* 8:23, therefore it is that this kind of law must be called eternal....

Promulgation is made by word of mouth or in writing, and in both ways the eternal law is promulgated, because both the divine Word and the writing of the Book of Life are eternal....

Whether There is in Us a Natural Law?

... As we have stated above, law, being a rule and measure, can be in a person in two ways: in one way, as in him that rules and measures; in another way, as in that which is ruled and measured, since a thing is ruled and measured in so far as it partakes of the rule or measure. Therefore, since all things subject to divine providence are ruled and measured by the eternal law, as was stated above, it is evident that all things partake in some way in the eternal law, in so far as, name-ly, from its being imprinted on them, they derive their respective inclinations to their proper acts and ends. Now among all others, the rational creature is sub-ject to divine providence in a more excellent way, in so far as it itself partakes of a share of providence, by being provident both for itself and for others. Therefore it has a share of the eternal reason, whereby it has a natural inclination to its proper act and end; and this participation of the eternal law in the rational crea-ture is called the natural law. Hence the Psalmist, after saying (Ps. 4:6): *Offer up the sacrifice of justice*, as though someone asked what the works of justice are, adds: *Many say, Who showeth us good things?* in answer to which question he says: *The light of Thy countenance, O Lord, is signed upon us.* He thus implies that the light of natural reason, whereby we discern what is good and what is evil, which is the function of the natural law, is nothing else than an imprint on us of the divine light. It is therefore evident that the natural law is nothing else than the rational creature's participation of the eternal law....

Whether the Natural Law Contains Several Precepts, or Only One?

... The precepts of the natural law are to the practical reason what the first prin-ciples of demonstrations are to the speculative reason, because both are self-evident principles. Now a thing is said to be self-evident in two ways: first, in itself; secondly, in relation to us. Any proposition is said to be self-evident in itself, if its predicate is contained in the notion of the subject; even though it may happen that to one who does not know the definition of the subject, such a proposition is not self-evident. For instance, this proposition, *Man is a rational being,* is, in its very nature, self-evident, since he who says *man,* says *a rational being;* and yet to one who does not know what a man is, this proposition is not self-evident. Hence it is that, as Boethius says, certain axioms or propositions are universally self-evident to all; and such are the propositions whose terms are known to all, as, *Every whole is greater than its part,* and *Things equal to one and the same are equal to one another.* But some propositions are self-evident only to the wise, who understand the meaning of the terms of such propositions. Thus to one who understands that an angel is not a body, it is self-evident that an angel is not circumscriptively in a place. But this is not evident to the unlearned, for they cannot grasp it.

Now a certain order is to be found in those things that are apprehended by men. For that which first falls under apprehension, is *being,* the understanding of which is included in all things whatsoever a man apprehends. Therefore the first indemonstrable principle is that *the same thing cannot be affirmed and denied at the same time,* which is based on the notion of *being and not-being:* and on this prin-ciple all others are based.... Now as *being* is the first thing that falls under the apprehension absolutely, so *good* is the first thing that falls under the apprehen-sion of the practical reason, which is directed to action (since every agent acts for an end, which has the nature of good). Consequently, the first principle in the practical reason is one founded on the nature of good, viz., that *good is that which all things seek after*. Hence, this is the first precept of law, that *good is to be done and promoted, and evil is to be avoided*. All other precepts of the natural law are based upon this; so that all the things which the practical reason naturally apprehends as man's good belong to the precepts of the natural law under the form of things to be done or avoided.

Since, however, good has the nature of an end, and evil, the nature of the contrary, hence it is that all those things to which man has a natural inclination are naturally apprehended by reason as being good, and consequently as objects of pursuit, and their contraries as evil, and objects of avoidance. Therefore, the order of the precepts of the natural law is according to the order of natural inclinations. For there is in man, first of all, an inclination to good in accordance with the nature which he has in common with all substances, inasmuch, namely, as every substance seeks the preservation of its own being, according to its nature; and by reason of this inclination, whatever is a means of preserving human life, and of warding off its obstacles, belongs to the natural law. Secondly, there is in man an inclination to things that pertain to him more specially, according to that nature which he has in common with other animals; and in virtue of this inclination, those things are said to belong to the natural law *which nature has taught to all animals,* such as sexual intercourse, the education of offspring, and so forth. Thirdly, there is in man an inclination to good according to the nature of his reason, which nature is proper to him. Thus man has a natural inclination to know the truth about God, and to live in society; and in this respect, whatever pertains to this inclination belongs to the natural law: *e.g.,* to shun ignorance, to avoid offending those among whom one has to live, and other such things regarding the above inclination....

All these precepts of the law of nature have the character of one natural law, inasmuch as they flow from one first precept....

Whether the Natural Law is the Same in All Men?

... As we have stated above, to the natural law belong those things to which a man is inclined naturally; and among these it is proper to man to be inclined to act according to reason. Now it belongs to the reason to proceed from what is common to what is proper.... The speculative reason, however, is differently situated, in this matter, from the practical reason. For, since the speculative reason is concerned chiefly with necessary things, which cannot be otherwise than they are, its proper conclusions, like the universal principles, contain the truth without fail. The practical reason, on the other hand, is concerned with contingent matters, which is the domain of human actions; and, consequently, although there is necessity in the common principles, the more we descend towards the particular, the more frequently we encounter defects. Accordingly, then, in speculative matters truth is the same in all men, both as to principles and as to conclusions; although the truth is not known to all as regards the conclusions, but only as regards the principles which are called *common notions.* But in matters of action, truth or practical rectitude is not the same for all as to what is particular, but only as to the common principles; and where there is the same rectitude in relation to particulars, it is not equally known to all.

It is therefore evident that, as regards the common principles whether of speculative or of practical reason, truth or rectitude is the same for all, and is equally known by all. But as to the proper conclusions of the speculative reason, the truth is the same for all, but it is not equally known to all. Thus, it is true for all that the three angles of a triangle are together equal to two right angles, although it is not known to all. But as to the proper conclusions of the practical reason, neither is the truth or rectitude the same for all, nor, where it is the same, is it equally known by all. Thus, it is right and true for all to act according to reason, and from this principle it follows, as a proper conclusion, that goods entrusted to another should be restored to their owner. Now this is true for the majority of cases. But it may happen in a particular case that it would be injurious, and therefore unreasonable, to restore goods held in trust; for instance, if they are claimed for the purpose of fighting against one's country. And this principle will be found to fail the more, according as we descend further towards the particular, e.g., if one were to say that goods held in trust should be restored with such and such a guarantee, or in such and such a way; because the greater the number of conditions added, the greater the number of ways in which the principle may fail, so that it be not right to restore or not to restore.

Consequently, we must say that the natural law, as to the first common principles, is the same for all, both as to rectitude and as to knowledge. But as to certain more particular aspects, which are conclusions, as it were, of those common principles, it is the same for all in the majority of cases, both as to rectitude and as to knowledge; and yet in some few cases it may fail, both as to rectitude, by reason of certain obstacles (just as natures subject to generation and corruption fail in some few cases because of some obstacle), and as to knowledge, since in some the reason is perverted by passion, or evil habit, or an evil disposition of nature. Thus at one time theft, although it is expressly contrary to the natural law, was not considered wrong among the Germans, as Julius Caesar relates.

THE ETHICS OF NATURAL LAW
C. E. Harris

C. E. Harris is professor of philosophy at Texas A & M University. In the selection below he presents a version of the natural-law theory, including a discussion of the principle of double effect, which plays an important role in modern natural-law thinking.

From *Applying Moral Theories*, 3rd edition by Harris © 1997. Reprinted with permission of Wadsworth, a division of Thomson Learning: www.thomsonrights.com

The Natural-Law Moral Standard

WHAT IS NATURAL LAW?

The name *natural law* can be misleading. It implies that ethical laws are like "laws of nature" or scientific laws. An example of a scientific law is Boyle's law in physics, which states that the product of the pressure and the specific volume of a gas at constant temperature is constant. But scientific laws are *descriptive;* they state how phenomena in nature do in fact always behave. Ethical laws, on the other hand, are *prescriptive;* they stipulate how people *should* behave, whether or not they do so. Natural-law theorists assume that human beings have free will and that they can decide whether to act as they ought to act. This discussion implies that the word *law* has more in common with civil laws than with natural laws, because both civil and ethical laws can be disobeyed. Natural phenomena presumably always act according to the laws of nature, whereas people are not necessarily compelled to behave legally or morally.

But the analogy with civil laws can also be misleading, for the point of the term *natural* is to contrast ethical laws with the laws of governments. When the Roman jurists were looking for legal concepts that could apply throughout the Roman empire, they turned to the philosophy of natural law precisely because it proposed that certain ethical laws are "natural" rather than "conventional;" that is, they apply equally to all human beings, regardless of the conventions, customs, or beliefs of their particular society. These natural laws for all human behavior thus could serve as a basis for judging the actions of people throughout the Roman empire. Therefore we can say that *natural law* refers to ethical guidelines or rules that stipulate what people ought to do rather than what they in fact do and that apply equally to all humanity because they are rooted in human nature itself.

The term *natural law* can be misleading because it inevitably brings to mind some kind of ethical legalism—the belief that hard-and-fast guidelines cover every possible detail of conduct. This characterization, however, is unfair to the natural-law tradition. The greatest exponent of natural law, Thomas Aquinas (1225–1274), believed that the basic outlines of proper human behavior are relatively clear. But he also taught that, the closer we come to particular moral judgments, the more prone we are to error and the more room we make for differences of opinion. Some contemporary natural-law theorists even believe that natural law has a historical dimension, so that what is right in one epoch may not be right in another. Whether or not this view is accepted, the lively discussions of ethical issues in the Roman Catholic Church, where natural-law thinking is especially prominent, show that natural-law theorists by no means believe that all ethical problems have already been solved. The word *law* merely refers to the prescriptive character of the rules that should govern human behavior.

The natural-law theorist does, however, believe in an objective standard for morality: Moral truth exists just as scientific truth exists. The natural-law theorist cannot be a radical ethical relativist or an ethical sceptic....He generally believes we know the basic outlines of this standard, but this belief does not mean we have interpreted the implications of this standard correctly in every case. In ethics, as in science, human beings continually search for truth. The belief in objective truth should be no more stifling of human freedom and creativity in ethics than it is in science.

Human Nature and Natural Inclinations

What is that standard of truth in ethics? As an approximation we can say that the standard is human nature. People should do whatever promotes the fulfillment of human nature. How then do we determine what human nature is?

Let us consider some analogous situations that illustrate the difficulty in describing human nature. We often find it useful to describe something's nature in terms of its function, the purpose it serves. For example, we can describe the nature of a pencil in terms of its function of enabling humans to make marks on paper. A "good" pencil is one that performs this function well, without smudging or scratching or breaking, for example. Similarly, if an automobile's function is to provide transportation, a good automobile is one that provides comfortable and reliable transportation. The function of a tomato plant is to produce tomatoes, and a good tomato plant is one that produces many high-quality tomatoes.

We can also determine the function of human beings if we confine a person to one particular social role. The function of a farmer is to grow food, and a good farmer produces food efficiently and with proper care for the animals and the land for which he has responsibility. By similar reasoning we can say that a good father is one who attends diligently to his children's welfare. But now let us take human beings out of their social roles and ask simply "What is the function of a human being?" Here we see the problem faced by those who attempt to base ethics on human nature. Generally speaking, the more complex the animal, the more varied its behavior and presumably the less clearly defined is its function. The freedom of action possessed by human beings makes it plausible to argue, as some philosophers have, that human beings are characterized precisely by the fact that they have no set nature or function. How can we make sense out of natural law in the face of these problems?

Fortunately we can take another, more promising approach to discovering what human nature is like. One way to determine a thing's characteristics is to observe its behavior. In chemistry, we learn about the nature of iron by observing how it reacts with other elements. Perhaps we can find out what human nature is like by ascertaining those "natural inclinations," as Aquinas put it, that human beings have in common. To phrase it another way, perhaps we can discover what human nature is by identifying those goals that human beings generally tend to seek. These values would presumably reflect the structure of our human nature, which natural law directs us to follow. Therefore we shall propose the following statement as the moral standard of natural law:

MS: Those actions are right that promote the values specified by the natural inclinations of human beings.

How do we find out what these natural inclinations are? We might first consult psychologists, sociologists, or anthropologists. Some contemporary natural-law theorists use studies from the social sciences to defend their conclusions. However, the natural-law tradition developed before the rise of the social sciences, and a more informal method of observation was used to discover the basic human inclinations. Most natural-law theorists would maintain that these observations are still valid. We can divide the values specified by natural human inclination into two basic groups: (1) biological values, which are strongly linked with our bodies and which we share with other animals, and (2) characteristically human values, which are closely connected with our more specifically human aspects. (We will not call this second group uniquely human values because some of the inclinations that point to these values, such as the tendency to live in societies, are not unique to human beings.) We can summarize the values and the natural inclinations that point to them as follows:

1. Biological Values
   a. *Life*—From the natural inclinations that we and all other animals have to preserve our own existence, we can infer that life is good, that we have an obligation to promote our own health, and that we have the right of self-defense. Negatively, this inclination implies that murder and suicide are wrong.
   b. *Procreation*—From the natural inclination that we and all animals have to engage in sexual intercourse and to rear offspring, we can infer that procreation is a value and that we have an obligation to produce and rear children. Negatively, this inclination implies that such practices as sterilization, homosexuality, and artificial contraception are wrong.

2. Characteristically Human Values
   a. *Knowledge*—From the natural tendency we have to know, including the tendency to seek knowledge of God, we can infer that knowledge is a value and that we have an obligation to pursue knowledge of the world and of God. Negatively, this inclination implies that the stifling of intellectual curiosity and the pursuit of knowledge, including the pursuit of the knowledge of God, is wrong. It also implies that a lack of religion is wrong.
   b. *Sociability*—From the natural tendency we have to form bonds of affection and love with other human beings and to form groups or societies, we can infer that friendship and love are good and that the state is a natural institution and therefore good. We thus have an obligation to pursue close relationships with other human beings and to submit to the legitimate authority of the state. We can also infer that war can be justified under certain conditions if it is necessary to defend the state. Negatively, this inclination implies that activities that interfere with proper human relationships, such as spreading slander and lies, are wrong. Actions that destroy the state's power are also wrong, so natural law finds a basis for an argument against revolution and treason, except when the state is radically unjust.

These natural inclinations are reflections of human nature, and the pursuit of the goods they specify is the way to individual fulfillment. Aquinas himself makes it clear that his enumeration of basic values, which closely parallels our account, is incomplete; other natural-law theorists have expanded the list to include such things as play and aesthetic experience. However, the list given here has had the greatest historical influence, and we shall assume it is basically complete.

The more important issue raised by this list is the potential for conflict between the various values. What should we do when our need to defend ourselves requires that we kill someone else? What should we do when sterilization is necessary to prevent a life-threatening pregnancy? What should be done when contraception seems necessary to limit family size so that families can properly educate the children they already have? In each of these examples, one aspect of natural law seems to conflict with another, and the question arises whether these values have a hierarchy on which a decision can be based. The answer to this question brings into focus one of the most important and controversial aspects of natural law—namely, its moral absolutism.

Moral Absolutism and Its Qualifying Principles

MORAL ABSOLUTISM

Suppose you are on a military convoy from the United States to England during World War II. Your ship is attacked and sunk. Your life raft is carrying twenty-four persons, although it was designed to carry only twenty. You have good reason to believe that the raft will sink unless four people are eliminated, and four people on board have been so seriously injured in the catastrophe that they are probably going to die anyhow. Because no one volunteers to jump overboard, you, as the ranking officer on the boat, decide to have them pushed overboard. Are you morally justified in doing so? Many of us would say that under the circumstances you were, but natural-law theorists would say that you were not justified, even if everyone on the raft would have died otherwise.

Consider another wartime example. Suppose you know that some prisoners have information that will save a large number of lives. The only way to obtain the information is to threaten to kill the prisoners, but you know that they will not reveal what they know unless your threat is absolutely serious. To show them how serious you are, you have another prisoner, who has done nothing to deserve death, shot before their eyes. As a result of your action, the information is revealed and many lives are saved. Is this action justified? Many people would say that under these extreme circumstances it is justified, but natural-law theorists would say that it is not.

These examples point out one of the most significant aspects of natural-law theory: its absolutism. *Moral absolutism* can refer either to the belief that some objective standard of moral truth exists independently of us (what we have referred to as moral realism) or to the view that certain actions are right or wrong regardless of their consequences. Natural law is an absolutist moral theory in both senses, but the second meaning of absolutism is highlighted by our wartime illustrations. Natural-law theorists believe that *none of the values specified by natural inclinations may be directly violated.* Innocent people may not be killed for any reason, even if other innocent people can thereby be saved. The procreative function that is a part of our biological nature may not be violated by such practices as contraception and sterilization, even if these practices are necessary to preserve other values, such as a child's education or even the mother's life. Similarly, homosexuality violates the value of procreation and is prohibited, even if it is the only kind of sex a person can enjoy.

Natural-law theorists believe that basic values specified by natural inclinations cannot be violated because *basic values cannot be measured or compared;* that is, basic values cannot be quantified or measured by some common unit, so they cannot be traded off for one another. For example, we cannot divide the good of knowledge into units of value and the good of procreation into units of value so that the two can be compared on a common scale. Nor can the good of a single life be compared with the good of several lives; thus we cannot say that a single life may be sacrificed to preserve many other lives. This idea is sometimes called the "absolute value" or "infinite value" of a human life, suggesting that a human life cannot be weighed against anything else, including another human life. Natural-law theorists also make this point by saying that basic values are *incommensurable.* Because we cannot measure values, we cannot calculate which consequences of an action are more important. Therefore consequences cannot be used to determine the moral status of actions.

Another characteristic of natural law is that it is nonconsequentialist in character, even though it may not rule out consideration of consequences. Natural-law theorists insist that *moral judgments must include an evaluation of the intentions of the person performing the action.* The intention of an action is what a person wants to accomplish or "has in mind," as we say, in performing the action. For example, a person can give money to charity because he wants a good reputation in the community. The consequences of the action are good, but the person's intention is not morally praiseworthy. Some moral philosophers distinguish between a moral evaluation of the action and a moral evaluation of the intention of the person performing the action. Using this distinction, we can say that the action of giving money to charity is praiseworthy, but the person giving the money is not to be commended, because his intention was not praiseworthy.

QUALIFYING PRINCIPLES

Because values are incommensurable and may not ever be directly violated, we may find ourselves in a moral dilemma in which any action we could perform violates some value and hence is immoral. For example, self-defense may sometimes require that we override the natural inclination of another human being to self-preservation. If we do nothing, we allow ourselves to be killed; if we defend ourselves, we kill someone else. To avoid the paralysis of action, natural-law theorists have developed two principles that are crucial in making moral judgments: the principle of forfeiture and the principle of double effect.

THE PRINCIPLE OF FORFEITURE

According to the *principle of forfeiture,* a person who threatens the life of an innocent person forfeits his or her own right to life. (An *innocent* person is one who has not threatened anyone's life.) Suppose you are a pioneer tilling his land one morning when two men approach you and say they are going to kill you and your family in order to take your land. Is it morally permissible for you to defend yourself, even to the point of killing them? Natural-law theorists answer the question in the affirmative. Even though you might have to kill your would-be assailants, they have forfeited their innocence by unjustifiably threatening your life. Therefore, they have forfeited their claim to have their natural inclination to self-preservation respected. We can make this point by distinguishing between killing and murder. *Killing* is taking the life of a noninnocent person, whereas *murder* is taking the life of an innocent person. When you take the life of a person who is attempting to kill you, you are killing him but not committing murder.

The principle of forfeiture can be used to justify not only acts of individual self-defense but also war and capital punishment. A defensive war may be justified under certain conditions, even though it involves killing other people, because the aggressors have forfeited their right to life. Similarly, murderers may justly be put to death because they have forfeited their right to life by killing others.

THE PRINCIPLE OF DOUBLE EFFECT

According to the *principle of double effect,* it is morally permissible to perform an action that has two effects, one good and the other bad, if the following criteria are met:

1. The act, considered in itself and apart from its consequences, is good, or at least morally permissible. An act of murder violates this criterion because murder is bad in itself and apart from its consequences.

2. The bad effect cannot be avoided if the good effect is to be achieved. The moral significance of this criterion lies in the belief that if an alternative method that does not produce the bad effect is available and not used, we must assume that the bad effect was intended. This criterion illustrates the important place that consideration of intent has in natural law. An action with improper intent is morally unacceptable even if it does not otherwise violate natural law. Another test must be passed, however, before we can say that an action is unintended. It is embodied in the next criterion.

3. The bad effect is not the means of producing the good effect but only a side effect. If the bad effect is a necessary means of achieving the good effect, the bad effect must be intended along with the good effect for which it is a necessary means, so the action is morally impermissible. This criterion also illustrates the importance of intention in natural law.

4. The criterion of proportionality is satisfied, in that the good effect and the bad effect are more or less equally balanced in importance. If the bad effect of an action is far more significant than any good effect, the action should not be done, even if the other criteria are met.

If these four criteria are met, the violation of a fundamental value may be considered as indirect rather than direct. Although we may still be said to *bring about an evil*, we cannot be said to *do* an evil, according to natural law. The best way to explain the principle of double effect is by example, so let us consider several applications.

In the first example, a pregnant woman who has tuberculosis wants to take a drug that will cure her disease, but the drug also has the effect of aborting the fetus. Is taking the drug morally permissible? The principle of double effect justifies taking the drug in this case, because all four of its conditions are met.

First, the act of taking the drug to cure a disease is itself morally permissible. In fact, considered in itself and apart from its consequences, it is morally obligatory for the mother to take the drug, for she is obligated to do what she can to preserve her own life.

Second, if we assume that the drug is the only one that will cure the disease and that the mother cannot put off taking the drug until after the baby is born, then the bad effect is unavoidable. By this criterion, then, the death of the child is not intended. We must clarify here what natural-law theorists mean. The bad effect is certainly foreseen; the woman knows the drug will produce an abortion. But an effect may be foreseen without also being intended, that is, without being the goal of the action. If another drug were available that would cure her tuberculosis without causing the abortion, presumably the woman would take it. Otherwise, it would be difficult to argue that she did not intend to have an abortion.

Third, the bad effect is not the means of achieving the good effect. An abortion is not a necessary step in curing a person of tuberculosis; rather, it just happens that the only drug that will cure the woman also causes an abortion. The abortion is an unfortunate and unintended side effect, due to the particular nature of the drug.

Fourth, a proportionally serious reason exists for performing the abortion. The death of the fetus is at least balanced by the saving of the mother's life. If the bad effect were serious (as in this case), but the good effect were relatively insignificant, the action would not be justifiable by the principle of double effect, even if the other conditions were met.

The criterion of proportionality is an exception to the earlier statement that values are incommensurable and that human lives cannot be weighed against one another. We have seen that it may also be considered an exception to the claim that consequences are not considered moral evaluation. Here, consequences do play a part in natural-law reasoning. But note that consequences can be considered *only* when the other three conditions have been met. A more accurate statement, therefore, is that in natural-law theory, the consideration of consequences occupies some place in moral evaluation, but they are of secondary importance.

Two other examples will further illustrate how the principle of double effect functions. Suppose I want to turn on a light so that I can read a book on ethics, but I know that throwing the switch on the wall that turns on the light will result in the electrocution of a workman on the floor below. Is it morally permissible to throw the switch?

First, turning on a light to read a book on ethics is in itself a permissible—even praiseworthy—action.

Second, the bad effect is unavoidable if the good effect is to be achieved. If another light could be turned on and I deliberately failed to use it, knowing the consequence is the death of the workman, then I cold not argue that I did not intend to kill the workman.

Third, the bad effect (killing the workman) is not a means to reading philosophy but rather only an unfortunate and unintended side effect. Killing someone is not ordinarily a consequence of turning on a light.

But the fourth condition of the principle of double effect is not satisfied. The killing of a human being is not outweighed by the value of reading a book on ethics. Therefore, turning on the light is not justified by the principle of double effect.

Consider another example. In the process of attempting to deliver a fetus, a physician discovers that the fetus is hydrocephalic. The fetus's large cranium makes normal vaginal delivery impossible; both the woman and the fetus would die in the attempt. Neither the mother nor the fetus would survive a cesarean section, so the only way to save the mother's life is to crush the skull of the fetus (craniotomy), thus rendering a vaginal delivery of the stillborn fetus possible. Would the craniotomy be justifiable by the principle of double effect?

First, the act of attempting to save the mother's life is morally permissible, even commendable.

Second, there is no way to save the mother's life except by killing the fetus. The bad effect cannot be avoided if the good effect is to be achieved.

Third, the bad effect can only be seen as the means of producing the good effect. It makes not sense to talk about crushing the head of the fetus without also killing it. Because the death of the fetus must be considered the means of achieving the good effect, the third criterion is not satisfied. Each of the four criteria must be met for the action to be permissible, so we already know that the craniotomy is impermissible. However, for the sake of completeness, we shall consider the fourth criterion.

Fourth, both the fetus and the mother will die if the abortion is not performed; thus, the criterion of proportionality is satisfied. But because the third criterion is not met, the craniotomy may not be performed, and the fetus and mother must both die.

Natural-law theorists admit that this is a tragic case, and various attempts have been made to justify the craniotomy on other grounds. For example, some natural-law theorists argue that the principle of forfeiture can be invoked, because the fetus should be considered an aggressor on the life of the mother. Even though the fetus is innocent of any conscious motive to harm its mother, the actual effect of its growth is to threaten the mother's life. Natural-law theorists sometimes say that the fetus, having no malicious intent, is *subjectively innocent* but not *objectively innocent,* because it does threaten the other's life. Whether this argument justifies an abortion will be left for you to decide.

Applying the Ethics of Natural Law

We can now apply natural law to some cases involving moral decision....

CASE 1: AIDS AND CONDOMS

Let us consider the controversy over the use of condoms as a way to prevent AIDS...

Because of the different moral issues that arise in various instances of the use of condoms to prevent AIDS, it will be helpful to treat first the use of condoms to prevent AIDS in heterosexual vaginal intercourse between married couples and then to consider all other uses of condoms to prevent AIDS. We shall refer to this first category of sexual relations as *procreative intercourse,* because married couples would have intercourse in a context in which procreation would be justified from the standpoint of natural law. Natural-law theorists hold that the natural mode for producing children for human beings is in the context of monogamous heterosexual marriage. Other sexual relationships would include nonvaginal intercourse between married partners, vaginal and nonvaginal intercourse between unmarried heterosexual partners, and oral and anal intercourse between homosexual partners. We shall refer to this second category of sexual relations as *nonprocreative intercourse,* because the mode of intercourse is incapable of producing children, or the partners would probably not wish to produce them. To sharpen the issue further, we shall focus on the morality of actually *using* condoms rather than the morality of *advocating* the use of condoms.

1. The use of condoms is an "artificial" mode of contraception and a violation of the natural tendency to procreation. Therefore, it is morally illegitimate unless the principles of forfeiture or double effect can be invoked.

2. The principle of forfeiture is inapplicable to either procreative or nonprocreative intercourse. A person with AIDS has done nothing worthy of death, so he has not forfeited his own right to life.

3. If the use of condoms to prevent AIDS is morally permissible, it must be because the principle of double effect is satisfied.

Let us begin by considering procreative intercourse. To apply the principle of double effect, we must describe the action and its effects. In this case, the action is the use of condoms in marital vaginal intercourse. The good or morally desirable effect is the prevention of the transfer of the HIV virus. The bad effect is the prevention of conception.

a. Married couples who have a long-standing monogamous relationship would not need to use condoms, but we can consider a newly married couple, where one or both of he partners had been sexually active before marriage. Here the use of condoms would be desirable to prevent the spread of the HIV virus, assuming the couple had not taken the test for its presence, or the test is not reliable, or some suspicion exists that the couple might still be sexually active outside the marriage. Although sexual activity outside the marriage cannot be justified by natural law, the use of condoms in marital intercourse is a different issue.

If it makes sense to consider the use of condoms apart from the consequence of preventing conception or the transmission of the HIV virus, then we should consider the action in itself morally permissible.

b. If one partner has the HIV virus, or there is a suspicion that he or she has, then the bad effect of using condoms can be avoided while achieving the good effect only by refraining from intercourse altogether. Because natural-law theorists usually consider intercourse an obligation of married partners, this alternative is not acceptable. Therefore, if there is reason to believe a partner might have the HIV virus, the use of condoms might be considered unavoidable.

c. The application of the third criterion is controversial. The prevention of conception is not, strictly speaking, the means of controlling the spread of AIDS. Condoms are used to prevent the entrance of the HIV virus into the other partner's body, not to prevent conception. From this perspective, the use of condoms might appear morally permissible. However, in attempting to control the spread of the HIV virus, the transmission of *all* bodily fluids from one sexual partner to the other must be stopped—including sperm, which carry the virus. Hence, the prevention of the transmission of sperm (and therefore the prevention of conception) must be a part of the means employed. So the use of condoms in heterosexual vaginal intercourse by a married couple would seem to violate the third criterion.

d. If we consider the risk of loss of life through HIV infection a greater evil than the violation of moral principles involved in the use of condoms, then the principle of proportionality is satisfied. Because criterion c is violated, procreative intercourse, using condoms to prevent AIDS, is morally impermissible.

Now let us consider nonprocreative intercourse in its various forms. To apply the principle of double effect, we must again describe the action and its effects. In this case, the action is the use of condoms in nonprocreative intercourse. The good or morally desirable effect is the prevention of the transfer of the HIV virus. The bad effect is the provision of a degree of safety that allows nonprocreative intercourse to occur more easily. That is, the bad effect is the encouragement of promiscuity.

a. The use of condoms, considered in itself and apart from its consequences, will again be considered morally permissible.

b. The transmission of the HIV virus can be prevented by refraining from nonprocreative intercourse, so the bad effect is not unavoidable in promoting the good effect.

c. The provision of an environment in which intercourse that is impermissible from natural law's standpoint can more easily take place is a means of preventing the spread of the HIV virus. Therefore, the bad effect is a means to the good effect.

d. If we consider the risk of loss of life through HIV infection a greater evil than the violation of moral principles involved in the use of condoms, then the principle of proportionality is satisfied. Because criteria b and c are violated, nonprocreative intercourse with condoms is also morally impermissible.

4. We can conclude that the use of condoms to prevent AIDS is morally impermissible in both procreative and nonprocreative intercourse.

CASE 2: THE MORALITY OF OBLITERATION BOMBING

During World War II, both the Germans and the Allied Forces bombed civilian residential areas, a practice called "obliteration bombing." Probably the two most famous examples of this practice, in which conventional explosives were used, were the German bombing of London and the Allied bombing of Dresden, Germany. Let us confine ourselves to the fire bombing of Dresden and ask whether this action was permissible by the principles of natural law.

1. The focus must be on the killing of civilians in Dresden. This feature of the action makes it an apparent violation of natural-law morality. Hence, we must ask whether the principles of forfeiture and double effect serve to make the bombing morally permissible.

2. The principle of forfeiture raises the conceptual problem of whether the civilians in Dresden should be considered innocent. If we assume that the criteria of just-war theory were met—that is, the Allied Forces were fighting a just war and the Germans were not fighting a just war—then the Germans in uniform were noninnocent, and attacking them was morally justified. But most civilians in large cities were connected with the war effort in a very indirect way. Unless civilians are employed in the production of military hardware, most natural-law theorists would probably count them as innocent. Many Germans may have had little direct knowledge of the reasons for the war; in a nondemocratic state, they certainly had no part in starting it. Therefore, the civilians in Dresden should be considered innocent, and the principle of forfeiture does not justify the bombing.

3. Some have argued that an appeal to the principle of double effect could justify the bombing. According to this argument, the direct and intended effect of the bombing was to destroy war industries, communications, and military installations, whereas the damage to civilian life was unintentional and indirect. But a careful analysis of the conditions of the bombing will not sustain this argument.

a. We shall consider the action under analysis to be the bombing of Dresden, the good effect to be the shortening of the war, and the bad effect to be the deaths of innocent civilians. Bombing an enemy city cannot be said to be intrinsically immoral. We have shown that war can be justified by natural law, and we shall assume that the Allied cause could be defended by just-war criteria. Therefore, the Allies had a right to attack German cities.

b. Let us assume that there was no other way to shorten the war except by bombing cities. If the desirable end is described as "shortening the war," bombing the cities would be unavoidable in achieving that end, so the second criterion of the principle of the double effect is met.

c. The third criterion asks whether the bad effect—namely, killing innocent civilians—was a means to the good effect. Destroying German morale through terror was, on the testimony of military documents themselves, an object of the bombing. And the means of inducing terror and consequent demoralization was the deaths of innocent civilians. Therefore, the third condition of double effect is not met.

d. We can also question the allegation that the principle of proportionality was satisfied by the belief that obliteration bombing would shorten the war. That goal was speculative, futuristic, and problematic, whereas the evil effect was definite, immediate, and widespread. Thus, we shall conclude that this criterion is also not met and that the principle of double effect does not apply.

4. Because the allied attack on Dresden involved the destruction of innocent human life, and because the principles of forfeiture and double effect do not excuse it, we must conclude that the action was morally impermissible by natural-law theory.

CASE 3: THE SUPPRESSION OF GALILEO

Galileo Galilei (1564–1642) has a strong claim to the title of founder of modern science. At first he accepted the Ptolemaic theory that the sun and planets revolved around the earth. But his invention of the telescope and the discovery of the satellites of Jupiter led him to confess his adherence to the Copernican system in 1610. In 1616, the Office of the Holy Inquisition took the important step of entering the works of Copernicus on the list of forbidden books and declaring his teaching heretical. In 1632, Galileo published his *Dialogue on the Two Principal Systems of the World,* in which he contrasted the Ptolemaic and Copernican systems of astronomy. He thought that, if he merely gave an "objective" account of the differences between the two systems, he would not offend the Inquisition and would thereby avoid persecution.

Galileo's sympathies with the Copernican system were all too evident, however, and the Inquisition banned his book and summoned him to Rome for a hearing. After being threatened with torture, Galileo was forced, on June 22, 1633, to go down on his knees and renounce the doctrine that the earth revolves around the sun and to swear that he would cease any further promotion of Copernican astronomy. He lived for several more years under conditions of virtual house arrest but was still able to produce his greatest scientific book. However, the spectacle of Galileo's persecution inhibited the advance of science. Can the silencing of Galileo be justified by the principles of natural law?

1. This issue raises the problem of how to properly promote the natural inclination to know. Natural law requires that we promote the natural inclination of humans to know, but the question is how best to accomplish this. The leaders of the Inquisition would no doubt have described their action of silencing Galileo as promoting the inclination to know, arguing that they were defending truth against error by defending the astronomical system that seems to be in agreement with Holy Scripture. From our perspective, their action should probably be described as obstructing the inclination to know by silencing free inquiry, which we regard as essential to the discovery of truth.

What is implied by the natural-law requirement to promote knowledge, defending the truths of Holy Scripture or defending free inquiry? In Galileo's time, there were different conceptions of the authority of Scripture in science and the value of free inquiry, and it is not clear that contemporary views are an appropriate basis for evaluating actions that took place centuries ago. However, adopting the contemporary perspective is probably more instructive for us today, so I shall assume that the proper way to promote the natural inclination to know is to promote free inquiry. However, I shall also assume that from the natural-law viewpoint, protecting Holy Scripture has some value as well. Because suppressing free inquiry is, by this account, a violation of a natural inclination, the only way to avoid the conclusion that the Inquisition's action was morally impermissible is to find an excusing condition in one of the two qualifying principles.

2. Galileo had not threatened anyone's life; he had done nothing to forfeit his own right to life. This consideration is important, because Galileo was threatened with torture and possible death. Natural-law theorists might argue that a person can do other things to forfeit his status as an innocent person, such as teach heretical doctrines that endanger the souls of others. However, this point presupposes that Galileo was wrong, so I shall assume that the principle of forfeiture is not relevant.

3. To analyze the action of the leaders of the Inquisition from the standpoint of the principle of double effect, we must be able to distinguish an action, a good effect, and a bad effect. The action, as we have described it, was forcing Galileo to renounce his adherence to Copernican astronomy. The good effect was promoting Scripture's authority. The bad effect was denying individual freedom to state one's views and seek truth. Can the action of the Inquisitors be justified by the principle of double effect?

a. Forcing Galileo to renounce his public adherence to a scientific view is an act that seems inherently contrary to the inclination to know, even if we consider the act apart from any future consequences regarding the inhibition of free inquiry. Therefore, I shall assume that the first criterion is not met. There is no need to continue the analysis, because the principle of double effect cannot be used here. But, in this case, it will be instructive to proceed with the rest of the analysis.

b. The Inquisitors would probably disagree with most people today on the question of whether denying freedom of expression was avoidable in promoting Scripture's authority. However, we shall assume that it was avoidable, so that the second criterion was not met. Denying individual freedom was probably unavoidable if the authority of Scripture was to be protected, so we shall assume that the second criterion is met.

c. The means used to achieve the end of protecting Scripture was the denial of freedom of inquiry. So this criterion is also not met.

d. The leaders of the Inquisition would probably have said that their action passed the test of proportionality, because the negative consequences of Galileo's suppression were outweighed by the fact that Scripture was defended. But this claim is questionable, because the suppression of opinion (even if it is false) is

probably not the best way to defend Scripture. Besides, the test of proportionality is relevant only if the other tests are met. We may conclude that this criterion
is also not passed.

4. Because the action of the leaders of the Inquisition violates the value of
knowledge by suppressing the right to dissent, and because the two qualifying
principles are inapplicable, we must conclude that the Inquisitors' action was
morally impermissible.

This case illustrates the difference that factual assumptions and conceptual
issues can make in the ethical analysis of a case. The Inquisitors had very different ideas from most of us about the place of free discussion and the authority of
Scripture in the pursuit of truth. I shall leave it to you to determine whether,
using the ideas prevalent in their time, the Inquisitors could have justified their
action from the standpoint of natural law.

Notes

1. This case was supplied by Harry S. Lipscomb, M.D. Used with permission.
2. Gerald Kelly, *Medico-Moral Problems* (St. Louis, Mo.: The Catholic Hospital
    Association, 1958), p. 120. Quoted in Paul Ramsey, *The Patient as Person*, p. 122.

THE DOCTRINE OF DOUBLE EFFECT
Philippa Foot

*Philippa Foot is Griffen Professor of Philosophy Emeritus at the University of California,
Los Angeles, and Honorary Fellow of Somerville College, Oxford. She has written many
influential essays in moral philosophy and is author of* Natural Goodness *(2001).
According to the doctrine (or principle) of double effect, it is sometimes permissible to perform an action that will knowingly bring about a bad effect so long as one does not directly intend the bad effect. Foot is critical of this doctrine. After explaining why some
philosophers have thought that certain problematic cases calling for moral response
require that we accept the doctrine, she goes on to argue that (1) those same cases can be
understood in terms of the distinction between the negative duty to avoid injury to others
and the positive duty to render aid (and so the cases in question do not require accepting
the doctrine), and (2) that because there are cases where the doctrine of double effect
yields counterintuitive results about what is morally right, we should reject it.*

I

I shall not, of course, discuss all the principles that may be used in deciding how
to act where the interests or rights of human beings conflict. What I want to do

From "The Problem of Abortion and the Doctrine of Double Effect," *Virtues and Vices and Other Essays in Moral
Philosophy* (1978). Reprinted by permission of the author.

is to look at one particular theory, known as the "doctrine of the double effect" which is invoked by Catholics in support of their views on abortion but supposed by them to apply elsewhere....

The doctrine of the double effect is based on a distinction between what a man foresees as a result of his voluntary action and what, in the strict sense, he intends. He intends in the strictest sense both those things that he aims at as ends and those that he aims at as means to his ends. The latter may be regretted in themselves but nevertheless desired for the sake of the end, as we may intend to keep dangerous lunatics confined for the sake of our safety. By contrast a man is said not strictly, or directly, to intend the foreseen consequences of his voluntary actions where these are neither the end at which he is aiming nor the means to this end. Whether the word "intention" should be applied in both cases is not of course what matters: Bentham spoke of "oblique intention," contrasting it with the "direct intention" of ends and means, and we may as well follow his terminology. Everyone must recognise that some such distinction can be made, though it may be made in a number of different ways, and it is the distinction that is crucial to the doctrine of the double effect. The words "double effect" refer to the two effects that an action may produce: the one aimed at, and the one foreseen but in no way desired. By "the doctrine of the double effect" I mean the thesis that it is sometimes permissible to bring about by oblique intention what one may not directly intend. Thus the distinction is held to be relevant to moral decision in certain difficult cases. It is said for instance that the operation of hysterectomy involves the death of the fetus as the foreseen but not strictly or directly intended consequence of the surgeon's act, while other operations kill the child and count as the direct intention of taking an innocent life, a distinction that has evoked particularly bitter reactions on the part of non-Catholics. If you are permitted to bring about the death of the child, what does it matter how it is done? The doctrine of the double effect is also used to show why in another case, where a woman in labour will die unless a craniotomy operation is performed, the intervention is not to be condoned. There, it is said, we may not operate but must let the mother die. We foresee her death but do not directly intend it, whereas to crush the skull of the child would count as direct intention of its death.[1]...

The first point that should be made clear, in fairness to the theory, is that no one is suggesting that it does not matter what you bring about as long as you merely foresee and do not strictly intend the evil that follows. We might think, for instance, of the (actual) case of wicked merchants selling, for cooking, oil they knew to be poisonous and thereby killing a number of innocent people, comparing and contrasting it with that of some unemployed gravediggers, desperate for custom, who got hold of this same oil and sold it (or perhaps they secretly gave it away) in order to create orders for graves. They strictly (directly) intend the deaths they cause, while the merchants could say that it was not part of their plan that anyone should die. In morality, as in law, the merchants, like the gravediggers, would be considered as murderers; nor are the supporters of the doctrine of the double effect bound to say that there is the least difference between them in respect of moral turpitude. What they are committed to is the thesis that *sometimes* it makes a difference to the permissibility of an action involving harm to others that this harm, although foreseen, is not part of the agent's direct intention. An end such as earning one's living is clearly not such as to justify *either* the direct or oblique intention of the death of innocent people, but in certain cases one is justified in bringing about knowingly what one could not directly intend.

It is now time to say why this doctrine should be taken seriously in spite of the fact that it sounds rather odd, that there are difficulties about the distinction on which it depends, and that it seems to yield one sophistical conclusion when applied to the problem of abortion. The reason for its appeal is that its opponents have often *seemed* to be committed to quite indefensible views. Thus the controversy has raged around examples such as the following. Suppose that a judge or magistrate is faced with rioters demanding that a culprit be found for a certain crime and threatening otherwise to take their own bloody revenge on a particular section of the community. The real culprit being unknown, the judge sees himself as able to prevent the bloodshed only by framing some innocent person and having him executed. Beside this example is placed another in which a pilot whose aeroplane is about to crash is deciding whether to steer from a more to a less inhabited area. To make the parallel as close as possible it may rather be supposed that he is the driver of a runaway tram which he can only steer from one narrow track on to another; five men are working on one track and one man on the other; anyone on the track he enters is bound to be killed. In the case of the riots the mob has five hostages, so that in both the exchange is supposed to be one man's life for the lives of five. The question is why we should say, without hesitation, that the driver should steer for the less occupied track, while most of us would be appalled at the idea that the innocent man could be framed. It may be suggested that the special feature of the latter case is that it involves the corruption of justice, and this is, of course, very important indeed. But if we remove that special feature, supposing that some private individual is to kill an innocent person and pass him off as the criminal we still find ourselves horrified by the idea. The doctrine of double effect offers us a way out of the difficulty, insisting that it is one thing to steer towards someone foreseeing that you will kill him and another to aim at his death as part of your plan....

Another pair of examples poses a similar problem. We are about to give a patient who needs it to save his life a massive dose of a certain drug in short supply. There arrive, however, five other patients each of whom could be saved by one-fifth of that dose. We say with regret that we cannot spare our whole supply of the drug for a single patient, just as we should say that we could not spare the whole resources of a ward for one dangerously ill individual when ambulances arrive bringing in victims of a multiple crash. We feel bound to let one man die rather than many if that is our only choice. Why then do we not feel justified in killing people in the interests of cancer research or to obtain, let us say, spare parts for grafting onto those who need them? We can suppose, similarly, that several dangerously ill people can be saved only if we kill a certain individual and make a serum from his dead body. (These examples are not over-fanciful considering present controversies about prolonging the life of mortally ill patients whose eyes or kidneys are to be used for others.) Why cannot we argue from the case of the scarce drug to that of the body needed for medical purposes? Once again the doctrine of the double effect comes up with an explanation. In one kind of case but not the other we aim at the death of an innocent man....

II

At one time I thought that these arguments in favour of the doctrine of the double effect were conclusive, but I now believe that the conflict should be solved in another way....

Let us speak of negative duties when thinking of the obligation to refrain from such things as killing or robbing, and of the positive duty, e.g., to look after children or aged parents. It will be useful, however, to extend the notion of positive duty beyond the range of things that are strictly called duties, bringing acts of charity under this heading. These are owed only in a rather loose sense, and some acts of charity could hardly be said to be *owed* at all, so I am not following ordinary usage at this point.

Let us now see whether the distinction of negative and positive duties explains why we see differently the action of the steering driver and that of the judge, of the doctors who withhold the scarce drug and those who obtain a body for medical purposes, of those who choose to rescue five men rather than one man from torture and those who are ready to torture the one man themselves in order to save five. In each case we have a conflict of duties, but what kind of duties are they? Are we, in each case, weighing positive duties against positive, negative against negative, or one against the other? Is the duty to refrain from injury, or rather to bring aid?

The steering driver faces a conflict of negative duties, since it is his duty to avoid injuring five men and also his duty to avoid injuring one. In the circumstances he is not able to avoid both, and it seems clear that he should do the least injury he can. The judge, however, is weighing the duty of not inflicting injury against the duty of bringing aid. He wants to rescue the innocent people threatened with death but can do so only by inflicting injury himself. Since one does not in general have the same duty to help people as to refrain from injuring them, it is not possible to argue to a conclusion about what he should do from the steering driver case. It is interesting that, even where the strictest duty of positive aid exists, this still does not weigh as if a negative duty were involved. It is not, for instance, permissible to commit a murder to bring one's starving children food. If the choice is between inflicting injury on one or many there seems only one rational course of action; if the choice is between aid to some at the cost of injury to others, and refusing to inflict the injury to bring the aid, the whole matter is open to dispute. So it is not inconsistent of us to think that the driver must steer for the road on which only one man stands while the judge (or his equivalent) may not kill the innocent person in order to stop the riots. Let us now consider the second pair of examples, which concern the scarce drug on the one hand and on the other the body needed to save lives. Once again we find a difference based on the distinction between the duty to avoid injury and the duty to provide aid. Where one man needs a massive dose of the drug and we withhold it from him in order to save five men, we are weighing aid against aid. But if we consider killing a man in order to use his body to save others, we are thinking of doing him an injury to bring others aid. In an interesting variant of the model, we may suppose that instead of killing someone we deliberately let him die. (Perhaps he is a beggar to whom we are thinking of giving food, but then we say "No, they need bodies for medical research.") Here it does seem relevant that in allowing him to die we are aiming at his death, but presumably we are inclined to see this as a violation of negative rather than positive duty. If this is right, we see why we are unable in either case to argue to a conclusion from the case of the scarce drug....

So far the conclusions are the same as those at which we might arrive following the doctrine of the double effect, but in others they will be different, and the advantage seems to be all on the side of the alternative. Suppose, for instance, that there are five patients in a hospital whose lives could be saved by the manufacture of a certain gas, but that this inevitably releases lethal fumes into the room of another patient whom for some reason we are unable to move. His death, being of no use to us, is clearly a side effect, and not directly intended. Why then is the case different from that of the scarce drug, if the point about that is that we foresaw but did not strictly intend the death of the single patient? Yet it surely is different. The relatives of the gassed patient would presumably be successful if they sued the hospital and the whole story came out. We may find it particularly revolting that someone should be *used* as in the case where he is killed or allowed to die in the interest of medical research, and the fact of *using* may even determine what we would decide to do in some cases, but the principle seems unimportant compared with our reluctance to bring such injury for the sake of giving aid.

My conclusion is that the distinction between direct and oblique intention plays only a quite subsidiary role in determining what we say in these cases, while the distinction between avoiding injury and bringing aid is very important indeed. I have not, of course, argued that there are no other principles. For instance it clearly makes a difference whether our positive duty is a strict duty or rather an act of charity: feeding our own children or feeding those in faraway countries. It may also make a difference whether the person about to suffer is one thought of as uninvolved in the threatened disaster, and whether it is his presence that constitutes the threat to the others. In many cases we find it very hard to know what to say, and I have not been arguing for any general conclusion such as that we may never, whatever the balance of good and evil, bring injury to one for the sake of aid to others, even when this injury amounts to death. I have only tried to show that even if we reject the doctrine of the double effect we are not forced to the conclusion that the size of the evil must always be our guide....

Note

1. For discussions of the Catholic doctrine on abortion see Glanville Williams, *The Sanctity of Life and the Criminal Law* (New York, 1957); also N. St. John Stevas, *The Right to Life* (London, 1963).

PROBLEMS FOR NATURAL LAW THEORY
Emmett Barcalow

Emmett Barcalow teaches at Western New England College and is author of Moral Philosophy: Theories and Issues *(1994). Natural law theory attempts to base moral principles on facts about human nature, and Barcalow raises two problems for this feature of natural-law thinking. First, it is doubtful that one can infer moral principles forbidding adultery, rape, homosexuality, and so forth, either from biological facts about human nature or from facts about the inherent nature of* Homo sapiens. *Second, it is questionable that behavior in accordance with human nature is morally right and behavior not in accord with human nature is morally wrong. For instance, if it turns out that human beings (at least the males) are naturally aggressive, should we infer that war and fighting are morally right?*

Human Nature

Natural law theorists argue in the following way.

Behavior/action X is not in accordance with a human being's inherent nature.
It is contrary to reason for a human being to act in a way that is not in accordance with a human being's inherent nature.
Whatever is contrary to reason is immoral.
Therefore, behavior/action X is immoral.

However, many critics of natural law theory doubt that human nature can provide moral guidance and they doubt that whatever is "natural" or in conformity with an organism's inherent nature must be morally right and good.

The concept of the inherent nature of an organism is complicated. On the one hand it can include purely biological features that all members of a species have. For example, it is part of the inherent nature of whales that they have lungs rather than gills, while it is part of the inherent nature of sharks that they have gills rather than lungs. Consequently, whales must breathe in air and cannot breathe in water while sharks must breathe in water and cannot breathe in air. Similarly, it is part of a chicken's inherent nature that it lays eggs, while it is part of a cow's nature that it bears live calves rather than lays eggs. It is part of a termite's inherent nature that its digestive system can gain nourishment from eating wood, while it is part of a crocodile's nature that its digestive system cannot gain nourishment from eating wood. In this sense of an organism's inherent nature, an organism either physically cannot do certain things because of its inherent nature (lay eggs, breathe in water, digest wood) or it cannot survive and flourish if it acts contrary to its inherent nature.

Human nature includes certain biological features. For example, all human beings have lungs rather than gills; therefore, they breathe in air and cannot breathe in water. Similarly, because of the nature of their digestive systems, human beings cannot digest and gain nourishment from wood or stones. Therefore, a human being who attempted to breathe in water or eat wood would not be acting in accordance with his inherent nature as a human being. However, the biological features of the species *Homo sapiens* do not establish the most common moral laws that natural law theorists claim to derive from human nature. For example, adultery, polygamy, homosexuality, theft, physical assault, cruelty, rape, and killing the innocent are not contrary to the biological nature of human beings the way that breathing in water or eating wood are; they obviously do not have the same effects on a person as eating wood or breathing in water. Therefore, they are not "unnatural" in the sense of being contrary to the biological nature of human beings. If natural law theorists wish to maintain that such behavior is contrary to reason and immoral for human beings because it is not in accordance with human nature, they must appeal to some other conception of what it is to act or not act, to live or not live, in accordance with human nature.

An organism's inherent nature as a member of a certain species often establishes characteristic patterns of behavior common to all or almost all members of the species. For example, spiders spin webs; sparrows build nests; bees construct hives; cats hunt mice and birds; hyenas tend to hunt in packs; polar bears hunt alone. It would be unnatural in the sense of unusual or uncharacteristic for a spider not to spin a web, for a sparrow to spin a web, for a hyena to hunt alone, or for a polar bear to hunt in a pack of polar bears. Similarly, it would be contrary to a lamb's nature to attack a lion, just as it would be contrary to a lion's nature to run from a lamb. In a sense, an organism's inherent nature as a member of a certain species establishes laws of behavior for it that are physical laws of nature.

Critics of natural law theory say that it is doubtful, however, that the inherent nature of *Homo sapiens* establishes laws of behavior for human beings in the same way as it may establish laws of behavior for cats, lions, and polar bears. Human nature is surprisingly diverse. For example, are human beings naturally as fearless and aggressive as lions or are they naturally as timid and pacific as rabbits and lambs? Human nature has room for both kinds of personality. Human beings also don't seem to have the relatively simple inherent or "instinctive" behavior patterns of some of the animals lower on the evolutionary tree. Cats "instinctively" chase mice and birds; therefore, such behavior is natural for them. It is not easy to identify "instinctive" behavior patterns in human beings that are akin to such behavior patterns as cats chasing mice and birds. It is especially difficult because so much of human behavior is shaped by the environment, that is, by deliberate and nondeliberate conditioning, training, and education.

In this sense of an organism's inherent nature, critics think that it is quite doubtful that polygamy, adultery, homosexuality, physical assault, cruelty, rape, or killing the innocent are contrary to the inherent nature of human beings. If that is so, then we cannot appeal to this sense of the inherent nature of human beings in order to show that such behavior is wrong. The challenge facing natural law theorists is to provide a plausible account of the inherent nature of human beings so that they can show that the kinds of behavior they condemn (for example, adultery, homosexuality, theft, and killing the innocent) are immoral because they are contrary to the inherent nature of human beings. Without that, it is not clear how appeals to the inherent nature of human beings can provide moral guidance.

What is Natural is Right and What is Unnatural is Wrong?

Natural law theorists assume that it is morally right and good for an organism to act in accordance with its inherent nature. Only on the basis of that assumption can the inherent nature of human beings provide moral laws of conduct for them. However, critics present reasons for doubting that all behavior that is in accordance with an organism's inherent nature is morally good and all behavior not in accordance with its inherent nature is morally bad. For example, biologist Stephen Jay Gould writes of a group of wasps named Ichneumonoidea comprising hundreds of thousands of different species. These wasps reproduce by laying their eggs inside the living body of another insect, most commonly a caterpillar. The wasp stings the caterpillar and then injects its eggs into it. As Gould writes, "Usually, the host is not otherwise inconvenienced for the moment, at least until the eggs hatch and the ichneumon larvae begin their grim work of interior excavation."[1] Then, the larvae slowly eat the helpless caterpillar from the inside out. "[T]he ichneumon larva eats fat bodies and digestive organs first, keeping the caterpillar alive by preserving intact that essential heart and central nervous system. Finally, the larva completes its work and kills its victim, leaving behind the caterpillar's empty shell."[2] Such behavior is in accordance with the inherent nature of Ichneumonoidea wasps. However, one may doubt that such natural behavior is morally praiseworthy.

It may be that human beings, or at least male human beings, are naturally aggressive and prone to violence. After all, war and fighting seem to be such universal pastimes of men in all ages that one might conclude that the inherent nature of male human beings includes a strong tendency to behave violently. If that is so, should men act in accordance with their inherent nature or should they try to resist their inherent natural tendencies? Similarly, many people believe that the image of childhood as a time of innocence and purity is sentimental nonsense. In their view, children are inherently cruel and are brought to extinguish or control their inherent cruelty only through education and socialization. Consider the tendency of children to mercilessly taunt or bully those who are weaker than or different from themselves. We might maintain that the purpose of moral education is not to encourage people to give their inherent natures free rein but rather to tame their inherent natures.

Similarly, suppose that human beings are inherently selfish or primarily self-interested and that altruism is not in accordance with the inherent nature of human beings. If this were true, would it follow that altruism is immoral and contrary to reason because it is not in accordance with the inherent nature of human beings? Many people would deny that altruism is wrong even if it is not in accordance with the inherent nature of human beings. They would say, "So much the worse for the inherent nature of human beings." In their view, moral education often needs to go against rather than with the inherent nature of human beings. They deny that actions in accordance with the inherent nature of human beings are always right and good for human beings and that actions not in accordance with the inherent nature of human beings are always wrong and bad for human beings.

Notes

1. Stephen Jay Gould, "Nonmoral Nature," in Stephen Jay Gould, *Hen's Teeth and Horse's Toes* (New York: W. W. Norton, 1983), p. 34.
2. Ibid., p. 35.

CHAPTER 5

Consequentialism

THE PRINCIPLE OF UTILITY
Jeremy Bentham

Jeremy Benthan (1748–1832) is often called the father of modern utilitarianism—a theory of right conduct that combines three elements. First, utilitarianism has a consequentialist structure in that the rightness of an action depends upon the net value of the consequences associated with that action. In moral theory, such views are versions of consequentialism. Second, for the utilitarian, what has intrinsic positive value is happiness and what has negative intrinsic value is unhappiness. This distinguishes utilitarianism from other forms of consequentialism. Finally, this view is impartialist in that it is the resulting level of happiness and unhappiness for everyone affected that determines the rightness or wrongness of an action. This element distinguishes utilitarianism from ethical egoism, which was the subject of Chapter 2. Let us use the term "utility" to refer to the overall value of the consequences associated with some action. Then, if we put all of this together, we have this basic utilitarian principle: An action is right if and only if the utility associated with that action is at least as high as the utility associated with any other alternative action open to the agent in the situation. But if rightness is understood in terms of the production of happiness (or in some unfortunate cases, the reduction of net unhappiness), how are we to understand happiness?

In this selection from his classic, The Principles of Morals and Legislation *(1789), Bentham understands happiness and unhappiness in terms of experiences of pleasure and pain respectively. Thus, Bentham is a value hedonist: Experiences of pleasure and pain alone are what have intrinsic value; anything else of value has merely instrumental value. If we plug a hedonistic theory of intrinsic value into the basic utilitarian principle just formulated, we have Bentham's principle of utility: An action is right if and only if it would (if performed) produce as high a balance of pleasure (or reduction of pain) as would any alternative action open to the agent in the circumstances in question. Because this principle is focused on the values of the consequences of concrete*

Reprinted from *The Principles of Morals and Legislation* by Jeremy Bentham (New York: Hafner Press, 1948).

actions, this view is referred to as "act utilitarianism." After defending this principle,
Bentham proceeds to set forth his famous "felecific calculus"—a list of seven consid-
erations to be used in calculating the utility of actions.

T he principle of utility is the foundation of the present work: it will be proper therefore at the outset to give an explicit and determinate account of what is
meant by it. By the principle of utility is meant that principle which approves or
disapproves of every action whatsoever, according to the tendency which it
appears to have to augment or diminish the happiness of the party whose interest is in question: or, what is the same thing in other words, to promote or to
oppose that happiness. I say of every action whatsoever; and therefore not only of
every action of a private individual, but of every measure of government.

By utility is meant that property in any object, whereby it tends to produce
benefit, advantage, pleasure, good, or happiness (all this in the present case
comes to the same thing), or (what comes again to the same thing) to prevent the
happening of mischief, pain, evil, or unhappiness to the party whose interest is
considered: if that party be the community in general, then the happiness of the
community: if a particular individual, then the happiness of that individual.

The interest of the community is one of the most general expressions that can
occur in the phraseology of morals: no wonder that the meaning of it is often lost.
When it has a meaning, it is this. The community is a fictitious *body*, composed of
the individual persons who are considered as constituting as it were its *members*.
The interest of the community then is, what?—the sum of the interests of the several members who compose it.

It is in vain to talk of the interest of the community, without understanding what
is the interest of the individual. A thing is said to promote the interest, or to be *for*
the interest, of an individual, when it tends to add to the sum total of his pleasures:
or, what comes to the same thing, to diminish the sum total of his pains.

An action then may be said to be conformable to the principle of utility, or, for
shortness sake, to utility (meaning with respect to the community at large), when
the tendency it has to augment the happiness of the community is greater than
any it has to diminish it.

A measure of government (which is but a particular kind of action, performed by a particular person or persons) may be said to be conformable to or
dictated by the principle of utility, when in like manner the tendency which it
has to augment the happiness of the community is greater than any which it has
to diminish it.

When an action, or in particular a measure of government, is supposed by a
man to be conformable to the principle of utility, it may be convenient, for the
purposes of discourse, to imagine a kind of law or dictate, called a law or dictate
of utility: and to speak of the action in question, as being conformable to such law
or dictate.

A man may be said to be a partisan of the principle of utility, when the approbation or disapprobation he annexes to any action, or to any measure, is determined
by and proportioned to the tendency which he conceives it to have to augment or

to diminish the happiness of the community: or in other words, to its conformity or unconformity to the laws or dictates of utility.

Of an action that is conformable to the principle of utility one may always say either that it is one that ought to be done, or at least that it is not one that ought not to be done. One may say also, that it is right it should be done; at least that it is not wrong it should be done: that it is a right action; at least that it is not a wrong action. When thus interpreted, the words *ought,* and *right* and *wrong,* and others of that stamp, have a meaning: when otherwise, they have none.

Has the rectitude of this principle been ever formally contested? It should seem that it had, by those who have not known what they have been meaning. Is it susceptible of any direct proof? it should seem not: for that which is used to prove every thing else, cannot itself be proved: a chain of proofs must have their commencement somewhere. To give such proof is as impossible as it is needless.

Not that there is or ever has been that human creature breathing, however stupid or perverse, who has not on many, perhaps on most occasions of his life, deferred to it. By the natural constitution of the human frame, on most occasions of their lives men in general embrace this principle, without thinking of it: if not for the ordering of their own actions, yet for the trying of their own actions, as well as of those of other men. There have been, at the same time, not many, perhaps, even of the most intelligent, who have been disposed to embrace it purely and without reserve. There are even few who have not taken some occasion or other to quarrel with it, either on account of their not understanding always how to apply it, or on account of some prejudice or other which they were afraid to examine into, or could not bear to part with. For such is the stuff that man is made of: in principle and in practice, in a right track and in a wrong one, the rarest of all human qualities is consistency.

When a man attempts to combat the principle of utility, it is with reasons drawn, without his being aware of it, from that very principle itself. His arguments, if they prove any thing, prove not that the principle is *wrong,* but that, according to the applications he supposes to be made of it, it is *misapplied.* Is it possible for a man to move the earth? Yes; but he must first find out another earth to stand upon.

To disprove the propriety of it by arguments is impossible; but, from the causes that have been mentioned, or from some confused or partial view of it, a man may happen to be disposed not to relish it. Where this is the case, if he thinks the setting of his opinions on such a subject worth the trouble, let him take the following steps, and at length, perhaps, he may come to reconcile himself to it.

Let him settle with himself, whether he would wish to discard this principle altogether; if so, let him consider what it is that all his reasonings (in matters of politics especially) can amount to?

If he would, let him settle with himself, whether he would judge and act without any principle, or whether there is any other he would judge and act by?

If there be, let him examine and satisfy himself whether the principle he thinks he has found is really any separate intelligible principle; or whether it be not a mere principle in words, a kind of phrase, which at bottom expresses neither more nor less than the mere averment of his own unfounded sentiments; that is, what in another person he might be apt to call caprice?

If he is inclined to think that his own approbation or disapprobation, annexed to the idea of an act, without any regard to its consequences, is a sufficient foundation for him to judge and act upon, let him ask himself whether his sentiment is to be a standard of right and wrong, with respect to every other man, or whether every man's sentiment has the same privilege of being a standard to itself?

In the first case, let him ask himself whether his principle is not despotical, and hostile to all the rest of human race?

In the second case, whether it is not anarchial, and whether at this rate there are not as many different standards of right and wrong as there are men? and whether even to the same man, the same thing, which is right today, may not (without the least change in its nature) be wrong tomorrow? and whether the same thing is not right and wrong in the same place at the same time? and in either case, whether all argument is not at an end? and whether, when two men have said, "I like this," and "I don't like it," they can (upon such a principle) have any thing more to say?

If he should have said to himself, No: for that the sentiment which he proposes as a standard must be grounded on reflection, let him say on what particulars the reflection is to turn? if on particulars having relation to the utility of the act, then let him say whether this is not deserting his own principle, and borrowing assistance from the very one in opposition to which he sets it up: or if not on those particulars, on what other particulars?

If he should be for compounding the matter, and adopting his own principle in part, and the principle of utility in part, let him say how far he will adopt it?

When he has settled with himself where he will stop, then let him ask himself how he justifies to himself the adopting it so far? and why he will not adopt it any farther?

Admitting any other principle than the principle of utility to be a right principle, a principle that it is right for a man to pursue; admitting (what is not true) that the word *right* can have a meaning without reference to utility, let him say whether there is any such thing as a *motive* that a man can have to pursue the dictates of it: if there is, let him say what that motive is, and how it is to be distinguished from those which enforce the dictates of utility: if not, then lastly let him say what it is this other principle can be good for?...

Pleasures then, and the avoidance of pains, are the *ends* which the legislator has in view: it behooves him therefore to understand their *value*. Pleasures and pains are the *instruments* he has to work with: it behooves him therefore to understand their force, which is again, in other words, their value.

To a person considered *by himself,* the value of a pleasure or pain considered *by itself,* will be greater or less, according to the four following circumstances:

1. Its *intensity.*

2. Its *duration.*

3. Its *certainty* or *uncertainty.*

4. Its *propinquity* or *remoteness.*

These are the circumstances which are to be considered in estimating a pleasure or a pain considered each of them by itself. But when the value of any pleasure or pain is considered for the purpose of estimating the tendency of any *act* by which it is produced, there are two other circumstances to be taken into the account; these are,

5. Its *fecundity,* or the chance it has of being followed by sensations of the *same* kind: that is, pleasures, if it be a pleasure: pains, if it be a pain.

6. Its *purity,* or the chance it has of *not* being followed by sensations of the *opposite* kind: that is, pains, if it be a pleasure: pleasures, if it be a pain.

These two last, however, are in strictness scarcely to be deemed properties of the pleasure or the pain itself, they are not, therefore, in strictness to be taken into the account of the value of that pleasure or that pain. They are in strictness to be deemed properties only of the act, or other event, by which such pleasure or pain has been produced; and accordingly are only to be taken into the account of the tendency of such act or such event.

To a *number* of persons, with reference to each of whom the value of a pleasure or a pain is considered, it will be greater or less, according to seven circumstances: to wit, the six preceding ones; viz.

1. Its *intensity.*

2. Its *duration.*

3. Its *certainty* or *uncertainty.*

4. Its *propinquity* or *remoteness.*

5. Its *fecundity.*

6. Its *purity.*

And one other; to wit:

7. Its *extent;* that is, the number of persons to whom it *extends;* or (in other words) who are affected by it.

To take an exact account then of the general tendency of any act, by which the interests of a community are affected, proceed as follows. Begin with any one person of those whose interests seem most immediately to be affected by it: and take an account,

1. Of the value of each distinguishable *pleasure* which appears to be produced by it in the *first* instance.

2. Of the value of each *pain* which appears to be produced by it in the *first* instance.

3. Of the value of each pleasure which appears to be produced by it *after* the first. This constitutes the *fecundity* of the first *pleasure* and the *impurity* of the first *pain*.

4. Of the value of each *pain* which appears to be produced by it after the first. This constitutes the *fecundity* of the first *pain,* and the *impurity* of the first pleasure.

5. Sum up all the values of all the *pleasures* on the one side, and those of all the pains on the other. The balance, if it be on the side of pleasure, will give the *good* tendency of the act upon the whole, with respect to the interests of that *individual* person; if on the side of pain, the *bad* tendency of it upon the whole.

6. Take an account of the *number* of persons whose interests appear to be concerned; and repeat the above process with respect to each. *Sum up* the numbers expressive of the degrees of *good* tendency, which the act has, with respect to each individual, in regard to whom the tendency of it is *good* upon the whole: do this again with respect to each individual, in regard to whom the tendency of it is *good* upon the whole: do this again with respect to each individual, in regard to whom the tendency of it is *bad* upon the whole. Take the *balance;* which, if on the side of *pleasure,* will give the general *good tendency* of the act, with respect to the total number or community of individuals concerned; if on the side of pain, the general *evil tendency,* with respect to the same community.

It is not to be expected that this process should be strictly pursued previously to every moral judgment, or to every legislative or judicial operation. It may, however, be always kept in view: and as near as the process actually pursued on these occasions approaches to it, so near will such process approach to the character of an exact one.

The same process is alike applicable to pleasure and pain, in whatever shape they appear: and by whatever denomination they are distinguished: to pleasure, whether it be called *good* (which is properly the cause or instrument of pleasure) or *profit* (which is distant pleasure, or the cause or instrument of distant pleasure), or *convenience,* or *advantage, benefit, emolument, happiness,* and so forth: to pain, whether it be called *evil* (which corresponds to *good*), or *mischief,* or *inconvenience,* or *disadvantage,* or *loss,* or *unhappiness,* and so forth.

Nor is this a novel and unwarranted, any more than it is a useless theory. In all this there is nothing but what the practice of mankind, wheresoever they have a clear view of their own interest, is perfectly conformable to. An article of property, an estate in land, for instance, is valuable, on what account? On account of the pleasures of all kinds which it enables a man to produce, and what comes to the same thing the pains of all kinds which it enables him to avert. But the value of such an article of property is universally understood to rise or fall according to the length or shortness of the time which a man has in it: the certainty or uncertainty of its coming into possession: and the nearness or remoteness of the time at which, if at all, it is to come into possession. As to the *intensity* of the pleasures which a man may derive from it, this is never thought of, because it depends upon the use which each particular person may come to make of it; which cannot be estimated till the particular pleasures he may come to derive from it, or the particular pains he may come to exclude by means of it, are brought to view. For the same reason, neither does he think of the *fecundity* or *purity* of those pleasures....

IN DEFENSE OF UTILITARIANISM
J. S. Mill

John Stuart Mill (1806–1873), a British philosopher, was a leading intellectual of the nineteenth century. In the following excerpt from his book, Utilitarianism *(1863), Mill considers three objections to the utilitarian theory. First, some opponents charge that the emphasis on the pursuit of pleasure makes utilitarianism "a doctrine worthy of swine." Mill responds by distinguishing higher from lower pleasures. Because utilitarianism considers pursuit of higher, distinctively human pleasures (such as enjoying great literature) as especially important, it is, Mill asserts, a doctrine worthy of human beings. Second, some argue that utilitarian moral theory sets standards that are "too high for humanity." Third, still others object that in ordinary circumstances that call for a moral decision, we lack the time needed for calculating the utility of actions. Mill argues that these latter two objections are based on misunderstandings of the utilitarian theory. After answering these objections, Mill offers what he calls an "indirect proof" of the principle of utility.*

The creed which accepts as the foundation of morals, Utility, or the Greatest Happiness Principle, holds that actions are right in proportion as they tend to promote happiness, wrong as they tend to produce the reverse of happiness. By happiness is intended pleasure, and the absence of pain; by unhappiness, pain, and the privation of pleasure. To give a clear view of the moral standard set up by the theory, much more requires to be said; in particular, what things it includes in the ideas of pain and pleasure; and to what extent this is left an open question. But these supplementary explanations do not affect the theory of life on which this theory of morality is grounded—namely, that pleasure, and freedom from pain, are the only things desirable as ends; and that all desirable things (which are as numerous in the utilitarian as in any other scheme) are desirable either for the pleasure inherent in themselves, or as means to the promotion of pleasure and the prevention of pain.

Now, such a theory of life excites in many minds, and among them in some of the most estimable in feeling and purpose, inveterate dislike. To suppose that life

Reprinted from *Utilitarianism* (1863).

has (as they express it) no higher end than pleasure—no better and nobler object of desire and pursuit—they designate as utterly mean and grovelling; as a doctrine worthy only of swine, to whom the followers of Epicurus were, at a very early period, contemptuously likened; and modern holders of the doctrine are occasionally made the subject of equally polite comparisons by its German, French, and English assailants.

When thus attacked, the Epicureans have always answered, that it is not they, but their accusers, who represent human nature in a degrading light; since the accusation supposes human beings to be capable of no pleasures except those of which swine are capable. If this supposition were true, the charge could not be gainsaid, but would then be no longer an imputation; for if the sources of pleasure were precisely the same to human beings and to swine, the rule of life which is good enough for the one would be good enough for the other. The comparison of the Epicurean life to that of beasts is felt as degrading, precisely because a beast's pleasures do not satisfy a human being's conceptions of happiness. Human beings have faculties more elevated than the animal appetites, and when once made conscious of them, do not regard anything as happiness which does not include their gratification. I do not, indeed, consider the Epicureans to have been by any means faultless in drawing out their scheme of consequences from the utilitarian principle. To do this in any sufficient manner, many Stoic, as well as Christian, elements require to be included. But there is no known Epicurean theory of life which does not assign to the pleasures of the intellect, of the feelings and imagination, and of the moral sentiments, a much higher value as pleasures than to those of mere sensation. It must be admitted, however, that utilitarian writers in general have placed the superiority of mental over bodily pleasures chiefly in the greater permanency, safety, uncostliness, etc., of the former—that is, in their circumstantial advantages rather than in their intrinsic nature. And on all these points utilitarians have fully proved their case; but they might have taken the other, and, as it may be called, higher ground, with entire consistency. It is quite compatible with the principle of utility to recognize the fact, that some *kinds* of pleasure are more desirable and more valuable than others. It would be absurd that while, in estimating all other things, quality is considered as well as quantity, the estimation of pleasures should be supposed to depend on quantity alone.

If I am asked, what I mean by difference of quality in pleasures, or what makes one pleasure more valuable than another, merely as a pleasure, except its being greater in amount, there is but one possible answer. Of two pleasures, if there be one to which all or almost all who have experience of both give a decided preference, irrespective of any feeling of moral obligation to prefer it, that is the more desirable pleasure. If one of the two is, by those who are competently acquainted with both, placed so far above the other that they prefer it, even though knowing it to be attended with a greater amount of discontent, and would not resign it for any quantity of the other pleasure which their nature is capable of, we are justified in ascribing to the preferred enjoyment a superiority in quality, so far outweighing quantity as to render it, in comparison, of small account.

Now it is an unquestionable fact that those who are equally acquainted with, and equally capable of appreciating and enjoying, both, do give a most marked preference to the manner of existence which employs their higher faculties. Few human creatures would consent to be changed into any of the lower animals, for a promise of the fullest allowance of a beast's pleasures; no intelligent human being would consent to be a fool, no instructed person would be an ignoramus, no person of feeling and conscience would be selfish and base, even though they should be persuaded that the fool, the dunce, or the rascal is better satisfied with his lot than they are with theirs. They would not resign what they possess more than he for the most complete satisfaction of all the desires which they have in common with him. If they ever fancy they would, it is only in cases of unhappiness so extreme, that to escape from it they would exchange their lot for almost any other, however undesirable in their own eyes. A being of higher faculties requires more to make him happy, is capable probably of more acute suffering, and is certainly accessible to it at more points than one of an inferior type; but in spite of these liabilities, he can never really wish to sink into what he feels to be a lower grade of existence. We may give what explanation we please of this unwillingness; we may attribute it to pride, a name which is given indiscriminately to some of the most and to some of the least estimable feelings of which mankind are capable; we may refer it to the love of liberty and personal independence, an appeal to which was with the Stoics one of the most effective means for the inculcation of it; to the love of power, or to the love of excitement, both of which do really enter into and contribute to it: but its most appropriate appellation is a sense of dignity, which all human beings possess in one form or other, and in some, though by no means in exact, proportion to their higher faculties, and which is so essential a part of the happiness of those in whom it is strong, that nothing which conflicts with it could be, otherwise than momentarily, an object of desire to them. Whoever supposes that this preference takes place at a sacrifice of happiness—that the superior being, in anything like the equal circumstances, is not happier than the inferior—confounds the two very different ideas, of happiness, and content. It is indisputable that the being whose capacities of enjoyment are low, has the greatest chance of having them fully satisfied; and a highly-endowed being will always feel that any happiness which he can look for, as in the world is constituted, is imperfect. But he can learn to bear its imperfections, if they are at all bearable; and they will not make him envy the being who is indeed unconscious of the imperfections, but only because he feels not at all the good which those imperfections qualify. It is better to be a human being dissatisfied than a pig satisfied; better to be Socrates dissatisfied than a fool satisfied. And if the fool, or the pig, is of a different opinion, it is because they only know their own side of the question. The other party to the comparison knows both sides....

... The objectors to utilitarianism cannot always be charged with representing it in a discreditable light. On the contrary, those among them who entertain anything like a just idea of its disinterested character, sometimes find fault with its standard as being too high for humanity. They say it is exacting too much to require that people shall always act from the inducement of promoting the general interests of society. But this is to mistake the very meaning of a standard of morals, and to confound the rule of action with the motive of it. It is the business of ethics to tell us what are our duties, or by what test we may know them; but no system of ethics requires that the sole motive of all we do shall be a feeling of duty; on the contrary, ninety-nine hundredths of all our actions are done from other motives, and rightly so done, if the rule of duty does not condemn them. It is the more unjust to utilitarianism that this particular misapprehension should be made a ground of objection to it, inasmuch as utilitarian moralists have gone beyond almost all others in affirming that the motive has nothing to do with the morality of the action, though much with the worth of the agent. He who saves a fellow creature from drowning does what is morally right, whether his motive be duty, or the hope of being paid for his trouble: he who betrays the friend that trusts him, is guilty of a crime, even if his object be to serve another friend to whom he is under greater obligations. But to speak only of actions done from the motive of duty, and in direct obedience to principle: it is a misapprehension of the utilitarian mode of thought, to conceive it as implying that people should fix their minds upon so wide a generality as the world, or society at large. The great majority of good actions are intended, not for the benefit of the world, but for that of individuals, of which the good of the world is made up; and the thoughts of the most virtuous man need not on these occasions travel beyond the particular persons concerned, except so far as is necessary to assure himself that in benefiting them he is not violating the rights—that is, the legitimate and authorized expectations—of any one else. The multiplication of happiness is, according to the utilitarian ethics, the object of virtue: the occasions on which any person (except one in a thousand) has it in his power to do this on an extended scale, in other words, to be a public benefactor, are but exceptional; and on these occasions alone is he called on to consider public utility; in every other case, private utility, the interest or happiness of some few persons, is all he has to attend to. Those alone the influence of whose actions extends to society in general, need concern themselves habitually about so large an object. In the case of abstinences indeed—of things which people forbear to do, from moral considerations, though the consequences in the particular case might be beneficial—it would be unworthy of an intelligent agent not to be consciously aware that the action is of a class which, if practiced generally, would be generally injurious, and that this is the ground of the obligation to abstain from it. The amount of regard for the public interest implied in this recognition, is no greater than is demanded by every system of morals; for they all enjoin to abstain from whatever is manifestly pernicious to society....

... Again, defenders of utility often find themselves called upon to reply to such objections as this—that there is not time, previous to action, for calculating and weighing the effects of any line of conduct on the general happiness. This is exactly as if any one were to say that it is impossible to guide our conduct by Christianity, because there is not time, on every occasion on which anything has to be done, to read through the Old and New Testaments. The answer to the objection is, that there has been ample time, namely, the whole past duration of ... the human species. During all that time mankind have been learning by experience the tendencies of actions; on which experience all the prudence, as well as all the morality of life, is dependent. People talk as if the commencement of this course of experience had hitherto been put off, and as if, at the moment when some man feels tempted to meddle with the property or life of another, he had to begin considering for the first time whether murder and theft are injurious to human happiness. Even then I do not think that he would find the question very puzzling; but, at all events, the matter is now done to his hand. It is truly a whimsical supposition that if mankind were agreed in considering utility to be the test of morality, they would remain without any agreement as to what *is* useful, and would take no measures for having their notions on the subject taught to the young, and enforced by law and opinion. There is no difficulty in proving any ethical standard whatever to work ill, if we suppose universal idiocy to be conjoined with it, but on any hypothesis short of that, mankind must by this time have acquired positive beliefs as to the effects of some actions on their happiness; and the beliefs which have thus come down are the rules of morality for the multitude, and for the philosopher until he has succeeded in finding better. That philosophers might easily do this, even now, on many subjects; that the received code of ethics is by no means of divine right; and that mankind have still much to learn as to the effects of actions on the general happiness, I admit, or rather, earnestly maintain. The corollaries from the principle of utility, like the precepts of every practical art, admit of indefinite improvement, and, in a progressive state of the human mind, their improvement is perpetually going on. But to consider the rules of morality as improvable, is one thing; to pass over the intermediate generalizations entirely, and endeavor to test each individual action directly by the first principle, is another. It is a strange notion that the acknowledgment of a first principle is inconsistent with the admission of secondary ones. To inform a traveller respecting the place of his ultimate destination, is not to forbid the use of landmarks and direction-posts on the way. The proposition that happiness is the end and aim of morality, does not mean that no road ought to be laid down to that goal, or that persons going thither should not be advised to take one direction rather than another. Men really ought to leave off talking a kind of nonsense on this subject, which they would neither talk nor listen to in other matters of practical concernment. Nobody argues that the art of navigation is not founded on astronomy, because sailors cannot wait to calculate the Nautical Almanack. Being rational creatures, they go to sea with it ready calculated; and all rational creatures go out upon the sea of life with their minds made up on the common questions of right and wrong, as well as on many of the far more difficult questions of wise and foolish. And this, as long as foresight is a human quality, is to be presumed they will continue to do. Whatever we adopt as the fundamental principle of morality, we require subordinate principles to apply it by: the impossibility of doing without them, being common to all systems, can afford no argument against any one in particular: but gravely to argue as if no such secondary principles could be had, and as if mankind had remained till now, and always must remain, without drawing any general conclusions from the experience of human life, is as high a pitch, I think, as absurdity has ever reached in philosophical controversy....

Of What Sort of Proof the Principle of Utility Is Susceptible

It has already been remarked, that questions of ultimate ends do not admit of proof, in the ordinary acceptation of the term. To be incapable of proof by reasoning is common to all first principles; to the first premises of our knowledge, as well as to those of our conduct. But the former, being matters of fact, may be the subject of a direct appeal to the faculties which judge of fact—namely, our senses, and our internal consciousness. Can an appeal be made to the same faculties on questions of practical ends? Or by what other faculty is cognizance taken of them?

Questions about ends are, in other words, questions what things are desirable. The utilitarian doctrine is, that happiness is desirable, and the only thing desirable, as an end; all other things being only desirable as means to that end. What ought to be required of this doctrine—what conditions is it requisite that the doctrine should fulfill—to make good its claim to be believed?

The only proof capable of being given that an object is visible, is that people actually see it. The only proof that a sound is audible, is that people hear it: and so of the other sources of our experience. In like manner, I apprehend, the sole evidence it is possible to produce that anything is desirable, is that people do actually desire it. If the end which the utilitarian doctrine proposes to itself were not, in theory and in practice, acknowledged to be an end, nothing could ever convince any person that it was so. No reason can be given why the general happiness is desirable, except that each person, so far as he believes it to be attainable, desires his own happiness. This, however, being a fact, we have not only all the proof which the case admits of, but all which it is possible to require, that happiness is a good: that each person's happiness is a good to that person, and the general happiness, therefore, a good to the aggregate of all persons. Happiness has made out its title as one of the ends of conduct, and consequently one of the criteria of morality.

But it has not, by this alone, proved itself to be the sole criterion. To do that, it would seem, by the same rule, necessary to show, not only that people desire happiness, but that they never desire anything else. Now it is palpable that they do desire things which, in common language, are decidedly distinguished from happiness. They desire, for example, virtue, and the absence of vice, no less really than pleasure and the absence of pain. The desire of virtue is not as universal, but it is as authentic a fact, as the desire of happiness. And hence the opponents of the utilitarian standard deem that they have a right to infer that there are other ends of human action besides happiness, and that happiness is not the standard of approbation and disapprobation.

But does the utilitarian doctrine deny that people desire virtue, or maintain that virtue is not a thing to be desired? The very reverse. It maintains not only that virtue is to be desired, but that it is to be desired disinterestedly, for itself. Whatever may be the opinion of utilitarian moralists as to the original conditions by which virtue is made virtue; however they may believe (as they do) that actions and dispositions are only virtuous because they promote another end than virtue; yet this being granted, and it having been decided, from considerations of this description, what is virtuous, they not only place virtue at the very head of the things which are good as means to the ultimate end, but they also recognize as a psychological fact the possibility of its being, to the individual, a good in itself, without looking to any end beyond it; and hold, that the mind is not in a right state, not in a state conformable to Utility, not in the state most conducive to the general happiness, unless it does love virtue in this manner—as a thing desirable in itself, even although, in the individual instance, it should not produce those other desirable consequences which it tends to produce, and on account of which it is held to be virtue. This opinion is not, in the smallest degree, a departure from the Happiness principle. The ingredients of happiness are very various, and each of them is desirable in itself, and not merely when considered as swelling an aggregate. The principle of utility does not mean that any given pleasure, as music, for instance, or any given exemption from pain, as for example health, are to be looked upon as a means to a collective something termed happiness, and to be desired on that account. They are desired and desirable in and for themselves; besides being means, they are a part of the end. Virtue, according to the utilitarian doctrine, is not naturally and originally part of the end, but it is capable of becoming so; and in those who love it disinterestedly it has become so, and is desired and cherished, not as a means to happiness, but as a part of their happiness....

UTILITARIANISM: ACT OR RULE?
Stephen Darwall

Stephen Darwall is John Dewey collegiate professor of philosophy at the University of Michigan, Ann Arbor, and author of Impartial Reason *(1983),* The British Moralists and the Internal "Ought": 1640–1740 *(1995),* Philosophical Ethics *(1998), and* Welfare and Rational Care *(2004). Darwall provisionally interprets Mill as holding a version of act utilitarianism (AU) and proceeds to explain various standard objections to AU. He then contrasts act utilitarianism with rule utilitarianism according to which (roughly) the rightness of an action is explained in terms of the utility of rules instead of the utilities of individual actions themselves. (In the next selection, Brad Hooker defends what he calls* rule consequentialism, *a near cousin of rule utilitarianism.)*

From Moral Good to Moral Right: Act-Utilitarianism

Suppose we grant Mill that the general happiness is the end of morality, and that outcomes can be ranked from the moral point of view by how much overall net happiness they involve. A state of affairs that involves more happiness than some other will then be better, overall, from the moral perspective. It will be morally better (or, perhaps more appropriately, morally "more fortunate").

But how could Mill argue from this statement to a principle that determines which acts are right and which are wrong? Here is what he said: "The creed which accepts as the foundation of morals 'utility' or 'the greatest happiness principle' holds that actions are right in proportion as they tend to promote happiness; wrong as they tend to produce the reverse of happiness" (U.II.2). Taken by itself, this passage might naturally be read as a statement of what is called *act-utilitarianism (AU)*: An act is right if, and only if, of those acts available to the agent in the circumstances, it would produce the greatest total net happiness. For the moment we will proceed, provisionally, as if the latter is Mill's view....

Whether it is Mill's view or not, AU can seem a sensible thing to believe if the end of morality is the general happiness. After all, if what morality is *about* is producing the greatest happiness for all, then why shouldn't this end also always determine what a person should do, what it would be morally right for him to do?

Before we begin to evaluate AU as the "criterion of right and wrong," we should note various features of it. First, although Mill was a qualitative hedonist, AU is a quantitative criterion. At this point, however, we would do better to ignore this problem. One way of doing so is to suppose that the quantitative measure of happiness that figures in AU is one that already takes account of intensity, duration, *and* quality.

Second, we have to assume that there can be a quantitative *interpersonal* measure of happiness, one that compares amounts of happiness and unhappiness across individuals. We don't have to assume that we know how to measure happiness. We just have to assume that there are facts about how much happiness or unhappiness one individual would experience in an outcome, compared to someone else. This is far from a trivial assumption, and there are some deep issues concerning it. Then again, people make rough-and-ready judgments about relative amounts of happiness all the time. In deciding to whom to give an extra ticket to a concert, for instance, you may well think something like "Joan would probably enjoy it more than Jerome." To get to the interesting ethical issues about utilitarianism, we will simply assume that there are such facts.

Third, we should note that AU holds that *whatever* effects on happiness and unhappiness an action would *actually have*—*wherever, whenever,* and to *whomever* they would occur—are all equally relevant to determining what the person should do. Let's consider each of these separately.

Wherever. If my action would cause happiness or unhappiness on the other side of the globe, this has the same relevance to whether I should do it as if it were to occur right next to me.

Whenever. If my action would cause happiness or unhappiness twenty centuries from now, that has the same relevance to whether I should do it as if it were to occur presently.

To Whomever. The happiness and unhappiness of all persons (or sentient beings) are equally morally relevant to what I should do.

Putting these together, we can reason as follows: If two alternative actions that I could perform would cause the same amount of aggregate happiness, but with one act causing benefits to be realized presently to neighbors about whom I care greatly, and with the other act causing benefits to be realized many years from now for people far from my home about whom I care not at all (assuming that my happiness has been taken account of, like everyone else's), then there is as good a moral reason to perform the second act as to perform the first. And if the second would produce slightly more happiness, I should do it. (N.B.: We have to assume that the benefits actually *would* be realized in the future; it is not enough that I set events in motion that would realize the benefits *unless* some obstacle arises, *if* some obstacle would arise.)

Fourth, AU holds that an action is right if, and only if, it would produce the greatest total *net* happiness—that is, after we have subtracted the unhappiness from the happiness that would result.

Finally, AU holds that I should perform that act, *of the ones available,* which would produce the *greatest* total net happiness. It is not enough to make an action right that it would produce happiness, since there may be some other alternative that would produce even more. Likewise, it is not enough to make an action wrong that it would produce net unhappiness, since there may be no alternative available that would produce net happiness.

The intuitive idea behind AU can be put this way. Actions have consequences. Whenever we act, there are things that happen as a result of our actions that wouldn't have occurred otherwise. Some of these consequences are proximate, but others can be quite remote in space, time, or both. C_i, referring to an action's consequences, is what we can call the set of things that would occur if a particular action A_i were taken. Within this set C_i there will be instances of people being happy and unhappy to various degrees. Suppose that for each set of consequences C we can associate a number H_i, which is the total net happiness in C_i.

Now, in any choice situation, there are many different things an agent could do. Each of these actions A_i will have a consequence set C_i with a total net happiness equal to H_i. Since what is best from the moral point of view is the greatest total net happiness, an agent should always perform the act that would cause the greatest total net happiness. Within the set of acts (A_i) there will be one or more (say, A_j) whose consequence set C_j produces a greatest total net happiness H_j. The right thing for the agent to do, then, is to perform that act (or one of the acts that tie for the highest H).

Defending AU Against Some Objections

The philosophical line of thought leading to AU is very powerful. Who can deny that, morally speaking, one person's welfare is the same as any other person's? Of course, we all care more about some people than about others. That is only natural. But can we defend the idea that these people are really more important than others about whom we happen to care less? To be sure, they are more important *to us.* But that doesn't make them more important, period, or more important morally. Of course, some people don't just happen to be more important to us; rather, it is inherent in various morally important relationships, such as those of mutual love, friendship, and family, that they be more important to us. But then what makes these relationships important can't be that they involve people important to us. There must be some way of defending them from a standpoint in which all people are taken to matter equally. And AU argues that this standpoint is one of equal concern for the happiness of all.

If you want to feel the force of this thought, imagine that someone steps on your toe. You protest, and he says, "But you are not important to me." Won't this seem beside the point? Might you not think something like "Well, I may not be very important to you, but I am no less important than you." If, however, everyone's welfare matters equally from the moral point of view, then each person's welfare would seem also to matter equally to what we morally should do. AU can seem a natural conclusion to this line of thought.

Still, there are many reasons why AU is difficult to accept, and Mill attempted to address some of these objections. He noted, for example, the frequent complaint that "there is not time, previous to action, for calculating and weighing the effects of any line of conduct on the general happiness" (U.II.24). But this objection mistakes what AU aims to be. AU is a criterion of what makes an action the right thing to do. If the objection's assumption is correct, it will follow from AU that there is not time before acting to *know* which action is right. But how is that an objection to AU, since the latter could still tell us what we should need to know in order to know which action is right?

Consider an analogy. Suppose someone offers as a theory of *prudent* action the principle that an action is the most prudent act if it is the one, of those available, that will produce the greatest total net happiness for the agent. If the objection applies in the moral case, then an analogous objection should apply here. But it would seem that the only thing we can conclude if this objection's assumption is correct is that there is not time before acting to know which action is most prudent. Would this conclusion pose an objection to the theory of prudence? It is hard to see how it would. In both cases, it might be urged, we would be best advised to do whatever is likeliest, according to available evidence, to promote the greatest happiness. That would be the *subjectively right (or prudent)* act, whereas the act that would actually promote the most happiness would be the *objectively right (or prudent)* act.

Neither does AU necessarily say that agents should attempt to follow AU in great detail in their *deliberations,* in terms of making difficult calculations and so on. How should agents deliberate? Deliberations are also things we *do.* So AU says that agents should deliberate in whatever way will have the best consequences. And here, Mill argued, we have the benefit of centuries of accumulated wisdom concerning what sorts of actions are likely to have what sorts of effects. Much of moral common sense, concerning the keeping of promises and being fair, honest, kind, and so on, can be viewed as "rules of thumb" or "secondary principles," as Mill called them, by which people sensibly guide their deliberations in the knowledge that, generally and in the long run, their doing so will have the best consequences for human happiness.

Nonetheless, according to AU these "intermediate generalizations" have no moral validity in themselves. The fact that an action falls under some such rule of thumb has nothing to do with whether it is the right action or not. That depends entirely on the consequences of the action for human happiness.

Another objection is that AU may seem to require that we love all people equally. But that is impossible—and probably undesirable even if it were possible. Personal relationships in which we care for each other in special ways are an important source of human happiness. Mill replied to this objection by saying that it mistakes a "rule of action with the motive of it" (U.II.19). AU, then, is a rule or principle of action that says what must be true in order for an action to be morally right. And, moreover, it says that the rightness of an action depends entirely on its consequences. So which motive an action is performed from is irrelevant to whether, according to AU, it is the right thing to do. Thus AU does not tell us that we must love all people equally.

Objections to AU: Some Case Studies

No doubt the most serious source of objection to AU is that it conflicts so clearly with moral common sense about particular cases. I will briefly describe four kinds of cases where objections of these sorts frequently arise.

1. *Promises.* Common sense holds that the fact that an act would break a promise is intrinsically relevant to its moral rightness, whereas AU maintains that only an act's consequences determine whether it is right or wrong. Whether an action would break a promise is a *backward-looking consideration,* whereas, according to AU, *only forward-looking* considerations matter to what a person morally should do.

Of course, AU will indirectly recognize many backward-looking considerations that are related to promising. Usually people to whom promises have been given have increased expectations that would be frustrated by breaking a promise. Also, trust is an important social resource, and breaking a promise usually tends to undermine trust. And so on.

But these consequences may be lacking in a particular case. A promise may have been given to someone no longer alive, or to someone who is alive but has forgotten about the promise (although she still continues to have a stake in it). Or no one else may know about the promise. And so on. In such cases, there may be few, if any, bad consequences attributable to the fact that a promise would be broken. And even in cases where there are such consequences, AU holds, contrary to common sense, that the fact that a promise was made has no moral weight in itself.

2. *Other Actions Thought to Be Wrong in Themselves.* Promise-breaking is only one example of a number of kinds of acts that are thought to be wrong in themselves, at least other things being equal. Don't you think, for example, that the fact that an action would amount to betrayal or dishonesty is a serious moral reason against it, a wrong-making consideration in itself? According to AU, however, such a fact is morally irrelevant, since it does not intrinsically concern consequences for human happiness.

3. *The Moral Asymmetry of Harm and Benefit.* According to AU, a harm can be compensated by an equal benefit. Suppose that an action of yours will create a

benefit for Brown, but at the cost of an exactly equal harm to Green. AU holds that there is no greater reason to avoid causing harm (to Green) than there is reason to create a benefit (for Brown). But don't you view the moral duty not to harm differently from the moral duty to benefit? Common sense seems to hold that the duty not to cause harm is stronger than the duty to benefit. The fact that causing harm to Green will cause an equal benefit to Brown is normally thought insufficient to justify the harm to Green.

4. *Distributive Justice.* Suppose that there are only two actions (A and B) you can perform, that only four people (w,x,y,z) will be affected, and that their happiness can be represented as follows:

	w	x	y	z
A	-2	2	2	2
B	1	1	1	1

According to AU, it is morally equivalent whether one does A or B, since both would produce the same total net happiness. It does not matter how happiness or unhappiness is distributed. However, common sense holds that goods can be distributed justly or unjustly. Especially if it doesn't make a difference to the total, don't you think it would be morally preferable to perform B rather than A? The benefits are spread equally in B, whereas some benefit and some lose in A.

Rule Utilitarianism

[According to] *rule utilitarianism (RU)*: An act is wrong if, and only if, it is contrary to a (possible) rule, such that were society to have a practice of enforcing that rule (formally or informally), this practice would maximize overall net happiness. To see the difference between AU and RU, consider a situation that Gilbert Harman has described. Suppose someone goes to the hospital for his yearly physical. As it happens, there are five patients in the hospital, each of whom needs a different organ (heart, kidney, etc.) to survive. Suppose that with the organ each person could look forward to roughly as many years of life as the healthy person would have. And suppose that otherwise the situations of all six people are roughly comparable in terms of the impact their lives would have on other people's happiness, and so on. Suppose, finally, that a doctor is in a position to kill the healthy person and distribute his organs to the five patients in a way that no one will suspect. Assume, therefore, that this action would create the most happiness overall and, accordingly, that AU would require it. Would RU?

To answer that question, we have to ask what sort of social practice governing the conduct of doctors, with what kinds of rules, would promote the greatest happiness. Consider three possibilities. In one practice, doctors are required by the rules to promote the general happiness, which would include killing patients and distributing their organs if that would best promote it. In a second, doctors are required never to kill patients for the purpose of organ distribution, even if it would have beneficial consequences in a particular instance. And in a third, doctors are neither required to kill patients to harvest their organs nor forbidden to do so. They may or may not kill patients at their own discretion when doing so would have better consequences. Now let's ask, which social practice is likely to have the best social consequences?

In other words, if you could write the code of ethics for the American Medical Association so that society's being governed by the resulting code would maximize happiness, what rules would you write into the code? Notice, specifically, that the question is which rule, *if publicly acknowledged as governing*, would maximize happiness. Thus a rule requiring or permitting doctors to harvest healthy patients for organs, if they could do so secretly, would not itself be a secret rule. And society's having a rule permitting secret organ harvesting might, for example, undermine trust in hospitals and doctors, even if a single secret organ harvesting might not. Would you trust doctors as much as you currently do if you knew that they were permitted or required to harvest organs from healthy patients when it would produce more general happiness to do so? Suppose you would not, and you think that others would not also. If so, then must you not think that according to RU it would be wrong for a doctor to harvest organs of healthy patients, even in cases where it would maximize happiness to do so?

It is generally believed that RU is much closer to moral common sense than AU and that, in the kinds of cases just described, its dictates would conflict with AU and coincide with common sense. You should think about these cases to see if you agree. And you should also ask yourself whether, if this were so, it would mean that RU is likelier to be a correct moral theory than is AU.

RULE-CONSEQUENTIALISM
Brad Hooker

Brad Hooker is senior lecturer in philosophy at the University of Reading, author of Ideal Code, Real World *(2000), and co-editor of* Moral Particularism *(2000) and* Morality, Rules, and Consequences *(2000). Whereas act consequentialism makes the rightness and wrongness of a particular action depend directly upon the value of its consequences, rule consequentialism, by contrast, makes the rightness or wrongness depend indirectly upon the value of consequences. It does so in the following way. According to the rule consequentialist, the deontic status of a concrete action (in a situation) depends upon whether it conforms to a correct moral rule that applies to the situation. Furthermore, what makes a rule "correct" is that the consequences of its general acceptance are at least as good as the consequences of other alternative rules for that situation. Because at bottom the explanation of rightness and wrongness appeals to considerations of the value of consequences of acceptance of rules, this view is properly classified as a version of consequentialism.*

In his article, Hooker defends a specific version of rule consequentialism against certain objections including the "demandingness" and "partial compliance" objections.

From Brad Hooker, "Rule-Consequentialism," *Mind* 99 (1990). Reprinted by permission of the publisher.

Suppose that accepting rules is a matter of having certain desires and dispositions. Now consider the theory that an act is morally right if and only if it is called for by the set of desires and dispositions the having of which by everyone would result in at least as good consequences judged impartially as any other. For lack of a better name, we might call this theory *disposition/rule-consequentialism,* or just rule-consequentialism for short. Two crucial features of this theory should be noted. One is that it assesses the rightness and wrongness of any particular act, not directly in terms of its consequences, but *indirectly* in terms of a set of desires, dispositions, and rules, which is then assessed in terms of the consequences of everyone's having that set.[1] The other is that it assesses the rightness of any given act, not in terms of the desires, dispositions, and rules which are such that *the agent's having them* would bring about the best overall consequences, but rather in terms of the desires, dispositions, and rules which are such that *everyone's having them* would bring about the best overall consequences. Let me refer to the set of desires, dispositions, and rules which are such that everyone's having them would bring about the best overall consequences as the *optimific* set.

To those who are attracted to consequentialism but want a moral theory that accords with at least most of our intuitions, rule-consequentialism should have considerable initial appeal. In section I of this paper, I try to bring out the attractions of rule-consequentialism by showing how it can be formulated so as to be safe from the main objections to other consequentialist theories. Yet, even if the best version of rule-consequentialism is immune to the objections that plague other consequentialist theories, rule-consequentialism has difficulties of its own—one of the most serious of which is the so-called partial compliance objection. In section II, I consider how rule-consequentialists might reply to the partial compliance objection. Then, in section III, I explore the question of whether rule-consequentialists can avoid the partial compliance objection without opening up their theory to the objection that it makes unreasonably severe demands on individuals.

I

[One] objection to act-utilitarianism is that it does not allow that fairness or equality in the distribution of benefits and burdens can be morally required even when a less fair or less egalitarian distribution would provide greater net welfare.[2] But it is possible to accommodate this objection without abandoning even act-consequentialism. For it might be held that, while the right act is still just whatever one will bring about the best outcome, outcomes are to be ranked in terms of not only how much well-being they contain but also how equally or fairly it is distributed.[3]

A prominent objection to standard kinds of act-consequentialism is that they give no direct weight to deontological, agent-relative considerations: standard kinds of act-consequentialism hold that it is morally right to harm people, or to ignore one's special obligations to those with whom one has some special connection, when such acts would bring about even slightly more good overall. Many people confidently believe that it is morally wrong to commit murder, to torture someone for information, to frame the innocent, to steal, to break one's promises, to fail to give special weight to the interests of those with whom one has some special connection, and so on, *even when doing one of these things would produce somewhat better consequences judged impartially.* But here, too, much can be said in defence of act-consequentialism.[4] Defenders of the theory usually start by pointing out that the kinds of act in question very rarely produce the best available outcome. They add that human limitations and biases are such that we are not accurate calculators of the expected consequences—for everyone—of our alternatives. That is, we frequently do not have the needed information, time, or the capacity to weight benefits and harms impartially (for example, most of us are biased in such a way that we tend to underestimate the harm to others of acts that would benefit us). For these reasons, a sophisticated act-consequentialism would prescribe that we inculcate and maintain in ourselves and others *both* firm dispositions not to commit some kinds of acts *and* dispositions to disapprove of others who do commit them. Indeed, given our psychological limitations, act-consequentialism may favour our moral dispositions' running so deep that we could not bring ourselves to do the kinds of act in question even in the rare cases in which they *would* bring about the best consequences impartially calculated. Such might be the dispositions—of those sets that are psychologically possible—which are such that one's having them would produce the most good. But all this notwithstanding, act-consequentialists insist that *right* acts are those which would result in the most overall good (even if morally good people could not bring themselves to perform some of these acts). And in making this claim act-consequentialism conflicts sharply with the deontological convictions I mentioned.

Rule-consequentialism, however, does not make that problematic claim. Rule-consequentialism claims instead that individual acts of murder, torture, promise-breaking, and so on, can be wrong even when those particular acts bring about better consequences than any alternative acts would have. For rule-consequentialism makes the rightness and wrongness of particular acts, not a matter of the consequences of those individual acts, but rather a matter of conformity with that set of fairly general rules whose acceptance by (more or less) everyone would have the best consequences. And, this acceptance of fairly general rules forbidding murder, torture, promise-breaking, and so on, would clearly have better consequences than everyone's accepting fairly general rules permitting such acts. (This point could just as easily be put in terms of dispositions rather than rules.)

Consider now one more objection to act-utilitarianism—that it is unreasonably demanding, construing as duties what one would have thought were supererogatory self-sacrifices. To fully appreciate this objection we need to keep in mind the following three things: (1) money and other material goods usually have diminishing marginal utility; (2) each dollar can buy vastly more food in, for example, Ethiopia than it can in a 'First-World' country; and (3) other relatively well-off people will not give much. We must thus accept that it would be utility-maximizing, and thus optimific according to most versions of act-consequentialism, if I gave away most of my material goods to the appropriate charities. I must, of course, take into account the effects of my present actions on my future capacity to give. In the light of that consideration, I should keep whatever proportion of my income and possessions is necessary for me to continue earning so that I can maximize the amount I can give over the course of my whole life. But, presumably, what I am allowed to keep for myself is still very little. And many of us may on reflection think that it would be *morally unreasonable* to demand this level of self-sacrifice for the sake of others.[5] This thought is not inconsistent with the realization that morality can from time to time require significant self-sacrifice for the sake of others; nor does it oppose the claim that giving most of what one has to the needy is both permissible and extremely praiseworthy. But most of us are quite confident that such self-sacrifice is supererogatory—that is, not something morality *requires* of us.

I admit that there is something unsavoury about objecting to a moral theory because of the severity of its requirements. One might be tempted to think that the demandingness objection will appeal to people whose self-interest is clouding their moral judgement, that it will appeal to people who have a lot to lose from a strong requirement to aid others. But it would be unfair to dismiss the objection on such grounds—to do so would be to find the objection 'guilty by association.' Furthermore, even after we acknowledge that the demandingness objection may appeal to some disreputable characters, the objection retains considerable force.

I have been discussing the act-utilitarian requirement to keep making sacrifices for others until further sacrifices would result in less overall welfare in the long run. Consider now an alternative and less demanding principle of aid. This principle is that we are required to come to the aid of others as long as the benefit to them is very great in comparison to the sacrifice to us.[6] Even this less demanding principle makes heavy demands on those of us with spare money: most of us would have to sacrifice most of our welfare in helping others before we reached the point at which the sacrifice to us would no longer be very much smaller than the benefits produced for them. And it might well be thought that a requirement that one sacrifice *most* of one's own welfare for the sake of strangers whose suffering is not one's fault is unreasonably demanding, particularly when most others in a position to help are not doing so.

Indeed, one of the notable initial attractions of rule-consequentialism is that it—unlike both act-consequentialism and the more modest principle of aid just mentioned—calls for an amount of self-sacrifice that is not unreasonable. If each relatively well-off person contributed some relatively small percentage of his or her income to famine relief, there would be enough to feed the world. Perhaps ten per cent from each of the well-off would be enough. Though giving that much may seem difficult enough for most of us, the demand that we do so does not seem unreasonable. Rule-consequentialism therefore seems to escape the demandingness objection. If so, it is acquitted of all of the main charges against act-utilitarianism.

I do not mean to suggest that there are not other powerful reasons for finding rule-consequentialism the most appealing form of consequentialism. One might well think that reflection on the nature of morality suggests that it must serve as a *public* system of principles to which we can appeal to justify our behaviour to one another, and that rule-consequentialism, but not act-consequentialism, does justice to this insight. Or one might well think that rule-consequentialism does justice to the importance of the common question 'what if everyone did that?' in a way that act-consequentialism cannot. I also do not mean to suggest that the only way of reacting to the excessive demands of act-consequentialism is to join up with the rule-consequentialists. But those are matters I do not want to explore here.

II

What is the partial compliance objection to rule-consequentialism? It is that following the moral code that would be optimal in a world in which everyone accepted it can be (in Brandt's words) 'counterproductive or useless' in the real world where there is actually only partial social acceptance of that code.[7] To use an example Brandt cites, suppose that what would produce optimal results would be for everyone to act in a race-blind way. But suppose also that you are surrounded by people with fierce racial prejudices. It is easy to imagine that your acting in a race-blind way in front of these rabid racists would have very bad consequences.

On the simplest rule-consequentialist view, the best set of rules, desires, and dispositions is whatever set is such that, if absolutely everyone accepted those rules and had those desires and dispositions, the results would be better than if absolutely everyone accepted other rules and had other desires and dispositions. But then how can it make sense to object that some dispositions which would produce the most good if *everyone* had them would be counterproductive or useless in situations where *not everyone* had them? It is clearly illogical to imagine both that everyone accepts a certain code of rules or has a certain set of dispositions and that at the same time some do not accept that code and do not have those dispositions. Brandt provides a neat solution to this problem: he defines the optimal moral code as the one that would result in the most good if it were accepted by 'all except those whose agreement is precluded by a description of some moral-problem situations.'[8]

But there remain problems with how to interpret the partial compliance objection to rule-consequentialism. Consider three possibilities:

(i) The objection might be that you might sometimes be required by the rules whose currency would produce the most good to do something that, because others are not complying, would produce *slightly* worse consequences viewed impartially.

(ii) Or the objection might be that you might sometimes be required by the rules to do something that, because others are not complying, would be *harmful or inconvenient to you and beneficial to the very people who are not complying.*

(iii) Or the objection might be that you might sometimes be required by these rules to do something that, because others are not complying, would produce *very much* worse consequences viewed impartially.

The first of these interpretations can, I think, be dismissed. The claim that one should follow certain rules even when breaking them would produce *slightly* more good does *not* seem counterintuitive (except to hard-line act-consequentialists).

So consider now the second interpretation of the objection—that, sometimes, because others are not complying, my following simple rules would be both harmful to me and beneficial to the very people who are not complying. The idea that the simple rules provide the criterion of rightness and wrongness for such cases does offend against our sentiments about fairness. But it is pretty obvious how rule-consequentialists can defuse this objection: they can agree it is not wrong to refuse to follow certain rules in one's dealings with those who do not reciprocate. The moral rules that would produce the most good in our partial compliance world would have provisions written into them designed to give incentives to those who are possible beneficiaries of our rule-following to do their part in following the rules. Such provisions would permit us to ignore the ordinarily appropriate rules when we are dealing with those who refuse to follow those rules.

The third interpretation of the objection seems the most powerful. Rule-consequentialism is less than credible if it claims one is required always to follow certain rules, even when not following these rules would prevent *very much* worse consequences for others. (Since from now on I shall ignore the first two ways of construing the partial compliance objection, I shall henceforth refer to the objection construed in the third way as simply the partial compliance objection.) Now, can rule-consequentialists provide a convincing reply to the objection?

Brandt articulates what would seem to be the natural reply for the rule-consequentialist to make. He suggests that rule-consequentialism would prescribe our having a set of moral motivations consisting of

(1) the standing motivations corresponding to the usual simple moral rules (that is, a standing desire to treat others fairly, another standing desire not to hurt others, another not to steal, another not to break one's promises, another not to lie, and so on),

(2) a standing desire to prevent great harm, and

(3) a standing desire to promote the wider acceptance of the optimific rules.

Rule-consequentialists would presumably say that an act is morally wrong if it is one that this set of motivations would oppose. We might summarize this reply to the partial compliance objection as follows: by including in their favoured code a particularly strong requirement that one prevent great harm, rule-consequentialists can escape having to maintain that it is morally right to stick to the (normally optimific) rules in those situations in which our doing so would result in very much worse consequences. (For the purposes of the rest of this paper, however, we can focus on (1) and (2) above and ignore (3). This is so because in at least many situations the desire to prevent great harm would not need the help of the desire to promote wider acceptance of the optimific rules in order to prevail in a battle with the motivations corresponding to the simple rules. And those are the cases I shall be focusing on.)

III

Unfortunately, relying on a strong principle of preventing harm in order to deal with the partial compliance problem threatens to make rule-consequentialism excessively demanding. Suppose that, of the various possible rules about coming to others' aid, the rule whose acceptance by absolutely everyone relatively well off would produce the most good requires one to donate a tenth of one's income to famine relief. Suppose that this is what I have just done. Knowing that most others in a position to donate are not complying with that requirement, I am now trying to decide whether I must donate more. There are still people dying who would be saved if I gave more. My doing so would thus prevent serious harm to others. Given these conditions, Brandt's proposal would require me to give more of my income. And even if I give another tenth, there would be other people whom I would save by giving more. So yet again serious harm would be avoided if I kept giving. In fact, I would have to make myself quite badly off before I myself would be so poor that the further sacrifices I could make would be too little to save others in desperate need from great harm. And so the code in question seems to require self-sacrifices up to that point. But to require self-sacrifices all the way up to this point seems unreasonably demanding, especially when others in a position to help are not doing their share.

So my argument might be put like this. The partial compliance objection to rule-utilitarianism is extremely important—after all, we live in a partial compliance world. Rule-consequentialism can be rescued from the partial compliance objection by bringing in a strong requirement that one prevent great harm. But this move seems to pull rule-consequentialism out of the mouth of one objection only to throw it into the mouth of another.

What might rule-consequentialists say in reply? They might try to claim that the optimific set of rules and dispositions *would permit* me to depart from a given rule in order to prevent great harm, but *would not require* me to do so. This reply might sound good when we think about the famine relief cases, but we can see it cannot be right when we think about the other partial compliance cases, the cases in which the agent's own welfare is not in play. To give an intuitively acceptable answer for the cases in which the agent's own welfare is not in play, rule-consequentialists must say that the optimific code requires the agent not to do what would result in great harm. And it would seem that the most natural way for rule-consequentialists to accomplish this is to maintain that we should obey the code of rules that would be optimific if everyone complied with it, except when our following that code would result in great harm because of others' non-compliance, and that in those cases we should do what would prevent that harm. But, as I have explained, this answer will make rule-consequentialism terribly demanding in the famine relief cases.

Here is a more promising reply that rule-consequentialists might try. Rule-consequentialists favour the code of rules whose currency would produce the most good. One of the factors counted in the cost-benefit assessment of any proposed code is what we might call its maintenance costs, that is, the costs of sustaining people's commitment to it and of teaching it to the young. Furthermore, many rule-consequentialists (Brandt among them) hold that wrong acts are those for-bidden by that moral code whose general currency among human beings *with their natural biases and limitations* would produce the best consequences.[9] And, given natural human selfishness, etc., it might well be true that an *extremely* demanding morality could be successfully taught to, and sustained in, people *only at great cost*. Therefore, the currency of a somewhat less demanding morality might have better consequences, all things considered. That is, the moral code whose currency would result in the greatest good overall might be less demand-ing than we would have thought if we had forgotten about maintenance costs.

The question now is: even after we take maintenance costs into account, would the optimific set of rules nevertheless be unreasonably demanding? It is hard to be sure. Part of the reason for this is that our sense of what counts as being unreasonably demanding is somewhat vague (though determinate enough to license the charges of excessive demandingness made earlier in this paper). But equally important is that we are uncertain which rule of the alternative possible ones about coming to the aid of others is such that its acceptance by everyone (except those whose acceptance is precluded by the description of the problem situation in question) would produce the most good. In other words, we do not know how demanding the optimific rule about coming to the aid of others would be. Just where the line is between reasonable and unreasonable demandingness and just how demanding the optimific rule would be are questions that require further work. But at least we can throw down the gauntlet, challenging rule-con-sequentialists to show that the rule about coming to the aid of others which is such that its general acceptance would produce better consequences on the whole than the general acceptance of any alternative would not be in conflict with our *fairly confident* convictions about what is above and beyond the call of duty.

Notes

This paper is much better than it would otherwise have been because of written com-ments on earlier drafts from Penelope Mackie, Mark Overvold, Peter Vallentyne, Anthony Ellis, Mark Nelson, and Richard Brandt. I am extremely grateful to these people, and to Alan Fuchs, James Griffin, R. M. Hare, Roger Crisp, David Dyzenhaus, Cheryl Misak, Eldon Soifer, Howard Robinson, Madison Powers, and Greg Trianosky for help-ful discussions about the ideas in the paper. Remaining defects, however, are my responsibility.

1. So rule-consequentialism is a kind of *indirect* consequentialism. It is a mistake to think that indirect consequentialism assesses not acts but only the rightness and wrongness of other things such as motives, standing dispositions, rules, and social practices. Indirect consequentialism does assess acts as well (see B. Williams, 'A Critique of Utilitarianism', in J. J. C. Smart and B. Williams, *Utilitarianism: For and Against*, Cambridge, Cambridge University Press, 1973, p. 121).

2. For an account of the main intuitive objections to act-utilitarianism, see S. Scheffler's 'Introduction' to his collection *Consequentialism and its Critics*, Oxford, Oxford University Press, 1988, pp. 1–13, esp. pp. 2–4.

3. See, for example, T. M. Scanlon, 'Rights, Goals, and Fairness', in *Public and Private Morality*, ed. S. Hampshire, Cambridge, Cambridge University Press, 1978, pp. 93–111,

especially sect. 2. This paper is reprinted in Scheffler's collection *Consequentialism and its Critics*. See also Scheffler, *The Rejection of Consequentialism,* Oxford, Clarendon Press, 1982, pp. 26–34, 70–9; and Parfit, *Reasons and Persons,* p. 26.

4.   Prominent among those associated with the defence I am about to summarize are H. Sidgwick, *The Methods of Ethics,* 7th ed, London, Macmillan, 7907, bk. IV, ch. III; R. M. Hare, *Moral Thinking,* Oxford, Clarendon Press, 1981, pp. 35–52, 130–59; Parfit, *Reasons and Persons,* pp. 27–8; and P. Railton, 'Alienation, Consequentialism, and Morality,' *Philosophy and Public Affairs,* 1984, pp. 134–71, esp. pp. 153–4, 157–9 (Railton's paper is also reprinted in Scheffler's Collection).

5.   See P. Singer, *Practical Ethics,* Cambridge, Cambridge University Press, 1979, p. 163.

6.   Scheffler and T. Nagel usefully set out a number of different ways moral theorists might respond to a very demanding moral conception (Scheffler, 'Morality's Demands and their Limits,' *Journal of Philosophy,* 1986, pp. 531–7; Nagel, *The View from Nowhere,* New York, Oxford University Press, 1986, ch. X.

7.   Brandt, 'Fairness to Indirect Optimific Theories in Ethics', *Ethics,* 1988, p. 357.

8.   'Fairness to Indirect Optimific Theories in Ethics,' p. 342; see also p. 358.

9.   See 'Indirect Optimific Theories,' pp. 346–7, 349–50; and 'Problems of Contemporary Utilitarianism,' p. 98. See also J. L. Mackie's remark that in devising a moral code 'we are to take men as they are and moral laws as they might be' (*Ethics: Inventing Right and Wrong,* Harmondsworth, Penguin Books, 1977, p. 133).

CHAPTER 6

Kantian Ethical Theory

THE MORAL LAW AND AUTONOMY OF THE WILL
Immanuel Kant

Kant (1724–1804) is one of the most important philosophers of the Western world. He wrote three major ethical works: Groundwork (Foundations) of the Metaphysic of Morals *(1785),* Critique of Practical Reason *(1788), and* The Metaphysics of Morals *(1797). Included below are selections from the first and third of these works. In the first selection, which I have entitled, "Foundations," Kant presents and defends what he takes to be the fundamental moral principle, the Categorical Imperative, which serves as a law for the behavior of all rational agents. He argues that this principle can be discovered by reflecting on the idea of a good will and that it can be formulated in different ways—in terms of the idea of* universal law *and in terms of the idea of* humanity as an end in itself. *He proceeds to explain how this principle (in its different formulations) can be used to derive a variety of moral duties, including the negative duties to refrain from suicide and false promises and the positive duties to develop one's talents and to help others (often referred to as a duty of beneficence).*

In the second selection that I have entitled "Casuistical Questions," taken from his final work in moral philosophy, Kant briefly explores certain questions of detail and casuistry (the art of applying principles to particular cases) that arise in connection with the four duties featured in the Foundations.

I. Foundations

THE GOOD WILL

Nothing can possibly be conceived in the world, or even out of it, which can be called good, without qualification, except a Good Will. Intelligence, wit, judgment, and the other *talents* of the mind, however they may be named, or courage, resolution, perseverance, as qualities of temperament, are undoubtedly good and

Part I, "Foundations," is reprinted from *The Foundations of the Metaphysic of Morals,* translated by T. K. Abbott (first published in 1873). Part II, "Casuistical Questions," is reprinted from *The Metaphysics of Morals,* translated by James W. Ellington and published in *Ethical Philosophy,* 2nd edition (Indianapolis, IN: Hackett, 1984). Reprinted by permission of Hackett Publishing Company, Inc. All rights reserved.

desirable in many respects; but these gifts of nature may also become extremely bad and mischievous if the will which is to make use of them, and which, therefore, constitutes what is called *character,* is not good. It is the same with the *gifts of fortune.* Power, riches, honor, even health, and the general well-being and contentment with one's condition which is called *happiness,* inspire pride, and often presumption, if there is not a good will to correct the influence of these on the mind, and with this also to rectify the whole principle of acting, and adapt it to its end. The sight of a being who is not adorned with a single feature of a pure and good will, enjoying unbroken prosperity, can never give pleasure to an impartial rational spectator. Thus a good will appears to constitute the indispensable condition even of being worthy of happiness.

There are even some qualities which are of service to this good will itself, and may facilitate its action, yet which have no intrinsic unconditional value, but always presuppose a good will, and this qualifies the esteem that we justly have for them, and does not permit us to regard them as absolutely good. Moderation in the affections and passions, self-control, and calm deliberation are not only good in many respects, but even seem to constitute part of the intrinsic worth of the person; but they are far from deserving to be called good without qualification, although they have been so unconditionally praised by the ancients. For without the principles of a good will, they may become extremely bad; and the coolness of a villain not only makes him far more dangerous, but also directly makes him more abominable in our eyes than he would have been without it.

A good will is good not because of what it performs or effects, not by its aptness for the attainment of some proposed end, but simply by virtue of the volition, that is, it is good in itself, and considered by itself is to be esteemed much higher than all that can be brought about by it in favor of any inclination, nay, even of the sum-total of all inclinations. Even if it should happen that, owing to special disfavor of fortune, or the niggardly provision of a step-motherly nature, this will should wholly lack power to accomplish its purpose, if with its greatest efforts it should yet achieve nothing, and there should remain only the good will (not, to be sure, a mere wish, but the summoning of all means in our power), then, like a jewel, it would still shine by its own light, as a thing which has its whole value in itself. Its usefulness or fruitlessness can neither add to nor take away anything from this value....

...Thus the moral worth of an action does not lie in the effect expected from it, nor in any principle of action which requires to borrow its motive from this expected effect. For all these effects—agreeableness of one's condition, and even the promotion of the happiness of others—could have been also brought about by other causes, so that for this there would have been no need of the will of a rational being; whereas it is in this alone that the supreme and unconditional good can be found. The pre-eminent good which we call moral can therefore consist in nothing else than *the conception of law* in itself, *which certainly is only possible in a rational being,* in so far as this conception, and not the expected effect, determines the will. This is a good which is already present in the person who acts accordingly, and we have not to wait for it to appear first in the result.

THE SUPREME PRINCIPLE OF MORALITY: THE CATEGORICAL IMPERATIVE

But what sort of law can that be, the conception of which must determine the will, even without paying any regard to the effect expected from it, in order that this will may be called good absolutely and without qualification? As I have deprived the will of every impulse which could arise to it from obedience to any law, there remains nothing but the universal conformity of its actions to law in general, which alone is to serve the will as a principle, i.e. I am never to act otherwise than *so that I could also will that my maxim should become a universal law.* Here, now, it is the simple conformity to law in general, without assuming any particular law applicable to certain actions, that serves the will as its principle, and must so serve it, if duty is not to be a vain delusion and a chimerical notion. The common reason of men in its practical judgments perfectly coincides with this, and always has in view the principle here suggested. Let the question be, for example: May I when in distress make a promise with the intention not to keep it? I readily distinguish here between the two significations which the question may have: Whether it is prudent, or whether it is right, to make a false promise? The former may undoubtedly often be the case. I see clearly indeed that it is not enough to extricate myself from a present difficulty by means of this subterfuge, but it must be well considered whether there may not hereafter spring from this lie much greater inconvenience than that from which I now free myself, and as, with all my supposed *cunning,* the consequences cannot be so easily foreseen but that credit once lost may be much more injurious to me than any mischief which I seek to avoid at present, it should be considered whether it would not be more *prudent* to act herein according to a universal maxim, and to make it a habit to promise nothing except with the intention of keeping it. But it is soon clear to me that such a maxim will still only be based on the fear of consequences. Now it is a wholly different thing to be truthful from duty, and to be so from apprehension of injurious consequences. In the first case, the very notion of the action already implies a law for me; in the second case, I must first look about elsewhere to see what results may be combined with it which would affect myself. For to deviate from the principle of duty is beyond all doubt wicked; but to be unfaithful to my maxim of prudence may often be very advantageous to me, although to abide by it is certainly safer. The shortest way, however, and an unerring one, to discover the answer to this question whether a lying promise is consistent with duty, is to ask myself, Should I be content that my maxim (to extricate myself from difficulty by a false promise) should hold good as a universal law, for myself as well as for others? and should I be able to say to myself, "Every one may make a deceitful promise when he finds himself in a difficulty from which he cannot otherwise extricate himself"? Then I presently become aware that while I can will the lie, I can by no means will that lying should be a universal law. For with such a law there would be no promises at all, since it would be in vain to allege my intention in regard to my future actions to those who would not believe this allegation, or if they over-hastily did so, would pay me back in my own coin. Hence my maxim, as soon as it should be made a universal law, would necessarily destroy itself....

IMPERATIVES: HYPOTHETICAL AND CATEGORICAL

Everything in nature works according to laws. Rational beings alone have the faculty of acting according *to the conception of laws,* that is according to principles, *i.e.,* have a *will.* Since the deduction of actions from principles requires *reason,* the will is nothing but practical reason. If reason infallibly determines the will, then the actions of such a being which are recognized as objectively necessary are subjectively necessary also, *i.e.,* the will is a faculty to choose *that only* which reason independent of inclination recognizes as practically necessary, *i.e.,* as good. But if reason of itself does not sufficiently determine the will, if the latter is subject also to subjective conditions (particular impulses) which do not always coincide with the objective conditions; in a word, if the will does not *in itself* completely accord with reason (which is actually the case with men), then the actions which objectively are recognized as necessary are subjectively contingent, and the determination of such a will according to objective laws is *obligation,* that is to say, the relation of the objective laws to a will that is not thoroughly good is conceived as the determination of the will of a rational being by principles of reason, but which the will from its nature does not of necessity follow.

The conception of an objective principle, in so far as it is obligatory for a will, is called a command (of reason), and the formula of the command is called an Imperative.

All imperatives are expressed by the word *ought* [or *shall*], and thereby indicate the relation of an objective law of reason to a will, which from its subjective constitution is not necessarily determined by it (an obligation). They say that something would be good to do or to forbear, but they say it to a will which does not always do a thing because it is conceived to be good to do it. That is practically *good,* however, which determines the will by means of the conceptions of reason, and consequently not from subjective causes, but objectively, that is on principles which are valid for every rational being as such. It is distinguished from the *pleasant,* as that which influences the will only by means of sensation from merely subjective causes, valid only for the sense of this or that one, and not as a principle of reason, which holds for every one.

A perfectly good will would therefore be equally subject to objective laws (*viz.,* laws of good), but could not be conceived as *obliged* thereby to act law fully, because of itself from its subjective constitution it can only be determined by the conception of good. Therefore no imperatives hold for the Divine will, or in general for a *holy* will; *ought* is here out of place, because the volition is already of itself necessarily in unison with the law. Therefore imperatives are only formulae to express the relation of objective laws of all volition to the subjective imperfection of the will of this or that rational being, *e.g.,* the human will.

Now all *imperatives* command either *hypothetically* or *categorically.* The former represent the practical necessity of a possible action as means to something else that is willed (or at least which one might possibly will). The categorical imperative would be that which represented an action as necessary of itself without reference to another end, *i.e.,* as objectively necessary....

FIRST FORMULATION OF THE CATEGORICAL IMPERATIVE: UNIVERSAL LAW

There is therefore but one categorical imperative, namely, this: *Act only on that maxim whereby thou canst at the same time will that it should become a universal law.*

Now if all imperatives of duty can be deduced from this one imperative as from their principle, then, although it should remain undecided whether what is called duty is not merely a vain notion, yet at least we shall be able to show what we understand by it and what this notion means.

Since the universality of the law according to which effects are produced constitutes what is properly called *nature* in the most general sense (as to form), that is the existence of things so far as it is determined by general laws, the imperative of duty may be expressed thus: *Act as if the maxim of thy action were to become by thy will a universal law of nature.*

FOUR ILLUSTRATIONS

We will now enumerate a few duties, adopting the usual division of them into duties to ourselves and to others, and into perfect and imperfect duties.

1. A man reduced to despair by a series of misfortunes feels wearied of life, but is still so far in possession of his reason that he can ask himself whether it would not be contrary to his duty to himself to take his own life. Now he inquires whether the maxim of his action could become a universal law of nature. His maxim is: From self-love I adopt it as a principle to shorten my life when its longer duration is likely to bring more evil than satisfaction. It is asked then simply whether this principle founded on self-love can become a universal law of nature. Now we see at once that a system of nature of which it should be a law to destroy life by means of the very feeling whose special nature it is to impel to the improvement of life would contradict itself, and therefore could not exist as a system of nature; hence that maxim cannot possibly exist as a universal law of nature, and consequently would be wholly inconsistent with the supreme principle of all duty.

2. Another finds himself forced by necessity to borrow money. He knows that he will not be able to repay it, but sees also that nothing will be lent to him, unless he promises stoutly to repay it in a definite time. He desires to make this promise, but he has still so much conscience as to ask himself: Is it not unlawful and inconsistent with duty to get out of a difficulty in this way? Suppose, however, that he resolves to do so, then the maxim of his action would be expressed thus: When I think myself in want of money, I will borrow money and promise to repay it, although I know that I never can do so. Now this principle of self-love or of one's own advantage may perhaps be consistent with my whole future welfare; but the question now is, Is it right? I change then the suggestion of self-love into a universal law, and state the question thus: How would it be if my maxim were a universal law? Then I see at once that it could never hold as a universal law of nature, but would necessarily contradict itself. For supposing it to be a universal law that everyone when he thinks himself in a difficulty should be able to promise whatever he pleases, with the purpose of not keeping his promise, the promise itself would become impossible, as well as the end that one might have in view

in it, since no one would consider that anything was promised to him, but would ridicule all such statements as vain pretenses.

3. A third finds in himself a talent which with the help of some culture might make him a useful man in many respects. But he finds himself in comfortable circumstances, and prefers to indulge in pleasure rather than to take pains in enlarging and improving his happy natural capacities. He asks, however, whether his maxim of neglect of his natural gifts, besides agreeing with his inclination to indulgence, agrees also with what is called duty. He sees then that a system of nature could indeed subsist with such a universal law although men (like the South Sea islanders) should let their talents rust, and resolve to devote their lives merely to idleness, amusement, and propagation of their species—in a word, to enjoyment; but he cannot possibly *will* that this should be a universal law of nature, or be implanted in us as such by a natural instinct. For, as a rational being, he necessarily wills that his faculties be developed, since they serve him, and have been given him, for all sorts of possible purposes.

4. A fourth, who is in prosperity, while he sees that others have to contend with great wretchedness and that he could help them, thinks: What concern is it of mine? Let everyone be as happy as Heaven pleases, or as he can make himself; I will take nothing from him nor even envy him, only I do not wish to contribute anything to his welfare or to his assistance in distress! Now no doubt if such a mode of thinking were a universal law, the human race might very well subsist, and doubtless even better than in a state in which everyone talks of sympathy and good-will, or even takes care occasionally to put it into practice, but, on the other side, also cheats when he can, betrays the rights of men, or otherwise violates them. But although it is possible that a universal law of nature might exist in accordance with that maxim, it is impossible to *will* that such a principle should have the universal validity of a law of nature. For a will which resolved this would contradict itself, inasmuch as many cases might occur in which one would have need of the love and sympathy of others, and in which, by such a law of nature, sprung from his own will, he would deprive himself of all hope of the aid he desires....

SECOND FORMULATION OF THE CATEGORICAL IMPERATIVE: HUMANITY AS AN END IN ITSELF

... Now I say: man and generally any rational being *exists* as an end in himself, *not merely as a means* to be arbitrarily used by this or that will, but in all his actions, whether they concern himself or other rational beings, must be always regarded at the same time as an end. All objects of the inclinations have only a conditional worth; for if the inclinations and the wants founded on them did not exist, then their object would be without value. But the inclinations themselves being sources of want are so far from having an absolute worth for which they should be desired, that, on the contrary, it must be the universal wish of every rational being to be wholly free from them. Thus the worth of any object which is *to be acquired* by our action is always conditional. Beings whose existence depends not on our will but on nature's, have nevertheless, if they are nonrational beings, only a relative value as means, and are therefore called *things;* rational beings, on the contrary, are called *persons,* because their very nature points them out as ends in themselves, that is as something which must not be used merely as means, and so far therefore restricts freedom of action (and is an object of respect). These, therefore, are not merely subjective ends whose existence has a worth *for us* as an effect of our action, but *objective ends,* that is things whose existence is an end in itself: an end moreover for which no other can be substituted, which they should subserve *merely* as means, for otherwise nothing whatever would possess *absolute worth;* but if all worth were conditioned and therefore contingent, then there would be no supreme practical principle of reason whatever.

If then there is a supreme practical principle or, in respect of the human will, a categorical imperative, it must be one which, being drawn from the conception of that which is necessarily an end for everyone because it is *an end in itself,* constitutes an *objective* principle of will, and can therefore serve as a universal practical law. The foundation of this principle is: *rational nature exists as an end in itself.* Man necessarily conceives his own existence as being so: so far then this is a *subjective* principle of human actions. But every other rational being regards its existence similarly, just on the same rational principle that holds for me: so that it is at the same time an objective principle from which as a supreme practical law all laws of the will must be capable of being deduced. Accordingly the practical imperative will be as follows: *So act as to treat humanity, whether in thine own person or in that of any other, in every case as an end withal, never as means only....*

We will now inquire whether this can be practically carried out.

To abide by the previous examples:

Firstly, under the head of the necessary duty to oneself: He who contemplates suicide should ask himself whether his action can be consistent with the idea of humanity *as an end in itself.* If he destroys himself in order to escape from painful circumstances, he uses a person merely as *a mean* to maintain a tolerable condition up to the end of life. But a man is not a thing, that is to say, something which can be used merely as a means, but must in all his actions be always considered as an end in himself. I cannot, therefore, dispose in any way of a man in my own person so as to mutilate him, to damage or kill him. (It belongs to ethics proper to define this principle more precisely so as to avoid all misunderstanding, *e.g.,* as to the amputation of the limbs in order to preserve myself; as to exposing my life to danger with a view to preserve it, &c. This question is therefore omitted here.)

Secondly, as regards necessary duties, or those of strict obligation, towards others; he who is thinking of making a lying promise to others will see at once that he would be using another man *merely as a mean,* without the latter containing at the same time the end in himself. For he whom I propose by such a promise to use for my own purposes cannot possibly assent to my mode of acting towards him, and therefore cannot himself contain the end of this action. This violation of the principle of humanity in other men is more obvious if we take in examples of attacks on the freedom and property of others. For then it is clear that he who transgresses the rights of men, intends to use the person of others merely as means, without considering that as rational beings they ought always to be esteemed also as ends, that is, as beings who must be capable of containing in themselves the end of the very same action.

Thirdly, as regards contingent (meritorious) duties to oneself; it is not enough that the action does not violate humanity in our own person as an end in itself, it must also *harmonize with* it. Now there are in humanity capacities of greater perfection which belong to the end that nature has in view in regard to humanity in ourselves as the subject: to neglect these might perhaps be consistent with the *maintenance* of humanity as an end in itself, but not with the *advancement* of this end.

Fourthly, as regards meritorious duties towards others: the natural end which all men have is their own happiness. Now humanity might indeed subsist, although no one should contribute anything to the happiness of others, provided he did not intentionally withdraw anything from it; but after all, this would only harmonize negatively not positively with *humanity as an end in itself,* if everyone does not also endeavor, as far as in him lies, to forward the ends of others. For the ends of any subject which is an end in himself, ought as far as possible to be *my* ends also, if that conception is to have its *full* effect with me.

...Looking back now on all previous attempts to discover the principle of morality, we need not wonder why they all failed. It was seen that man was bound to laws by duty, but it was not observed that the laws to which he is subject are *only those of his own giving,* though at the same time they are *universal,* and that he is only bound to act in conformity with his own will; a will, however, which is designed by nature to give universal laws. For when one has conceived man only as subject to a law (no matter what), then this law required some interest, either by way of attraction or constraint, since it did not originate as a law from *his own* will, but this will was according to a law obliged by *something else* to act in a certain manner. Now by this necessary consequence all the labor spent in finding a supreme principle of *duty* was irrevocably lost. For men never elicited duty, but only a necessity of acting from a certain interest. Whether this interest was private or otherwise, in any case the imperative must be conditional, and could not by any means be capable of being a moral command. I will therefore call this the principle of *Autonomy* of the will, in contrast with every other which I accordingly reckon as *Heteronomy.*

THE KINGDOM OF ENDS

The conception of every rational being as one which must consider itself as giving in all the maxims of its will universal laws, so as to judge itself and its actions from this point of view—this conception leads to another which depends on it and is very fruitful, namely, that of a *kingdom of ends.*

By a *kingdom* I understand the union of different rational beings in a system by common laws. Now since it is by laws that ends are determined as regards their universal validity, hence, if we abstract from the personal differences of rational beings, and likewise from all the content of their private ends, we shall be able to conceive all ends combined in a systematic whole (including both rational beings as ends in themselves, and also the special ends which each may propose to himself), that is to say, we can conceive a kingdom of ends, which on the preceding principles is possible.

For all rational beings come under the *law* that each of them must treat itself and all others *never merely as means,* but in every case *at the same time as ends in themselves.* Hence results a systematic union of rational beings by common objective laws, *i.e.,* a kingdom which may be called a kingdom of ends, since what these laws have in view is just the relation of these beings to one another as ends and means....

II. Casuistical Questions

[SUICIDE]

Is it self-murder to plunge oneself into certain death (like Curtius) in order to save one's country? Or is martyrdom—the deliberate sacrifice of oneself for the good of mankind—also to be regarded, like the former case, as a heroic deed?

Is committing suicide permitted in anticipation of an unjust death sentence from one's superior? Even if the sovereign permitted such a suicide (as Nero permitted of Seneca)?

Can one attribute a criminal intention to a great, recently deceased monarch [Frederick the Great] because he carried a fast-acting poison with him, presumably so that if he was captured in war (which he always conducted personally), he might not be forced to submit to conditions of ransom which might be harmful to his country? (For he can be credited with such a purpose without one's being required to presume that he carried the poison out of mere arrogance.)

Bitten by a mad dog, a man already felt hydrophobia coming upon him. He declared that since he had never known anybody cured of it, he would destroy himself in order that, as he said in his testament, he might not in his madness (which he already felt gripping him) bring misfortune to other men too. The question is whether or not he did wrong.

Whoever decides to let himself be inoculated against smallpox risks his life on an uncertainty, although he does it to preserve his life. Accordingly, he is in a much more doubtful position with regard to the law of duty than is the mariner, who does not in the least create the storm to which he entrusts himself. Rather, the former invites an illness which puts him in the danger of death. Consequently, is smallpox inoculation allowed?

[LYING]

Can an untruth from mere politeness (e.g., "your most obedient servant" at the end of a letter) be taken as lying? Nobody is deceived by it. An author asks one of this readers, "How do you like my work?" To be sure, the answer might be given in an illusory way inasmuch as one might jest concerning the captiousness of such a question. But who always has his wits about him? The slightest hesitation with the answer is already a mortification for the author. May one flatter him, then?

If I utter an untruth in actual business affairs, which come to questions of mine and thine, must I answer for all the consequences that might spring from it? For instance, a householder has instructed his servant that, if a certain person should ask for him, the servant should deny knowing anything about him. The servant does this, but in doing so is the occasion of the master's slipping away and committing a great crime, which would otherwise have been prevented by the watchman who was sent out to take him. Upon whom (according to ethical principles) does the blame fall? To be sure, also upon the servant, who here violates a duty to himself by lying, the consequence of which will now be imputed to him by his own conscience.

[SELF-PERFECTION: NATURAL AND MORAL]

It is a duty of man to himself to cultivate his natural powers (of the spirit, of the mind, and of the body) as means to all kinds of possible ends. Man owes it to himself (as an intelligence) not to let his natural predispositions and capacities (which his reason can use some day) remain unused, and not to leave them, as it were, to rust. Let it even be supposed that he is satisfied with the inborn range of his capacities for meeting his natural needs. Nevertheless, it is his reason which, by means of principles, points out to him this satisfaction with the meager compass of his capacities; for he (as a being capable of having ends or of making objects ends for himself) must owe the use of his powers not merely to natural instinct, but also to the freedom with which he determines their scope. It is thus not for the advantage which the cultivation of his capacity (for all kinds of ends) can provide that man should concern himself with such cultivation, even though, in view of the roughness of nature's requirements, this advantage would perhaps (according to Rousseau's principles) turn out to be profitable. But it is a command of morally practical reason and a duty of man to himself to build up his capacities (one more than another according to the variety of his ends), and to be a man fit (in a pragmatic sense) for the end of his existence.

Powers of the spirit are those whose exercise is possible only through reason. They are creative as far as their use is not obtained from experience but is derived a priori from principles. Such are mathematics, logic, and the metaphysics of nature. The latter two can also be counted as theoretical philosophy, which, to be sure, does not literally mean wisdom, but only science. However, philosophy can be favorable to the end of wisdom.

Powers of the mind are those which are at the disposal both of the understanding and of the rule which the understanding uses to satisfy purposes of its own liking, and in this they follow the lead of experience. Such are memory, imagination, and the like, upon which learnedness, taste (internal and external beautification), and so on can be established. These latter offer tools for many purposes.

Finally, the cultivation of the powers of the body (the true gymnastics) is care for that which constitutes the stuff (the matter) of man, without which the ends of man would remain unfulfilled. Consequently, the continual deliberate stimulation of the animal in man is a duty of man to himself.

Which of these natural perfections may be preferable, and in what proportions, in comparison with one another, it may be man's duty to himself to make them his aim, are matters left to one's own rational reflection upon his desire for a certain mode of life, and his evaluation of the powers requisite for it. This reflection and evaluation are necessary in order to choose what his mode of life should be, e.g., a handicraft, commerce, or a learned profession. For apart from the necessity of self-preservation, which in itself can establish no duty, man owes it to himself to be a useful member of the world, because being one belongs also to the worth of the humanity in his own person, which he should not degrade.

However, man's duty to himself regarding his physical perfection is only a broad and imperfect duty. This is so because such a duty contains, to be sure, a law for the maxim of actions, but determines nothing so far as the actions themselves are concerned—nothing as to their kind and degree. Rather, it allows a latitude for free choice.

[Moral] perfection consists subjectively in the purity (*puritas moralis*) of one's disposition toward duty: when, without any admixture of aims taken from sensibility, the law is its own incentive, and one's actions occur not only in accordance with duty but also from duty. "Be holy" [I Peter 1:16] is here the command. Secondly, such perfection consists objectively in doing one's full duty and in attaining the completeness of one's moral end regarding himself. "Be perfect!" [Matthew 5:48] For man, striving for this goal is always only a progression from one stage of perfection to another. "If there is any virtue, if there is any praise, aspire to it" [Philippians 4:8].

This duty to oneself is in quality strict and perfect, though in degree it is broad and imperfect because of the frailty (*fragilitas*) of human nature.

Such perfection, which it is indeed a duty to strive after but not to attain (in this life)—the obedience to this duty consisting thus only in a constant progression toward this perfection—is in reference to the object (the idea whose fulfillment one must make his end) a strict and perfect duty, but in reference to the subject, a broad and only imperfect duty to oneself.

The depths of the human heart are unfathomable. Who knows himself well enough, when he feels an incentive for observing duty, to tell whether the incentive arises wholly from the representation of the law, or whether many other sensible impulses contribute to it? Such impulses aim at advantage (or aim at preventing disadvantage) and might well, on another occasion, also serve vice. But as for what concerns perfection as a moral end, there is indeed in idea (objectively) only one virtue (as moral strength of one's maxims); but in fact (subjectively) there is a multitude of virtues of heterogeneous qualities, among which, if one wanted to look for it, one might possibly discover some lack of virtue (although this would not bear the name of vice since it is in the company of many virtues). However, a sum of virtues, whose completeness or deficiency our self-knowledge never lets us adequately discern, can establish nothing but an imperfect duty to be perfect.

Thus, all the duties to oneself regarding the end of the humanity in one's own person are only imperfect duties.

[BENEFICENCE]

How far should one push the expenditure of his means in beneficence? Certainly not to the point where he would finally need the beneficence of others. How valuable is the benefit which one bestows impersonally (as when, in departing from his life, he leaves a will)? Can he who exercises a legal power over another deprive this other of freedom by acting according to his own option as to what will make this other person happy (a serf of his estate, for instance)? I say, can this man regard himself as a benefactor when he looks after such a person paternally, as it were, according to his own concepts of happiness? Or, rather, is not the unrighteousness of depriving someone of his freedom something so contrary to juridical duty in general, that to count upon the beneficence of one's master and to surrender oneself to it on such conditions would be the greatest throwing away of one's humanity? And, further, would not then the greatest care of the master for such a person be no beneficence at all? Or can the merit of such beneficence perhaps be so great that the rights of humanity might be outweighed by comparison with it? I can benefit no one (with the exception of minors and the mentally deranged) according to my own concepts of happiness, but only according to the concepts of him whom I think of benefiting; I actually do not benefit him when I urge a gift upon him.

The wherewithal for doing good, which depends upon the gifts of fortune, is for the most part a result of the patronage of various men owing to the injustice of government, which introduces an inequality of wealth that makes beneficence necessary. Under such circumstances, does the assistance which the rich render the needy deserve at all the name of beneficence, with which one so gladly plumes himself as merit?

KANT'S PRINCIPLE OF UNIVERSAL LAW
Joshua Glasgow

Joshua Glasgow is assistant professor at Victoria University of Wellington, New Zealand and has published articles on Kant's ethics, philosophy of race, and metaphysics. In his contribution, Glasgow first explains some basic elements of Kant's moral theory needed for understanding Kant's supreme moral principle, the Categorical Imperative, and then proceeds to explain how one of the "universal law" formulations of this principle is to be used as a decision procedure in reasoning one's way to conclusions about our duties. Among the well-known objections to Kant's principle of universal law are the problems of false positives and false negatives (cases in which Kant's universalization procedure yields the wrong moral verdicts) and the associated problem of relevant descriptions. Glasgow explains these objections and ends by discussing a recently proposed solution to them.

Introduction: The Good Will

Kant develops his theory of ethics by considering some of our most fundamental commonsense intuitions about the nature of morality. On the basis of such intuitions, he articulates a basic moral principle that is strikingly different from the

Printed by permission of the author.

principles of other moral theories, such as utilitarianism, egoism, or virtue ethics. In order to see how Kant arrives at this principle, which he calls the *Categorical Imperative,* we can begin where he begins, with the concept of the good will.

The first commonsense intuition that Kant notes is that we don't usually change our evaluation of how good someone is merely because of how successful she is in pursuing her ends, as long as she is in fact sincerely pursuing them. For instance, imagine that two of the President's Secret Service guards see a would-be assassin pull out a gun and aim it at the President. Each of the guards is standing the same distance from the president, one to the right and one to the left, and neither has time to prevent the shooter from pulling the trigger. Thus, the most each can do is to dive in front of the President, in the hopes of taking a bullet. They both dive at the same time; however, at just the same moment the Vice President, who is sitting between the guard on the left and the President, stretches his legs. As a result, the guard on the left trips and fails to stop the bullet, while the guard on the right, unobstructed, successfully prevents the assassination by taking the bullet in the shoulder.

Now we might bestow certain honors on the guard on the right that we do not give to the guard on the left. But Kant's question is a more basic one: just by virtue of being successful, is the guard on the right somehow *morally better* than the (unsuccessful) guard on the left? Kant believes that our intuitions here suggest that the two agents are morally equal, because, after all, their intentions were the same. As he puts it, even if a good will—that is, the will of an agent who is committed to doing her duty for the sake of duty—were unsuccessful in achieving its ends, "like a jewel, it would still shine by itself" nonetheless.[1] This, then, is the first commonsense intuition of Kant's ethics: whether or not an agent's will is good is independent of her actual success in achieving her ends.

Two Kinds of Principles: Maxims and Imperatives

The claim that the successful good will is as good as the unsuccessful good will suggests a second basic intuition we have about ethics, namely that our moral evaluations focus on the agent's *intentions,* rather than her outward behavior. (Contrast this with classical utilitarianism, which focuses on whether the agent's outward act actually brings about happiness.)

The term of art that Kant uses to capture the intentional feature of one's will is "maxim." A *maxim,* in brief, is an abstract description of the action one intends to perform. There are three things to note about maxims. First, when a maxim is explicitly formulated in Kant's technical sense, it will include three components. Namely, each maxim has (1) a description of the physical act you are performing (e.g., "washing my hair"); (2) a description of the circumstances in which you are performing the act (e.g., "when I'm in the shower getting ready for school"); and (3) the purpose or end of your action (e.g., "to present myself in a cleanly manner"). With these three components, we can express the general form of all maxims as follows:[2]

GENERAL (ACE) FORM OF MAXIMS: I will do act A, in circumstances C, for end E

Before we consider the second main point about maxims, there are two more things to note about the ACE form of maxims. First, *A, C,* and *E* are *variables*—they can be replaced with whatever would accurately describe the act you intend to perform, no matter what that action is. Second, the *end (E)* is different from the *motive* of an act. For instance, say that your end in diving into the ocean is to save a drowning person. This end might be aimed at from all sorts of motives: perhaps you seek it because you think it is your duty, or simply because the drowning person is your friend, or perhaps because you believe that you'll get some reward for doing so. It doesn't matter here what the motive is; the point to keep in mind is that the motive is different from the end. In short, an end is what the agent hopes to achieve in a given action, while the motive is why the agent hopes to achieve it.

The second main point about maxims is that every action has some maxim, whether or not the agent explicitly thinks of it. For example, if you plan to see the dentist, you might explicitly think about what you are doing, and that thought will (barring cognitive error) contain your maxim. (You might not normally think of it in the precise ACE form, but of course it could be formulated in this way.) At the same time, as you go through the morning routine of washing your hair in the shower, you probably don't think about what you are doing. Nevertheless, that action still has a maxim—there is some description of what you are doing.

So far, then, we have seen that since the good will "shines like a jewel" independently of whether it succeeds in achieving its ends, moral evaluation focuses on intentions rather than outward bodily acts. We have also seen that every intended act has a maxim and that each maxim can be presented in the ACE format. The final main point to emphasize is that a maxim is a *description* of whatever action you intend to perform. It is not a principle about what you *should do;* rather it is a principle that describes the action you *actually intend.* Thus both the assassin and the guard have maxims (again, every action has an abstract description, or maxim). One reason for emphasizing the point that maxims are *descriptive* principles is that in this respect maxims differ from another main kind of principle. These principles are *prescriptive,* or *normative.* Rather than describing what we actually intend to do, they tell us what we *should* intend to do—they prescribe, rather than describe. Kant, following traditional ways of talking, calls such normative principles, about what we ought to do, *imperatives.*

Two Kinds of Imperatives: Hypothetical and Categorical

Here is where a third ordinary intuition about morality enters into Kant's ethical theory: moral claims are imperatives, rather than maxims. That is, when we say "It is wrong to torture puppies just for kicks" or "The right thing to do is to donate some of my income to charity," we are not describing the way we act. (Though, of course, people do act in these ways.) Instead, when we use words like "right" and "wrong," we are expressing the thought that people *should* or *should not* act in certain ways, and claims about what people should or should not do can be expressed as imperatives.

To fully appreciate this point, we must consider a more basic claim that Kant makes, namely, that moral principles are *rational* principles. If you have a moral obligation to keep your promises, then keeping your promises is the rational thing to do. (To say that an action is the rational action to perform is to say that it is the one that you have *reason* to perform.) At the same time, of course, we do not always do what is rational; we sometimes let our "inclinations"—roughly, our desires and aversions—influence us independently of what reason tells us to do. Kant's way of making this point is to distinguish between imperfectly rational beings like us and perfectly rational or "holy" beings (such as God, if God exists). By definition, perfectly rational beings always and necessarily do what is rational. Imperfect rational beings like humans (and perhaps aliens or non-human animals that also have rational capacities) do not necessarily do what is rational.

This explains why moral principles come in the form of imperatives for creatures like us. A rational principle details what it is rational to do, and as such it will simply *describe* the choices of a perfectly rational being. Since we are not perfectly rational (that is, we do not necessarily do what is rational), rational principles do not necessarily describe what we do. Rather, they detail what we *should* do and accordingly can be expressed in imperative form. So, since moral principles are rational principles, they too come in imperative form.

This brings us to the next main stage on the road to the Categorical Imperative, where Kant distinguishes between different kinds of imperatives. An imperative, remember, expresses an "ought-claim," a claim about what we should do. There are, of course, several kinds of ought-claims, of which Kant focuses on two: hypothetical and categorical imperatives.

A *hypothetical imperative* expresses an ought-claim that applies to you by virtue of your subjective (or personal) ends.[3] For instance, someone might say "If you want to get an 'A' on the exam, then you should study for it." In general, hypothetical imperatives all have this form: you should take all of the necessary, and some sufficient, means to your subjective ends. Thus, if you have the end of getting an 'A' on the exam, and if the means to that end involve studying for the exam, then you should study. But now imagine that you don't have the subjective end of getting an 'A', perhaps because you don't care about getting an 'A,' or perhaps because you are not even in school. If you lack such an end—one that is relevant to your studying, then when you choose not to study, you aren't violating the hypothetical imperative to study.

A *categorical imperative*, by contrast, expresses an ought-claim that applies to you independently of your subjective, personal ends. We will get to examples of categorical imperatives shortly. For now the key thing to note is the basic difference between the two kinds of imperatives: hypothetical imperatives apply to you because of your subjective ends, while categorical imperatives apply to you independently of your subjective ends.

Moral Principles are Categorical Imperatives

The next main stage in Kant's moral theory is to claim that moral principles must be (when formulated for imperfectly rather than perfectly rational beings) categorical imperatives. This claim is again supported by our ordinary thinking about moral obligation. Consider the hypothetical imperative "If you want to get an 'A', you should study." There is, again, an easy way to get yourself out from under such a hypothetical imperative: all you have to do is abandon the end. That is, you can escape any hypothetical imperative simply by avoiding the ends that make it apply to you. If you do not have an end that requires studying, then you don't violate the hypothetical imperative to study when you end up spending the day hiking instead. If you do not seek to lose weight or improve your health, you don't have to change your diet. If you do not seek to become a world-renowned pianist, you don't have to practice the piano for several hours per day. Again, the point is straightforward: the obligation placed on you by any given hypothetical imperative can be escaped simply by changing your subjective ends.

As Kant points out, however, ordinary thinking about ethics suggests that *moral* obligations are not like these hypothetical imperatives. If I have a moral duty to, say, keep my promise, I can't escape this obligation simply by changing my subjective ends so that this duty doesn't apply to me. Even if I say, "I don't care if other people trust me," it is still the case that I have a moral duty to keep my promise. This, then, is the fourth ordinary moral intuition identified by Kant: moral imperatives obligate me independently of whatever subjective ends I might have. That is, moral obligations are categorical imperatives, rather than hypothetical imperatives.

The Categorical Imperative: Kant's Formula of Universal Law

Now that we have seen Kant's analysis of ordinary moral concepts, such that moral obligations are categorical imperatives, we can appreciate his supreme principle of morality. We can begin by clarifying a few more points.

Kant thinks that there is only *one* Categorical Imperative. That is, he thinks there is only one supreme principle of morality: whether an act is right or wrong will ultimately be determined by whether or not it accords with this single supreme principle. However, we must make two caveats to this point about there being only one supreme principle of morality. First, there can be several derivative, or non-supreme, principles of morality. Thus while there can only be one Categorical Imperative (with a capital "C" and capital "I") as the *supreme* principle of morality, there can be several categorical imperatives (with a lower-case "c" and "i"), that is, several *derivative* principles that obligate us independently of our ends. These categorical imperatives are our moral *duties,* the specific types of act that we either must or must not perform (e.g., "be beneficent" or "do not make false promises"), and these duties are derived from the Categorical Imperative.

Secondly, Kant is also clear that while there is only one Categorical Imperative, it comes in several different formulations. Commentators have long puzzled over how to make sense of this claim and how to understand the relations between the different formulations. But here we need only note that while there are several formulations of the Categorical Imperative, we are only going to focus on two of them. The Kant scholar H. J. Paton dubbed the first formulation the "Formula of Universal Law," or FUL for short.[4] Let us now see how Kant arrives at FUL.

We already know that the supreme principle of morality cannot depend on our ends—for that would make it a hypothetical imperative, when we know it must be a categorical imperative. But here's the rub: if the supreme principle of morality cannot depend on our ends, it is hard to see what such a principle would demand of us. That is, it is often easy to identify hypothetical imperatives as long as we identify our ends—once you know that you want an 'A,' it follows pretty quickly that you need to study. But categorical imperatives (by definition) can't use our subjective ends to tell us what we need to do. According to Kant, what follows from this is that all we can say about the supreme principle of morality (the Categorical Imperative) is that it must require our maxims to be compatible with its essential nature, and its essential nature has two parts. First, Kant thinks that morality's categorical nature has the force of *law:* unlike hypothetical imperatives, which don't necessarily obligate us (because we can avoid the ends that make them apply to us), moral imperatives bind us *necessarily,* like a law (because their applicability isn't contingent on our subjective ends). So this pushes the question one step further: What is the character of law? In a word, *universality.* All laws (laws of nature, civil laws, etc.) are universal in the sense that within their domains (nature, civil society, etc.) they cover everything. Second, the Categorical Imperative is an *imperative,* that is, it prescribes to, or obligates, us. So, if we put these two ideas—the universality and necessity of law and the prescriptive nature of imperatives—together with the claim that morality focuses on maxims, then we get the result that the Categorical Imperative must categorically obligate us to have maxims that can be universal laws.[5]

The fact that the Categorical Imperative cannot use our subjective ends to generate our obligations, and so can only require us to act in a manner compatible with the universality of law, is the basis for FUL:

FUL: "Act only in accordance with that maxim through which you can at the same time will that it become a universal law."[6]

Kant follows his presentation of FUL by noting that our actions take place in the natural world. So he gives us a second, related formulation of the Categorical Imperative, which Paton labeled the Formula of the Law of Nature (or FLN):

FLN: "Act as if the maxim of your action were to become by your will a universal law of nature."

So far, then, we have seen that from our basic intuitions about the categorical nature of morality Kant generates FUL and FLN as two ways of formulating the supreme moral principle, the Categorical Imperative. With this we can turn to two questions. First, how is the Categorical Imperative to be applied to our lives? That is, how can it function as a decision procedure, a way of determining the right thing to do? Second, are there any problems with this principle? These two questions are taken up in the next two sections.

FLN and Our Duties

Kant proceeds to discuss how we can get various duties (or categorical imperatives) from the Categorical Imperative. Rather than continuing on with FUL, he
proceeds to use FLN, and we shall follow suit here.

When Kant says that we should act as if our maxims are going to become universal laws of nature, he is asking us to try to imagine a hypothetical world. That is,
for any act you might perform, you should try to imagine a world where your maxim
is going to be a law of nature, which everyone had to conform to, just like everyone
in the real world must conform to the law of gravity. The question to ask, then, is
whether your maxim could in fact be such a law. Kant's test for whether an act is
morally permissible, then, is deceptively simple: if the maxim can be a universal law
of nature, then acting on it is morally permissible; if the maxim cannot be a universal law of nature, acting on it is morally forbidden. (Morally obligatory acts are the
opposites of morally forbidden acts. For example, if it is forbidden to neglect the
needs of others, then it is obligatory to attend to the needs of others.)

To see how this works, let's look at Kant's treatment of the duty to not make false
promises. Kant has us imagine a person who has an urgent need to get some cash.
This person knows that he cannot pay back a loan, but he also knows that the only
way he can get the cash is if a second party loans it to him on the promise that he
will repay it tomorrow. So, he decides to make a false promise to the second party
to repay borrowed money knowing full well that he will not fulfill this promise.

According to FLN, what this person should do is try to imagine that the maxim
of this action is a universal law of nature. That is, he should ask, "What if, as a law
just like the law of gravity, everyone had to make false promises, when they needed
money, to serve their own self-interest?" Kant's verdict is that *it is impossible to
imagine this as a universal law of nature.* For if everyone had to do this when in
need of money, we all would know that each of us was lying when we promised to
pay back loans (just like we all know that none of us can fly simply by flapping
our arms); in turn, this would mean that we wouldn't believe anyone's promises,
which would mean that the practice of promising would collapse into nonexis-
tence. So the "false promise" maxim cannot be universal law, because such a law
would require that promises are possible (so that our false promisor can make his
false promise) but also that promises are impossible (because the practice of promising collapses). The problem is not that we'd have a world with no promising;
rather, the problem is that this hypothetical world would impossibly contain the
contradiction that everyone makes false promises but false promises (indeed all
promises) cannot be made. Therefore, since it is impossible to imagine a world
with a contradiction like this, false promising is morally forbidden.

We can be more precise about this procedure for generating not only the duty
to not make false promises, but any duty whatsoever. There are three steps to this
procedure:

(1) First, you must figure out your maxim. At its most precise, this will come
in the ACE format.

(2) Second, you must "universalize" your maxim. To *universalize* your maxim is just to pretend that it is a universal law of nature, like the law of gravity—to try to think of a world where everyone does what you are doing.

(3) Finally, you then see if this universalization is successful. Again, if the maxim cannot be successfully universalized, acting on it is morally wrong. If it can be successfully universalized, acting on it is morally permissible. Maxims that can be successfully universalized are called *universalizable* maxims.

One more point is crucial here. In step (3), when you examine whether your maxim can be successfully universalized, Kant means something very specific by this, namely, he means that you should see if *you run into a contradiction*. You are *not* supposed to ask, "Would *bad results* follow if everyone acted according to my maxim?" For example, a world where false promising was universally practiced would contain some bad states of affairs, because some people might get used or hurt in the process. But on Kant's view bad results do not of themselves show that the action is immoral. Instead, what you should ask is, "Is it *contradictory* for everyone to act according to my maxim?" So Kant's point with the false promising maxim is not that universalizing it would have bad results, but that it is simply contradictory to imagine such a state of affairs. The contradiction that emerges upon universalizing the "false promise" maxim is that it entails a state of affairs where the following are both true:

(p) It must be possible to make promises. (After all, this is required if the agent is to make a false promise.)
(~p) Promises cannot be made. (Because upon universalizing the false promising maxim the practice of promising collapses.)

This is one place where Kant clearly differs with consequentialists. Roughly put, consequentialists say that it is wrong to do what would bring about bad states of affairs. Historically, the most prominent consequentialist view has been utilitarianism, according to which bad states of affairs are those that contain unhappiness; so utilitarians say that the wrong act is the one the produces less than maximally available happiness.[7] For Kant, what reveals the wrongness of making false promises is not that it makes people unhappy (though it no doubt does in many cases); rather, false promising is shown to be wrong because it cannot be universal law. Kant's ethics is similarly distinguished from rule-consequentialism, which roughly holds that an act is wrong when it violates the rules that, when widely internalized, would best promote well-being. While both rule-consequentialism and Kantianism would prohibit false promising, each view offers a unique theoretical account of the wrongness of false promising. For rule-consequentialism, false promising is wrong because when widely internalized it wouldn't maximize well-being, and for Kantianism it is wrong because a maxim of false promising cannot be universalized.

It is worth recalling why we should care about whether or not a maxim is universalizable. For Kant, two ordinary intuitions about morality are particularly salient on this question. First, we ought to focus on the agent's maxims, rather than her outward acts. Second, moral obligations come in the form of categorical imperatives, and therefore moral requirements cannot depend on the agent's subjective ends, but only on whether her maxims have the form of law, that is, universality. (Later, Kant adds to the appeal of his principle by noting that what it shows is that it is wrong to be a "free rider." For instance, the only way you can make false promises is if everyone else plays by the rules and keeps their promises—false promising cannot be something that everyone always does as a matter of universal law. Put more generally, people who act immorally are parasitically free riding on the morally upright behavior of others.[8])

The contradiction involved in the false promising maxim is what has become known as a *contradiction in conception:* what shows us that false promising is immoral is that it is impossible to even *conceive* of a world in which false promising is universally practiced as a way of securing loans. Kant has another duty that is generated by a contradiction in conception, namely, the duty to not commit suicide. Here Kant imagines someone who is, perhaps, feeling sorry for himself, and this person decides to commit suicide out of 'self-love.' But, Kant thinks that the purpose of self-love is to preserve the self. Many have questioned whether Kant is right to think this about the purpose of self-love, but let's grant it here so that we may focus on how he generates the duty against suicide. If he were right that the purpose of self-love is self-preservation, then it would be impossible to imagine a world where the motive of self-preservation leads to self-extermination. Therefore, suicide based on self-love is morally forbidden.

Kant thinks that when a duty is derived from a contradiction in conception, that duty is a *narrow duty*. A narrow duty is narrow in the sense that the agent has no leeway in deciding when, how, and in what circumstances she will comply with it. So this means, for example, that an agent couldn't say "Well, I fulfilled my duty against suicide on Monday, so it's okay for me to commit suicide on Tuesday." But Kant also offers some *wide duties*. Wide duties allow latitude in deciding when, how, and in what circumstances the agent will fulfill them. Consider, for example, the duty of beneficence. One way of being beneficent is to give money to charity. Since this is a wide duty, the agent has leeway here—she can decide which (reputable) charity to give to, she can decide to do it only when she has the available wealth, and she can do it on Tuesday instead of Monday.

Just as narrow duties are derived from contradictions in conception, wide duties are derived from what are known as *contradictions in the will*. A contradiction in the will arises not when a potential hypothetical world is impossible to conceive (as with contradictions in conception); rather, a contradiction in the will arises when the maxim contradicts something else that the agent must will. To see this, consider the duty of beneficence.

Kant has us imagine a person who could help others, but decides not to. This agent won't place demands on others; rather, she merely wishes to not be burdened by the needs of others. So let's put it to Kant's test: could we imagine a world in which no one helps anyone else? In one sense, we can imagine such a world. It might not be a very nice world, but there's nothing contradictory about it in the way we cannot imagine a world where everybody makes false promises. So there is no contradiction in conception here. But there is a contradiction in the will. For, according to Kant, every agent at some point will need the love or aid of someone else. So the question becomes: Can one will the help of others in a world in which no one helps anyone else? The answer is that we cannot, because those two willings are incompatible: if no one is helping anyone, then our agent cannot receive help from others when she needs it. Thus, though a non-beneficent world is possible, and so there is no contradiction in conception, the maxim of non-beneficence does generate a contradiction in the will, because an agent who willed universal non-beneficence would be contradicting her willing help for herself. Thus, non-beneficence is forbidden (and, therefore, beneficence is an obligation).

Finally, Kant holds that a maxim of neglecting one's talents generates a contradiction in the will. Again he offers a purposive premise about our talents (which, as with the purposive premise about self-love, many have questioned): the purpose of our talents is to enable us to handle any of the manifold tasks we might face in life. So now imagine someone who just wants to sit around all day, watching cartoons and letting her talents rust. Certainly it is *conceivable* that everyone could do this: even if it made for a pretty pathetic world with few resources and short life spans, there is no contradiction in conception here upon universalization. But the rusting-talents maxim contradicts something else that we must will, namely that we are able to handle life's challenges and tasks. So our agent gets a contradiction in the will: it is impossible both to completely neglect one's talents and to prepare oneself for life's challenges. This contradiction in the will generates a wide duty: we have to develop our talents, though we have leeway in determining which talents we want to develop (perhaps you're a better carpenter than violinist), when we'll work on our skills, and so forth.

What Kant offers, then, are four duties: prohibitions on false-promising, suicide, non-beneficence, and letting one's talents rust. Two are derived from contradictions in conception and are therefore narrow duties, while two are derived from contradictions in the will and are therefore wide duties. And two are duties to the self, while two are duties to others. The relationships between these concepts and duties are displayed in Figure 6.1. Given this system of duties, Kant thinks that his

FIGURE 6.1   Categories of Duty in Kant's Ethics.

	DUTIES TO OTHERS	DUTIES TO SELF
NARROW DUTIES	Prohibition on False Promising	Prohibition on Suicide
WIDE DUTIES	Prohibition on Non-Beneficence	Prohibition on Neglecting One's Talents

Categorical Imperative is quite fruitful as a way of guiding action. We can now proceed to examine whether there are any problems with this theory.

Two Potential Problems

Commentators on Kant's ethics have long recognized two related problems facing Kant's universalizability test. The first problem is that it might generate erroneous results in some cases. Recall here the three-step procedure for determining moral permissibility: (1) formulate your maxim, (2) universalize it, and (3) look for a contradiction (if there is none, acting on that maxim is permissible).

But now consider, for instance, someone who likes to collect model trains.[9] Since she likes to collect (rather than trade) trains, when she goes to buy them her maxim will be "I will buy model trains and not sell them." But when she universalizes this maxim, she'll be imagining a world in which everybody buys model trains but nobody sells them. And this is impossible: it is contradictory to have a world where no one sells model trains but everyone buys them.

This is where the problem for Kant enters in: this contradiction means that collecting model trains is morally wrong according to FLN. But, of course, there is nothing morally wrong about collecting model trains. So something must be incorrect about FLN.

Cases like this are called *false negatives*, because they get a negative result from the test (i.e., they get a verdict of being morally wrong), but falsely so. We will see shortly that FLN also faces problem maxims in the form of *false positives*, that is, cases that get a positive result (of being morally permissible) from the test, but that are obviously morally wrong.

Whether or not a maxim fails the universalizability test depends in part on how we formulate our maxims. The question of maxim formulation points us to the second problem with the universalizability test, known as the *problem of relevant descriptions*. This problem is that for any action, there are innumerable (perhaps infinite) ways of describing it. So, since a maxim is just a description of an action, there are innumerable maxims for any one action, and since it appears that we have no good way of figuring out which maxim to focus on, the potential problem is that we have no good way to run the FLN test. Let's look at an example.

Say that I intend to rob a bank. We could formulate the maxim for this action in several ways. Here are some, formulated in the ACE format:

(a) "I will rob a bank at gun-point, when I am in need of cash, to satisfy my self-interest."

(b) "I will get some money from the bank, when I am in need of cash, to satisfy my self-interest."

(c) "I, Joshua Glasgow, author of the present article, will rob a bank at gun-point, when I am in need of cash, to satisfy my self-interest."

One problem here is that the universalization procedure yields different results for the three maxims. It seems that the universalization of maxim (a) would be contradictory, because if everyone robbed banks at gun-point when they needed cash, the banking system would collapse, in which case we'd be imagining a contradictory world in which there are banks (as required by maxim (a)) and there are no banks (because the banking system has collapsed). Thus it seems that FLN would imply that acting on maxim (a) is morally forbidden.

But maxim (b), *which also describes the very same action of robbing the bank,* seems to pass the test. For what would happen if everyone got money from the bank when they needed it? Well, we can imagine such a world without contradiction—there is no impossibility in everyone doing this. (In fact, this maxim is followed with near universality in the real world.) But this means that we have a false positive: presumably it is wrong to rob a bank at gun-point, but the FLN test seems to imply that maxim (b), which is one way of formulating the bank-robbing maxim, is morally permissible.

Now consider maxim (c). What if everyone named Joshua Glasgow, who is also the author of this article, robs banks at gun-point to get some cash? Well, since I happen to be the only one who fits this description, and since the banking system won't collapse just from one person robbing banks, we won't get the contradiction that we got with maxim (a). So it seems possible that maxim (c) can be a universal law of nature without contradiction, which means that (c) is a false positive as well: if there is no contradiction, acting on maxim (c) would be morally permissible according to the FLN universalizability test, but it clearly is morally wrong.

The problem of relevant descriptions therefore actually generates three potential objections to FLN. First, the problem of relevant descriptions is at least one factor in the other main problem, the problem of false positives/negatives: until we know how to properly describe our actions, we'll keep getting objectionable results, such that it's morally wrong to collect model trains or permissible to rob banks at gun-point. Second, because any action, like robbing a bank, can be described in any number of ways, it can have different maxims, which means that in principle one action can get different results on the universalizability test. But this is a problem—robbing a bank is either right or wrong, but it can't be both. If this objection is on target, then FLN will not satisfy the desideratum of being *consistent*. Finally, if there are innumerable ways of describing my action, Kant's test seems woefully inadequate as a decision procedure, since I won't know which of my action's maxims to test. And the theory isn't very practical if we can't get *determinate* results. In short, it seems that FLN requires a *determinate* and *relevant* maxim for each action, and the problem is that it is not obvious that there is one determinate and relevant description for each action (hence the name "the problem of relevant descriptions"). Given the three objections involved in the problem of relevant descriptions, FLN seems problematic at best.

Conclusion

By way of conclusion, we should consider whether the problems of false negatives/positives and relevant descriptions are truly devastating for Kant's supreme principle of morality, as stated in FLN.[10] Two points are important here. First, recall that FLN is independently motivated, that is, we have a plausible basis for believing it.

The basis for FUL and FLN is the ordinary intuition that moral obligations are categorical imperatives—they tell us what we should do independently of our subjective ends. And if our ends are made irrelevant, then all that is left to morally constrain our actions is to demand that our maxims have the form of law, or universality. So even if opponents of Kant can point out some problems for FLN, Kantians can always reply that their principle nevertheless captures some important features of morality. (Some who hold non-Kantian moral theories—such as perfectionists, including natural law theorists, who hold that right acts are those that realize the *objective* end of human perfection—maintain that their views also can generate categorical requirements. This remains a matter of ongoing debate in ethical theory.)

Second, there may be solutions to the two problems we have examined here. Ever since Onora O'Neill (then writing under the surname 'Nell') published her book, *Acting on Principle,* in 1975, in which she fully exposed the problems discussed here, Kantians have been working hard to find creative ways to solve them. This is an interesting area of research, and while it would be too ambitious to try to cover all of the Kantian proposals, we can look at one of them.

Barbara Herman proposes dealing with the problem of relevant descriptions as follows.[11] She (plausibly) thinks that Kant's insight about morality focusing on maxims suggests that maxims are *general policies* for actions. This means that when we are formulating maxims for testing under FLN, we should think of them in a fairly general way. This would rule out, for instance, maxim (c) above, since it is *too specific* in referencing me in particular. Also, on this account, we must represent maxims *as they are willed*. This means, for example, that we cannot use maxim (b), since it *suppresses a basic fact about what I am willing,* namely that I am willing not merely to get money from the bank, but actually to rob it at gun-point.

Notice, then, that Herman's solution rules out maxims (b) and (c), and so it seems to rule out at least some of the false positives, which is a welcome result for Kantians. Now add to this a second virtue of Herman's account. Since FLN will be testing general policies only, we should not think of it as a decision procedure for *particular* actions. Rather, FLN will be used to get what Herman calls "deliberative presumptions," which are general duties about what is morally forbidden (such as "do not make false promises"). For Herman, these deliberative presumptions set the ground rules that provide the starting point for deliberating about particular cases' morality, though they can be overridden in some cases (much like Ross' *prima facie* duties and Aristotle's virtues). Then, if an act falls under two or more competing deliberative presumptions, we use judgment, rather than any algorithmic test, to determine whether or not it is morally permissible.[12] So Herman's account also avoids the problem of needing a determinate and relevant maxim for every specific action, since on her interpretation FLN is not to be used for specific actions. Instead, we simply use FLN to generate basic policies, which then would set the ground rules for further deliberation about the moral permissibility of our specific actions. Finally, this means that it won't suffer the third problem involved in the problem of relevant descriptions, namely that of getting incompatible results for different maxims that describe the same specific action. For, again, what we will be testing are basic deliberative presumptions for general act-types, not maxims for specific actions.

In short, Herman's account seems to neutralize the three potential objections that stem from the problem of relevant descriptions. So, while Kant's principle of universality faces certain problems, it is independently motivated, and Kantians are presenting arguments to fully defend it.

Notes

1. Immanuel Kant, *Groundwork of the Metaphysics of Morals*, ed. and trans. Mary Gregor, (Cambridge: Cambridge University Press, 1997), p. 394. (Here, as elsewhere, I cite the standard Academy pagination.)
2. This way of formulating maxims was codified in Onora Nell, *Acting on Principle* (New York: Columbia University Press, 1975), p. 37.
3. For our purposes, we can roughly characterize *subjective* ends as the ends that depend on your personal constitution, while *objective* ends would be those ends that are not particular to you but instead are common to all rational beings.
4. H. J. Paton, *The Categorical Imperative*, (Philadelphia: University of Pennsylvania Press, 1947), p. 129.
5. I would be remiss not to note that commentators have long struggled with this argument. They often find it plausible to claim that morality involves prescriptivity, universality, and (more controversially) necessity. But it's an open question whether that then implies that the supreme principle of morality simply states that one's maxims should be fit for universal law.
6. Immanuel Kant, *Groundwork*, p. 421.
7. More precisely, this is the claim of maximizing, act-utilitarians.
8. See Kant, *Groundwork*, p. 424.
9. This example is taken from Nell, *Acting on Principle*, p. 76.
10. There are, recall, other formulations of the Categorical Imperative. So even if these problems are devastating for FLN, one might turn to those other formulations to defend Kantian ethics.
11. See Barbara Herman, "Moral Deliberation and the Derivation of Duties," in Herman, *The Practice of Moral Judgment* (Cambridge, MA: Harvard University Press, 1993), Chapter 7.
12. Despite the prevalent stereotype, Kant (like Aristotle and Ross) placed a high premium on non-algorithmic judgment. For example, at one point Kant writes that moral philosophy furnishes "laws a priori, which no doubt still require a judgment sharpened by experience, partly to distinguish in what cases they are applicable and partly to provide them with access to the will of the human being and efficacy for his fulfillment of them" (*Groundwork*, p. 389).

KANT ON TREATING PEOPLE AS ENDS IN THEMSELVES
Onora O'Neill

Onora O'Neill is professor of philosophy and principal of Newnham College, Cambridge University. She is author of The Faces of Hunger *(1985),* Constructions

From *Matters of Life and Death*, edited by Tom Regan (New York: McGraw-Hill, 1986). Reprinted with permission of the McGraw-Hill Companies.

*of Reason (1989), and Towards Justice and Virtue (1996). O'Neill provides an expli-
cation of the ideas and implications of Kant's formula of the End-in-Itself formulation
of the categorical imperative.*

Kant's moral theory has acquired the reputation of being forbiddingly difficult
to understand and, once understood, excessively demanding in its requirements.
I don't believe that this reputation has been wholly earned, and I am going to try
to undermine it....

The main method by which I propose to avoid some of the difficulties of Kant's
moral theory is by explaining only one part of the theory. This does not seem to
me to be an irresponsible approach in this case. One of the things that makes
Kant's moral theory hard to understand is that he gives a number of different versions of the principle that he calls the Supreme Principle of Morality, and these
different versions don't look at all like one another. They also don't look at all like
the utilitarians' Greatest Happiness Principle. But the Kantian principle is supposed to play a similar role in arguments about what to do.

Kant calls his Supreme Principle the *Categorical Imperative*; its various versions
also have sonorous names. One is called the Formula of Universal Law; another is
the Formula of the Kingdom of Ends. The one on which I shall concentrate is
known as the *Formula of the End in Itself*. To understand why Kant thinks that these
picturesquely named principles are equivalent to one another takes quite a lot of
close and detailed analysis of Kant's philosophy. I shall avoid this and concentrate
on showing the implications of this version of the Categorical Imperative.

The Formula of the End in Itself

Kant states the Formula of the End in Itself as follows:

*Act in such a way that you always treat humanity, whether in your own person or in
the person of any other, never simply as a means but always at the same time as an end.*

To understand this we need to know what it is to treat a person as a means or as
an end. According to Kant, each of our acts reflects one or more *maxims*. The
maxim of the act is the principle on which one sees oneself as acting. A maxim
expresses a person's policy, or if he or she has no settled policy, the principle
underlying the particular intention or decision on which he or she acts. Thus, a
person who decides "This year I'll give 10 percent of my income to famine relief"
has as a maxim the principle of tithing his or her income for famine relief. In
practice, the difference between intentions and maxims is of little importance, for
given any intention, we can formulate the corresponding maxim by deleting references to particular times, places, and persons. In what follows I shall take the
terms "maxim" and "intention" as equivalent.

Whenever we act intentionally, we have at least one maxim and can, if we
reflect, state what it is. (There is of course room for self-deception here—"I'm
only keeping the wolf from the door" we may claim as we wolf down enough to

keep ourselves overweight, or, more to the point, enough to feed someone else who hasn't enough food.)

When we want to work out whether an act we propose to do is right or wrong, according to Kant, we should look at our maxims and not at how much misery or happiness the act is likely to produce, and whether it does better at increasing happiness than other available acts. We just have to check that the act we have in mind will not use anyone as a mere means, and, if possible, that it will treat other persons as ends in themselves.

Using Persons as Mere Means

To use someone as a *mere means* is to involve them in a scheme of action *to which they could not in principle consent*. Kant does not say that there is anything wrong about using someone as a means. Evidently we have to do so in any cooperative scheme of action. If I cash a check I use the teller as a means, without whom I could not lay my hands on the cash; the teller in turn uses me as a means to earn his or her living. But in this case, each party consents to her or his part in the transaction. Kant would say that though they use one another as means, they do not use one another as *mere* means. Each person assumes that the other has maxims of his or her own and is not just a thing or a prop to be manipulated.

But there are other situations where one person uses another in a way to which the other could not in principle consent. For example, one person may make a promise to another with every intention of breaking it. If the promise is accepted, then the person to whom it was given must be ignorant of what the promisor's intention (maxim) really is. If one knew that the promisor did not intend to do what he or she was promising, one would, after all, not accept or rely on the promise. It would be as though there had been no promise made. Successful false promising depends on deceiving the person to whom the promise is made about what one's real maxim is. And since the person who is deceived doesn't know that real maxim, he or she can't in principle consent to his or her part in the proposed scheme of action. The person who is deceived is, as it were, a prop or a tool—a mere means—in the false promisor's scheme. A person who promises falsely treats the acceptor of the promise as a prop or a thing and not as a person. In Kant's view, it is this that makes false promising wrong.

One standard way of using others as mere means is by deceiving them. By getting someone involved in a business scheme or a criminal activity on false pretenses, or by giving a misleading account of what one is about, or by making a false promise or a fraudulent contract, one involves another in something to which he or she in principle cannot consent, since the scheme requires that he or she doesn't know what is going on. Another standard way of using others as mere means is by coercing them. If a rich or powerful person threatens a debtor with bankruptcy unless he or she joins in some scheme, then the creditor's intention is to coerce; and the debtor, if coerced, cannot consent to his or her part in the creditor's scheme. To make the example more specific: If a moneylender in an Indian village threatens not to renew a vital loan unless he is given the debtor's land, then he uses the debtor as a mere means. He coerces the debtor, who cannot truly consent to this "offer he can't refuse." (Of course the outward form of such transactions may look like ordinary commercial dealings, but we know very well that some offers and demands couched in that form are coercive.)

In Kant's view, acts that are done on maxims that require deception or coercion of others, and so cannot have the consent of those others (for consent precludes both deception and coercion), are wrong. When we act on such maxims, we treat others as mere means, as things rather than as ends in themselves. If we act on such maxims, our acts are not only wrong but unjust: such acts wrong the particular others who are deceived or coerced.

Treating Persons as Ends in Themselves

Duties of justice are, in Kant's view (as in many others'), the most important of our duties. When we fail in these duties, we have used some other or others as mere means. But there are also cases where, though we do not use others as mere means, still we fail to use them as ends in themselves in the fullest possible way. To treat someone as an end in him or herself requires in the first place that one not use him or her as mere means, that one respect each as a rational person with his or her own maxims. But beyond that, one may also seek to foster others' plans and maxims by sharing some of their ends. To act beneficently is to seek others' happiness, therefore to intend to achieve some of the things that those others aim at with their maxims. If I want to make others happy, I will adopt maxims that not merely do not manipulate them but that foster some of their plans and activities. Beneficent acts try to achieve what others want. However, we cannot seek everything that others want; their wants are too numerous and diverse, and, of course, sometimes incompatible. It follows that beneficence has to be selective.

There is then quite a sharp distinction between the requirements of justice and of beneficence in Kantian ethics. Justice requires that we act on *no* maxims that use others as mere means. Beneficence requires that we act on *some* maxims that foster others' ends, though it is a matter for judgment and discretion which of their ends we foster. Some maxims no doubt ought not to be fostered because it would be unjust to do so. Kantians are not committed to working interminably through a list of happiness-producing and misery-reducing acts; but there are some acts whose obligatoriness utilitarians may need to debate as they try to compare total outcomes of different choices, to which Kantians are stringently bound. Kantians will claim that they have done nothing wrong if none of their acts is unjust, and that their duty is complete if in addition their life plans have in the circumstances been reasonably beneficent.

In making sure that they meet all the demands of justice, Kantians do not try to compare all available acts and see which has the best effects. They consider only the proposals for action that occur to them and check that these proposals use no other as mere means. If they do not, the act is permissible; if omitting the act would use another as mere means, the act is obligatory. Kant's theory has less scope than utilitarianism. Kantians do not claim to discover whether acts whose maxims they don't know fully are just. They may be reluctant to judge others' acts or policies that cannot be regarded as the maxim of any person or institution. They cannot rank acts in order of merit. Yet, the theory offers more precision than utilitarianism when data are scarce. One can usually tell whether one's act would use others as mere means, even when its impact on human happiness is thoroughly obscure.

The Limits of Kantian Ethics: Intentions and Results

Kantian ethics differs from utilitarian ethics both in its scope and in the precision with which it guides action. Every action, whether of a person or of an agency, can be assessed by utilitarian methods, provided only that information is available about all the consequences of the act. The theory has unlimited scope, but, owing to lack of data, often lacks precision. Kantian ethics has a more restricted scope. Since it assesses actions by looking at the maxims of agents, it can only assess intentional acts. This means that it is most at home in assessing individuals' acts; but it can be extended to assess acts of agencies that (like corporations and governments and student unions) have decision-making procedures. It can do nothing to assess patterns of action that reflect no intention or policy, hence it cannot assess the acts of groups lacking decision-making procedures, such as the student movement, the women's movement, or the consumer movement.

It may seem a great limitation of Kantian ethics that it concentrates on intentions to the neglect of results. It might seem that all conscientious Kantians have to do is to make sure that they never intend to use others as mere means, and that they sometimes intend to foster others' ends. And, as we all know, good intentions sometimes lead to bad results, and correspondingly, bad intentions sometimes do no harm, or even produce good.... If some traditional arguments in favor of capitalism are right, the greed and selfishness of the profit motive have produced unparalleled prosperity for many.

But such discrepancies between intentions and results are the exception and not the rule. For we cannot just *claim* that our intentions are good and do what we will. Our intentions reflect what we expect the immediate results of our action to be. Nobody credits the "intentions" of a couple who practice neither celibacy nor contraception but still insist "we never meant to have (more) children." Conception is likely (and known to be likely) in such cases. Where people's expressed intentions ignore the normal and predictable results of what they do, we infer that (if they are not amazingly ignorant) their words do not express their true intentions. The Formula of the End in Itself applies to the intentions on which one acts—not to some prettified version that one may avow. Provided this intention—the agent's real intention—uses no other as mere means, he or she does nothing unjust. If some of his or her intentions foster others' ends, then he or she is sometimes beneficent. It is therefore possible for people to test their proposals by Kantian arguments even when they lack the comprehensive causal knowledge that utilitarianism requires. Conscientious Kantians can work out whether they will be doing wrong by some act even though they know that their foresight is limited and that they may cause some harm or fail to cause some benefit. But they will not cause harms that they can foresee without this being reflected in their intentions.

Kant and Respect for Persons

Kantians reach different conclusions about human life. Human life is valuable because humans (and conceivably other beings, e.g., angels or apes) are the bearers of rational life. Humans are able to choose and to plan. This capacity and its exercise are of such value that they ought not to be sacrificed for anything of lesser value. Therefore, no one rational or autonomous creature should be treated as mere means for the enjoyment or even the happiness of another. We may in Kant's view justifiably—even nobly—risk or sacrifice our lives for others. For in doing so we follow our own maxim and nobody uses us as mere means. But no others may use either our lives or our bodies for a scheme that they have either coerced or deceived us into joining. For in doing so they would fail to treat us as rational beings; they would use us as mere means and not as ends in ourselves.

It is conceivable that a society of Kantians, all of whom took pains to use no other as mere means, would end up with less happiness or with fewer persons alive than would some societies of complying utilitarians. For since the Kantians would be strictly bound only to justice, they might without wrongdoing be quite selective in their beneficence and fail to maximize either survival rates or happiness, or even to achieve as much of either as a strenuous group of utilitarians, who somehow make the right calculations. On the other hand, nobody will have been made an instrument of others' survival or happiness in the society of complying Kantians.

ON TREATING PEOPLE AS ENDS IN THEMSELVES: A CRITIQUE OF KANT
Fred Feldman

Fred Feldman is professor of philosophy at the University of Massachusetts, Amherst. His books include Doing the Best We Can *(1986),* Confrontations with the Reaper *(1991),* Utilitarianism, Hedonism and Desert: Essays in Moral Philosophy *(1997), and* Pleasure and the Good Life *(2004). Feldman argues that the main problem with Kant's End-in-Itself formula of the categorical imperative is that the meaning of treating someone as a mere means is never made adequately clear and so cannot function as a criterion of right action.*

The Formula of the End in Itself

We can draw a broad distinction between things that are good as means, and things that are good as ends. The distinction emerges clearly enough if we select some good thing and ask why it is good. Take sunlight. Sunlight is surely a good thing. But why is it good? Some would say that sunlight is good because, among other things, it makes plants grow, and it is a good thing that plants grow. But why

From *Introductory Ethics* by Fred Feldman (Prentice Hall, 1978). Reprinted by permission of the publisher.

is it good that plants grow? It is good that plants grow, it could be maintained, because without plants there would be no life on the earth, and it is good that there is life. But why is it good that there is life? Life, many would say, is good in itself. Its goodness does not arise as a result of what it leads to, or contributes to. It is good not because of its results, but because of itself. If these reflections about life are correct, then we can say that sunlight is good as a *means*, whereas life is good as an *end*. Another way to put this would be to say that sunlight is extrinsically good, whereas life is intrinsically good. Still another way to put it would be to say that sunlight is a means, whereas life is an end in itself.

We can define "means" in terms of "end in itself":

D_1: *x is a means* − *df. there is something, y, that is an end in itself, and x contributes, directly or indirectly, to the existence of y.*

Thus, according to D_1, sunlight is a means, since it contributes to the existence of life, which we are assuming to be an end in itself. If life is an end in itself, then money, health, education, and abundant natural resources may be taken to be good as means. Each of these things contribute to life, something that may be good in itself.

Kant claims that "rational nature exists as an end in itself."[1] By this, he seems to mean that all rational beings, including people, are ends in themselves. In other words, every person is intrinsically good. From this, Kant infers that it can never be morally right to treat any person merely as a means. That is, it is never morally right to treat a person as if he were simply a useful object for your own purposes. This view, which is the second version of the categorical imperative, is stated by Kant in a variety of ways:

Act in such a way that you always treat humanity, whether in your own person or in the person of any other, never simply as a means, but always at the same time as an end.[2]

A rational being, by his very nature an end and consequently an end in himself, must serve for every maxim as a condition limiting all merely relative and arbitrary ends.[3]

So act in relation to every rational being (both to yourself and to others) that he may at the same time count in your maxim as an end in himself.[4]

Let us understand Kant to be saying in these passages that one ought never to act in such a way as to treat anyone merely as a means. In other words:

CI_2: *An act is morally right if and only if the agent, in performing it, refrains from treating any person merely as a means.*

According to CI_2, there is a moral prohibition against treating anyone merely as a means. We should recognize that CI_2 does not rule out treating a person as a means. That is, CI_2 must not be confused with this rather implausible view:

CI_2': *An act is morally right if and only if, in performing it, the agent refrains from treating any person as a means.*

CI_2' rules out any act in which the agent treats anyone as a means. But this is absurd, since we use other people as means to our ends all the time, and we cannot avoid doing so. A student uses his teacher as a means to gaining an education; a teacher uses her students as a means to gaining a livelihood; a customer in a restaurant uses his waiter as a means to gaining his dinner. None of these acts is ruled out by CI_2. For in each of these cases the agent of the act may also treat the others involved, *at least in part,* as ends in themselves. Thus, although these acts would violate a preposterous principle such as CI_2', it is not clear that they would have to violate the more plausible principle, CI_2. For as we are understanding it, this second version of the categorical imperative only rules out treating persons *merely* as means.

CI_2 embodies an important moral insight, one that many would find plausible. It is the idea that it is wrong to "use" people. People are not mere objects, to be manipulated to serve our purpose. We cannot treat people as we treat wrecked cars, or wilted flowers, or old tin cans. Such things can be thrown out or destroyed when we no longer have any use for them. People, on the other hand, have dignity and worth, and must be treated accordingly.

Thus, what CI_2 says seems fairly plausible. Nevertheless, many moral philosophers would be uneasy about the claim that CI_2 is a formulation of "the supreme principle of morality." Can it really be the case that *all* wrong action is action in which people are used merely as means? Can all of our moral obligations be seen as obligations to treat people as ends? Some philosophers, admitting that it is important to treat people with respect, will deny that CI_2 captures the whole of our moral obligation. Others may even have their doubts about the acceptability of the insight embodied in CI_2, even if that insight were interpreted rather generously.

Problems for CI_2

The greatest problem for CI_2 is not, however, the lack of a convincing proof. Nor is it that CI_2 is subject to obvious counterexamples. Rather, the main difficulty with CI_2 is that its meaning is never made sufficiently clear. The most troublesome concept in this version of the categorical imperative is the concept of "treating someone merely as a means." It is pretty clear that if you own and mistreat slaves, then you treat them as means. But what about some more typical cases? What about a patron in a diner who grunts out his order to the waitress without even looking at her? What about a "freeloader" who lives with relatives? What about a factory owner who pays minimum wages and refuses to install safety equipment? Are these people treating others merely as means? Suppose the patron smiles and leaves a tip. Suppose the freeloader offers to do some work around the house. Suppose the factory owner gives a bonus at Christmas. Would they still be treating others merely as means? Would they be treating them, in part, as ends in themselves? It is very hard to tell.

When a concept is left unclear, one way to gain some clarification is by looking closely at the author's examples. Often, the examples will shed light on the more important general concept. Fortunately, Kant has given several examples of the application of CI_2. Close consideration of these may help to clarify the intent of the principle....

The first example is the man who contemplates committing suicide. As we saw previously, Kant's view is that suicide in this particular case would be wrong. Hence, he tries to show that the contemplated act would violate CI_2:

If he does away with himself in order to escape from a painful situation, he is making use of a person merely as a means to maintain a tolerable state of affairs till the end of his life. But man is not a thing—not something to be used merely as a means: he must always in all his actions be regarded as an end in himself. Hence I cannot dispose of man in my person by maiming, spoiling, or killing.[5]

Kant's point here seems to be that if the man were to commit suicide, then he would be using himself merely as a means to the end of making his life tolerable until its end. If this is Kant's point, it certainly seems quite strained. Surely, the man could claim that in order to treat himself as an end, he must commit suicide. For if he does not commit suicide, he will suffer. And, he could insist, it is not appropriate for a person who is an end in himself to suffer.

So Kant's comments on this example are not very helpful. He does not say anything that gives us a new insight into the concept of treating someone merely as a means. Hence, we turn to the second example.

Kant's comments on the second example are more revealing. This is the case of the lying promise. Kant suggests that the man who makes the lying promise is "intending to make use of another man merely as a means to an end he does not share."[6] Kant goes on to point out the other man "cannot possibly agree with my way of behaving to him."[7] Kant's point here seems to be this: The man to whom the lie is told does not want to be used in the way the liar uses him. If he knew what was going on, he would refuse to lend the money. Thus, the liar is using him merely as a means. For this reason, his act is in violation of CI_2, and so is wrong.

Understood in this way, Kant's comments suggest a definition of what is meant by saying that a person, A, treats a person, B, merely as a means:

D_2: A treats B merely as a means = df. A treats B in such a way that if B knew all about it, B would not want A to treat him in that way.

Thus, if you do not agree to being treated in a certain way, then if I treat you in that way I use you merely as a means. I use you for my purposes, but not for your own. Hence, according to CI_2, I act wrongly.

This line of reasoning may be plausible, but it leads to unacceptable results in a wide variety of cases. A large group of these cases have a similar pattern: B wants to do something morally wrong. A prevents B from doing this wrong act. According to D_2, A is then using B merely as a means, since B would not agree to A treating him that way. According to CI_2, then, A is acting wrongly. This seems absurd.

Let us consider an example. Suppose B is planning to steal A's motorcycle. A learns of B's plans and decides to chain his motorcycle to a lamppost, thereby making it impossible for B to achieve his goal. Surely, if B knew what A was doing, B would not agree to it. B would not want A to chain up the motorcycle. For if A's motorcycle is chained, B cannot steal it. According to D_2, therefore, in chaining the motorcycle A is using B merely as a means. This, together with CI_2, entails that A's act of chaining the motorcycle is morally wrong. This result is surely incorrect.

As long as we interpret "treating a person merely as a means" according to D_2, it will not be clear how this problem can be avoided. It appears, then, that we should not accept this second account of the crucial concept. It does not provide us with a plausible view about what Kant might have meant. Let us consider the next example to see if we can find a more helpful suggestion....

Since the third example is rather questionable anyway, let us move on and try to find some illumination in the final example. This is the example of the man who refuses to give to charity. Kant's comments here are more helpful. He apparently holds that the man who refuses to give to charity thereby acts wrongly. His error is that he fails to "agree positively with humanity as an end in itself."[8] If the man were to have done this, Kant suggests, he would have had to try, as much as he could have, to "further the ends of others."[9] Kant claims that since other people are ends in themselves, we act rightly only if we make their ends our own. This is an interesting idea, so let us examine it more closely.

Kant's comments on the final example suggest another interpretation of what is meant by "A treats B merely as a means." Kant explicitly says that we must further the ends of others. By this he seems to mean that unless we try, as much as we can, to see to it that others achieve their goals, we are not treating them as ends in themselves. We are treating them merely as means. Thus, if another person is trying to be happy, we must not only refrain from making him unhappy, we must try to help him become happy. The man who gives nothing to charity obviously violates this requirement. He treats those who need aid merely as means. We can define this concept as follows:

D_3: A treats B merely as a means = df. B has some goal, and A could help B achieve that goal, but A refrains from doing so.

When we combine CI_2 with D_3, we seem to get the correct result in the charity case. Those who need charity have a certain goal—happiness. The agent can help them to achieve that goal, but he decides to refrain from doing so. Hence, according to D_3, he treats them merely as means. But CI_2 says that one acts rightly only if he treats no one merely as a means. So, in this case CI_2 entails that the man who refuses to give charity does not act rightly. His selfish act is morally wrong. This result seems acceptable.

However, the problem with D_3 should be obvious. It is, in effect, the same as the problem with D_2. If other people want, for example, to destroy the environment, then according to D_3, we must help them to achieve their misguided goal; otherwise, we are treating them merely as means. Thus, CI_2 and D_3 entail that if we refrain from helping such people to destroy the environment, we are acting wrongly. This seems preposterous.

So the trouble with D_3 is that, together with CI_2, it requires us to help others to achieve their goals, whatever those goals may be. If the others have morally acceptable goals, this may seem to be a reasonable doctrine. But if the goals of the others are morally wrong, then it is absurd to insist that we should try to help them to achieve these goals. Yet this is just what D_3 and CI_2 require.

Before we leave CI_2, we may find it worthwhile to consider one final proposal. Kant does not make this proposal himself, but some sympathetic readers may find hints of it in the *Groundwork*. The basic idea is that there are some goals that it is rational for a person to have, and others that it is irrational for a person to have. For example, it might be said that it is rational for a person to have happiness as his goal, whereas it is irrational of him to have the destruction of the environment as his goal. Perhaps Kant would say that we are under no moral obligation to help others achieve irrational goals, but if another person is attempting to achieve a rational goal, then we should "make his end our own."

One way to develop this idea would be as follows. First, we must introduce a new definition:

D_4: *A treats B merely as a means = df. B has some rational goal, and A can help B achieve that goal, but A refrains from doing so.*

The difference between D_3 and D_4 is small, but significant. According to D_3, we treat another person merely as a means if we fail to help him achieve his goal, whatever that goal may be. According to D_4, we treat him merely as a means if we fail to help him achieve a rational, or reasonable, goal. Thus, the concept defined in D_4 may be more promising.

When we combine D_4 with CI_2, we get what may seem to be a more plausible moral doctrine. For under this interpretation, CI_2 requires us only to help others to achieve their *rational* goals. So there would be no need to help another person to destroy the environment, or commit a crime. On the other hand, there would be a need to help another to become happy—assuming that it is rational for that person to want to become happy.

Although the use of D_4 helps to make this version of the categorical imperative somewhat more successful, very great problems remain. For one, it often happens that there are several different persons who might benefit from one person's action. For example, suppose a man has an unbreakable piece of candy that he can give to either of two twins, Jean and Joan. If he gives the candy to Jean, he will make her happy. This will help Jean to achieve a rational goal she has. However, if he gives the candy to Jean, he will not be helping Joan to achieve a rational goal she has, for he will fail to help her to become happy. Similarly, if he gives it to Joan, he will fail to help Jean achieve a rational goal. Thus, according to D_4, whichever twin the man helps, he treats the other merely as a means. CI_2, then, implies that his act of giving the candy is morally wrong.

The general point should be clear. I can help each of many different persons achieve his rational goals. However, I cannot simultaneously help *all* of these individuals achieve their rational goals. I must choose some to help and some to ignore. According to D_4, it would follow that I have to treat some of them merely as means. CI_2 then yields the inevitable result that I act wrongly. This seems much too severe.

The second main problem with D_4 is that it makes use of a rather obscure concept—the concept of a "rational goal." If you think about it for a minute, you will see that where ultimate goals are concerned, it is hard to distinguish the rational from the irrational. Normally, we would say that a person who aims to collect a large amount of money is pursuing a rational goal, whereas a person who aims to collect a large number of bent nails is pursuing an irrational goal. But what is the difference? If each can gain happiness from his collection, why is one more rational than the other? Perhaps the only rational goal is happiness itself.

It is interesting to note that if we assume that happiness is the only rational goal, and if we also assume that Kant's view is the more moderate view that we should do the most we can to help other people achieve their rational goals, then Kant's view becomes indistinguishable from act utilitarianism. Of course, there is nothing in Kant's writing to suggest that he ever made either of these assumptions. With these reflections, we have strayed quite far from Kant's text. Perhaps it would be better to avoid such speculations.

It appears, then, that CI_2 is not a very successful principle. The insight behind it is vague, although plausible. There surely is something morally objectionable about using people. However, Kant's discussion of this view does not do enough to clarify this vague insight. Whether we interpret "A treats B merely as a means" according to D_2, D_3, or D_4, CI_2 yields obviously incorrect results in many cases. Until some more plausible account of the meaning of CI_2 is proposed, we must conclude that it is not an acceptable moral doctrine.

Notes

1. Immanuel Kant, *Groundwork of the Metaphysic of Morals*, translated and analyzed by H. J. Paton (New York: Harper & Row, 1964), p. 96.
2. Ibid.
3. Ibid., p. 104.
4. Ibid., p. 105.
5. Ibid., p. 97.
6. Ibid.
7. Ibid.
8. Ibid., p. 98.
9. Ibid.

CHAPTER 7

Virtue Ethics

VIRTUE AND CHARACTER
Aristotle

Aristotle (384–322 B.C.E.) is one of the most important philosophers ever to have lived. The son of a physician, he was a student of Plato and served as tutor to Alexander the Great. He contributed important works on logic, the sciences, and virtually every area of philosophy.

In the following selection from his Nicomachean Ethics, *Aristotle begins by arguing that a happy or good life essentially involves a life of activity in accordance with virtue. He then goes on to define virtue as a disposition to avoid extremes in feeling and action. For example, in matters relating to money, the virtue of generosity stands between the extremes of extravagance and stinginess.*

Characteristics of the Good

1. The good is the end of action.

But let us return once again to the good we are looking for, and consider just what it could be, since it is apparently one thing in one action or craft, and another thing in another; for it is one thing in medicine, another in generalship, and so on for the rest.

What, then, is the good in each of these cases? Surely it is that for the sake of which the other things are done; and in medicine this is health, in generalship victory, in house-building a house, in another case something else, but in every action and decision it is the end, since it is for the sake of the end that everyone does the other things.

And so, if there is some end of everything that is pursued in action, this will be the good pursued in action; and if there are more ends than one, these will be the goods pursued in action.

From *Nicomachean Ethics,* trans. Terence Irwin (Hackett, 1974). Reprinted by permission of Hackett Publishing Company, Inc. All rights reserved.

Our argument has progressed, then, to the same conclusion [as before, that the highest end is the good]; but we must try to clarify this still more.

2. The good is complete.

Though apparently there are many ends, we choose some of them, e.g., wealth, flutes and, in general, instruments, because of something else; hence it is clear that not all ends are complete. But the best good is apparently something complete. Hence, if only one end is complete, this will be what we are looking for; and if more than one are complete, the most complete of these will be what we are looking for.

Criteria for Completeness

An end pursued in itself, we say, is more complete than an end pursued because of something else; and an end that is never choiceworthy because of something else is more complete than ends that are choiceworthy both in themselves and because of this end; and hence an end that is always [choiceworthy, and also] choiceworthy in itself, never because of something else, is unconditionally complete.

3. Happiness meets the criteria for completeness, but other goods do not.

Now happiness more than anything else seems unconditionally complete, since we always [choose it, and also] choose it because of itself, never because of something else. Honor, pleasure, understanding and every virtue we certainly choose because of themselves, since we would choose each of them even if it had no further result, but we also choose them for the sake of happiness, supposing that through them we shall be happy. Happiness, by contrast, no one ever chooses for their sake, or for the sake of anything else at all.

4. The good is self-sufficient; so is happiness.

The same conclusion [that happiness is complete] also appears to follow from self-sufficiency, since the complete good seems to be self-sufficient.

Now what we count as self-sufficient is not what suffices for a solitary person by himself, living an isolated life, but what suffices also for parents, children, wife and in general for friends and fellow-citizens, since a human being is a naturally political [animal]. Here, however, we must impose some limit; for if we extend the good to parents' parents and children's children and to friends of friends, we shall go on without limit; but we must examine this another time.

Anyhow, we regard something as self-sufficient when all by itself it makes a life choiceworthy and lacking nothing; and that is what we think happiness does.

5. The good is most choiceworthy; so is happiness.

Moreover, [the complete good is most choiceworthy, and] we think happiness is most choiceworthy of all goods, since it is not counted as one good among many. If it were counted as one among many, then, clearly, we think that the addition of the smallest of goods would make it more choiceworthy; for [the smallest good] that is added becomes an extra quantity of goods [so creating a good larger than the original good], and the larger of two goods is always more choiceworthy. [But we do not think any addition can make happiness more choiceworthy; hence it is most choiceworthy.]

Happiness, then, is apparently something complete and self-sufficient, since it is the end of the things pursued in action.

A clearer account of the good: the human soul's activity expressing virtue.

But presumably the remark that the best good is happiness is apparently something [generally] agreed, and what we miss is a clearer statement of what the best good is.

1. If something has a function, its good depends on its function.

Well, perhaps we shall find the best good if we first find the function of a human being. For just as the good, i.e., [doing] well, for a flautist, a sculptor, and every craftsman, and, in general, for whatever has a function and [characteristic] action, seems to depend on its function, the same seems to be true for a human being, if a human being has some function.

2. What sorts of things have functions?

Then do the carpenter and the leatherworker have their functions and actions, while a human being has none, and is by nature idle, without any function? Or, just as eye, hand, foot and, in general, every [bodily] part apparently has its functions, may we likewise ascribe to a human being some functions besides all of theirs?

3. The human function.

What, then, could this be? For living is apparently shared with plants, but what we are looking for is the special function of a human being; hence we should set aside the life of nutrition and growth. The life next in order is some sort of life of sense-perception; but this too is apparently shared, with horse, ox and every animal. The remaining possibility, then, is some sort of life of action of the [part of the soul] that has reason.

Clarification of "has reason" and "life."

Now this [part has two parts, which have reason in different ways], one as obeying the reason [in the other part], the other as itself having reason and thinking. [We intend both.] Moreover, life is also spoken of in two ways [as capacity and as activity], and we must take [a human being's special function to be] life as activity, since this seems to be called life to a fuller extent.

4. The human good is activity expressing virtue.

(a) We have found, then, that the human function is the soul's activity that expresses reason [as itself having reason] or requires reason [as obeying reason]. (b) Now the function of F, e.g., of a harpist, is the same in kind, so we say, as the function of an excellent F, e.g., an excellent harpist. (c) The same is true unconditionally in every case, when we add to the function the superior achievement that expresses the virtue; for a harpist's function, e.g., is to play the harp, and a good harpist's is to do it well. (d) Now we take the human function to be a certain kind of life, and take this life to be the soul's activity and actions that express reason. (e) [Hence by (c) and (d)] the excellent man's function is to do this finely and well. (f) Each function is completed well when its completion expresses the proper virtue. (g) Therefore [by (d), (e) and (f)] the human good turns out to be the soul's activity that expresses virtue.

5. The good must also be complete.

And if there are more virtues than one, the good will express the best and most complete virtue. Moreover, it will be in a complete life. For one swallow does not make a spring, nor does one day; nor, similarly, does one day or a short time make us blessed and happy....

Virtues of Character in General

HOW A VIRTUE OF CHARACTER IS ACQUIRED

Virtue, then, is of two sorts, virtue of thought and virtue of character. Virtue of thought arises and grows mostly from teaching, and hence needs experience and time. Virtue of character [i.e., of *ethos*] results from habit [*ethos*]; hence its name "ethical," slightly varied from *"ethos."*

Virtue comes about, not by a process of nature, but by habituation.

Hence it is also clear that none of the virtues of character arises in us naturally.

1. What is natural cannot be changed by habituation.

For if something is by nature [in one condition], habituation cannot bring it into another condition. A stone, e.g., by nature moves downwards, and habituation could not make it move upwards, not even if you threw it up ten thousand times to habituate it; nor could habituation make fire move downwards, or bring anything that is by nature in one condition into another condition.

Thus the virtues arise in us neither by nature nor against nature, but we are by nature able to acquire them, and reach our complete perfection through habit.

2. Natural capacities are not acquired by habituation.

Further, if something arises in us by nature, we first have the capacity for it, and later display the activity. This is clear in the case of the senses; for we did not acquire them by frequent seeing or hearing, but already had them when we exercised them, and did not get them by exercising them.

Virtues, by contrast, we acquire, just as we acquire crafts, by having previously activated them. For we learn a craft by producing the same product that we must produce when we have learned it, becoming builders, e.g., by building and harpists by playing the harp; so also, then, we become just by doing just actions, temperate by doing temperate actions, brave by doing brave actions.

3. Legislators concentrate on habituation.

What goes on in cities is evidence for this also. For the legislator makes the citizens good by habituating them, and this is the wish of every legislator; if he fails to do it well he misses his goal. [The right] habituation is what makes the difference between a good political system and a bad one.

4. Virtue and vice are formed by good and bad actions.

Further, just as in the case of a craft, the sources and means that develop each virtue also ruin it. For playing the harp makes both good and bad harpists, and it is analogous in the case of builders and all the rest; for building well makes good builders, building badly, bad ones. If it were not so, no teacher would be needed, but everyone would be born a good or a bad craftsman.

It is the same, then, with the virtues. For actions in dealings with [other] human beings make some people just, some unjust; actions in terrifying situations and the acquired habit of fear or confidence make some brave and others cowardly. The same is true of situations involving appetites and anger; for one or another sort of conduct in these situations makes some people temperate and gentle, others intemperate and irascible.

Conclusion: The Importance of Habituation.

To sum up, then, in a single account: A state [of character] arises from [the repetition of] similar activities. Hence we must display the right activities, since differences in these imply corresponding differences in the states. It is not unimportant, then, to acquire one sort of habit or another, right from our youth; rather, it is very important, indeed all-important....

But our claims about habituation raise a puzzle: How can we become good without being good already?

However, someone might raise this puzzle: "What do you mean by saying that to become just we must first do just actions and to become temperate we must first do temperate actions? For if we do what is grammatical or musical, we must already be grammarians or musicians. In the same way, then, if we do what is just or temperate, we must already be just or temperate."

First reply: Conformity versus understanding.

But surely this is not so even with the crafts, for it is possible to produce something grammatical by chance or by following someone else's instructions. To be a grammarian, then, we must both produce something grammatical and produce it in the way in which the grammarian produces it, i.e., expressing grammatical knowledge that is in us.

Second reply: Crafts versus virtues.

Moreover, in any case what is true of crafts is not true of virtues. For the products of a craft determine by their own character whether they have been produced well; and so it suffices that they are in the right state when they have been produced. But for actions expressing virtue to be done temperately or justly [and hence well] it does not suffice that they are themselves in the right state. Rather, the agent must also be in the right state when he does them. First, he must know [that he is doing virtuous actions]; second, he must decide on them, and decide on them for themselves; and, third, he must also do them from a firm and unchanging state.

As conditions for having a craft these three do not count, except for the knowing itself. As a condition for having a virtue, however, the knowing counts for nothing, or [rather] for only a little, whereas the other two conditions are very important, indeed all-important. And these other two conditions are achieved by the frequent doing of just and temperate actions.

Hence actions are called just or temperate when they are the sort that a just or temperate person would do. But the just and temperate person is not the one who [merely] does these actions, but the one who also does them in the way in which just or temperate people do them.

It is right, then, to say that a person comes to be just from doing just actions and temperate from doing temperate actions; for no one has even a prospect of becoming good from failing to do them.

Virtue requires habituation, and therefore requires practice, not just theory.

The many, however, do not do these actions but take refuge in arguments, thinking that they are doing philosophy, and that this is the way to become excellent people. In this they are like a sick person who listens attentively to the doctor, but acts on none of his instructions. Such a course of treatment will not improve the state of his body; any more than will the many's way of doing philosophy improve the state of their souls.

A Virtue of Character Is a State Intermediate Between Two Extremes, and Involving Decision

THE GENUS

Feelings, capacities, states. Next we must examine what virtue is. Since there are three conditions arising in the soul—feelings, capacities and states—virtue must be one of these.

By feelings I mean appetite, anger, fear, confidence, envy, joy, love, hate, longing, jealousy, pity, in general whatever implies pleasure or pain.

By capacities I mean what we have when we are said to be capable of these feelings—capable of, e.g., being angry or afraid or feeling pity.

By states I mean what we have when we are well or badly off in relation to feelings. If, e.g., our feeling is too intense or slack, we are badly off in relation to anger, but if it is intermediate, we are well off; and the same is true in the other cases.

Virtue is not a feeling...

First, then, neither virtues nor vices are feelings. (a) For we are called excellent or base in so far as we have virtues or vices, not in so far as we have feelings. (b) We are neither praised nor blamed in so far as we have feelings; for we do not praise the angry or the frightened person, and do not blame the person who is simply angry, but only the person who is angry in a particular way. But we are praised or blamed in so far as we have virtues or vices. (c) We are angry and afraid without decision; but the virtues are decisions of some kind, or [rather] require decision. (d) Besides, in so far as we have feelings, we are said to be moved; but in so far as we have virtues or vices, we are said to be in some condition rather than moved.

Or a capacity...

For these reasons the virtues are not capacities either; for we are neither called good nor called bad in so far as we are simply capable of feelings. Further, while we have capacities by nature, we do not become good or bad by nature; we have discussed this before.

But a state

If, then, the virtues are neither feelings nor capacities, the remaining possibility is that they are states. And so we have said what the genus of virtue is.

THE DIFFERENTIA

But we must say not only, as we already have, that it is a state, but also what sort of state it is.

Virtue and the human function. It should be said, then, that every virtue causes its possessors to be in a good state and to perform their functions well; the virtue of eyes, e.g., makes the eyes and their functioning excellent, because it makes us see well; and similarly, the virtue of a horse makes the horse excellent, and thereby good at galloping, at carrying its rider and at standing steady in the face of the enemy. If this is true in every case, then the virtue of a human being will likewise be the state that makes a human being good and makes him perform his function well....

The numerical mean and the mean relative to us. In everything continuous and divisible we can take more, less and equal, and each of them either in the object itself or relative to us; and the equal is some intermediate between excess and deficiency.

By the intermediate in the object I mean what is equidistant from each extremity; this is one and the same for everyone. But relative to us the intermediate is what is neither superfluous nor deficient; this is not one, and is not the same for everyone.

If, e.g., ten are many and two are few, we take six as intermediate in the object, since it exceeds [two] and is exceeded [by ten] by an equal amount, [four]; this is what is intermediate by numerical proportion. But that is not how we must take the intermediate that is relative to us. For if, e.g., ten pounds [of food] are a lot for someone to eat, and two pounds a little, it does not follow that the trainer will prescribe six, since this might also be either a little or a lot for the person who is to take it—for Milo [the athlete] a little, but for the beginner in gymnastics a lot; and the same is true for running and wrestling. In this way every scientific expert avoids excess and deficiency and seeks and chooses what is intermediate—but intermediate relative to us, not in the object.

Virtue seeks the mean relative to us: Argument from craft to virtue.

This, then, is how each science produces its product well, by focusing on what is intermediate and making the product conform to that. This, indeed, is why people regularly comment on well-made products that nothing could be added or subtracted, since they assume that excess or deficiency ruins a good [result] while the mean preserves it. Good craftsmen also, we say, focus on what is intermediate when they produce their product. And since virtue, like nature, is better and more exact than any craft, it will also aim at what is intermediate.

Arguments from the nature of virtue of character. By virtue I mean virtue of character; for this [pursues the mean because] it is concerned with feelings and actions, and these admit of excess, deficiency and an intermediate condition. We can be afraid, e.g., or be confident, or have appetites, or get angry, or feel pity, in general have pleasure or pain, both too much and too little, and in both ways not well; but [having these feelings] at the right times, about the right things, towards the right people, for the right end, and in the right way, is the intermediate and best condition, and this is proper to virtue. Similarly, actions also admit of excess, deficiency and the intermediate condition.

Now virtue is concerned with feelings and actions, in which excess and deficiency are in error and incur blame, while the intermediate condition is correct and wins praise, which are both proper features of virtue. Virtue, then, is a mean, in so far as it aims at what is intermediate.

Moreover, there are many ways to be in error, since badness is proper to what is unlimited, as the Pythagoreans pictured it, and good to what is limited; but there is only one way to be correct. That is why error is easy and correctness hard, since it is easy to miss the target and hard to hit it. And so for this reason also excess and deficiency are proper to vice, the mean to virtue; "for we are noble in only one way, but bad in all sorts of ways."

Definition of virtue. Virtue, then, is (a) a state that decides, (b) [consisting] in a mean, (c) the mean relative to us, (d) which is defined by reference to reason, (e) i.e., to the reason by reference to which the intelligent person would define it. It is a mean between two vices, one of excess and one of deficiency.

It is a mean for this reason also: Some vices miss what is right because they are deficient, others because they are excessive, in feelings or in actions, while virtue finds and chooses what is intermediate.

Hence, as far as its substance and the account stating its essence are concerned, virtue is a mean; but as far as the best [condition] and the good [result] are concerned, it is an extremity.

The definition must not be misapplied to cases in which there is no mean.

But not every action or feeling admits of the mean. For the names of some automatically include baseness, e.g., spite, shamelessness, envy [among feelings], and adultery, theft, murder, among actions. All of these and similar things are called by these names because they themselves, not their excesses or deficiencies, are base.

Hence in doing these things we can never be correct, but must invariably be in error. We cannot do them well or not well—e.g., by committing adultery with the right woman at the right time in the right way; on the contrary, it is true unconditionally that to do any of them is to be in error.

[To think these admit of a mean], therefore, is like thinking that unjust or cowardly or intemperate action also admits of a mean, an excess and a deficiency. For then there would be a mean of excess, a mean of deficiency, an excess of excess and a deficiency of deficiency.

Rather, just as there is no excess or deficiency of temperance or of bravery, since the intermediate is a sort of extreme [in achieving the good], so also there is no mean of these [vicious actions] either, but whatever way anyone does them, he is in error. For in general there is no mean of excess or of deficiency, and no excess or deficiency of a mean.

The Definition of Virtue as a Mean
Applies to the Individual Virtues

However, we must not only state this general account but also apply it to the particular cases. For among accounts concerning actions, though the general ones are common to more cases, the specific ones are truer, since actions are about particular cases, and our account must accord with these. Let us, then, find these from the chart.

CLASSIFICATION OF VIRTUES OF CHARACTER

Virtues concerned with feelings. 1. First, in feelings of fear and confidence the mean is bravery. The excessively fearless person is nameless (and in fact many cases are nameless), while the one who is excessively confident is rash; the one who is excessively afraid and deficient in confidence is cowardly.

2. In pleasures and pains, though not in all types, and in pains less than in pleasures, the mean is temperance and the excess intemperance. People deficient in pleasure are not often found, which is why they also lack even a name; let us call them insensible.

Virtues concerned with external goods. 3. In giving and taking money the mean is generosity, the excess wastefulness and the deficiency ungenerosity. Here the vicious people have contrary excesses and defects; for the wasteful person spends to excess and is deficient in taking, whereas the ungenerous person takes to excess and is deficient in spending. At the moment we are speaking in outline and summary....

4. In questions of money there are also other conditions. Another mean is magnificence; for the magnificent person differs from the generous by being concerned with large matters, while the generous person is concerned with small. The excess is ostentation and vulgarity, and the deficiency niggardliness, and these differ from the vices related to generosity....

5. In honor and dishonor the mean is magnanimity, the excess something called a sort of vanity, and the deficiency pusillanimity.

6. And just as we said that generosity differs from magnificence in its concern with small matters, similarly there is a virtue concerned with small honors, differing in the same way from magnanimity, which is concerned with great honors. For honor can be desired either in the right way or more or less than is right. If someone desires it to excess, he is called an honor-lover, and if his desire is deficient he is called indifferent to honor, but if he is intermediate he has no name. The corresponding conditions have no name either, except the condition of the honor-lover, which is called honor-loving.

This is why people at the extremes claim the intermediate area. Indeed, we also sometimes call the intermediate person an honor-lover, and sometimes call him indifferent to honor; and sometimes we praise the honor-lover, sometimes the person indifferent to honor....

Virtues concerned with social life. 7. Anger also admits of an excess, deficiency and mean. These are all practically nameless; but since we call the intermediate person mild, let us call the mean mildness. Among the extreme people let the excessive person be irascible, and the vice be irascibility, and let the deficient person be a sort of inirascible person, and the deficiency be inirascibility.

There are three other means, somewhat similar to one another, but different. For they are all concerned with association in conversations and actions, but differ in so far as one is concerned with truth-telling in these areas, the other two with sources of pleasure, some of which are found in amusement, and the others in daily life in general. Hence we should also discuss these states, so that we can better observe that in every case the mean is praiseworthy, while the extremes are neither praiseworthy nor correct, but blameworthy. Most of these cases are also nameless, and we must try, as in the other cases also, to make names ourselves, to make things clear and easy to follow.

8. In truth-telling, then, let us call the intermediate person truthful, and the mean truthfulness; pretense that overstates will be boastfulness, and the person who has it boastful; pretense that understates will be self-deprecation, and the person who has it self-deprecating.

9. In sources of pleasure in amusements let us call the intermediate person witty, and the condition wit; the excess buffoonery and the person who has it a buffoon; and the deficient person a sort of boor and the state boorishness.

10. In the other sources of pleasure, those in daily life, let us call the person who is pleasant in the right way friendly, and the mean state friendliness. If someone goes to excess with no [further] aim he will be ingratiating; if he does it for his own advantage, a flatterer. The deficient person, unpleasant in everything, will be a sort of quarrelsome and ill-tempered person.

Mean states that are not virtues. 11. There are also means in feelings and concerned with feelings: shame, e.g., is not a virtue, but the person prone to shame as well as the virtuous person we have described receives praise. For here also one person is called intermediate, and another—the person excessively prone to shame, who is ashamed about everything—is called excessive; the person who is deficient in shame or never feels shame at all is said to have no sense of disgrace; and the intermediate one is called prone to shame.

12. Proper indignation is the mean between envy and spite; these conditions are concerned with pleasure and pain at what happens to our neighbors. For the properly indignant person feels pain when someone does well undeservedly; the envious person exceeds him by feeling pain when anyone does well, while the spiteful person is so deficient in feeling pain that he actually enjoys [other people's misfortunes].

NORMATIVE VIRTUE ETHICS
Rosalind Hursthouse

Rosalind Hursthouse is head of the philosophy department at the Open University. Her publications include Beginning Lives *(1987) and* On Virtue Ethics *(1999). Hursthouse contrasts the theory of right conduct distinctive of virtue ethics, contrasting it with both utilitarian and deontological theories. She then defends her version of virtue ethics against the charge that such a view is not sufficiently action guiding. Finally, she considers the issue of how virtue ethics deals with moral dilemmas.*

A common belief concerning virtue ethics is that it does not tell us what we should do. This belief is sometimes manifested merely in the expressed assumption

Reprinted from Rosalind Hursthouse, "Normative Virtue Ethics," *How Should One Live? Essays on the Virtues*, edited by Roger Crisp (Oxford: Clarendon Press, 1996). Reprinted by permission of the publisher.

that virtue ethics, in being 'agent-centred' rather than 'act-centred,' is concerned with Being rather than Doing, with good (and bad) character rather than right (and wrong) action, with the question 'What sort of person should I be?' rather than the question 'What should I do?' On this assumption, 'virtue ethics' so-called does not figure as a normative rival to utilitarian and deontological ethics; rather, its (fairly) recent revival is seen as having served the useful purpose of reminding moral philosophers that the elaboration of a normative theory may fall short of giving a full account of our moral life. Thus prompted, deontologists have turned to Kant's long neglected 'Doctrine of Virtue,' and utilitarians, largely abandoning the old debate about rule- and act-utilitarianism, are showing interest in the general-happiness-maximizing consequences of inculcating such virtues as friendship, honesty, and loyalty.

On this assumption, it seems that philosophers who 'do virtue ethics', having severed this purpose, must realize that they have been doing no more than supplementing normative theory, and should now decide which of the two standard views they espouse. Or, if they find that too difficult, perhaps they should confine themselves to writing detailed studies of particular virtues and vices, indicating where appropriate that 'a deontologist would say that an agent with virtue X will characteristically..., whereas a utilitarian would say that she will characteristically....' But anyone who wants to espouse virtue ethics as a rival to deontological or utilitarian ethics (finding it distinctly bizarre to suppose that Aristotle espoused either of the latter) will find this common belief voiced against her as an objection: 'Virtue ethics does not, because it cannot, tell us what we should do. Hence it cannot be a normative rival to deontology and utilitarianism.'

This paper is devoted to defending virtue ethics against this objection.

1. Right Action

What grounds might someone have for believing that virtue ethics cannot tell us what we should do? It seems that sometimes the ground is no more than the claim that virtue ethics is concerned with good (and bad) character rather than right (and wrong) action. But that claim does no more than highlight an interesting contrast between virtue ethics on the one hand, and deontology and utilitarianism on the other; the former is agent-centred, the latter (it is said) are act-centred. It does not entail that virtue ethics has nothing to say about the concept of right action, nor about which actions are right and which wrong. Wishing to highlight a different contrast, the one between utilitarianism and deontology, we might equally well say, 'Utilitarianism is concerned with good (and bad) states of affairs rather than right (and wrong) action,' and no one would take that to mean that utilitarianism, unlike deontology, had nothing to say about right action, for what utilitarianism does say is so familiar.

Suppose an act-utilitarian laid out her account of right action as follows:

U1. An action is right iff [if and only if] it promotes the best consequences.

This premise provides a specification of right action, forging the familiar utilitarian link between the concepts of *right action* and *best consequences,* but gives one no guidance about how to act until one knows what to count as the best consequences. So these must be specified in a second premise, for example:

U2. *The best consequences are those in which happiness is maximized,*

which forges the familiar utilitarian link between the concepts of *best consequences* and *happiness.*[1]

Many different versions of deontology can be laid out in a way that displays the same basic structure. They begin with a premiss providing a specification of right action:

D1. *An action is right iff it is in accordance with a correct moral rule or principle.*

Like the first premiss of act-utilitarianism, this gives one no guidance about how to act until, in this case, one knows what to count as a correct moral rule (or principle). So this must be specified in a second premiss which begins

D2. *A correct moral rule (principle) is one that…,*

and this may be completed in a variety of ways, for example:

  (i) is on the following list (and then a list does follow)

or

  (ii) is laid on us by God

or

  (iii) is universalizable

or

  (iv) would be the object of choice of all rational beings

and so on.

Although this way of laying out fairly familiar versions of utilitarianism and deontology is hardly controversial, it is worth noting that it suggests some infelicity in the slogan 'Utilitarianism begins with (or takes as its fundamental concept etc.) the Good, whereas deontology begins with the Right.' If the concept a normative ethics 'begins with' is the one it uses to specify right action, then utilitarianism might be said to begin with the Good (if we take this to be the 'same' concept as that of the *best*), but we should surely hasten to add 'but only in relation to consequences; not, for instance, in relation to *good* agents, or to living *well*.' And even then, we shall not be able to go on to say that most versions of deontology 'begin with' the Right, for they use the concept of moral rule or principle to specify right action. The only versions which, in this sense, 'begin with' the Right would have to be versions of what Frankena calls 'extreme act-deontology,'[2] which (I suppose) specify a right action as one which just is right.

And if the dictum is supposed to single out, rather vaguely, the concept which is 'most important', then the concepts of *consequences* or *happiness* seem as deserving of mention as the concept of the Good for utilitarianism, and what counts as most important (if any one concept does) for deontologists would surely vary from case to case. For some it would be God, for others universalizability, for others the Categorical Imperative, for others rational acceptance, and so on.

It is possible that too slavish an acceptance of this slogan, and the inevitable difficulty of finding a completion of 'and virtue ethics begins with ...' which does not reveal its inadequacy, has contributed to the belief that virtue ethics cannot provide a specification of right action. I have heard people say, 'Utilitarianism defines the Right in terms of the Good, and deontology defines the Good in terms of the Right; but how can virtue ethics possibly define both in terms of the (virtuous) Agent?', and indeed, with no answer forthcoming to the questions 'Good *what?* Right *what?*,' I have no idea. But if the question is 'How can virtue ethics specify right action?', the answer is easy:

V1. An action is right if it is what a virtuous agent would characteristically (i.e. acting in character) do in the circumstances.

This specification rarely, if ever, silences those who maintain that virtue ethics cannot tell us what we should do. On the contrary, it tends to provoke irritable laughter and scorn. '*That's* no use', the objectors say. 'It gives us no guidance whatsoever. Who are the virtuous agents?' But if the failure of the first premiss of a normative ethics which forges a link between the concept of right action and a concept distinctive of that ethics may provoke scorn because it provides no practical guidance, why not direct a similar scorn at the first premisses of act-utilitarianism and deontology in the form in which I have given them? Of each of them I remarked, apparently *en passant* but with intent, that they gave us no guidance. Utilitarianism must specify what are to count as the best consequences, and deontology what is to count as a correct moral rule, producing a second premiss, before any guidance is given. And similarly, virtue ethics must specify who is to count as a virtuous agent. So far, the three are all in the same position.

Of course, if the virtuous agent can only be specified as an agent disposed to act in accordance with moral rules, as some have assumed, then virtue ethics collapses back into deontology and is no rival to it. So let us add a subsidiary premiss to this skeletal outline, with the intention of making it clear that virtue ethics aims to provide a non-deontological specification of the virtuous agent via a specification of the virtues, which will be given in its second premiss:

V1a. A virtuous agent is one who acts virtuously, that is, one who has and exercises the virtues.

V2. A virtue is a character trait that...

This second premiss of virtue ethics might, like the second premiss of some versions of deontology, be completed simply by enumeration ('a virtue is one of the following,' and then the list is given). Or we might, not implausibly, interpret the Hume of the second *Enquiry* as espousing virtue ethics. According to him, a virtue is a character trait (of human beings) that is useful or agreeable to its possessor or to others (inclusive 'or' both times). The standard neo-Aristotelian completion claims that a virtue is a character trait a human being needs for *eudaimonia*, to flourish or live well.

Here, then, we have a specification of right action, whose structure closely resembles those of act-utilitarianism and many forms of deontology. Given that virtue ethics can come up with such a specification, can it still be maintained that it, unlike utilitarianism and deontology, cannot tell us what we should do? Does the specification somehow fail to provide guidance in a way that the other two do not?

At this point, the difficulty of identifying the virtuous agent in a way that makes V1 action-guiding tends to be brought forward again. Suppose it is granted that deontology has just as much difficulty in identifying the correct moral rules as virtue ethics has in identifying the virtues and hence the virtuous agent. Then the following objection may be made.

'All the same,' it may be said, 'if we imagine that that has been achieved—perhaps simply by enumeration—deontology yields a set of clear prescriptions which are readily applicable ("Do not lie," "Do not steal," "Do not inflict evil or harm on others", "Do help others," "Do keep promises," etc.). But virtue ethics yields only the prescription "Do what the virtuous agent (the one who is honest, charitable, just, etc.) would do in these circumstances." And this gives me no guidance unless I am (and know I am) a virtuous agent myself (in which case I am hardly in need of it). If I am less than fully virtuous, I shall have no idea what a virtuous agent would do, and hence cannot apply the only prescription that virtue ethics has given me. (Of course, act-utilitarianism also yields a single prescription, "Do what maximises happiness," but there are no *parallel* difficulties in applying that.) So there is the way in which V1 fails to be action-guiding where deontology and utilitarianism succeed.'

It is worth pointing out that, if I acknowledge that I am far from perfect, and am quite unclear what a virtuous agent would do in the circumstances in which I find myself, the obvious thing to do is to go and ask one, should this be possible. This is far from being a trivial point, for it gives a straightforward explanation of an aspect of our moral life which should not be ignored, namely the fact that we do seek moral guidance from people who we think are morally better than ourselves. When I am looking for an excuse to do something I have a horrid suspicion is wrong, I ask my moral inferiors (or peers if I am bad enough), 'Wouldn't you do such and such if you were in my shoes?' But when I am anxious to do what is right, and do not see my way clear, I go to people I respect and admire—people who I think are kinder, more honest, more just, wise, than I am myself—and ask them what they would do in my circumstances. How utilitarianism and deontology would explain this fact, I do not know; but, as I said, the explanation within the terms of virtue ethics is straightforward. If you want to do what is right, and doing what is right is doing what a virtuous agent would do in the circumstances, then you should find out what she would do if you do not already know.

Moreover, seeking advice from virtuous people is not the only thing an imperfect agent trying to apply the single prescription of virtue ethics can do. For it is simply false that, in general, 'if I am less than fully virtuous, then I shall have no idea what a virtuous agent would do', as the objection claims. Recall that we are assuming that the virtues have been enumerated, as the deontologist's rules have been. The latter have been enumerated as, say, 'Do not lie', 'Do not inflict evil or harm', etc.; the former as, say, honesty, charity, justice, etc. So, *ex hypothesi*, a virtuous agent is one who is honest, charitable, just, etc. so what she characteristically does is act honestly, charitably, justly, etc., and not dishonestly, uncharitably, unjustly. So given an enumeration of the virtues, I may well have a perfectly good idea of what the virtuous person would do in my circumstances despite my own imperfection. Would she lie in her teeth to acquire an unmerited advantage? No, for that would be to act both dishonestly and unjustly. Would she help the naked man by the roadside or pass by on the other side? The former, for she acts charitably. Might she keep a deathbed promise even though living people would benefit from its being broken? Yes, for she acts justly. And so on.

2. Moral Rules

The above response to the objection that V1 fails to be action-guiding clearly amounts to a denial of the oft-repeated claim that virtue ethics does not come up with any rules (another version of the thought that it is concerned with Being rather than Doing and needs to be supplemented with rules). We can now see that it comes up with a large number; not only does each virtue generate a prescription—act honestly, charitably, justly—but each vice a prohibition—do not act dishonestly, uncharitably, unjustly. Once this point about virtue ethics is grasped (and it is remarkable how often it is overlooked), can there remain any reason for thinking that virtue ethics cannot tell us what we should do? Yes. The reason given is, roughly, that rules such as 'Act honestly', 'Do not act uncharitably', etc. are, like the rule 'Do what the virtuous agent would do', still the wrong sort of rule, still somehow doomed to fail to provide the action guidance supplied by the rules (or rule) of deontology and utilitarianism.

But how so? It is true that these rules of virtue ethics (henceforth 'v-rules') are couched in terms, or concepts, which are certainly 'evaluative' in *some* sense, or senses, of that difficult word. Is it this which dooms them to failure? Surely not, unless many forms of deontology fail too. If we concentrate on the single example of lying, defining lying to be 'asserting what you believe to be untrue, with the intention of deceiving your hearer(s)', then we might, for a moment, preserve the illusion that a deontologist's rules do not contain 'evaluative' terms. But as soon as we remember that few deontologists will want to forego principles of non-maleficence or beneficence, the illusion vanishes. For those principles, and their corresponding rules ('Do no evil or harm to others', 'Help others', 'Promote their well-being'), rely on terms or concepts which are at least as 'evaluative' as those employed in the v-rules. Few deontologists rest content with the simple quasi-biological 'Do not kill', but more refined versions of that rules such as 'Do not murder', or 'Do not kill the innocent', once again employ 'evaluative' terms, and 'Do not kill unjustly' is itself a particular instantiation of a v-rule.

Supposing this point were granted, a deontologist might still claim that the v-rules are markedly inferior to deontological rules as far as providing guidance for children is concerned. Granted, adult deontologists must think hard about what really constitutes harming someone, or promoting their well-being, or respecting their autonomy, or murder, but surely the simple rules we learnt at our mother's knee are indispensable? How could virtue ethics plausibly seek to dispense with these and expect toddlers to grasp 'Act charitably, honestly, and kindly', 'Don't act unjustly', and so on? Rightly are these concepts described as 'thick'. Far too thick for a child to grasp.

Strictly speaking, this claim about learning does not really support the *general* claim that v-rules fail to provide action-guidance, but the claim about learning, arising naturally as it does in the context of the general claim, is one I am more than happy to address. For it pinpoints a condition of adequacy that any normative ethics must meet, namely that such an ethics must not only come up with action-guidance for a clever rational adult but also generate some account of moral education, of how one generation teaches the next what they should do. But an ethics inspired by Aristotle is unlikely to have forgotten the question of moral education, and the objection fails to hit home. First, the implicit empirical claim that toddlers are taught *only* the deontologist's rules, not the 'thick' concepts, is false. Sentences such as 'Don't do that, it hurts, you mustn't be *cruel*', 'Be *kind* to your brother, he's only little', 'Don't be so *mean*, so *greedy*' are commonly addressed to toddlers. Secondly, why should a proponent of virtue ethics deny the significance of such mother's-knee rules as "Don't lie', 'Keep promises', 'Don't take more than your fair share', 'Help others'? Although it is a mistake, I have claimed, to define a virtuous agent simply as one disposed to act in accordance with moral rules, it is a very understandable mistake, given the obvious connection between, for example, the exercise of the virtue of honesty and refraining from lying. Virtue ethicists want to emphasize the fact that, if children are to be taught to be honest, they must be taught to prize the truth, and that *merely* teaching them not to lie will not achieve this end. But they need not deny that to achieve this end teaching them not to lie is useful, even indispensable.

So we can see that virtue ethics not only comes up with rules (the v-rules, couched in terms derived from the virtues and vices), but further, does not exclude the more familiar deontologists' rules. The theoretical distinction between the two is that the familiar rules, and their applications in particular cases, are given entirely different backings. According to virtue ethics, I must not tell this lie, since it would be dishonest, and dishonesty is a vice; must not break this promise, since it would be unjust, or a betrayal of friendship, or, perhaps (for the available virtue and vice terms do not neatly cover every contingency), simply because no virtuous person would.

However, the distinction is not merely theoretical. It is, indeed, the case that, with respect to a number of familiar examples, virtue ethicists and deontologists tend to stand shoulder to shoulder against utilitarians, denying that, for example, this lie can be told, this promise broken, this human being killed because the consequences of so doing will be generally happiness-maximizing. But, despite a fair amount of coincidence in action-guidance between deontology and virtue ethics, the latter has its own distinctive approach to the practical problems involved in dilemmas.

3. The Conflict Problem

It is a noteworthy fact that, in support of the general claim that virtue ethics cannot tell us what we should do, what is often cited is the 'conflict problem'. The requirements of different virtues, it is said, can point us in opposed directions. Charity prompts me to kill the person who would (truly) be better off dead, but justice forbids it. Honesty points to telling the hurtful truth, kindness and compassion to remaining silent or even lying. And so on. So virtue ethics lets us down just at the point where we need it, where we are faced with the really difficult dilemmas and do not know what to do.

In the mouth of a utilitarian, this may be a comprehensible criticism, for, as is well known, the only conflict that classical utilitarianism's one rule can generate is the tiresome logical one between the two occurrences of 'greatest' in its classical statement. But it is strange to find the very same criticism coming from deontologists, who are notoriously faced with the same problem. 'Don't kill', 'Respect autonomy', 'Tell the truth', 'Keep promises' may all conflict with 'Prevent suffering' or 'Do no harm', which is precisely why deontologists so often reject utilitarianism's deliverances on various dilemmas. Presumably, they must think that deontology can solve the 'conflict problem' and, further, that virtue ethics cannot. Are they right?

With respect to a number of cases, the deontologist's strategy is to argue that the 'conflict' is merely apparent, or *prima facie*. The proponent of virtue ethics employs the same strategy: according to her, many of the putative conflicts are merely apparent, resulting from a misapplication of the virtue or vice terms. Does kindness require not telling hurtful truths? Sometimes, but in *this* case, what has to be understood is that one does people no kindness by concealing this sort of truth from them, hurtful as it may be. Or, in a different case, the importance of the truth in question puts the consideration of hurt feelings out of court, and the agent does not show herself to be unkind, or callous, by speaking out. Does charity require that I kill the person who would be better off dead but who wants to stay alive, thereby conflicting with justice? Not if, in Foot's words, '[a] man does not lack charity because he refrains from an act of injustice which would have been for someone's good'.[3]

One does not have to agree with the three judgements expressed here to recognize this as a *strategy* available to virtue ethics, any more than one has to agree with the particular judgements of deontologists who, for example, may claim that one rule outranks another, or that a certain rule has a certain exception clause build in, when they argue that a putative case of conflict is resolvable. Whether an individual has resolved a putative moral conflict or dilemma rightly is one question; whether a normative ethics has the wherewithal to resolve it is an entirely different question, and it is the latter with which we are concerned here.

The form the strategy takes within virtue ethics provides what may plausibly be claimed to be the deep explanation of why, in some cases, agents do not know the answer to 'What should I do in these circumstances?' despite the fact that there *is* an answer. Trivially, the explanation is that they lack moral knowledge of what to do in this situation; but why? In what way? The lack, according to virtue ethics' strategy, arises from lack of moral wisdom, from an inadequate grasp of what is involved in acting *kindly* (unkindly) or *charitable* (uncharitably), in being *honest*, or *just*, or *lacking in charity*, or, in general, of how the virtue (and vice) terms are to be correctly applied.

Here we come to an interesting defence of the v-rules, often criticized as being too difficult to apply for the agent who lacks moral wisdom.[4] The defence relies on an (insufficiently acknowledged) insight of Aristotle's—namely that moral knowledge, unlike mathematical knowledge, cannot be acquired merely by attending lectures and is not characteristically to be found in people too young to have much experience of life.[5] Now *if* right action were determined by rules that any clever adolescent could apply correctly, how could this be so? Why are there not moral whiz-kids, the way there are mathematical (or quasi-mathematical) whiz-kids? But if the rules that determine right action are, like the v-rules, very difficult to apply correctly, involving, for instance, a grasp of the *sort* of truth that one does people no kindness by concealing, the explanation is readily at hand. Clever adolescents do not, in general, have a good grasp of that sort of thing.[6] And *of course* I have to say 'the sort of truth that ...' and 'that sort of thing', relying on my readers' knowledgeable uptake. For if I could define either sort, then, once again, clever adolescents could acquire moral wisdom from textbooks.

So far, I have described one strategy available to virtue ethics for coping with the 'conflict problem', a strategy that consists in arguing that the conflict is merely apparent, and can be resolved. According to one—only one of many—versions of 'the doctrine of the unity of the virtues', this is the only possible strategy (and ultimately successful), but this is not a claim I want to defend. One general reason is that I still do not know what I think about 'the unity of the virtues' (all those different versions!); a more particular, albeit related, reason is that, even if I were (somehow) sure that the requirements of the particular virtues could never conflict, I suspect that I would still believe in the possibility of moral dilemmas. I have been talking so far as though examples of putative dilemmas and examples of putative conflict between the requirements of different virtues (or deontologists' rules) coincided. But it may seem to many, as it does to me, that there are certain (putative) dilemmas which can only be described in terms of (putative) conflict with much artifice and loss of relevant detail.

Let us, therefore, consider the problem of moral dilemmas without bothering about whether they can be described in the simple terms of a conflict between the requirements of two virtues (or two deontologists' rules). Most of us, it may be supposed, have our own favoured example(s), either real or imaginary, of the case (or cases) where we see the decision about whether to do A or B as a very grave matter, have thought a great deal about what can be said for and against doing A, and doing B, and have still not managed to reach a conclusion which we think is the right one. How, if at all, does virtue ethics direct us to think about such cases?

4. Dilemmas and Normative Theory

...The [question] I want to focus on here is the issue of whether a normative ethics should provide a decision procedure which enables us to resolve all moral dilemmas....

Let us return to V1—'An action is right iff it is what a virtuous agent would characteristically do in the circumstances.' This makes it clear that if two people disagree about the possibility of irresolvable moral dilemmas, their disagreement will manifest itself in what they say about the virtue of agents. So let us suppose that two candidates for being virtuous are each faced with their own case of the same dilemma. (I do not want to defend the view that each situation is unique in such a way that nothing would count as two agents being in the same circumstances and faced with the same dilemma.) And, after much thought, one does A and the other does B.

Now, those who believe that there cannot be irresolvable dilemmas (of the sort described) can say that, in the particular case, at least one agent, say the one who did A, thereby, showed themselves to be lacking in virtue, perhaps in that practical wisdom which is an essential aspect of each of the 'non-intellectual' virtues....

But those who believe that there are, or may be, irresolvable dilemmas can suppose that both agents are not merely candidates for being, but actually are, virtuous agents. For to believe in such dilemmas is to believe in cases in which even the perfect practical wisdom that the most idealized virtuous agent has does not direct her to do, say, A rather than B. And then the fact that these virtuous agents acted differently, despite being in the same circumstances, *determines* the fact that there is no answer to the question 'What is *the* right thing to do in these circumstances?' For if it is true both that *a* virtuous agent would do A, and that *a* virtuous agent would do B (as it is, since, *ex hypothesi*, one did do A and the other B), then both A and B are, in the circumstances, right, according to V1.

The acceptance of this should not be taken as a counsel of despair, nor as an excuse for moral irresponsibility. It does not license coin-tossing when one is faced with a putative dilemma, for the moral choices we find most difficult do not come to us conveniently labelled as 'resolvable' or 'irresolvable'. I was careful to specify that the two candidates for being virtuous agents acted only 'after much thought'. It will always be necessary to think very hard before accepting the idea that a particular moral decision does not have one right issue, and, even on the rare occasions on which she eventually reached the conclusion that this is such a case, would the virtuous agent toss a coin? Of course not.

No doubt someone will say, 'Well, if she really thinks the dilemma is irresolvable, why not, according to virtue ethics?', and the answer must, I think, be *ad hominem*. If their conception of the virtuous agent—of someone with the character traits of justice, honesty, compassion, kindness, loyalty, wisdom, etc.—really is of someone who would resort to coin-tossing when confronted with what she believed to be an irresolvable dilemma, then that is the bizarre conception they bring to virtue ethics, and they must, presumably, think that there is nothing morally irresponsible or light-minded about coin-tossing in such cases. So they should not want virtue ethics to explain 'why not'. But if their conception of the virtuous agent does not admit of her acting thus—if they think such coin-tossing would be irresponsible, or light-minded, or indeed simply insane—then they have no need to ask the question. My question was, 'Would the virtuous agent toss a coin?'; they agree that of course she would not. Why not? Because it would be irresponsible, or light-minded, or the height of folly.

The acceptance of the possibility of irresolvable dilemmas within virtue ethics (by those of us who do accept it) should not be seen in itself as conceding much to 'pluralism'. If I say that I can imagine a case in which two virtuous agents are faced with a dilemma, and one does A while the other does B, I am not saying that I am imagining a case in which the two virtuous agents each think that what the other does is wrong (vicious, contrary to virtue) because they have radically different views about what is required by a certain virtue, or about whether a certain character trait is a vice, or about whether something is to be greatly valued or of little importance. I am imagining a case in which my two virtuous agents have the same 'moral views' about everything, up to and including the view that, in this particular case, neither decision is *the* right one, and hence neither is wrong. Each recognizes the propriety of the other's reason for doing what she did—say, 'To avoid *that* evil', 'To secure *this* good'—for her recognition of the fact that this is as good a moral reason as her own (say, 'To avoid *this* evil', 'To secure *that* good') is what forced each to accept the idea that the dilemma was irresolvable in the first place. Though each can give such a reason for what they did (A in one case, B in the other), neither attempts to give 'the moral reason' why they did one *rather than* the other. The 'reason' for or explanation of *that* would be, if available at all, in terms of psychological autobiography ('I decided to sleep on it, and when I woke up I just found myself thinking in terms of doing A', or 'I just felt terrified at the thought of doing A: I'm sure this was totally irrational, but I did, so I did B).[7]

The topic of this chapter has been the view that virtue ethics cannot be a normative rival to utilitarianism and deontology because 'it cannot tell us what we should do'. In defending the existence of normative virtue ethics I have not attempted to argue that it can 'tell us what we should do' in such a way that the difficult business of acting well is made easy for us. I have not only admitted but welcomed the fact that, in some cases, moral wisdom is require if the v-rules are to be applied correctly and apparent dilemmas thereby resolved (or indeed identified, since a choice that may seem quite straightforward to the foolish or wicked may rightly appear difficult, calling for much thought, to the wise). Nor have I attempted to show that virtue ethics is guaranteed to be able to resolve every dilemma. It seems bizarre to insist that a normative ethics must be able to do this prior to forming a reasonable belief that there cannot be irresolvable dilemmas, but those who have formed such a belief may share a normative ethics with those who have different views concerning realism, or the existence of God. A normative ethics, I suggested, should be able to accommodate both views on this question, as virtue ethics does, not model itself mindlessly on scientific theory.

Notes

1. Variations on utilitarianism are not my concern here. I am ignoring rule-utilitarianism, and assuming my reader to be well aware of the fact that different utilitarians may

specify *best consequences* in different ways. See the introduction to A. Sen and B. Williams (eds.), *Utilitarianism and Beyond* (Cambridge, 1982), from which I have (basically) taken the characterization of utilitarianism given here.

2. W. Frankena, *Ethics*, 2nd ed. (Englewood Cliffs, NJ, 1973), 16.

3. P. Foot, *Virtues and Vices* (Oxford, 1978), p. 60, n. 12.

4. This could well be regarded as another version of the criticism discussed earlier, that the v-rules somehow fail to provide action-guidance.

5. *Nicomachean Ethics* (= *NE*) 1142^{a}12–16.

6. In defending the thesis that virtue ethics is a normative *rival* to utilitarianism and deontology, I am not simultaneously aiming to establish the far more ambitious thesis that it beats its rivals hollow. Utilitarians and deontologists may well take the Aristotelian point on board and provide an account, appropriate to their ethics, of why we should not consult whiz-kids about difficult moral decisions.

7. It must be remembered that, *ex hypothesi*, these are things said by virtuous agents about what they did when confronted with an irresolvable dilemma. Of course they would be very irresponsible accounts of why one had done A rather than B in a resolvable case.

A VIRTUE ETHICAL ACCOUNT OF RIGHT ACTION
Christine Swanton

Christine Swanton is professor of philosophy at the University of Auckland and author of Virtue Ethics: A Pluralistic View *(2003). Swanton defends a virtue-based account of right action that features the notion of the "target" of a virtue at its core. After raising objections to competing virtue ethical accounts of right action (including the one defended by Rosalind Hursthouse in the previous selection), Swanton proceeds to develop her "target-centered" account, which involves two central theses: (1) an action is virtuous in a certain respect V if and only if it hits the target of virtue V; (2) and an action is right if and only if it is overall virtuous.*

I. Introduction

It is a common view of virtue ethics that it emphasizes the evaluation of agents and downplays or ignores the evaluation of acts, especially their evaluation as right or wrong. Despite this view, some contemporary proponents of virtue ethics have explicitly offered a virtue ethical criterion of the right, contrasting that criterion with Kantian and consequentialist criteria.[1] I too believe that though the virtues themselves require excellence in affective and motivational states, they can also provide the basis of accounts of rightness of actions, where the criteria for rightness can deploy notions of success extending beyond such agent-centered excellences. They can do this, I shall claim, through the notion of the target or aim of a virtue. This notion can provide a distinctively virtue ethical notion of rightness of actions. In this article I make two basic assumptions:

From "A Virtue Ethical Account of Right Action," *Ethics* 112 (2001). Reprinted by permission of the University of Chicago Press and the author. An updated version of Swanton's article is published as a chapter in *Virtue Ethics: A Pluralistic View* (Oxford: Oxford University Press, 2003).

first, that a virtue ethical search for a virtue ethical criterion of rightness is an appropriate search, and second, since virtue ethics in modern guise is still in its infancy, relatively speaking, more work needs to be done in the exploration of virtue ethical criteria of the right.

I wish to show in particular that a virtue ethics can offer a criterion of rightness that has certain structural similarities with act conseqentialism. These are (i) a criterion of rightness offers an account of success in action not entirely reducible to inner properties of a virtuous agent; (ii) such a criterion allows a virtue ethics to distinguish between rightness of acts and praiseworthiness of acts, wrongness of acts and blameworthiness of acts; and (iii) such a criterion is not tantamount to a decision procedure or a method of guiding actions.

My aim is not to defend the need for a criterion of rightness of this kind in virtue ethics. Rather, I appeal to those who share (as I do) commonly held intuitions of both consequentialists and W. D. Ross that moral goodness and rightness are not the same thing. I aim to show how a virtue ethicist, too often accused of being too "agent-centered," can accommodate such intuitions.

This article offers a virtue ethical criterion of rightness of acts as an alternative to certain other virtue ethical criteria, which are discussed in Section II. Indeed, there are two types of explicit, developed, virtue ethical accounts of right action in modern virtue ethics. One I call a 'qualified agent' account of rightness;[2] the other is motive-centered. In "Virtue Theory and Abortion," Rosalind Hursthouse proposed the following 'qualified agent' account, which has received widespread attention and which has often been thought canonical for a virtue ethical account of rightness: "An act is right if and only if it is what a virtuous agent would do in the circumstances."[3] In a later article, Hursthouse modified the above as follows: "An act is right if and only if it is what a virtuous agent would characteristically (i.e., acting in character) do in the circumstances."[4]

A second kind of virtue ethical account of rightness is proposed in Michael Slote's 'agent-based virtue ethics,' according to which an action is right if and only if it exhibits or expresses a virtuous (admirable) motive, or at least does not exhibit or express a vicious (deplorable) motive.[5]

In this article I propose a third account, whose central theses are (1) an action is virtuous in respect V (e.g., benevolent, generous) if and only if it hits the target of (realizes the end of) virtue V (e.g., benevolence, generosity); (2) an action is right if and only if it is overall virtuous.

In Section II, I consider difficulties in Hursthouse's and Slote's accounts. In Section III, I explain what it is for an act to be virtuous, by explaining what it is to hit the target of (realize the end of) the relevant virtue. In Section IV, I offer an account of what it is for an action to be overall virtuous, and thereby right.

II. Rival Accounts

The following problem arises in Hursthouse's notion of rightness. The rightness of an act is criterially determined by a qualified agent, but how qualified is a virtuous agent? If 'virtue' is a threshold concept, then it is possible that you, I, and our friends are virtuous, but it is also possible (indeed likely) that others are yet more virtuous.

The problem has both a vertical and a horizontal dimension. On the latter dimension, a standardly temperate, courageous, just, generous individual does not have expertise in all areas of endeavor. She may be inexperienced in medicine, or law, or in child rearing. She may therefore lack practical wisdom in those areas. Even though we may call her virtuous *tout court,* she is not a qualified agent in the areas where she lacks practical wisdom. On the vertical dimension, our virtuous agents (you, I, and our friends) are surpassed in temperance, courage, generosity, and justice by greater moral paragons. So even though on a threshold concept of 'virtue', you, I, and our friends are virtuous, we are not as virtuous as we might be, let alone ideally so, and maybe we should defer to our betters in moral decision making.

Hursthouse could resolve the above problem in the following ways. She may assume that 'virtue' is a threshold notion, but where the threshold is set depends on context. For example, in the field of medical ethics not any virtuous agent will be a qualified agent. A medical ethicist, for example, needs to be not merely benevolent, kind, and a respecter of autonomy, but also knowledgeable about medicine or, at the very least, in excellent communication with those who are. She needs to possess the full array of dialogical virtues. Another resolution is to drop the threshold concept of virtue in the definition of rightness. Perhaps 'virtue' is an idealized notion. However, it seems clear that Hursthouse wants actual human agents to be qualified agents. In her later account of rightness, Hursthouse realizes the danger that actual virtuous agents may at times judge and act out of character, so she inserts into the definition a qualification to rule out this possibility.

However, the above resolutions do not completely resolve the problem of whether a virtuous agent is a qualified agent. Actual human agents, no matter how virtuous and wise, are not omniscient. As a result, an important end of a virtue may be something about which there is large-scale ignorance and for which no blame can be attached to individuals or even cultures. To illustrate the point I am making, consider the relatively newly discovered virtue, that of environmental friendliness. As the debates in journals like *Scientific American* show, controversy rages about whether or not environmental friendliness requires various drastic measures to reduce a perceived threat—for example, global warming. The Aristotelian virtuous agent possesses phronesis, but phronesis, with its connotations of fine sensibilities and discriminatory powers, is impotent in the face of massive ignorance of the entire human species. No matter how well motivated and practically wise the virtuous policy maker, if her policies prove environmentally disastrous, one would think, they cannot be regarded as right. Here is another example. Wise, suitably cautious, and benevolent policy makers may decide to severely restrict genetically modified food on the grounds that large-scale ignorance about genetic modification still persists. But it may be that though the caution expresses practical wisdom, it does not exhibit knowledge. For though the possible dangers of genetically modified products of various kinds may not, in fact, be realized, reasonable people in the face of ignorance should guard against such possible dangers. The caution, even if wise, may have the result that important ends of the virtue of benevolence, such as the production of cheaper and more plentiful food, may be missed.

The above problem has a more general manifestation. Any virtuous agent is necessarily limited, and in a variety of ways. Janna Thompson puts the problem this way: "The belief that the right answer to an ethical problem is what the virtuous person judges is right is not compatible with the recognition that ethical judgments of individuals are limited and personal. It would be irrational for us to place our trust in what a single individual, however virtuous, thinks is right."[6]

The problems facing Slote's account are quite different from those facing Hursthouse's. Slote does not aspire to a "qualified agent" account of rightness, and so avoids the above difficulties. Rightness is tied firmly to quality of motive, but this arguably leads to counterintuitive results. A foolish but well-motivated agent may not be blameworthy in her misguided actions, but should we call such actions morally right? Slote deals with this problem in the following way. The well-motivated agent is concerned to determine facts: an agent genuinely desirous of being helpful is concerned that her help reaches its target, in a suitable way.[7] To a reply that such an agent may not be aware of her ignorance, Slote would claim that a motive to help contaminated with intellectual arrogance is not an admirable motive. However, not all ignorance about one's expertise need be so contaminated.[8]

In general, it could be argued that Slote has failed to take account of a distinction between rightness and goodness of action. For W. D. Ross, quality of motive has nothing to do with rightness (although, as will be seen, my own view will not be so stark). Ross claims:

Suppose, for instance, that a man pays a particular debt simply from fear of the legal consequences of not doing so, some people would say he had done what was right, and others would deny this: they would say that no moral value attaches to such an act, and that since 'right' is meant to imply moral value, the act cannot be right. They might generalize and say that no act is right unless it is done from a sense of duty, or if they shrank from so rigorous a doctrine, they might at least say that no act is right unless done from *some* good motive, such as either sense of duty or benevolence.[9]

Ross distinguishes between a right act and a morally good act understood as one which is well motivated. Virtue ethicists are inclined to sidestep or belittle this distinction by speaking of acting well, but this idea does not obliterate, or even downgrade the importance of, the distinction Ross is trying to draw. Unsurprisingly, however, on my view, a virtue ethical employment of the distinction between right act and good act is not going to be quite the same as Ross's. First, on my view, quality of motive can sometimes make a difference to rightness,[10] and second, as Aristotle believes, goodness of motive is not the only inner state of the agent relevant to acting well. Since this article is about rightness and not about acting well generally, I shall not elaborate further on the latter point.

III. A Target-Centered Virtue Ethical Conception of Rightness

The first stage in the presentation of my virtue ethical account of rightness is the provision of an account of a virtuous act (or more precisely an act which is virtuous in respect V).[11] The basis of my account of such an act is Aristotle's distinction between virtuous act and action from (a state of) virtue. On my account, rightness (as opposed to full excellence) of action is tied not to action from virtue but to virtuous act.

Let me first present Aristotle's distinction, before elaborating further on the notion of virtuous act. Aristotle introduces the distinction thus:

A difficulty, however, may be raised as to how we can say that people must perform just actions if they are to become just, and temperate ones if they are to become temperate; because if they do what is just and temperate, they are just and temperate already, in the same way that if they use words or play music correctly they are already literate or musical. But surely this is not true even of the arts. It is possible to put a few words together correctly by accident, or at the prompting of another person; so the agent will only be literate if he does a literate act in a literate way, viz. in virtue of his own literacy. Nor, again, is there an analogy between the arts and the virtues. Works of art have their merit in themselves; so it is enough for them to be turned out with a certain quality of their own. But virtuous acts are not done in a just or temperate way merely because they have a certain quality, but only if the agent also acts in a certain state, viz. (1) if he knows what he is doing, (2) if he chooses it, and chooses it for its own sake, and (3) if he does it from a fixed and permanent disposition.[12]

How can an action be just or temperate if it does not exhibit a just or temperate state? The answer I shall propose is this: an action can be just or temperate if it hits the target of the virtues of justice or temperance, and an action may hit those targets without exhibiting a just or temperate state. According to Robert Audi, one 'dimension' of virtue is "the characteristic targets it aims at."[13] This idea requires explication if it is to be employed in the service of an account of rightness. The task of the remainder of this article is precisely to offer what may be termed a 'target centered' virtue ethical account of rightness.

...

...Let me now explicate the idea of hitting the target of a virtue. To understand the idea of hitting the target of a virtue it is necessary to propose a schematic definition of a virtue:

(V₁): A virtue is a good quality or excellence of character. It is a disposition of acknowledging or responding to items in the field of a virtue in an excellent (or good enough) way.

Three points need to be made about this definition. The qualification 'good enough' is intended to accommodate the possibility that 'virtue', especially in worlds full of evil, catastrophe, neediness, and conflict, is a threshold concept. Second, the definition is intended to be neutral with respect to a variety of virtue theories and virtue ethics. In particular, it entails neither eudaemonistic nor noneudaemonistic virtue ethics. Third, the definition is neutral about the issue of how broadly or how narrowly we should understand the notion of (moral) virtue.

I can now present schematic definitions of an act from virtue and a virtuous act in the light of (V1). First, a definition of action from virtue:

(V₂): An action from *virtue* is an action which displays, expresses, or exhibits all (or a sufficient number of) the excellences comprising virtue in sense (V₁), to a sufficient degree.

In the light of (V_1) also, we can understand what it is to hit the target of a virtue:

(V_3): Hitting the target of a virtue is a form (or forms) of success in the moral acknowledgment of or responsiveness to items in its field or fields, appropriate to the aim of the virtue in a given context.

A virtuous act can now be defined:

(V_4): An act is virtuous (in respect V) if and only if it hits the target of V.

In the remainder of this section, I first elucidate the idea of hitting the target of a virtue, before showing how a virtuous act differs from an action from virtue.

Recall that to hit the target of a virtue is to respond successfully to items in its field according to the aim of a virtue. I need now to discuss this idea further in order to clarify the distinction between virtuous act and action from virtue. What counts as hitting the target of a virtue is relatively easy to grasp when the aim of a virtue is simply to promote the good of individuals and hitting that target is successfully promoting that good. However, this relatively simple paradigm is complicated by several features. I shall discuss five. These are: (1) there are several modes of moral response or acknowledgment appropriate to one kind of item in a virtue's field, so hitting the target of a virtue may involve several modes of moral response; (2) the target of a virtue may be internal to the agent; (3) the target of a virtue may be plural; (4) what counts as the target of a virtue may depend on context; (5) the target of a virtue may be to avoid things. Features 1–5 are discussed in turn.

1. *Hitting the targets of virtue may involve several modes of moral response.*— Given that hitting the target of a virtue is constituted by successful response to items in its field, according to the virtue's aim, I need briefly to explain the ideas of a virtue's field and the types of response to items in it.

The field of a virtue consists of the items which are the sphere of concern of the virtue. These items may be within the agent, for example, the bodily pleasures which are the focus of temperance, or outside the agent, for example, human beings, property, money, honors. They may be situations, for example, the dangerous situations which are the focus of courage; abstract items such as knowledge or beauty; physical objects, such as one's children, friends, sentient beings in general; art works or cultural icons; or the natural objects which are the focus of the environmental virtues.

What are the types of response to items in a virtue's field? That responsiveness to, or acknowledgment of, items in the field of a virtue required by a virtue may take several forms is at least suggested by an investigation of individual virtues. These forms I shall call modes of moral responsiveness or acknowledgment. They include not only promoting or bringing about (benefit or value) but also honoring value (roughly, not dirtying one's hands with respect to a value, e.g., by not being unjust in promoting justice);[14] honoring things such as rules; producing; appreciating; loving; respecting; creating; being receptive or open to; using or handling. One may respect an individual in virtue of her status as an elder or one's boss; promote or enhance value; promote the good of a stranger or friend; appreciate the value of an artwork, nature, or the efforts of a colleague; create a valuable work of art; creatively solve a moral problem; love an individual in ways appropriate to various types of bonds; be open or receptive to situations and individuals; use money, or natural objects.

The modes of moral acknowledgment of items are richly displayed in the virtues. The virtue of justice is primarily concerned with the honoring of rules of justice by adhering to those rules oneself and with respect for the status of individuals. The virtues of connoisseurship are concerned not with the promoting of, for example, art (by giving money to art foundations, say) but with the appreciation of valuable items such as art. Virtues of creativity require more than appreciation. Thrift is a virtue concerned with use of money; temperance, a virtue concerned with handling of and pursuit of pleasure; consideration, politeness, appropriate deference, virtues concerned with respect for others and their status. Many virtues, for example, that of friendship, exhibit many modes of moral acknowledgment. A good friend does not merely promote the good of her friend: she appreciates her friend, respects, and even loves her friend. Caring as a virtue involves receptivity, perhaps love in some sense, and to a large extent promotion of good.

What I shall call the profile of a virtue is that constellation of modes of moral responsiveness which comprise the virtuous disposition. On my view, not only do the virtues exhibit many modes of moral acknowledgment, but a single virtue, such as benevolence, friendship, or justice, may require that we acknowledge items in its field through several different modes. The plurality of modes of moral acknowledgment comprising the profiles of the virtues reflects the complexity of human responsiveness to the world. The virtues, with their complex profiles, recognize that we are beings who are not only agents of change in the attempt to promote good but also agents of change in the attempt to produce and to create. They also recognize that we are not only agents who are active in changing the world by promoting good (often at the expense of causing harm) but also agents who love and respect (often at the expense of maximizing good). And they recognize that we are not only active beings hell-bent on change but also are passive in a sense: in our openness, receptivity to, and appreciation of value and things. Not all ethics is "task-oriented." In short, attention to the profiles of the virtues reminds us of the complexity of our human nature and our modes of moral response. This complexity will feed into the account of rightness.

What counts as success in exhibiting modes of moral responsiveness appropriate to the aim of a virtue is a complex matter, requiring discussion of each mode. Of course, to give a full account of each mode of moral acknowledgment as it is manifested in the profiles of the virtues is a very large undertaking. I cannot, therefore, within the confines of this article provide such an account but shall instead be briefly illustrative in the service of my discussion of rightness.

2. *The targets of some virtues are internal.*—It is granted that the target of many virtues is external, for example, the target of beneficence, efficiency, justice. A just act is one that, for example, conforms to legitimate rules of procedure; an efficient act is timely and poses little cost for a worthwhile gain; a beneficent act successfully

promotes human welfare. We sometimes speak too of a generous act of giving without any knowledge of, or even interest in, the motivation of the donor. The same point applies to wrongness. Consider the action of former Prime Minister Keating of Australia, who ushered the Queen to her place by putting his arm round her waist. Many considered this action wrong—even egregious, even outrageous—because it was disrespectful or impolite. He did not suitably keep his distance (as Kant puts it), and his action was therefore deemed wrong because disrespectful by many, regardless of his motivations. He may have been innocently operating within Australian mores of informality and egalitarianism, or he may have been striking another blow for turning Australia into a republic by subtly undermining the Queen's prestige or mystique.

However, the supposition that the target of all virtue is external to the agent or is only external to the agent is false. Though the target of some virtues is external or is external in many contexts, the target of others seems to be entirely internal, for example, determination or (mental) strength. The target of the former virtue is trying hard in a sustained way, and that target may be reached even if the agent fails rather consistently in her endeavors. More commonly, the targets of virtues such as caring are a mixture of features within the agent's mind, features of an agent's behavior (her manner) and features external to the agent. Similarly, the target of the virtue of (racial) toleration is not merely external: the pro forma respecting of the rights of people in certain racial groups. We may call an act wrong because racist if the agent, in respecting a right, possessed racist motivation, even if that motivation was not displayed.[15] Notice, however, that the application of terms such as "racist" to acts is controversial, and what is required for an act not to be racist may be more or less demanding, depending on context. Though the full virtue of racial toleration may demand that we morally acknowledge those of other races through a variety of different modes (e.g., respect, promotion of good, appreciation, even a form of love), the conditions under which we call an act racist and thereby wrong may be more or less stringent.

3. *Some targets of virtue are plural.*—According to Robert Audi, the target of courage is the control of fear.[16] However, one may have thought that hitting the target of courage is to successfully handle dangerous or threatening situations. Perhaps then, the target of courage is plural, embracing both regulating certain inner states and handling certain sorts of external situations. On my view, regardless of what one wants to say about courage, there is no requirement for a virtue to have only one target, for a virtue may have more than one field. Even with respect to inner states, Aristotle thought that courage involved the regulation of both fear and confidence.

4. *Contextual variability of targets.*—One might wonder how the target of a virtue is to be determined if the profile of a virtue is complex. Part of the answer to this question lies in the contextual variability of the target of a virtue. What counts as a virtuous act is more heavily contextual than what counts as an action from virtue. In some contexts, for example, where there is considerable need, one may be

said to have performed a generous act if one donates a large amount of money, say, even if that donation is made with bad grace. However, in other contexts, we may deny that an act of giving is generous on the grounds that it was not made in a generous spirit. Here the target of generosity is to alleviate need, in the right way, where "in the right way" makes reference to manner of giving and even motivation. Perhaps the context is a more personal one, and the hostility or ill grace noticed by the recipients. We may at other times mark the fact that the target of a virtue is reached, but only in a minimalist sense, by claiming of an action that it is all right but not right *tout court*. At yet other times we may mark the fact that the target of a virtue has been reached in its richest sense, by claiming of an action not merely that it was right but that it was splendid or admirable because lavish, nobly performed, or performed in the face of great difficulty or cost.

...

5. *Some targets of virtue are to avoid things.*—Talk of "hitting the target" of a virtue suggests that the aim of a virtue is always positive, as opposed to the avoiding of certain things. However, some virtues seem to be targeted at the avoidance of certain states, and to illustrate this, let me briefly discuss the controversial virtue of modesty. There is disagreement about the targets aimed at by the virtue of modesty, and such disagreement may be explained by differing views about what makes a trait a virtue. On a consequentialist view, such as Julia Driver's, a trait is a virtue if and only if its exercise tends to bring about valuable states of affairs.[17] According to Driver, what makes modesty a virtue is that it "stops problems from arising in social situations," such problems as jealousy.[18] It does not follow that this is the aim of the virtue, but a *consequentialist* view of what makes a trait of virtue may drive the account of its aim, and this is the case with Driver's account of modesty.

On Driver's view, the modest agent avoids spending time ranking herself and avoids seeking information to enable her to have a correct estimation of her worth. But so far, modesty as a virtue has not been distinguished from laziness as a vice. Driver goes further. The target of modesty is not just to avoid these things, it is to attain something positive: the ignorance of underestimation. The agent need not directly aim at this but must achieve it if the target of the virtue of modesty is to be reached. And it is the hitting of this target which leads to the valuable social consequences of absence of jealousy.

On my view, by contrast, the target of modesty is simply to avoid certain things. The modest agent avoids certain behaviors, including those mentioned by Driver, but it is also the case (if modesty is to be distinguished from laziness) that the modest agent avoids drawing attention to herself, talking about herself excessively, boasting, and so forth. One might accept all this without buying into the consequentialist justification of modesty as a virtue and without buying into an account of its target as something positive: the ignorance of underestimation. One may reject that account because one may believe (as I do) that what makes modesty a virtue is not its tendency to promote valuable states of affairs (absence of jealousy, etc.) but its being the expression of a valuable or flourishing state of the agent—namely, an agent who has self-love and who does not need therefore to get a sense of self-worth from comparisons with others. Though this is what makes modesty a virtue on my view, that is not its target, however. Its target is simply to avoid certain things—the kinds of behavior mentioned above.

I am now in a position to give an account of the distinction between an action from (a state of) virtue and a virtuous act. The requirements for hitting the target of a virtue and for action from virtue are demanding in different kinds of ways. We have seen already that an act from virtue may fail to hit the target of a virtue if the virtuous agent's practical wisdom does not amount to complete knowledge. So an agent with virtues of benevolence or environmental friendliness may act out of those virtues and miss the targets of those virtues.

Second, for an action to be from a state of virtue, in an ideal case, all modes of acknowledgment of items in a virtue's field, constituting the profile of the relevant virtue, must be displayed. However, this is not always, or even standardly, a requirement for virtuous action, even in an ideal case. Furthermore, for an act to be from a state of virtue (in an ideal case), not only must all modes of moral acknowledgment comprising the virtuous disposition be displayed, they must be displayed in an excellent way, in a way which expresses fine inner states. For Aristotle, this involves fine motivation (including having fine ends), fine emotions, practical wisdom, and the possession of a stable disposition of fine emotions, feelings, and other affective states. But even though the targets of some virtues are internal (at least in part), it is not generally the case that they involve the expression of all those fine inner states required for action from virtue. For example, we might say that obedience (to legitimate authority) as a virtue requires the existence of fine depth states: not only the practical wisdom which distinguishes obedience as a virtue from related vices such as blind obedience but also the absence of deep-seated hostile resentment of all authority figures, whether legitimate or not. However, the end or target of that virtue is compliance with legitimate rules and instructions, not the elimination of such deep-seated feelings.

I now summarize the key differences between action from virtue and virtuous act.

1. An action from a state of virtue may not be a virtuous act because it misses the target of (the relevant) virtue.

2. A virtuous act may fail to be an action from virtue because it fails to manifest aspects of the profile of the relevant virtue at all.

3. A virtuous act may fail to be an action from virtue because it fails to manifest the profile of a virtue in a good enough way, namely, it fails to express sufficiently fine inner states (such as practical wisdom, fine motivation, or dispositions of fine emotion).

4. What counts as a virtuous act is more heavily contextual than what counts as an act from virtue.

We have seen how it is possible to draw a distinction between virtuous act and action from virtue. We have also seen that the drawing of this distinction in particular cases is by no means easy, for there is a constellation of modes of moral acknowledgment constituting the profiles of the virtues, and it is often a matter of context which aspects of the profile of a virtue are salient in determining the target of a virtue. It is time now to discuss rightness as the overall virtuousness of an act.

IV. Overall Virtuousness

According to my account, an act is right if and only if it is overall virtuous. There is much ambiguity about the idea of rightness. In particular, a target centered virtue ethical view is compatible with three possible accounts which are now discussed. I illustrate with the virtue of generosity.

1. An act is right if and only if it is overall virtuous, and that entails that it is the (or a) best action possible in the circumstances. Assuming that no other virtues or vices are involved, we could say that a given act is right insofar as it was the most generous possible. The target of generosity on this view is very stringent: there is no large penumbra such that any act which falls within it is deemed right.

2. An act is right if and only if it is overall virtuous, and that entails that it is good enough even if not the (or a) best action. Here it is assumed that there is much latitude in hitting the target of virtues such as generosity. Right acts range from the truly splendid and admirable to acts which are "all right."

3. An act is right if and only if it is not overall vicious. Here it is assumed that not being overall vicious does not entail being overall virtuous. An act may avoid the vices of meanness or stinginess, for example, without hitting the target of generosity, which demands more than mere avoidance of stingy, mean acts. This may be true even if the target of generosity is interpreted as in 2, rather than 1.

My own target-centered view rules out 3, since rightness is understood in terms of overall virtuousness rather than the avoidance of overall viciousness. This leaves open a choice between 1 and 2. I prefer 1. Provided a distinction is made between rightness and praiseworthiness, and wrongness and blameworthiness, it seems natural to think of the targets of a virtue as best acts (relative to the virtue) though it does not follow that a rational agent should always aim at such a target directly or should necessarily deliberate about reaching that target.

It should also be noted that a belief in 1 is compatible with considerable indeterminacy about what is best. "What is best" may not be a single action but any of a number of actions, none of which are ruled out by reasons that could be defeated.

Finally, the distinction between 1, 2, and 3 raises the issue of what should be called wrong. Should wrong actions include or exclude actions which fall short of rightness in sense 1 but are "all right" in the sense of "good enough"? My own preference is to employ three categories: right actions (conforming to 1), "all right" actions (which exclude actions which are overall vicious), and wrong actions (actions which are overall vicious).

We turn now to the account of rightness as overall virtuousness. Assume that it is determined whether an act is properly describable as hitting the target of an individual virtue, such as justice, generosity, friendship, and so forth. Disagreement about overall virtuousness centers on the resolution of conflict when an action is said to be virtuous in respect V and nonvirtuous or even vicious in respect W. Given that an act can be virtuous in respect V if merely certain aspects of the profile of V are displayed, it is not necessary that such an act is in all ways excellent. It is possible for vice terms to also apply. Actions, for example, can be both just and weak, or just and malicious, or friendly and unjust, or self-protective and nonbeneficent, or independent and unkind, or cruel and environmentally sound, or assertive and hurtful, or efficient and uncaring. Of course, it is possible for an action to be right (overall) simply because it is friendly, or generous.

How is overall virtuousness determined? Like Jonathan Dancy, I wish to highlight the holism of right making features of action.[19] Dancy subscribes to a form of particularism according to which "the behaviour of a reason (or of a consideration which serves as a reason) in a new case cannot be predicted from its behaviour elsewhere.[20] The point is this. We cannot claim that certain features always contribute positively (or negatively) to the overall virtuousness of an act, even if those kinds of feature characteristically contribute positively (or negatively).

. . .

Let us now see how virtue-based reasons function holistically in the assessment of actions as overall virtuous. Say that we have a bunch of virtues, such as kindness, generosity, frankness, tactfulness, assertiveness, justice. Remember that for an action to be described as virtuous (insofar as it is frank, tactful, kind, generous, just, etc.), it has to hit the target of the relevant virtue, but it does not characteristically have to display all the excellences which would make it an act from the relevant virtuous state. Indeed, the agent who performs a tactful action on an occasion may not possess the virtue of tact at all. It is possible even for such terms as 'tactful' and 'kind', which normally contribute positively to the rightness of actions, to contribute neutrally or even negatively on occasion. I want now to show how this can be possible, using two illustrations.

Consider an act which hits the target of the virtue of kindness. We are at a conference where a stranger looks lonely. It turns out he is a person from overseas with a poor command of English and cannot participate in the scintillating and sophisticated discussion on moral theory. Our agent Tim performs a kind act, namely, going to talk to the stranger. However, let us look at further features of this situation. Tim is exceptionally keen to participate in the discussion but leaves in order to talk to the stranger who could have made more effort to amuse himself in other ways and whose hangdog expression is expressive of a rather weak, spoiled approach to life. The conversation with the stranger is difficult, and Tim does not enjoy it. Furthermore, Tim is always doing this kind of thing, sacrificing his interests in the performance of such kind acts. He has resolved to be more self-protective and strong, and encourage others to do their share of burdensome tasks. But he consistently fails to abide by the resolution. In this context, the kindness of the act contributes negatively to the overall virtuousness of the act.

The second example concerns intrafamilial justice. I have been training my children not to be obsessive about justice or fairness, particularly in an intrafamily context and where the stakes are not high. I want them to be more caring, magnanimous, generous. Despite my personal tendencies to be overly concerned with justice, I resolve to drive the lesson home at the next opportunity. An opportunity soon arises. A family tradition of "fair shares" requires that the person making the division has last choice. There is a cake to be cut. I allow my older son to cut the cake. I notice that he has cut carelessly, but in a state of unawareness takes the biggest piece. The target of (procedural) justice has not been reached. My younger son, apparently unnoticing and uncaring, looks delightedly at the smaller piece that he has been left with. Instead of praising my younger son, I make my older son swap pieces telling him that the division, and his action in going first, having cut, is unjust. My intervention is just, but in the circumstances that is a wrong-making feature of the situation. The justice of the intervention is in this context expressive of the obsessive, weak quality of my behavior.

My point in the above examples is that the virtuousness of an act in a given respect (e.g., its friendliness, justice, kindness) can be wrong making (i.e., can contribute negatively to the rightness of an act). My point is not that the virtuousness of an act is not characteristically right making. Indeed, if the virtuousness of acts were not characteristically right making, we could not subsume features under virtue concepts.

V. Objections

A number of objections to my target-centered virtue ethical notion of rightness might be raised. The first objection is that virtuousness (or viciousness) may not feature at all in the list of right making properties. In the claim "it's wrong because it is distasteful," it may be thought that 'distasteful' is not a vice term.[21] In reply one should note the following. It should first be determined how properties such as being distasteful are to be understood as relevant to rightness. The notion of distastefulness, for example, needs to be unpacked. One would need to say, for example, "it is distasteful because indecent." Ideally, the vice term 'indecent' needs itself to be further unpacked into such notions as 'manipulative', 'dishonest', 'disrespectful', 'lacking integrity'.

Another example is "it's right to stop considering this problem because there isn't enough time." It may be supposed that "because there is not enough time" is a right-making property not involving virtue. However, to know the impact of "lack of time" on rightness, we need to see how it affects virtues and vices. The sense that there is no time may reflect laziness. Or it may involve self-indulgence or lack of temperance. Perhaps we are wanting to rush off to a party. On the other hand, the reason may implicate the virtues of courage, self-protection, or parental virtue. Virtues such as these need to operate in the face of a pressuring administration which thinks that we have limitless capacities to cope with stress or no families to go back to.

Second, it may be objected that my account of rightness is too agent centered. Rightness, it may be claimed, has nothing to do with an agent's motives or reasons but has entirely to do with success in the external realm. However, my target-centered virtue ethical view (by comparison with some virtue ethical and Kantian views) does accommodate this consequentialist intuition about rightness. My problem with consequentialism is that it has too narrow a conception of modes of moral acknowledgment or response that are relevant to rightness. Once the plurality of modes of moral response is accepted, it can be appreciated that the target of some virtues, such as caring, can include the internal.

...

Another objection to my account of rightness is this: if the claim that an act is virtuous in respect V is the claim that the act falls under a virtue term 'V', then, it may be argued, the idea of rightness does not track the truth but merely culturally dependent beliefs. For virtue terms reflect our culturally determined and possibly false beliefs about virtue.

Notice, however, that to say that an act is virtuous in respect V if and only if it hits the target of V is not quite the same as saying that an act is virtuous in respect V if and only if it falls under a virtue-term 'V'. This is so for two reasons. First, some virtue terms refer to states which only approximate to virtue. Take for example 'honest'. We are happy to say that 'honest' is a virtue term, but 'honesty' is arguably not an accurate description of a virtue. Honesty is a disposition to tell the truth, or at least a disposition to not lie. We do not describe an act of evasiveness or an act of telling a lie as honest acts. Yet such acts may hit the target of a virtue—namely, a virtue of a correct disposition with respect to the field of divulging information. Certainly, this disposition involves being a respecter of truth and is normally manifested in honest acts, but arguably practical wisdom in this area does not always mandate honest acts. Furthermore, some of our virtue terms may not refer even to states which approximate virtues, and a correct theory of virtue may demonstrate this. Nietzsche's "revaluation of values," for example, called into question pity as a virtue and (egalitarian conceptions of) justice as a virtue, on the assumption that 'justice' refers to egalitarian propensities expressive of resentment. Second, as Aristotle remarks, not all virtues have names. The fact that our language is insufficiently rich to capture all forms of virtue does not tell against (V_4).

. . .

Finally, it is sometimes claimed that since virtue ethical accounts of rightness are not rule-based, they lack resources for resolving moral dilemmas. In fact virtue ethics has more resources for determining overall rightness of acts in dilemmatic situations than may be appreciated.

The question is whether it is possible that an agent cannot do something which is virtuous overall and therefore right, when faced with alternatives, all of which are extremely repugnant. The richness of virtue and vice vocabulary allows us to admit the possibility of right action, even in such cases. For virtue-based act evaluations allow us to think of "actions" as embracing demeanor, motivation, processes of deliberation and thought, reactions and attitudes. We can describe demeanor, motivation, thought processes, and reactions as callous, arrogant, or light minded, or as anguished. We can describe them as strong, or decisive, or courageous; or as cowardly, feeble, pathetic, vacillating. We can describe them as dignified or weak.[22] In short, the choice of a repugnant option can be understood as right (virtuous overall) when we take account of the full nature of the action, including the way it was done. In *Sophie's Choice* for example, it is possible that Sophie acted virtuously overall.[23] One might argue that she acted virtuously because she acted as a good mother in that situation. Or (someone may argue) in such a tragic situation, Sophie had to rise above the normal traits of goodness in mothers, and virtuous action required a certain coolness and deliberateness. One might in that case say her choice was not overall virtuous because it failed to display virtuous calmness and strength in the process of choice. This kind of question (of how a good mother would react) cannot be answered from within the resources of the philosopher. For a start, research on the behavior of mothers required to make life and death decisions for their children, in different kinds of contexts of scarcity and evil, would be required.

Finally, the idea that virtue ethics is not rule-based should not be misunderstood. On my account, the determination of rightness is partly a matter of publicly accessible rules, rather than the essentially private deliberations and intuitions of a virtuous agent. For rightness depends on the applicability of terms like 'caring', 'efficient', 'kind', 'friendly' and their applicability is rule-governed. But I do want to express an important caveat here. The correct applicability of virtue concepts in any sophisticated context is not a matter of the application of relatively perspicuous rules. When, for example, I praise an act as right because strong, or right because caring, or wrong because weak or uncaring, ensuing controversy may precipitate entire accounts of the concepts of strength, weakness, and caring. And good accounts will extend into terrain well beyond the expertise of the analytic philosopher.

Notes

I wish to thank Marcia Baron, Jonathan Dancy, Vanya Kovach, Walter Sinnott-Armstrong, Linda Zagzebski, and especially Rosalind Hursthouse for helpful comments; and also the audiences of a symposium at the Pacific Division of the American Philosophical Association, March 1998; the Australasian Association of Philosophy conference, Brisbane, July 2000; a philosophy colloquium at Oklahoma University, Norman, October 2000; and the New Zealand Division Philosophy Conference, Wellington, December 2000, at which I presented earlier versions of this article. I am also very grateful to the editors and reviewers of *Ethics* for their useful criticisms.

1. Most self-consciously, Rosalind Hursthouse in *On Virtue Ethics* (Oxford: Oxford University Press, 2000).
2. I thank Linda Zagzebski for this terminological suggestion.
3. Rosalind Hursthouse, "Virtue Theory and Abortion," *Philosophy & Public Affairs* 20 (1991): 223–46.
4. Rosalind Hursthouse, "Normative Virtue Ethics," in *How Should One Live? Essays in the Philosophy of Virtue*, ed. Roger Crisp (Oxford: Clarendon Press, 1996).
5. Michael Slote, "Agent-Based Virtue Ethics," in *Midwest Studies in Philosophy*, vol. 20, *Moral Concepts*, ed. Peter A. French, Theodore E. Uehling, Jr., and Howard K Wettstein (Notre Dame, Ind.: University of Notre Dame Press, 1996), pp. 85–101.
6. Janna Thompson, *Discourse and Knowledge: A Defence of Collectivist Ethics* (London: Routledge, 1988), p. 79.
7. Slote, "Agent-Based Virtue Ethics," and "The Justice of Caring," *Social Philosophy and Policy* 15 (1998): 171–95.
8. For further criticism of Slote's failure to incorporate notions of successful relation to the external world in his criterion of rightness, see Julia Driver, "Monkeying with Motives: Agent-Basing Virtue Ethics," *Utilitas* 7 (1995): 281–88.
9. W. D. Ross, *The Right and the Good* (Oxford: Oxford University Press, 1930), p. 2.
10. Indeed, I agree with Stephen Sverdlik's view that sometimes the quality of a motive can change the deontic status of an action from right to wrong. See his "Motive and Rightness," *Ethics* 106 (1996): 527–49.
11. Henceforth, 'virtuous act'.
12. Aristotle, *Nicomachean Ethics*, trans. J. A. K. Thomson (New York: Penguin Classics, 1976), p. 97, sec. 2 iv.

13. Robert Audi, *Moral Knowledge and Ethical Character* (New York: Oxford University Press, 1997), p. 180.

14. The idea of honoring value is introduced by Philip Pettit in "Consequentialism," in *A Companion to Ethics,* ed. Peter Singer (Oxford: Blackwell, 1991), pp. 230–40.

15. See Sverdlik.

16. Audi, p. 180.

17. Julia Driver, "The Virtues and Human Nature," in *How Should One Live? Essays in the Philosophy of Virtue,* ed. Roger Crisp (Oxford: Clarendon Press, 1996), pp. 111–29.

18. Julia Driver, "Modesty and Ignorance," *Ethics* 109 (1999): 827–34, p. 828.

19. Jonathan Dancy, *Moral Reasons* (Oxford: Blackwell, 1993).

20. Ibid., p. 60. Dancy does not mean to imply that we cannot make reasonable estimates on the basis of characteristic (as opposed to universal) properties of things, e.g., the characteristic badness of pain.

21. An example suggested to me in conversation by Jonathan Dancy.

22. For more on a virtue ethical understanding of "irresolvable dilemmas," see Hursthouse, *On Virtue Ethics.*

23. William Styron, *Sophie's Choice* (New York: Random House, 1979).

VIRTUE AND RIGHT
Robert N. Johnson

Robert N. Johnson is associate professor of philosophy at the University of Missouri, Columbia, and author of many articles in ethics. Johnson is critical of virtue ethical accounts of right action. Against the version of virtue ethics defended by Rosalind Hursthouse according to which right action is characterized in terms of what a virtuous agent (acting in character) would do, Johnson describes cases involving moral self-improvement in which what an agent ought to do would be uncharacteristic of a virtuous agent. Such cases, then, purport to show that right action cannot be explained in terms of what it would be characteristic for a virtuous agent to do, contrary to Hursthouse's view. Johnson then explains how these same problems arise for Christine Swanton's "target-centered" version of virtue ethics.

I s the morally right action the action that a virtuous person would perform? Many may think so, even that this is an uninteresting truism. The only question of consequence may seem to be whether moral philosophy does best to begin by theorizing about right actions or about the virtues. But the claim that right actions are those of a virtuous person is so far from being an uninteresting truism as to be utterly false, or so I believe. In particular, I think that it is inconsistent with the commonsense idea that we ought to become better people. If I am right, then not only is this claim about virtue and right action false, but any theory that relies on it to construct a virtue-oriented theory of right action will be unable to explain moral distinctions we regularly make regarding behavior appropriate for those who could better themselves.

From Robert N. Johnson, "Virtue and Right," *Ethics* 113 (2003): 810–834. Reprinted by permission of the University of Chicago Press and the author.

In what follows, I begin by discussing views espoused by Rosalind Hursthouse and John McDowell.[1] I describe in broad strokes the account of right action that views such as theirs offer, views based on the idea that right actions are those characteristic of the virtuous. I then give three examples of right conduct that would be utterly uncharacteristic of the virtuous and argue that this shows that the account should be rejected.... I end by discussing the account of right action offered by Christine Swanton[2]...[which] fail[s] to take into account the fact that we should morally improve ourselves.

Although I argue that [this] virtue-oriented account of right action in [its] current form [is] unsatisfactory, I stop short of claiming that no virtue-oriented account can work. As Swanton points out, "virtue ethics in modern guise is still in its infancy,"[3] and so it would be premature to conclude that the whole project must founder on the problems I discuss. My message is in fact broader than this: however an ethical theory combines its account of the virtues with its account of right action, it must make room for a genuine moral obligation to improve your character and to act in other ways that are appropriate only because you could be a better person than you are.

Why construct a theory of right action out of a conception of virtue in the first place? After all, some who have favored a virtue-oriented approach to ethics have resisted doing so on the grounds that moral philosophy does better simply to stick with virtue concepts. Such concepts are too "thick," they think, and virtuous behavior too "uncodifiable" to make such a project profitable. But even so there is also a strong interest among many other virtue ethicists in developing an account of right action that is a genuine alternative to standard deontological and consequentialist theories.[4]...Hursthouse's view... is the most fully developed account of this kind. In summary, her view is:

V: An action A is right for S in circumstances C if and only if a completely virtuous agent would characteristically A in C.[5]

...

What V offers us is the means to construct a theory of right conduct out of a conception of virtue and, thus, a desirable alternative to the standard utilitarian and deontological theories. One begins by developing an account of the virtues independently of a conception of right action. One then conceives of right actions as first and foremost virtuous actions, or actions characteristic of an agent possessed of the virtues. Moreover, one represents moral facts as being necessarily practical, in that they are themselves at bottom constituted (even if not wholly or even primarily) by dispositions to action. Finally, these facts are themselves constituted by ordinary natural facts, for instance, psychological states of a human being. Let us now turn to the plight of the less than fully virtuous.

II

A

Consider this person: he is mendacious, lying even about unimportant things such as the films he has seen or books he has read. The lies cause little harm, nor are they meant to, and he doesn't lie merely to extricate himself out of difficult situations. That is, lying is not a means by which he expresses other vices such as malice or cowardice. Rather, it is a habit operating more or less independently of other vices, engendered by an insufficient appreciation of the value of truthfulness. Indeed, he occasionally rationalizes lies to himself as a "social lubricant" to keep those around him happy, or perhaps as a way of "getting things done." Even so, often lies pass his lips almost without his notice.

Suppose now that a friend calls him on the carpet for lying, and as a result he decides that he must change. He must change, he thinks, not to avoid further embarrassment or because it would be "the best policy," but because it is after all rotten to behave in the way that he has. His task will not be simple. Lying has become habitual and has permeated his attitudes so deeply that no "decision to do better" can by itself change him. What sorts of steps might he take?

Some virtue theorists, including Aristotle himself, tend to be pessimistic about the possibility of character change.[6] But I will assume for the sake of argument that this person's character is within the range of those that are changeable. With enough effort and persistence he could change. Given this, there are many things he might do, but again for the sake of argument, suppose he does the following: he begins by resolving to tell the truth and exerting his will in that direction. But he soon caves in to temptation, given that lying is so easy and "natural." So after consulting with a therapist he decides to begin writing down lies that he tells, no matter how insignificant, to become more aware of his habits and to keep track of improvements. Further, whenever he is aware of temptations to lie, he tries to develop a concrete idea of what would happen if he told the truth. Who, exactly, is protected by my lie? Why do I want to protect her? Who, exactly, would be dismayed if my lie were discovered? He also tries to remind himself that people often do not react badly to the person who tells them unpleasant truths. Finally, since he suspects that his mendacity may have something to do with low self-esteem, he engages in activities that enhance it.

The above sketches a range of kinds of actions: "self-monitoring" and keeping track of one's progress toward becoming a better person, trying to change one's thinking about one's situation and the consequences of one's actions, enhancing one's self-esteem, and so on. Common sense would regard these kinds of things as what he morally ought to do in circumstances such as these, at least insofar as they will improve his character. Yet all are utterly uncharacteristic of completely virtuous agents. Note well: it makes absolutely no difference whether these particular things are what this particular person ought to do. Perhaps there are better ways to improve himself. But surely he ought to do things of this sort, things over and above simply "deciding to tell the truth from now on." This would in large part consist in behavior that a completely virtuous person would not characteristically engage in. That he ought to do such things goes directly counter to the claim that right conduct is conduct characteristic of the virtuous.

Or so it seems. For some might think that Aristotle has a ready reply: it is by performing the very same actions that a virtuous person would characteristically perform, he argued, that we cultivate the virtues in ourselves and, hence, better ourselves. In summary, the argument would be:

1. Virtues are states of character arising in the novice "neither by nor against nature."[7]

2. "A state results from similar activities."[8] Therefore,

3. "We become just by doing just actions, temperate by doing temperate actions, brave by doing brave actions."[9]

The first premise ensures that virtues are the sorts of things—states—that can and must be cultivated in a person over time, ideally from childhood. The second is a general claim about how states develop, so, applying this to the virtues qua states, the virtues arise from performing similar actions. Hence, it is by acting as the virtuous agent acts that we develop the states that the virtuous agent possesses. It may seem to follow, then, that there are no actions other than simply acting as the virtuous person himself acts that develop the virtues, and so no set of right actions uncharacteristic of the virtuous.

But this does not follow. The argument only implies that acting as the virtuous agent acts does produce them. But, even were this true, V is vulnerable *merely if there are actions producing the virtues that one morally ought to perform, and these actions are not part of the characteristic behavior of virtuous persons.* I think that common sense recognizes many such actions.

...

There is … a second problem with V that I want to discuss. Even if there were no obligation to improve ourselves morally, there certainly is one at least to take account of: our shortcomings when we act. In particular, the novice at virtue ought to perform self-controlling acts. But these acts will again be utterly uncharacteristic of the virtuous, who, by contrast, are temperate.... My next example develops these points.

B

Imagine someone whose moral upbringing was inadequate, but after many years of lessons learned the hard way manages to keep his life in moral order. To put it simply, he struggles to do what he should. Most who know him would agree that his character lacks grace. His day-to-day life reveals a pattern of behavior characteristic of a person who is at war with malicious and cowardly desires. One might even think less of him for this, but we would find it difficult to fault his actions themselves. He never intentionally harms others, nor does he evade worthy tasks or causes because of risks to himself.

He is able to overcome his unsavory desires not because of any special inner surge of motivation that he is able to muster at the instant duty calls. Far from it. Since he knows that he will fail if he leaves it to a fortuitous surge, he plans ahead when he foresees potential struggles. He thinks of ways to avoid behaving badly for those times when he thinks that temptation may strike, such as alternative ways of phrasing difficult truths that he must tell others. Further, he tries to create social support for behaving well. For example, when he decided to help move his elderly mother across town one weekend, he didn't simply make a private inner "decision to help." He told friends ahead of time that he was going to do it, that he had the free time to help, that he thought he ought to help, that he wouldn't be around to go out with them, and so on.

He also tries to be specific about exactly what he should do, so that he knows exactly what counts as movement toward fulfilling obligations. Instead of meditating on puerile aphorisms such as "I ought to help others in need" and then leaving it to impulse to determine what he will do and when and where he will do it, he brainstorms about exactly where, how, when, and to what he can contribute. Indeed, he does this in part to avoid projects that will require him to rely too heavily on the weaknesses in his character. This of course helps to create the very pattern of action that reveals that character to those who know him. No doubt, he would like to be more "natural" and admires those who are. And although he often must work around his weaknesses, he tries hard not to pander to them. He just has come to know himself well enough to know that, at least in certain situations, he is not at his best.

In order to perform a just, brave, kind, or otherwise virtuous action, a nonvirtuous person will have to control himself in many ways. Indeed, if he didn't have to, he would already possess the kind of psychological makeup that would make virtuous action second nature. In other words, he would not be a novice at all. Notice in particular that a novice's virtuous action is typically embedded in a web of self-controlling actions. That makes the virtuous action itself shrink in significance when viewed within this web. By contrast, a temperate person performs none of these acts of self-control. The virtuous act for the virtuous is not embedded in any such web. Again, how one ought to behave is here utterly uncharacteristic of the virtuous.

The virtuous would also characteristically behave in a fair number of further ways, and not in others, that are at odds with how it seems most of us should. Consider, for instance, this final example.

C

Imagine a person who lacks moral sensitivity in some area. The problem is not that he faces more than his share of dilemmas. Nor is it that he is so malicious that he runs roughshod over the interests, rights, and feelings of others with pleasure. Rather, he faces most of the same sorts of moral situations as the rest of us and means well, but, perhaps because of his upbringing or culture, he has a moral blind spot.[10] Suppose, however, that he possesses enough self-awareness to know this. Therefore, when he has reason to doubt his perception he asks for guidance from a friend who is in these respects more virtuous and whose vision is in these respects unhindered. The friend, by contrast, is able to see precisely what these situations call for. The person I want you to imagine, however, first tries to rely on his own judgment and is determined not to be dependent on his friend's perception. Indeed, given enough time, he might be able to work out many of the problems for himself. But many situations call for immediate steps. In these situations, he surely ought to ask for guidance.

The virtuous are supposed to appreciate fully their circumstances—who has been harmed and how, what is called for in terms of a response, and so on. Indeed, some even think of moral education as itself mostly a matter of perceptual improvement. In any case, the less sensitive ought to try to improve their moral perception and in particular seek guidance from the more sensitive. Hence, what one morally ought to do—seek guidance and try to improve one's perceptual capacities—is again utterly uncharacteristic of the completely virtuous....

IV

To my mind, the view represented by V is the most natural way of grounding a theory of right action in a prior conception of virtue. But there are [other] ways of doing it [including] Swanton's "target-centered" view....

...Swanton argues that a virtuous act is an act that hits the characteristic target of a virtue.[11]

A right act, however, is not merely an act that is virtuous with respect to a single virtue, but an act that is overall virtuous, which she takes to be the best act possible in the circumstances, taking the other virtues into account in a holistic way.[12] Like Hursthouse's view,...an action can be virtuous without being brought about by an admirable motive, disposition, or trait. This is because an action can hit the characteristic target of a virtue without being brought about by that virtue. Indeed, the actions characteristically brought about by a given virtue may not characteristically hit the target of that virtue. Hence, a just action is an action that hits the target of justice, even if not motivated by the virtue of justice, and some traits, such as environmental friendliness, may well not produce environmentally friendly actions, given that they may well not characteristically hit their own targets.[13]

Now whether Swanton's view can account for the areas of moral behavior I have discussed above depends entirely on (a) whether there is a virtue—or are virtues—whose target is self-improvement, self-control and like strategies, and gaining advice from those better placed and, equally important, (b) whether hitting the characteristic target of this virtue is consistent with overall virtue, where this is understood as the best act possible. Now a depends on Swanton's general theory of virtue—that is, her theory of what puts something on the list of virtues. It may be possible to develop or extend a virtue theory in such a way that it includes traits with the relevant targets. But it is not obvious how. One might, for instance, argue from a general theory of what makes a trait a virtue to the conclusion that there is a special virtue whose target is self-improvement. Alternatively, one might argue that the target of some of the virtues on the standard list—courage, fortitude, benevolence, and so on—already encompasses the various right actions appropriate for the various nonoptimal conditions I discuss above.

On the Aristotelian theory of how traits get on the list of virtues, however, the target of any virtue does not include the acquisition of those self-same virtues, self-control, or the improvement in one's moral perception, nor could there be a special virtue of self-improvement. For virtues are excellences on this view, in the sense that seeing well is the excellence of the eyes and cutting well is the excellence of the knife.[14] That is, they are traits that constitute well-functioning in a human being. But self-improvement, self-control, advice seeking, and so on, do not themselves constitute well-functioning in a human being.

On the other hand, even if one successfully argues for a virtue of self-improvement, a regress problem might remain: for suppose there were a virtue whose aim is the acquisition of the other virtues. Surely one ought to acquire such a virtue if one lacks it. And if one ought, then we need a further virtue whose aim is to acquire the virtue of self-improvement, a virtue the lack of which would, moreover, in turn make it right to acquire it, and so on.

Suppose, however, that we could establish that self-improvement, and so on, are virtues. There would still be the further point to establish, *b,* that an act that hits the target of this trait could also be overall virtuous in Swanton's sense. I have already argued that at least self-improving actions, and perhaps other actions of the sort I've discussed above, can be morally excellent even if not the actions of a completely virtuous character. In that sense, they can be morally "best." But I suspect that while they can be morally excellent, they may often at the same time not be "morally best" in Swanton's sense—that is, if she means the act that hits the target of whichever standard virtue (i.e., the virtues excluding any traits defined by the counterexamples given above) it would be best to hit, determined holistically. Suppose that self-improvement is a virtue and suppose that there is an action available that hits the target of this virtue. There is at least a prima facie case that hitting the target of that virtue will be incompatible with being an overall virtuous act. For if I am right, then in a given circumstance, hitting the target of self-improvement and other such traits would be one sort of act, while hitting the target of whichever standard virtue it would be best to hit would be quite a different sort of act. Again, to return to Aristotle's advice, if those who lack virtue should take the lesser of evils, drag themselves off in the direction contrary to their natural tendencies, and beware of pleasure and its sources, it is difficult to see how such an act could also hit the target of whichever standard virtue it would be best to hit.

V

If self-improvement and other actions of the sort that I have discussed are genuinely morally right, then no ethical theory should accept V, whether to generate a theory of right action out of an account of the virtues or, indeed, to generate a theory of the virtues out of a theory of right action. Further, any alternative virtue-oriented theory of right action must take account of the fact that many actions are morally required of us only because we fail to possess the character traits or motives that we ought to possess. But, again, my argument leaves untouched the position of virtue ethicists who make no claim to offer any conception of right action. It also leaves a large question about how to combine right and virtue in such a way that it takes seriously the thought that we have a moral obligation to better ourselves. But I must leave that question for another time.

Notes

Earlier versions of this article were improved by comments from audiences at Humboldt-Universität zu Berlin department of philosophy; Münster Universität department of philosophy; the Royal Institute of Philosophy "Conference on the Emotions" in Manchester, England; the British Society for Ethical Theory 2001 Conference in

Glasgow; the University of California, Davis, department of philosophy; and Simpson College. Discussions early on with Rosalind Hursthouse were exceedingly helpful. Others whose input improved earlier drafts are Katja Vogt, Marcus Willaschek, Ralph Schumacher, Richard Dean, Karen Jones, Michael Smith, John Pauley, Jon Kvanvig, Jack Kultgen, Robert Audi, Meg Klein-Trull, Peter Markie, Eric Wiland, Stephen Darwall, an anonymous referee, and the associate editors of *Ethics*. Work on this article was made possible by a research leave in the academic year 2000–2001 funded by a grant from the University of Missouri Research Board.

1.   Rosalind Hursthouse, *On Virtue Ethics* (Oxford: Oxford University Press, 2000), p. 28; John McDowell, "Virtue and Reason," in *Virtue Ethics,* ed. Roger Crisp and Michael Slote (Oxford: Oxford University Press, 1997), pp. 141–62. The seeds of the kind of theory that they espouse can be found (naturally) in Aristotle: "Actions are called just or temperate when they are the sort that a just or temperate person would [characteristically] do" (*Nicomachean Ethics,* trans. T. R. Irwin [Indianapolis: Hackett, 1993], 1105b6).

2.   Michael Slote, "Agent-Based Virtue Ethics," in Crisp and Slote, eds., pp. 239–62, pp. 239–41, and *Morals from Motives* (New York: Oxford University Press, 2001), pp. 3–37; Christine Swanton, "A Virtue Ethical Account of Right Action," *Ethics* 112 (2001): 32–52.

3.   Swanton, p. 32.

4.   Most prominently Hursthouse, *On Virtue Ethics;* Slote, "Agent-Based Virtue Ethics"; and Swanton. For an alternative view, see Edmund Pincoffs, *Quandaries and Virtues* (Lawrence: University Press of Kansas, 1986).

5.   Hursthouse, *On Virtue Ethics,* p. 28, and her "Virtue Ethics and Abortion," in Crisp and Slote, eds., pp. 217–38.

6.   See Aristotle, *Nicomachean Ethics,* 1114a1–1114b25.

7.   Aristotle, *Nicomachean Ethics,* 1103a25.

8.   Ibid., 1103b21.

9.   Ibid., 1103b1.

10.   I myself am not convinced that there is such a thing as "moral blindness." I take it that virtue-oriented views, however, are committed to its existence. In any case, racism, sexism, or homophobia might be good candidates for moral blindness.

11.   Swanton, p. 39.

12.   Ibid., pp. 46–49.

13.   Hence, I take it, the target of a given virtue may not be the outcome that it characteristically produces.

14.   Aristotle, *Nicomachean Ethics,* 1106a15–1106b5.

CHAPTER 8

The Ethics of Care

MORAL ORIENTATION AND MORAL DEVELOPMENT
Carol Gilligan

Carol Gilligan is professor of education at the Harvard Graduate School of Education. Her books include In a Different Voice *(1982), and* Mapping the Moral Domain *coedited with Janie Victoria Ward, Jill McLean Taylor, and Betty Bardige (1988). In her 1982 book, Gilligan cited empirical evidence for the hypothesis that there is, in addition to the so-called* justice *perspective, a moral perspective focused on* care. *Her work has been the basis for the articulation of an ethic of care by such theorists as Nel Noddings (see the second selection). In this article, Gilligan compares the justice and care perspectives. The justice perspective finds articulation in the moral theories of Aquinas, Mill, and Kant, in which morality is conceived to be a matter of autonomous individuals settling conflicting claims against standards of equal and impartial respect. By contrast, the care perspective conceives morality to be a matter of creating and maintaining relationships in which agents respond to the perceived needs of others.*

The difference of focus between justice and care approaches to morality is illustrated in connection with abortion decisions and other situations calling for a moral response. The existence of two moral perspectives raises various questions that Gilligan considers about whether people tend, in their moral thinking, to focus on those concerns associated with one moral perspective at the expense of those concerns associated with the alternative perspective, and the extent to which this focus might be related to gender.

When one looks at an ambiguous figure like the drawing that can be seen as a young or old woman, or the image of the vase and the faces, one initially sees it in

From Carol Gilligan, *Women and Moral Theory,* edited by Eva F. Kittay and Diana T. Meyers (Lanham, MD: Rowman & Littlefield Publishers, 1987). Reprinted by permission of the publisher.

only one way. Yet even after seeing it in both ways, one way often seems more compelling. This phenomenon reflects the laws of perceptual organization that favor certain modes of visual grouping. But it also suggests a tendency to view reality as unequivocal and thus to argue that there is one right or better way of seeing.

The experiments of the Gestalt psychologists on perceptual organization provide a series of demonstrations that the same proximal pattern can be organized in different ways so that, for example, the same figure can be seen as a square or a diamond, depending on its orientation in relation to a surrounding frame. Subsequent studies show that the context influencing which of two possible organizations will be chosen may depend not only on the features of the array presented but also on the perceiver's past experience or expectation. Thus, a bird-watcher and a rabbit-keeper are likely to see the duck-rabbit figure in different ways; yet this difference does not imply that one way is better or a higher form of perceptual organization. It does, however, call attention to the fact that the rabbit-keeper, perceiving the rabbit, may not see the ambiguity of the figure until someone points out that it can also be seen as a duck.

This paper presents a similar phenomenon with respect to moral judgment, describing two moral perspectives that organize thinking in different ways. The analogy to ambiguous figure perception arises from the observation that although people are aware of both perspectives, they tend to adopt one or the other in defining and resolving moral conflict. Since moral judgments organize thinking about choice in difficult situations, the adoption of a single perspective may facilitate clarity of decision. But the wish for clarity may also imply a compelling human need for resolution or closure, especially in the face of decisions that give rise to discomfort or unease. Thus, the search for clarity in seeing may blend with a search for justification, encouraging the position that there is one right or better way to think about moral problems. This question, which has been the subject of intense theological and philosophical debate, becomes of interest to the psychologist not only because of its psychological dimensions—the tendency to focus on one perspective and the wish for justification—but also because one moral perspective currently dominates psychological thinking and is embedded in the most widely used measure for assessing the maturity of moral reasoning.

In describing an alternative standpoint, I will reconstruct the account of moral development around two moral perspectives, grounded in different dimensions of relationship that give rise to moral concern. The justice perspective, often equated with moral reasoning, is recast as one way of seeing moral problems and a care perspective is brought forward as an alternate vision or frame. The distinction between justice and care as alternative perspectives or moral orientations is based empirically on the observation that a shift in the focus of attention from concerns about justice to concerns about care changes the definition of what constitutes a moral problem, and leads the same situation to be seen in different ways. Theoretically, the distinction between justice and care cuts across the familiar divisions between thinking and feeling, egoism and altruism, theoretical and practical reasoning. It calls attention to the fact that all human relationships, public and private, can be characterized *both* in terms of equality and in terms of attachment, and that both inequality and detachment constitute grounds for moral concern. Since everyone is vulnerable both to oppression and to abandonment, two moral visions—one of justice and one of care—recur in human experience. The moral injunctions, not to act unfairly toward others, and not to turn away from someone in need, capture these different concerns.

The conception of the moral domain as comprised of at least two moral orientations raises new questions about observed differences in moral judgment and the disagreements to which they give rise. Key to this revision is the distinction between differences in developmental stage (more or less adequate positions within a single orientation) and differences in orientation (alternative perspectives or frameworks). The findings reported in this paper of an association between moral orientation and gender speak directly to the continuing controversy over sex differences in moral reasoning. In doing so, however, they also offer an empirical explanation for why previous thinking about moral development has been organized largely within the justice framework.

My research on moral orientation derives from an observation made in the course of studying the relationship between moral judgment and action. Two studies, one of college students describing their experiences of moral conflict and choice, and one of pregnant women who were considering abortion, shifted the focus of attention from the ways people reason about hypothetical dilemmas to the ways people construct moral conflicts and choices in their lives. This change in approach made it possible to see what experiences people define in moral terms, and to explore the relationship between the understanding of moral problems and the reasoning strategies used and the actions taken in attempting to resolve them. In this context, I observed that women, especially when speaking about their own experiences of moral conflict and choice, often define moral problems in a way that eludes the categories of moral theory and is at odds with the assumptions that shape psychological thinking about morality and about the self.[1] This discovery, that a different voice often guides the moral judgments and the actions of women, called attention to a major design problem in previous moral judgment research: namely, the use of all-male samples as the empirical basis for theory construction.

The selection of an all-male sample as the basis for generalizations that are applied to both males and females is logically inconsistent. As a research strategy, the decision to begin with a single-sex sample is inherently problematic, since the categories of analysis will tend to be defined on the basis of the initial data gathered and subsequent studies will tend to be restricted to these categories. Piaget's work on the moral judgment of the child illustrates these problems since he defined the evolution of children's consciousness and practice of rules on the basis of his study of boys playing marbles, and then undertook a study of girls to assess the generality of his findings. Observing a series of differences both in the structure of girls' games and "in the actual mentality of little girls," he deemed these differences not of interest because "it was not this contrast which we proposed to study." Girls, Piaget found, "rather complicated our interrogatory in relation to what we know about boys," since the changes in their conception of rules, although following the same sequence observed in boys, did not stand in the same relation to social experience. Nevertheless, he concluded that "in spite of these differences in the structure of the game and apparently in the players' mentality, we find the same process at work as in the evolution of the game of marbles."[2]

Thus, girls were of interest insofar as they were similar to boys and confirmed the generality of Piaget's findings. The differences noted, which included greater tolerance, a greater tendency toward innovation in solving conflicts, a greater willingness to make exceptions to rules, and a lesser concern with legal elaboration, were not seen as germane to "the psychology of rules," and therefore were regarded as insignificant for the study of children's moral judgment. Given the confusion that currently surrounds the discussion of sex differences in moral judgment, it is important to emphasize that the differences observed by Piaget did not pertain to girls' understanding of rules *per se* or to the development of the idea of justice in their thinking, but rather to the way girls structured their games and their approach to conflict resolution—that is, to their use rather than their understanding of the logic of rules and justice.

Kohlberg, in his research on moral development, did not encounter these problems since he equated moral development with the development of justice reasoning and initially used an all-male sample as the basis for theory and test construction. In response to his critics, Kohlberg has recently modified his claims, renaming his test a measure of "justice reasoning" rather than of "moral maturity" and acknowledging the presence of a care perspective in people's moral thinking.[3] But the widespread use of Kohlberg's measure as a measure of moral development together with his own continuing tendency to equate justice reasoning with moral judgment leaves the problem of orientation differences unsolved. More specifically, Kohlberg's efforts to assimilate thinking about care to the six-stage developmental sequence he derived and refined by analyzing changes in justice reasoning (relying centrally on his all-male longitudinal sample) underscores the continuing importance of the points raised in this paper concerning (1) the distinction between differences in developmental stage within a single orientation and differences in orientation, and (2) the fact that the moral thinking of girls and women was not examined in establishing either the meaning or the measurement of moral judgment within contemporary psychology.

An analysis of the language and logic of men's and women's moral reasoning about a range of hypothetical and real dilemmas underlies the distinction elaborated in this paper between a justice and a care perspective. The empirical association of care reasoning with women suggests that discrepancies observed between moral theory and the moral judgments of girls and women may reflect a shift in perspective, a change in moral orientation. Like the figure-ground shift in ambiguous figure perception, justice and care as moral perspectives are not opposites or mirror-images of one another, with justice uncaring and care unjust. Instead, these perspectives denote different ways of organizing the basic elements of moral judgment: self, others, and the relationship between them. With the shift in perspective from justice to care, the organizing dimension of relationship changes from inequality/equality to attachment/detachment, reorganizing thoughts, feelings, and language so that words connoting relationship like "dependence" or "responsibility" or even moral terms such as "fairness" and "care" take on different meanings.

To organize relationships in terms of attachment rather than in terms of equality changes the way human connection is imagined, so that the images or metaphors of relationship shift from hierarchy or balance to network or web. In addition, each organizing framework leads to a different way of imagining the self as a moral agent.

From a justice perspective, the self as moral agent stands as the figure against a ground of social relationships, judging the conflicting claims of self and others against a standard of equality or equal respect (the Categorical Imperative, the Golden Rule). From a care perspective, the relationship becomes the figure, defining self and others. Within the context of relationship, the self as a moral agent perceives and responds to the perception of need. The shift in moral perspective is manifest by a change in the moral question from "What is just?" to "How to respond?"

For example, adolescents asked to describe a moral dilemma often speak about peer or family pressure in which case the moral question becomes how to maintain moral principles or standards and resist the influence of one's parents or friends. "I have a right to my religious opinions," one teenager explains, referring to a religious difference with his parents. Yet, he adds, "I respect their views." The same dilemma, however, is also construed by adolescents as a problem of attachment, in which case the moral question becomes: how to respond both to oneself and to one's friends or one's parents, how to maintain or strengthen connection in the face of differences in belief. "I understand their fear of my new religious ideas," one teenager explains, referring to her religious disagreement with her parents, "but they really ought to listen to me and try to understand my beliefs."

One can see these two statements as two versions of essentially the same thing. Both teenagers present self-justifying arguments about religious disagreement; both address the claims of self and of others in a way that honors both. Yet each frames the problem in different terms, and the use of moral language points to different concerns. The first speaker casts the problem in terms of individual rights that must be respected within the relationship. In other words, the figure of the considering is the self looking on the disagreeing selves in relationship, and the aim is to get the other selves to acknowledge the right to disagree. In the case of the second speaker, figure and ground shift. The relationship becomes the figure of the considering, and relationships are seen to require listening and efforts at understanding differences in belief. Rather than the right to disagree, the speaker focuses on caring to hear and to be heard. Attention shifts from the grounds for agreement (rights and respect) to the grounds for understanding (listening and speaking, hearing and being heard). This shift is marked by a change in moral language from the stating of separate claims to rights and respect ("I have a right ... I respect their views.") to the activities of relationship—the injunction to listen and try to understand ("I understand ... they ought to listen ... and try to understand."). The metaphor of moral voice itself carries the terms of the care perspective and reveals how the language chosen for moral theory is not orientation neutral.

The language of the public abortion debate, for example, reveals a justice perspective. Whether the abortion dilemma is cast as a conflict of rights or in terms of respect for human life, the claims of the fetus and of the pregnant woman are balanced or placed in opposition. The morality of abortion decisions thus construed hinges on the scholastic or metaphysical question as to whether the fetus is a life or a person, and whether its claims take precedence over those of the pregnant woman. Framed as a problem of care, the dilemma posed by abortion shifts. The connection between the fetus and the pregnant woman becomes the focus of attention and the question becomes whether it is responsible or irresponsible, caring or careless, to extend or to end this connection. In this construction, the abortion dilemma arises because there is no way not to act, and no way of acting that does not alter the connection between self and others. To ask what actions constitute care or are more caring directs attention to the parameters of connection and the costs of detachment, which become subjects of moral concern.

Finally, two medical students, each reporting a decision not to turn in someone who has violated the school rules against drinking, cast their decision in different terms. One student constructs the decision as an act of mercy, a decision to override justice in light of the fact that the violator has shown "the proper degrees of contrition." In addition, this student raises the question as to whether or not the alcohol policy is just, i.e., whether the school has the right to prohibit drinking. The other student explains the decision not to turn in a proctor who was drinking on the basis that turning him in is not a good way to respond to this problem, since it would dissolve the relationship between them and thus cut off an avenue for help. In addition, this student raises the question as to whether the proctor sees his drinking as a problem.

This example points to an important distinction, between care as understood or construed within a justice framework and care as a framework or a perspective on moral decision. Within a justice construction, care becomes the mercy that tempers justice; or connotes the special obligations or supererogatory duties that arise in personal relationships; or signifies altruism freely chosen—a decision to modulate the strict demands of justice by considering equity or showing forgiveness; or characterizes a choice to sacrifice the claims of the self. All of these interpretations of care leave the basic assumptions of a justice framework intact: the division between the self and others, the logic of reciprocity or equal respect.

As a moral perspective, care is less well elaborated, and there is no ready vocabulary in moral theory to describe its terms. As a framework for moral decision, care is grounded in the assumption that self and other are interdependent, an assumption reflected in a view of action as responsive and, therefore, as arising in relationship rather than the view of action as emanating from within the self and, therefore, "self governed." Seen as responsive, the self is by definition connected to others, responding to perceptions, interpreting events, and governed by the organizing tendencies of human interaction and human language. Within this framework, detachment, whether from self or from others, is morally problematic, since it breeds moral blindness or indifference—a failure to discern or respond to need. The question of what responses constitute care and what responses lead to hurt draws attention to the fact that one's own terms may differ from those of others. Justice in this context becomes understood as respect for people in their own terms.

The medical student's decision not to turn in the proctor for drinking reflects a judgment that turning him in is not the best way to respond to the drinking problem, itself seen as a sign of detachment or lack of concern. Caring for the proctor thus raises the question of what actions are most likely to ameliorate this problem, a decision that leads to the question of what are the proctor's terms.

The shift in organizing perspective here is marked by the fact that the first student does not consider the terms of the other as potentially different but instead assumes one set of terms. Thus the student alone becomes the arbiter of what is *the* proper degree of contrition. The second student, in turn, does not attend to the question of whether the alcohol policy itself is just or fair. Thus each student discusses an aspect of the problem that the other does not mention.

These examples are intended to illustrate two cross-cutting perspectives that do not negate one another but focus attention on different dimensions of the situation, creating a sense of ambiguity around the question of what is the problem to be solved. Systematic research on moral orientation as a dimension of moral judgment and action initially addressed three questions: (1) Do people articulate concerns about justice and concerns about care in discussing a moral dilemma? (2) Do people tend to focus their attention on one set of concerns and minimally represent the other? and (3) Is there an association between moral orientation and gender? Evidence from studies that included a common set of questions about actual experiences of moral conflict and matched samples of males and females provides affirmative answers to all three questions.

When asked to describe a moral conflict they had faced, 55 out of 80 (69 percent) educationally advantaged North American adolescents and adults raised considerations of both justice and care. Two-thirds (54 out of 80) however, focused their attention on one set of concerns, with focus defined as 75 percent or more of the considerations raised pertaining either to justice or to care. Thus the person who presented, say, two care considerations in discussing a moral conflict was more likely to give a third, fourth, and fifth than to balance care and justice concerns—a finding consonant with the assumption that justice and care constitute organizing frameworks for moral decision. The men and the women involved in this study (high school students, college students, medical students, and adult professionals) were equally likely to demonstrate the focus phenomenon (two-thirds of both sexes fell into the outlying focus categories). There were, however, sex differences in the direction of focus. With one exception, all of the men who focused, focused on justice. The women divided, with roughly one third focusing on justice and one third on care.[4]

These findings clarify the different voice phenomenon and its implications for moral theory and for women. First, it is notable that if women were eliminated from the research sample, care focus in moral reasoning would virtually disappear. Although care focus was by no means characteristic of all women, it was almost exclusively a female phenomenon in this sample of educationally advantaged North Americans. Second, the fact that the women were advantaged means that the focus on care cannot readily be attributed to educational deficit or occupational disadvantage—the explanation Kohlberg and others have given for findings of lower levels of justice reasoning in women.[5] Instead, the focus on care in women's moral reasoning draws attention to the limitations of a justice-focused moral theory and highlights the presence of care concerns in the moral thinking of both women and men. In this light, the Care/Justice group composed of one third of the women and one third of the men becomes of particular interest, pointing to the need for further research that attends to the way people organize justice and care in relation to one another—whether, for example, people alternate perspectives, like seeing the rabbit and the duck in the rabbit-duck figure, or integrate the two perspectives in a way that resolves or sustains ambiguity.

Third, if the moral domain is comprised of at least two moral orientations, the focus phenomenon suggests that people have a tendency to lose sight of one moral perspective in arriving at moral decision—a liability equally shared by both sexes. The present findings further suggest that men and women tend to lose sight of different perspectives. The most striking result is the virtual absence of care-focused reasoning among men. Since the men raised concerns about care in discussing moral conflicts and thus presented care concerns as morally relevant, a question is why they did not elaborate these concerns to a greater extent.

In summary, it becomes clear why attention to women's moral thinking led to the identification of a different voice and raised questions about the place of justice and care within a comprehensive moral theory. It also is clear how the selection of an all-male sample for research on moral judgment fosters an equation of morality with justice, providing little data discrepant with this view. In the present study, data discrepant with a justice-focused moral theory comes from a third of the women. Previously, such women were seen as having a problem understanding "morality." Yet these women may also be seen as exposing the problem in a justice-focused moral theory. This may explain the decision of researchers to exclude girls and women at the initial stage of moral judgment research. If one begins with the premise that "all morality consists in respect for rules,"[6] or "virtue is one and its name is justice,"[7] then women are likely to appear problematic within moral theory. If one begins with women's moral judgments, the problem becomes how to construct a theory that encompasses care as a focus of moral attention rather than as a subsidiary moral concern.

Notes

1. C. Gilligan, "In a Different Voice: Women's Conceptions of Self and of Morality." *Harvard Educational Review* (1982) 47: 481–517; *In a Different Voice: Psychological Theory and Women's Development* (Cambridge, Mass.: Harvard University Press, 1977).
2. J. Piaget, *The Moral Judgment of the Child* (New York, N.Y.: The Free Press Paperback Edition, 1965), pp. 76–84.
3. L. Kohlberg, *The Psychology of Moral Development* (San Francisco, Calif.: Harper & Row, 1984).
4. C. Gilligan and J. Attanucci, *Two Moral Orientations* (Harvard University, unpublished manuscript, 1986).
5. L. Kohlberg, *Moral Development;* also L. Walker, "Sex Differences in the Development of Moral Reasoning: A Critical Review of the Literature," *Child Development* (1984) 55(3): 677–691.
6. J. Piaget, *Moral Judgment.*
7. L. Kohlberg, *Moral Development.*

AN ETHIC OF CARING
Nel Noddings

Nel Noddings is professor of philosophy and education at Teachers College, Columbia University, and Lee L. Jacks professor of child education emerita at Stanford University. Her books include Caring: A Feminine Approach to Ethics and Moral Education *(1984),* Awakening the Inner Eye: Intuition and Education *(with Paul J. Shore, 1984), and* Women and Evil *(1989). According to Noddings, moral obligation is rooted in a sentiment or feeling of "natural care"—a sentiment typified by the care a woman has for her infant. Natural caring together with one's reflective evaluation of the caring relation as good gives rise to a second, specifically moral, sentiment experienced as an obligation to respond to anyone in need with whom we come into contact in concrete, real-life situations. Furthermore, two criteria govern our obligation to care: (1) the existence of or potential for presently being related to another, and (2) the potentiality of the cared-for individual to reciprocate the care of the one caring. After examining the implications of this ethic of care for the case of making an abortion decision, Noddings considers the role of judgments of right and wrong in an ethic of care and what sort of justification one can provide for such an ethic.*

From Natural to Ethical Caring

David Hume long ago contended that morality is founded upon and rooted in feeling—that the "final sentence" on matters of morality, "that which renders morality an active virtue—... this final sentence depends on some internal sense or feeling, which nature has made universal in the whole species. For what else can have an influence of this nature?"[1]

What is the nature of this feeling that is "universal in the whole species"? I want to suggest that morality as an "active virtue" requires two feelings and not just one. The first is the sentiment of natural caring. There can be no ethical sentiment without the initial, enabling sentiment. In situations where we act on behalf of the other because we want to do so, we are acting in accord with natural caring. A mother's caretaking efforts in behalf of her child are not usually considered ethical but natural. Even maternal animals take care of their offspring, and we do not credit them with ethical behavior.

The second sentiment occurs in response to a remembrance of the first. Nietzsche speaks of love and memory in the context of Christian love and Eros, but what he says may safely be taken out of context to illustrate the point I wish to make here:

There is something so ambiguous and suggestive about the word love, something that speaks to memory and to hope, that even the lowest intelligence and the coldest heart still feel something of the glimmer of this word. The cleverest woman and the most vulgar man recall the relatively least selfish moments of their whole life, even if Eros has taken only a low flight with them.[2]

This memory of our own best moments of caring and being cared for sweeps over us as a feeling—as an "I must"—in response to the plight of the other and our conflicting desire to serve our own interests. There is a transfer of feeling analogous to transfer of learning. In the intellectual domain, when I read a certain kind of mathematical puzzle, I may react by thinking, "That is like the sailors, monkey, and coconuts problem," and then, "Diophantine equations" or "modulo arithmetic" or "congruences." Similarly, when I encounter an other and feel the natural pang conflicted with my own desires— "I must—I do not want to"—I recognize the feeling and remember what has followed it in my own best moments. I have a picture of those moments in which I was cared for and in which I cared, and I may reach toward this memory and guide my conduct by it if I wish to do so.

Recognizing that ethical caring requires an effort that is not needed in natural caring does not commit us to a position that elevates ethical caring over natural caring. Kant has identified the ethical with that which is done out of duty and not out of love, and that distinction in itself seems right. But an ethic built on caring strives to maintain the caring attitude and is thus dependent upon, and not superior to, natural caring. The source of ethical behavior is, then, in twin sentiments— one that feels directly for the other and one that feels for and with that best self, who may accept and sustain the initial feeling rather than reject it.

We shall discuss the ethical ideal, that vision of best self, in some depth. When we commit ourselves to obey the "I must" even at its weakest and most fleeting, we are under the guidance of this ideal. It is not just any picture. Rather, it is our best picture of ourselves caring and being cared for. It may even be colored by acquaintance with one superior to us in caring, but, as I shall describe it, it is both constrained and attainable. It is limited by what we have already done and by what we are capable of, and it does not idealize the impossible so that we may escape into ideal abstraction....

Obligation

There are moments for all of us when we care quite naturally. We just do care; no ethical effort is required. "Want" and "ought" are indistinguishable in such cases. I want to do what I or others might judge I ought to do. But can there be a "demand" to care? There can be, surely, no demand for the initial impulse that arises as a feeling, an inner voice saying "I must do something," in response to the need of the cared-for. This impulse arises naturally, at least occasionally, in the absence of pathology. We cannot demand that one have this impulse, but we shrink from one who never has it. One who never feels the pain of another, who never confesses the internal "I must" that is so familiar to most of us, is beyond our normal pattern of understanding. Her case is pathological, and we avoid her.

But even if I feel the initial "I must," I may reject it. I may reject it instantaneously by shifting from "I must do something" to "Something must be done," and removing myself from the set of possible agents through whom the action should be accomplished. I may reject it because I feel that there is nothing I can do. If I do either of these things without reflection upon what I might do in behalf of the cared-for, then I do not care. Caring requires me to respond to the initial impulse with an act of commitment: I commit myself either to overt action on behalf of the cared-for (I pick up my crying infant) or I commit myself to thinking about what I might do. In the latter case, as we have seen, I may or may not act overtly in behalf of the cared-for. I may abstain from action if I believe that anything I might do would tend to work against the best interests of the cared-for. But the test of my caring is not wholly in how things turn out; the primary test lies in an examination of what I considered, how fully I received the other, and whether the free pursuit of his projects is partly a result of the completion of my caring in him.

But am I obliged to embrace the "I must"? In this form, the question is a bit odd, for the "I must" carries obligation with it. It comes to us as obligation. But accepting and affirming the "I must" are different from feeling it, and these responses are what I am pointing to when I ask whether I am obliged to embrace the "I must." The question nags at us; it is a question that has been asked, in a variety of forms, over and over by moralists and moral theorists. Usually, the question arises as part of the broader question of justification. We ask something of the sort: Why must I (or should I) do what suggests itself to reason as "right" or as needing to be done for the sake of some other? We might prefer to supplement "reason" with "and/or feeling." This question is, of course, not the only thorny question in moral theory, but it is one that has plagued theorists who see clearly that there is no way to derive an "I ought" statement from a chain of facts. I may agree readily that "things would be better"—that is, that a certain state of affairs commonly agreed to be desirable might be attained—if a certain chain of events were to take place. But there is still nothing in this intellectual chain that can produce the "I ought." I may choose to remain an observer on the scene.

Now I am suggesting that the "I must" arises directly and prior to consideration of what it is that I might do. The initial feeling is the "I must." When it comes to me indistinguishable from the "I want," I proceed easily as one-caring. But often it comes to me conflicted. It may be barely perceptible, and it may be followed almost simultaneously by resistance. When someone asks me to get something for him or merely asks for my attention, the "I must" may be lost in a clamor of resistance. Now a second sentiment is required if I am to behave as one-caring. I care about myself as one-caring and, although I do not care naturally for the person who has asked something of me—at least not at this moment—I feel the genuine moral sentiment, the "I ought," that sensibility to which I have committed myself.

Let me try to make plausible my contention that the moral imperative arises directly. And, of course, I must try to explain how caring and what I am calling the "moral imperative" are related. When my infant cries in the night, I not only feel that I must do something but I want to do something. Because I love this child, because I am bonded to him, I want to remove his pain as I would want to remove my own. The "I must" is not a dutiful imperative but one that accompanies the "I want." If I were tied to a chair, for example, and wanted desperately to get free, I might say as I struggled, "I must do something; I must get out of these bonds." But this "must" is not yet the moral or ethical "ought." It is a "must" born of desire.

The most intimate situations of caring are, thus, natural. I do not feel that taking care of my own child is "moral" but, rather, natural. A woman who allows her own child to die of neglect is often considered sick rather than immoral; that is, we feel that either she or the situation into which she has been thrust must be pathological. Otherwise, the impulse to respond, to nurture the living infant, is overwhelming. We share the impulse with other creatures in the animal kingdom. Whether we want to consider this response as "instinctive" is problematic, because certain patterns of response may be implied by the term and because suspension of reflective consciousness seems also to be implied (and I am not suggesting that we have no choice), but I have no difficulty in considering it as innate. Indeed, I am claiming that the impulse to act in behalf of the present other is itself innate. It lies latent in each of us, awaiting gradual development in a succession of caring relations. I am suggesting that our inclination toward and interest in morality derives from caring. In caring, we accept the natural impulse to act on behalf of the present other. We are engrossed in the other. We have received him and feel his pain or happiness, but we are not compelled by this impulse. We have a choice; we may accept what we feel, or we may reject it. If we have a strong desire to be moral, we will not reject it, and this strong desire to be moral is derived, reflectively, from the more fundamental and natural desire to be and to remain related. To reject the feeling when it arises is either to be in an internal state of imbalance or to contribute willfully to the diminution of the ethical ideal.

But suppose in a particular case that the "I must" does not arise, or that it whispers faintly and disappears, leaving distrust, repugnance, or hate. Why, then, should I behave morally toward the object of my dislike? Why should I not accept feelings other than those characteristic of caring and, thus, achieve an internal state of balance through hate, anger, or malice?

The answer to this is, I think, that the genuine moral sentiment (our second sentiment) arises from an evaluation of the caring relation as good, as better than, superior to, other forms of relatedness. I feel the moral "I must" when I recognize that my response will either enhance or diminish my ethical ideal. It will serve either to increase or decrease the likelihood of genuine caring. My response affects me as one-caring. In a given situation with someone I am not fond of, I may be able to find all sorts of reasons why I should not respond to his need. I may be too busy. He may be undiscerning. The matter may be, on objective analysis, unimportant. But, before I decide, I must turn away from this analytic chain of thought and back to the concrete situation. Here is this person with this perceived need to which is attached this importance. I must put justification aside temporarily. Shall I respond? How do I feel as a duality about the "I" who will not respond?

I am obliged, then, to accept the initial "I must" when it occurs and even to fetch it out of recalcitrant slumber when it fails to awake spontaneously. The source of my obligation is the value I place on the relatedness of caring. This value itself arises as a product of actual caring and being cared-for and my reflection on the goodness of these concrete caring situations.

Now, what sort of "goodness" is it that attaches to the caring relation? It cannot be a fully moral goodness, for we have already described forms of caring that are natural and require no moral effort. But it cannot be a fully nonmoral goodness either, for it would then join a class of goods many of which are widely separated from the moral good. It is, perhaps, properly described as a "premoral good," one that lies in a region with the moral good and shades over into it. We cannot always decide with certainty whether our caring response is natural or ethical. Indeed, the decision to respond ethically as one-caring may cause the lowering of barriers that previously prevented reception of the other, and natural caring may follow.

I have identified the source of our obligation and have said that we are obligated to accept, and even to call forth, the feeling "I must." But what exactly must I do? Can my obligation be set forth in a list or hierarchy of principles? So far, it seems that I am obligated to maintain an attitude and, thus, to meet the other as one-caring and, at the same time, to increase my own virtue as one-caring. If I am advocating an ethic of virtue, do not all the usual dangers lie in wait: hypocrisy, self-righteousness, withdrawal from the public domain? We shall discuss these dangers as the idea of an ethical ideal is developed more fully.

Let me say here, however, why it seems preferable to place an ethical ideal above principle as a guide to moral action. It has been traditional in moral philosophy to insist that moral principles must be, by their very nature as moral principles, universifiable. If I am obligated to do X under certain conditions, then under sufficiently similar conditions you also are obligated to do X. But the principle of universifiability seems to depend, as Nietzsche pointed out, on a concept of "sameness."[3] In order to accept the principle, we should have to establish that human predicaments exhibit sufficient sameness, and this we cannot do without abstracting away from concrete situations those qualities that seem to reveal the sameness. In doing this, we often lose the very qualities or factors that gave rise to the moral question in the situation. That condition which makes the situation different and thereby induces genuine moral puzzlement cannot be satisfied by the application of principles developed in situations of sameness.

This does not mean that we cannot receive any guidance from an attempt to discover principles that seem to be universifiable. We can, under this sort of plan, arrive at the doctrine of "prima facie duty" described by W. D. Ross.[4] Ross himself, however, admits that this doctrine yields no real guidance for moral conduct in concrete situations. It guides us in abstract moral thinking; it tells us, theoretically, what to do, "all other things being equal." But other things are rarely if ever equal. A and B, struggling with a moral decision, are two different persons with different factual histories, different projects and aspirations, and different ideals. It may indeed be right, morally right, for A to do X and B to do not-X. We may, that is, connect "right" and "wrong" to faithfulness to the ethical ideal. This does not cast us into relativism, because the ideal contains at its heart a component that is universal: Maintenance of the caring relation....

Our obligation is limited and delimited by relation. We are never free, in the human domain, to abandon our preparedness to care; but practically, if we are meeting those in our inner circles adequately as ones-caring and receiving those linked to our inner circles by formal chains of relation, we shall limit the calls upon our obligation quite naturally. We are not obliged to summon the "I must" if there is no possibility of completion in the other. I am not obliged to care for starving children in Africa, because there is no way for this caring to be completed in the other unless I abandon the caring to which I am obligated. I may still choose to do something in the direction of caring, but I am not obliged to do so....

Now, this is very important, and we should try to say clearly what governs our obligation. On the basis of what has been developed so far, there seem to be two criteria: the existence of or potential for present relation, and the dynamic potential for growth in relation, including the potential for increased reciprocity and, perhaps, mutuality. The first criterion establishes an absolute obligation and the second serves to put our obligations into an order of priority.

If the other toward whom we shall act is capable of responding as cared-for and there are no objective conditions that prevent our receiving this response—if, that is, our caring can be completed in the other—then we must meet that other as one-caring. If we do not care naturally, we must call upon our capacity for ethical caring. When we are in relation or when the other has addressed us, we must respond as one-caring. The imperative in relation is categorical. When relation has not yet been established, or when it may properly be refused (when no formal chain or natural circle is present), the imperative is more like that of the hypothetical: I must if I wish to (or am able to) move into relation.

The second criterion asks us to look at the nature of potential relation and, especially, at the capacity of the cared-for to respond. The potential for response in animals, for example, is nearly static; they cannot respond in mutuality, nor can the nature of their response change substantially. But a child's potential for increased response is enormous. If the possibility of relation is dynamic—if the relation may clearly grow with respect to reciprocity—then the possibility and degree of my obligation also grows. If response is imminent, so also is my obligation. This criterion will help us to distinguish between our obligation to members of the nonhuman animal world and, say, the human fetus. We must keep in mind, however, that the second criterion binds us in proportion to the probability of increased response and to the imminence of that response. Relation itself is fundamental in obligation.

I shall give an example of thinking guided by these criteria, but let us pause for a moment and ask what it is we are trying to accomplish. I am working deliberately toward criteria that will preserve our deepest and most tender human feelings. The caring of mother for child, of human adult for human infant, elicits the tenderest feelings in most of us. Indeed, for many women, this feeling of nurturance lies at the very heart of what we assess as good. A philosophical position that has difficulty distinguishing between our obligation to human infants and, say, pigs is in some difficulty straight off. It violates our most deeply cherished feeling about human goodness. This violation does not, of course, make the position logically wrong, but it suggests that especially strong grounds will be needed to support it....

Now, let's consider an example: the problem of abortion. Operating under the guidance of an ethic of caring, we are not likely to find abortion in general either right or wrong. We shall have to inquire into individual cases. An incipient embryo is an information speck—a set of controlling instructions for a future human being. Many of these specks are created and flushed away without their creators' awareness. From the view developed here, the information speck is an information speck; it has no given sanctity. There should be no concern over the waste of "human tissue," since nature herself is wildly prolific, even profligate. The one-caring is concerned not with human tissue but with human consciousness—with pain, delight, hope, fear, entreaty, and response.

But suppose the information speck is mine, and I am aware of it. This child-to-be is the product of love between a man deeply cared-for and me. Will the child have his eyes or mine? His stature or mine? Our joint love of mathematics or his love of mechanics or my love of language? This is not just an information speck; it is endowed with prior love and current knowledge. It is sacred, but I—humbly, not presumptuously—confer sacredness upon it. I cannot, will not destroy it. It is joined to loved others through formal chains of caring. It is linked to the inner circle in a clearly defined way. I might wish that I were not pregnant, but I cannot destroy this known and potentially loved person-to-be. There is already relation albeit indirect and formal. My decision is an ethical one born of natural caring.

But suppose, now, that my beloved child has grown up; it is she who is pregnant and considering abortion. She is not sure of the love between herself and the man. She is miserably worried about her economic and emotional future. I might like to convey sanctity on this information speck; but I am not God—only mother to this suffering cared-for. It is she who is conscious and in pain, and I as one-caring move to relieve the pain. This information speck is an information speck and that is all. There is no formal relation, given the breakdown between husband and wife, and with the embryo, there is no present relation; the possibility of future relation—while not absent, surely—is uncertain. But what of this possibility for growing response? Must we not consider it? We must indeed. As the embryo becomes a fetus and, growing daily, becomes more nearly capable of response as cared-for, our obligation grows from a nagging uncertainty—an "I must if I wish"—to an utter conviction that we must meet this small other as one-caring.

If we try to formalize what has been expressed in the concrete situation described so far, we arrive at a legal approach to abortion very like that of the Supreme Court: abortions should be freely available in the first trimester, subject to medical determination in the second trimester, and banned in the third, when the fetus is viable. A woman under the guidance of our ethic would be likely to recognize the growing possibility of relation; the potential is clearly dynamic. Further, many women recognize the relation as established when the fetus begins to move about. It is not a question of when life begins but of when relation begins.

But what if relation is never established? Suppose the child is born and the mother admits no sense of relatedness. May she commit infanticide? One who asks such questions misinterprets the concept of relatedness that I have been struggling to describe. Since the infant, even the near-natal fetus, is capable of relation—of the sweetest and most unselfconscious reciprocity—one who encounters the infant is obligated to meet it as one-caring. Both parts of this claim are essential; it is not only the child's capability to respond but also the encounter that induces obligation. There must exist the possibility for our caring to be completed in the other. If the mother does not care naturally, then she must summon ethical caring to support her as one-caring. She may not ethically ignore the child's cry to live....

Our ethic of caring—which we might have called a "feminine ethic"—begins to look a bit mean in contrast to the masculine ethics of universal love or universal justice. But universal love is illusion. Under the illusion, some young people retreat to the church to worship that which they cannot actualize; some write lovely poetry extolling universal love; and some, in terrible disillusion, kill to establish the very principles which should have entreated them not to kill. Thus are lost both principles and persons.

Right and Wrong

How are we to make judgments of right and wrong under this ethic? First, it is important to understand that we are not primarily interested in judging but, rather, in heightening moral perception and sensitivity. But "right" and "wrong" can be useful.

Suppose a mother observes her young child pulling the kitten's tail or picking it up by the ears. She may claim, "Oh, no, it is not nice to hurt the kitty," or, "You must not hurt the kitty." Or she may simply say, "Stop. See—you are hurting the kitty," and she may then take the kitten in her own hands and show the child how to handle it. She holds the kitten gently, stroking it, and saying, "See? Ah, ah, kitty, nice kitty...." What the mother is supposing in this interaction is that the realization that his act is hurting the kitten supplemented by the knowledge of how to avoid inflicting hurt, will suffice to change the child's behavior. If she believes this, she has no need for the statement, "It is wrong to hurt the kitty." She is not threatening sanctions but drawing dual attention to a matter of fact (the hurting) and her own commitment (I will not hurt). Beyond this, she is supposing that her child, well-cared-for-himself, does not want to inflict pain....

The one-caring, clearly, applies "right" and "wrong" most confidently to her own decisions. This does not, as we have insisted before, make her a relativist. The caring attitude that lies at the heart of all ethical behavior is universal....

... [I]n general the one-caring evaluates her own acts with respect to how faithfully they conform to what is known and felt through the receptivity of caring. But she also uses "right" and "wrong" instructively and respectfully to refer to the judgments of significant others. If she agrees because the matter at hand can be assessed in light of caring, she adds her personal commitment and example; if she has doubts—because the rule appealed to seems irrelevant or ambiguous in the light of caring—she still acknowledges the judgment but adds her own dissent or demurrer. Her eye is on the ethical development of the cared-for and, as she herself withholds judgment until she has heard the "whole story," she wants the cared-for to encounter others, receive them, and reflect on what he has received. Principles and rules are among the beliefs he will receive, and she wants him to consider these in the light of caring.

But is this all we can say about right and wrong? Is there not a firm foundation in morality for our legal judgments? Surely, we must be allowed to say, for example, that stealing is wrong and is, therefore, properly forbidden by law. Because it is so often wrong—and so easily demonstrated to be wrong—under an ethic of caring, we may accede that such a law has its roots *partly* in morality. We may legally punish one who has stolen, but we may not pass moral judgment on him until we know why he stole. An ethic of caring is likely to be stricter in its judgment, but more supportive and corrective in following up its judgment, than ethics otherwise grounded. For the one-caring, stealing is almost always wrong:

Ms. A talks with her young son. *But, Mother,* the boy pleads, *suppose I want to make you happy and I steal something you want from a big chain store. I haven't hurt anyone, have I? Yes, you have,* responds his mother, and she points to the predicament of the store managers who may be accused of poor stewardship and to the higher prices suffered by their neighbors. *Well, suppose I steal from a rich, rich person? He can replace what I take easily, and...Wait,* says Ms. A. *Is someone suffering? Are you stealing to relieve that suffering, and will you make certain that what you steal is used to relieve it?...But can't I steal to make someone happy?* her son persists. Slowly, patiently, Ms. A explains the position of one-caring. *Each one* who comes under our gaze must be met as one-caring. When I want to please X and I turn toward Y as a means for satisfying my desire to please X, I must now meet Y as one-caring. I do not judge him for being rich—for treasuring what I, perhaps, regard with indifference. I may not cause him pain by taking or destroying what he possesses. *But what if I steal from a bad guy—someone who stole to get what he has?* Ms. A smiles at her young son, struggling to avoid his ethical responsibility: *Unless he is an immediate threat to you or someone else, you must meet him, too, as one-caring.*

The lessons in "right" and "wrong" are hard lessons—not swiftly accomplished by setting up as an objective the learning of some principle. We do not say: It is wrong to steal. Rather, we consider why it was wrong or may be wrong in this case to steal. We do not say: It is wrong to kill. By setting up such a principle, we also imply its exceptions, and then we may too easily act on authorized exceptions. The one-caring wants to consider, and wants her child to consider, the act itself in full context. She will send him into the world skeptical, vulnerable, courageous, disobedient, and tenderly receptive. The "world" may not depend upon him to obey its rules or fulfill its wishes, but you, the individual he encounters, may depend upon him to meet you as one-caring.

The Problem of Justification

... Why should I be committed to not causing pain? Now, clearly, in one sense, I cannot answer this better than we already have. When the "Why?" refers to motivation, we have seen that the one-caring receives the other and acts in the other's behalf as she would for herself; that is, she acts with a similar motive energy. Further, I have claimed that, when natural caring fails, the motive energy in behalf of the other can be summoned out of caring for the ethical self. We have discussed both natural caring and ethical caring. Ethical caring, as I have described it, depends not upon rule or principle but upon the development of an ideal self. It does not depend upon just any ideal of self, but the ideal developed in congruence with one's best remembrance of caring and being cared-for.

So far, in recommending the ethical ideal as a guide to ethical conduct, I have suggested that traditional approaches to the problem of justification are mistaken. When the ethical theorist asks, "Why should I behave thus-and-so?" his question is likely to be aimed at justification rather than motivation and at a logic that resides outside the person. He is asking for reasons of the sort we expect to find in logical demonstration. He may expect us to claim that moral judgments can be tested as claims to facts can be tested, or that moral judgments are derived from divine commandment, or that moral truths are intuitively apprehended. Once started on this line of discussion, we may find ourselves arguing abstractly about the status of relativism and absolutism, egoism and altruism, and a host of other positions that, I shall claim, are largely irrelevant to moral conduct. They are matters of considerable intellectual interest, but they are distractions if our primary interest is in ethical conduct.

Moral statements cannot be justified in the way that statements of fact can be justified. They are not truths. They are derived not from facts or principles but from the caring attitude. Indeed, we might say that moral statements come out of the moral view or attitude, which, as I have described it, is the rational attitude built upon natural caring. When we put it this way, we see that there can be no justification for taking the moral viewpoint—that in truth, the moral viewpoint is prior to any notion of justification.

Notes

1. David Hume, "An Enquiry Concerning the Principles of Morals," in *Ethical Theories,* ed. A. I. Melden (Englewood Cliffs, N.J.: Prentice-Hall, Inc., 1967), p. 275.
2. Friedrich Nietzsche, "Mixed Opinions and Maxims," in *The Portable Nietzsche,* ed. Walter Kaufmann (New York: The Viking Press, Inc., 1954), p. 65.
3. Friedrich Nietzsche, *The Will to Power,* trans. Walter Kaufmann (New York: Random House, 1967), pp. 476, 670. For a contemporary argument against strict application of universalizability, see Peter Winch, *Ethics and Action* (London: Routledge & Kegan Paul, 1972).
4. W. D. Ross, *The Right and the Good* (Oxford: Clarendon Press, 1930).

CARING AND EVIL
Claudia Card

Claudia Card is professor of philosophy at the University of Wisconsin, Madison, and faculty affiliate in women's studies and environmental studies. Her publications include Adventures in Lesbian Philosophy *(1994),* Lesbian Choices *(1995) and* The Unnatural Lottery *(1996). Card raises two related objections to Noddings' ethic of care. First, it does not seem that an ethic of care without justice can make good sense of our ethical responsibilities to strangers and, second, it runs the danger of "valorizing" exploitative relationships. These problems indicate, according to Card, the importance of supplementing and limiting care with considerations of justice.*

N el Noddings' "feminine approach to ethics"[1] is something like Carol Gilligan's "care perspective" in ethics.... Gilligan has recognized the need for both justice and care in a fully mature ethic.[2] Nel Noddings apparently disagrees. She presents her ethic of care as an *alternative* to an ethic of principle, rejecting universalizability except in the universal accessibility of the caring attitude. This rejection of justice as a fundamental ethical concept raises issues so important that I focus on it, rather than on topics where I find more with which to agree.

My question is: Can an ethic of care without justice enable us adequately to resist evil? By resisting evil, I have in mind something relatively modest: resisting complicity in evil-doing. I have long since abandoned ambitions of reducing evil in the world at large (leaving it a better place than I found it); such ambitions are usually dangerous as well as arrogant. Still, we can and ought to resist complicity in the evils around us. I have in mind evils of two kinds: the evils strangers do to strangers and the evils intimates do to intimates. Each raises different problems. Issues of racism and sexism can illustrate the two.

On the one hand, resting all of ethics on caring threatens to exclude as ethically insignificant our relationships with most people in the world, because we do not know them individually and never will. Regarding as ethically insignificant our relationships with people remote from ourselves is a constituent of racism and xenophobia. On the other hand, resting all of ethics on caring also seems in danger of valorizing relationships that are sheerly exploitative of our distinctively human capacity to take another's point of view. It thereby threatens to exacerbate the positions of women and other care-takers in a sexist society. By "sheer exploitation" I mean valuing others and their capacities sheerly for what they contribute to ourselves or our projects, by contrast with valuing them for themselves, apart from our own development and projects.

Our Relations with Strangers

Consider the first problem, our ethical relations with most people in the world. Nel Noddings grants (even insists) that no one has the responsibility even to try

Reprinted from Claudia Card, "Caring and Evil," *Hypatia* 5, 1990, by permission of Indiana University Press.

to care for everyone, in the full-blown sense of "caring" that her book develops. I agree. But that leaves the question of what ethical notions *are* relevant to our relationships with strangers, persons whose lives we may significantly affect although we will never know them as individuals, never encounter them. Where we have no responsibility to care *for* others, I should think that we still have responsibilities to refrain from doing them harm—to be *careful,* in a sense that does *not* require encounters with those for whose sakes we ought to take care.

On Nel Noddings' analysis caring requires real encounters with individuals. My ethical responsibility is to meet those whom I encounter as one-caring. The ideal, apparently, is to reproduce the quality of caring experienced in infancy, an experience lacking what most of us would recognize as reciprocity. (I will say more about that shortly). She is concerned not to dilute caring to include just any positive concern we can have for another. Her "caring for" is not just "being concerned about"; it has three elements: motivational engrossment—or "displacement"—in another, a regard for or inclination toward the other (she speaks of "being present to" them), and an action component, *care-taking,* such as protection or maintenance. Ideally, the reception of caring involves a responsiveness of spontaneously sharing with the carer one's aspirations, appraisals, and accomplishments, in particular, sharing the development that caring made possible.

The strengths of this analysis, which distinguishes caring from other ways of being concerned, also suggest certain limitations of caring as the basis for an ethic. Technology has made it possible for the effects of our actions to extend far beyond the range of our personal encounters. We can affect drastically, even fatally, people we will never know as individuals. What does a caring ethic say about our relations with them?

By means of what she calls "chains" of connection, Nel Noddings holds that we can be *prepared to care* for others who are presently outside our "circles" of connection—for outsiders such as our children's spouses-to-be. "Chains" are defined as "personal or formal relationships." The latter, however, are not defined, and the "chains" offered as examples suggest differing interpretations. The example of the spouse of one's child suggests that a "chain" has as a connecting link an individual whom one *has* encountered. This is also suggested by the idea of a preparedness to care because of others for whom we already care. This example makes sense of the metaphor of a "chain": individuals known to us are the links. However, to restrict ethics to such connections in a nuclear age would be preposterous.

A different example, one's future students who are simply potential placeholders in a formal relationship of teacher-student, extends our connections further but does not make sense of the chain metaphor. On this model, I as a teacher am apparently connected ("chainwise?") to my potential students. But what are the "links"? My present students may be connected with future students through me. But what links *me* with future students? To avoid circularity, my present students need *another* connection with future ones in order to link me to those future students. Still, if nearly anyone might enter into a relationship with me that I presently have to others, perhaps we have an answer to the question about our ethical relationships to strangers: they are "potentially" not strangers. Is that answer satisfactory? I have several questions.

First, what if the potentiality is never realized, as it never will be with regard to most people in the world? Does the existence of a potential relationship mean that *potentially* I have an ethical relationship with those who are presently strangers? Or does it mean that because of the potentiality, I have such a relationship now?

If the latter, how can caring in the sense requiring encounter apply? Are we to *imagine* an encounter? If an imagined encounter can substitute for a real one, what does the so-called "motivational displacement" of caring really have to do with the particularities of others? Nel Noddings has objected to the abstractness of an ethic of principle. It seems that here, however, ethical relationships are being defined by abstract potentialities, or even speculations, and if by such abstractions, why not by those in the idea of justice? And if the present potentiality for future encounters makes my relationship with strangers ethically significant now, how has universality been rejected?

On the other hand, if the existence of a potential relationship means only that *potentially* I have an ethical relationship with those who are presently strangers, am I free to act in ways that will veritably insure the unrealizability of that potentiality? Just what are the implications of a potential ethical relationship for one's actual responsibilities?

Second, *which* relationships linking us to strangers count as ethically significant? Are formal relationships *kinds* of relationship, as opposed to particular relationships? If so, *which* kinds of relationship? The examples suggest *institutionally* defined relationships, such as marriages and the relationships defined by educational institutions. However, if "formal relationships" are institutionally defined, we need justice to evaluate them. Some institutions unjustly exclude whole groups of people. If my formal relationships to others were defined by such institutions, it would seem to follow that I had no formal relationships to those excluded and therefore no ethical relationships to them, unless I were connected by personal relationships. But that is not plausible. If "formal relationships" are not institutionally defined, then how are they defined? What is the "form"?

The notion of "chains" is left at too intuitive a level. I have no intuitive sense of these "chains" that explains the examples. Why, for example, is the embryo a woman carries not connected with her by indefinitely *many* "chains," independently of her relationship with its father? It has indefinitely many potentialities for entering into relationships with her. Yet, in the case of an embryo carried by a woman not sure of the love between herself and the man, Nel Noddings says (referring to the embryo as an "information speck"), "This information speck is an information speck and that is all. There is no formal relation, given the breakdown between husband and wife, and with the embryo, there is no present relation...," but that there is a "growing possibility of relation."[3] Why is there no formal relation? (Is it not, for example, potentially its mother's student?) How does a connection by "formal relation" differ from "the possibility of relation"? Is the difference significant?...

Part of the point of justice is to make possible cooperative relationships with more people than one can or should even try to care for. It applies to interactions among many who are not bound by ties of affection but who have a stake in securing certain common advantages by mutual cooperation. This is especially important in a society plagued by racism, ethnocentrism, and xenophobia. In a poorly integrated multicultural society dominated by phobic stereotypes, opportunities for interracial caring relationships are not what they should be. In such a context, if one's ethical repertoire is exhausted by caring, there is nothing left to operate with respect to many of the interracial consequences of one's conduct. Normally, this is one place for justice and respect for others....

Personal Relationships and Problems of Abuse

If the care ethic threatens to exclude too much, it also threatens to include too much by valorizing relationships that sheerly exploit carers. Elevating caring into an ethical ideal threatens to valorize the maintenance by carers of relationships that ought to be dissolved or those from which a carer should be able to withdraw without being in any way "ethically diminished." Consider the problem of intimate partner abuse....

The care ethic seems to lack a basis for objecting to an abused carer's remaining in the relationship when leaving becomes possible. Referring to a famous burning bed case, Nel Noddings holds that if we must exclude from our caring someone for whom we have cared, we thereby act under a "diminished ethical ideal."[4] I should have thought the richness of our ethical ideals *enabled* us to reject bad relationships and freed us up for ethically fuller ones. After all, it is by contrasting abusive relationships with such ideals that we are finally able to see the abuse for what it is.

Getting stuck in the "pre-act" consciousness of the attitude of one-caring can be ethically disastrous. Caring has the consequence of supporting people in their projects. Caring unrestrained by other values is not necessarily a good thing. It can be better to cease caring than to allow one's caring to be exploited in the service of immoral ends.

Perhaps the case of abusive relationships also points to a gap in Professor Noddings' account of caring itself. That account does not explicitly include the idea of *valuing* individuals for themselves. Motivational displacement is not the same. We can take up the perspectives of others out of sheer necessity for survival, the necessity to anticipate others' needs in order to be a good servant or slave, for example. Women learn well to do this with men; slaves have learned well to do it with masters. To be the valuers that ethical caring requires we need to preserve in ourselves, as well as value in others, a certain spiritual integrity. Otherwise, we risk becoming simply tools or extensions of others. With a capacity for "motivational displacement"—receiving others into oneself—but lacking integrity as a self who chooses and rejects relationships, one is in danger of dissolving into a variety of personalities, changing one's colors (or values) like a chameleon in changing environments. Women know this danger intimately, as does anyone whose personal safety has regularly depended upon how well they were able to "receive others into themselves."

This last is not so much a disagreement as a suggestion for further development in analyzing caring as an ethical ideal. Where I disagree is on the need to both supplement and limit care with justice. In one sense caring *is* more basic to human life than justice: we can *survive* without justice more easily than without caring. However, this is part of the human tragedy because, in another sense, justice is also basic: life can be *worth* living despite the absence of caring from most people in the world, but in a densely populated high-tech world, life is not apt to be *worth* living without justice from a great many people, including many whom we will never know.

Notes

1. Nel Noddings, *Caring: A Feminine Approach to Ethics and Moral Education* (Berkeley, CA: University of California Press, 1984).
2. At least, she did in *In a Different Voice* (Cambridge, MA: Harvard University Press, 1982), but it is no longer clear that she holds this view. In her essay, "Moral Orientation and Moral Development" (*Women and Moral Theory,* Eva Kittay and Diana T. Meyers, eds. [Totawa, NJ: Rowman and Littlefield, 1987]), she develops the idea that the justice and care orientations are related to one another as alternative gestalts. It is not clear from the account of these gestalts whether each has a place for the basic concept in the other or not, nor if so, what place it has.
3. *Caring,* p. 88.
4. Ibid., p. 114.

CARE ETHICS AND VIRTUE ETHICS
Raja Halwani

Raja Halwani is associate professor of philosophy in the Liberal Arts Department at the School of the Art Institute in Chicago and is author of Virtuous Liasons *(2003) as well as articles in ethics, philosophy of sex, and philosophy of art. Halwani proposes to integrate care ethics and its focus on the value of relationships into a more comprehensive version of virtue ethics. In so doing, Halwani explains how various objections to care ethics, including those presented in the previous selection by Claudia Card, can be answered by the proponent of care ethics.*

The issue of the status of care ethics (CE) as a moral theory is still unresolved. If, as has been argued, CE cannot, and should not, constitute a comprehensive moral theory, and if care cannot be the sole foundation of such a theory, the question of the status of CE becomes a pressing one, especially given the plausibility of the idea that caring does constitute an important and essential component of moral thinking, attitude, and behavior. Furthermore, the answers given to solve this issue are inadequate. For instance, the suggestion that CE has its own moral domain to operate in (for example, friendship), while, say, an ethics of justice has

From Raja Halwani, "Ethics of Care and Ethics of Virtue," *Hypatia* 18 (2003). Reprinted by permission of the Indiana University Press. This essay is now part of the first chapter of *Virtuous Liaisons* (Chicago: Open Court, 2003).

another (public policy), seems to encounter difficulties when we realize that in the former domain justice is required.

I want to suggest that CE be part of a more comprehensive moral framework, namely, virtue ethics (VE). Doing so allows us to achieve two general, desirable goals. First, by incorporating care within VE, we will be able to imbed CE within a comprehensive moral theory and so accommodate the criticism that such an ethics cannot stand on its own.... Second, we can preserve those elements of CE thought to be most valuable, namely, its appeal to partiality as a legitimate moral concern, its application to specific individuals in the agent's life, its emotive component, and its relevance to areas in moral life that have been neglected by some traditional moral theories.

I will first explain the type of CE on which I focus and review two important objections to it. I then explain how subsuming CE under VE helps us achieve the desired goals mentioned above.... Throughout this discussion, I focus on Nel Noddings's views of care, and I assume a general familiarity with VE on the part of the reader.

I. Noddings's Care Ethics

Nel Noddings[1] formulated an influential attempt to build a comprehensive moral approach on the concept of care. It is important to look at her attempt because it allows us to see what is lacking in her approach and to delineate the concept of care. Starting with the claim that relations between human beings are ontologically basic, Noddings construes caring relations as ethically basic. In order to be moral, according to Noddings, one must maintain one's self as caring. She calls this view of oneself the "ethical ideal": "We want to be moral in order to remain in the caring relationship and to enhance the ideal of ourselves as one-caring [that is, as givers of care]. It is this ethical ideal...that guides us as we strive to meet the other morally" (5). This ethical ideal comes from the two sentiments of natural and ethical caring (104). The former is the natural sympathy we feel for others; it is the sentiment expressed when we want and desire to attend to those we care for, such as a mother's caring for her child. The latter occurs "in response to a remembrance of the first" (79), and it forms the basis of ethical obligation: it is the "I must" that we adhere to when we want to maintain our ethical ideal as one-caring. So even in situations when I find it difficult to engage in caring action, I am under an obligation to do so if I want to be moral, that is, to maintain myself as one-caring (82).

What, however, is involved in caring relations? Noddings claims that for caring to be genuine it has to be for persons in definite relations with the one-caring. Though she makes room for the idea that one can expand one's circle of those cared-for (that is, those who are the recipients of care), she insists that genuine caring is not caring for abstract ideas or causes (112). More specifically, genuine caring involves what Noddings calls "engrossment and motivational displacement." In engrossment, the one-caring attends to the cared-for without judgment and evaluation, and she allows herself to be transformed by the other, while in motivational displacement the one-caring adopts the goals of the cared-for and helps the latter to promote them, directly or indirectly (15–20, 33–34). This account has the result, as Noddings emphasizes, that caring has its limits. If genuine caring is not to be corrupted, the one-caring simply cannot care for everyone (18, 86). This, moreover, is not simply a practical consequence but a conceptual one: given Noddings's requirements of engrossment and displacement, it is impossible for any one person to engage a large number of people in such caring relations.

Noddings's views have been subject to severe criticism. Two of these are crucial to bringing out what is essentially missing in a moral view built simply on the notion of care. Claudia Card takes as her starting point the fact that in Noddings's view caring cannot be extended to everyone. If so, Card asks, how are we to think of our moral obligation to the people that we are not in caring relations with? We seem to need another moral concept that would ground our moral obligations to those who are not cared-for, and Card opts for justice: "…in a densely populated world life is not apt to be worth living without justice from a great many people, including many whom we will never know."[2]

Victoria Davion's criticism of Noddings has as its starting point the moral dangers attending engrossment and motivational displacement. If one cares for someone who is evil, then the one-caring might himself become evil. For if engrossment and displacement are, respectively, allowing oneself to be transformed by the cared-for and adopting the goals of the cared-for, then in caring for someone who is evil the one-caring allows himself to be transformed by the cared-for and to adopt immoral goals, and such a person, the one-caring, simply cannot be viewed as a moral paradigm. Hence, something is needed to regulate care and to ward off the possibility of such moral corruption. Davion opts for integrity, and her argument is that integrity is essential to one's ethical ideal, since "[s]eeing oneself as a being with moral integrity is part of seeing oneself as one's best self."[3] Since caring is sometimes incompatible with maintaining integrity, caring simply cannot be the only absolute moral value, as Noddings would have us believe.

These two objections point to an important conclusion: any ethics that attempts to build itself simply on the concept of care is bound to face severe difficulties. Though my discussion relied only on Noddings's account, the conclusion holds. For it is implausible to believe that caring is the only basic component that goes into an ethical life: if one understands "care" as Noddings does, it is clear that in being one-caring one can nevertheless act morally wrong. (7) In this regard, Carol Gilligan's views are more plausible than Noddings's, because Gilligan is not committed to the idea that an ethics built solely on care would yield a comprehensive moral theory. Indeed, Gilligan[4] often claims that a care approach needs to be combined with other approaches. However, it is precisely this issue that makes the problem of the status of CE within moral theory pressing, for it is not clear how this combination is to be articulated....

II. CE as Part of VE

My suggestion now is to think of care as a virtue, as one virtue, albeit an important one, among those that go into constituting a flourishing life. As a virtue, care would not simply be a natural impulse, but to use Noddings's terminology, also ethical (in Aristotelian terms, it would not be a natural virtue, but one harnessed by reason). This position allows us to maintain what is most desirable about CE. First, consider CE's insistence on the idea that human beings are not abstract individuals who morally relate to each other following principles such as justice and nonviolation of autonomy. One of VE's main claims is that we are social animals who need to negotiate the ways we are to deal and live with each other. With this general claim about our sociality, VE also claims that without certain types of relationships we will not flourish. Without friends and family members, human beings will lead impoverished lives, being unable to partake in the pleasures of associating with people with whom they can trust and share their joys, sorrows, and activities. It is not just that intimate relationships are instrumental to flourishing, but that they are also part and parcel of a flourishing life: the ends and goals of intimate others constrain the very ends and goals of the agent, and the very conception of the agent's life: intimate relationships "are not external conditions of [virtuous] activities, like money or power. Rather, they are the form virtuous activity takes when it is especially fine and praiseworthy."[5] VE, then, gives pride of place to CE's insistence on the sociality of human life and to its emphasis on the importance of certain types of relations such as those of friendship and family....

...Davion's worry is... about the ethical standing of the relationships themselves. I turn to [this] issue next.

III. Caring Relationships, Reason, and Davion's Criticism

I will begin addressing the issue of the moral desirability of intimate relationships by looking at some remarks Aristotle gave on friendship; these offer a good segue into my account.

Aristotle claims that the virtuous person's friend is another self: "The excellent person is related to his friend in the same way he is related to himself, since a friend is another himself. Therefore, just as his own being is choiceworthy for him, his friend's being is choiceworthy for him in the same or a similar way."[6] In the *Eudemian Ethics*, Aristotle states, "For friendship seems something stable, and this alone is stable. For a formed decision is stable, and where we do not act quickly or easily, we get the decision right. There is no stable friendship without confidence, but confidence needs time. One must then make trial....Nor is a friend made except through time...."[7] Though Aristotle does not explicitly speak of choosing our friends, his remarks indicate that there is a choice involved in friendships, a choice to the effect that we choose our friends given certain standards, such as having a morally desirable character (his remarks commit him to choosing our friends because without the notion of choice, his points about building confidence and making trial would not be plausible: Why test the character of our potential friends if we do not have the option to choose not to be their friends?). The choice need not be about initiating friendships, though this is true in many cases, but is about opting to continue or to quit them. Furthermore, the choice takes time and needs to be tested until a certain amount of confidence and trust is established. In addition, the friend, who is "another self," will share "a sense of our commitments and ends, and a sense of what we take to be ultimately 'good and pleasant' in living."[8]

It is important to note that the notion of choice is important not just for its own sake, but for what it indicates, namely, that with choice comes rational deliberation, and this implies that we can use reason to evaluate and regulate friendships (indeed, the notion of choice as such provides a poor basis for intimate relationships that do not involve much choice for their parties in initiating the relationships, such as siblings, and children in parental ones). Reason, then, plays a crucial role in our choice of friends. In choosing X for a friend, I need to make sure that he has a character compatible with mine, that his goals and activities are morally in the clear, and that I can even share them and be willing to (indirectly, at least) support them. Such a choice, of course, requires the time needed to evaluate my friend's character, actions, and goals. With time, my choice of X as a friend is either cemented or shaken. If the former, then, in caring for him, I need not always deliberate about whether my action is right. In caring for X by, say, helping him to achieve a certain goal, I need not think whether doing so is ethically correct, for this has already been established. He would not have been my friend if his goals were deemed unworthy. We have to remember that friendships contain a good amount of trust between the friends. If I come to know that my friend is a morally decent person, and given my intimate knowledge of his character and his life (he is, after all, my friend), then I can trust that his goals are morally in the clear, especially in those cases when he adopts new goals.

This account need not deny the possibility that a friend's character changes. If this were to occur, we use reason to re-evaluate not only our actions toward him, but the relationship itself. Aristotle recognizes that friends sometimes change,[9] and if a friend changes to the point were he is no longer the same person, the grounds of the friendship dissolve. The point is that reason plays a crucial regulative role: it assesses the goals and the general character of a friend, and in doing so, it offers a generally reliable mechanism with which we can check that the friendship is morally in the clear.

The above account applies as well to married couples and lovers, and to other relations that do not involve as much choice in initiating the relationship, such as child-parent ones, but that also essentially involve caring. The regulative role of reason would allow the one-caring, be it the offspring or the parent, to decide whether to continue to be in such a relationship and so to continue to be caring or not. And surely this is a result that ought to be welcome. For insofar as CE has been criticized on the grounds that it does not leave room for a mechanism by which the caring relation is evaluated as good or not, such an account of the role of reason would, in principle, supply such a mechanism. Furthermore, we can here see a role, though a limited one, for choice: if the emphasis is placed not so much on the choice to enter a relationship but on the ability to leave it, or at least to withhold care, then the one-caring would have some choice in the decision to minimize care, withhold it altogether, or even suspend the relationship entirely.

But one might find the idea that a parent or a child can opt to leave a parent-child relationship to be highly unrealistic or implausible. It might be thought unrealistic not because it is sometimes difficult to leave such a relationship due to factors specific to the case, but because, in addition to social pressures, few parents or children can just simply decide to leave such a relationship, even after much deliberation. For aside from the rare case in which the child or parent is thoroughly evil, children and parents find themselves to be, for good or ill, emotionally attached to their parents and children, respectively, in ways that spouses— perhaps—do not. Furthermore, opting to leave such relationships might be thought implausible because children-parent relationships have special obligations. Even if my mother, say, is self-centered and rarely shows concern for me, it is still my obligation to tend to and care for her.

The above reflections are plausible. However, we must keep in mind that the main idea in the above account is giving a regulative role for reason in intimate relationships. In those cases of parent-child relationships in which one (or both) of the parties shows signs of moral corruption, and if opting to leave is an implausible solution, then reason will have to play a more direct role, much like it would have to in cases of friendship that exhibit signs of going awry. Reason would have to play a role in how best to care for the other party in the relationship in order to make sure, for example, that the moral integrity of the one-caring is not compromised, or that the one-caring does not open himself up to corruption. So a son might decide to do the minimum required in terms of his duties to his father but maintain his emotional distance from him as much as possible. And a mother might lie to her son about how much money she has so that he won't forcefully take it and spend it on alcohol and gambling, even though she continues to perform her household activities, including those that tend to her son's domestic life (for example, his laundry).

To summarize, VE requires that caring relationships be subjected to a regulative role of reason to ensure their moral desirability. VE's emphasis on moral wisdom and on the virtues supplies us with an in-principle mechanism with which to morally scrutinize such intimate relationships. This, moreover, should be a welcome result given the need to supply care with a method of self-evaluation. I should, moreover, emphasize that this account is not a temporal one; that is, it is not an account that states that first reason must evaluate a potential friendship or relationship, and then the virtuous person can rest assured that her caring actions are morally okay. This would be implausible because evaluating relationships is not done in this way, since the evaluation typically goes temporally hand in hand with the development of the relationship. Rather, my account is a conceptual one: it makes room for the role of reason in the evaluation of relationships by giving reason a regulative role to play.

The account of the regulative role of reason should supply us with an adequate way of accommodating Davion's criticism of Noddings's ethics of care, namely, that one can care for someone who is evil and so open oneself to moral corruption. We can put this point in terms of integrity, the concept that Davion herself uses. A virtuous person is one who is concerned with her character and her life: she is someone who cares that she maintains an ethical character and that her dealings with others are moral. Put in this way, no person can be virtuous and yet lack moral integrity. To think otherwise is to think of someone as having what Aristotle calls "natural virtue," of someone who acts rightly, desires to do so, yet does and is so accidentally, so to speak. To be virtuous one must subject one's conduct and desires to the scrutiny, and shaping, of reason. And so, if a virtuous person finds herself in a relationship such that the one-cared for is turning evil (whether this is due to malicious reasons or to bad luck, such as oppression, is not the issue here), and if she fails to reverse or at least prevent such a change from being completed, then her concern for her character would imply severing such a relationship.

We can even go a bit further. Davion recognizes the role of integrity in her account as one of necessity but not sufficiency.[10] In other words, while integrity is necessary to maintain a morally good relationship, it is not sufficient, because two evil people can have integrity (so long as their actions, say, cohere with their principles) and so maintain a strong relationship. But VE can avoid this possibility. For under VE, integrity comes after certain conditions have been met. Simply put, a virtuous person is someone who is virtuous (excuse the banality). Her integrity will, ipso facto, be that of a person who is good, not evil. So the sufficiency condition is met.

IV. Partiality and Card's Criticism

Card's objection to CE is that it does not give us a way to ground our obligations to non-intimate others, especially strangers, who, as far as the one-caring is concerned, comprise the bulk of humanity. However, once CE is incorporated within VE, Card's worry would be adequately addressed: for a virtuous person has the virtue of justice, and justice is the primary virtue in which our obligations to strangers (and to a good extent intimate others as well) are grounded. Thus, while VE is able to account for our caring relations to others, it does not neglect justice. It is, furthermore, within a discussion of justice that the issue of partiality arises in full force, for it is here that we see the need to find a way to justifiably adjudicate between the claims of partiality and impartiality.

CE advocates usually construe the demand of impartiality as the claim that all persons should be treated on equal footing and that displaying favoritism in one's moral actions is morally prohibited. They then claim that such a demand is not plausible when it comes to our family members and friends. The idea is that it is not only morally permissible but also praiseworthy that we attend to our cared-fors, and that in (at least some) cases of conflict between partiality and the demands of impartiality, being partial is ethically acceptable, if not even laudable. Partiality, then, is not a limit on morality, but part and parcel of it. Still, since, as we have seen, we cannot endorse all forms of partiality and partial behavior, and since partiality and impartiality conflict, we need to plausibly situate the former within an overall moral theory. The issue, then, is this: Can VE supply us with a principled way to justify those cases of partiality that one could, indeed, reasonably consider justified? If VE can do this, then, given its emphasis on the virtue of justice, VE can offer us one theoretical framework within which our treatment of strangers and intimate others is balanced in a morally justified way. And in doing this, it can both incorporate CE and improve on it, in, respectively, inasmuch as CE has emphasized the importance of partiality, and has proven to be deficient in treating the claims of strangers upon the moral agent convincingly. The answer to this issue is clear and straightforward: VE includes, among others, the virtues of practical wisdom, of justice, and, on my proposal, of care. Because of this, it has an in-principle way of distinguishing between justified and unjustified partiality, and of distinguishing between justified and unjustified claims of strangers on the agent. I will illustrate this claim in what follows.

First, we should not exaggerate the conflict between partiality and impartiality. For one thing, it is not usual that our attention to our loved ones conflicts with the demands of impartiality, because the moral domains of our dealings with intimates and with strangers are usually separate from each other. It is not typically the case that one is conflicted between the demands of friends and of strangers. Furthermore, even given a duty of general benevolence toward people, this is not usually understood as the claim that we ought to divide our attention to everyone equally. There is a good reason for this (in addition to the fact that it is humanly impossible to do so): in order for individuals to lead happy and rich lives, they need to be able to pursue their own goals, activities, and interests, and this ability would be thwarted were individuals to divide their time and energy equally with others. And VE recognizes this: in its emphasis on flourishing, VE gives ample room to the above idea, and insofar as it insists on friendship as an essential factor that goes into flourishing, it also recognizes the importance of having friends and family relationships, and the importance of the attention such relationships require.

But cases of conflict between the demands of friendship and those of others do arise, and it is important to see whether VE would adequately deal with such types of cases. First, there are resolvable cases of conflict. These are exemplified by cases such as (1) breaking a promise to meet someone for lunch so as to attend to a friend who has just had a crisis; (2) being involved in an accident such that both the agent's spouse and a stranger require immediate medical attention but the agent can attend to only one; (3) being involved in an accident along the lines of (2) but such that the spouse is not in need of immediate medical attention; and (4) considering bribing a school official in order to secure a place for one's child in the school.[11] If the idea behind CE's insistence on partiality is that in cases (1) and (2) the agent should attend to his near and dear, then no (sane) philosopher would wish to argue against such a conclusion, and no (sophisticated) moral theory would, since we recognize that loved ones have special claims upon us. VE is no exception, for it recognizes that friends, spouses, and children have special claims.

In case (2) for instance (and supposing I were the agent), given my love for my spouse, his importance to my life and to my well-being, I simply cannot be morally faulted if I help him. That VE accommodates this type of case needs, I take it, no explanation.

Consider briefly case (3): Should I attend to my spouse, knowing that the other person is in need of immediate assistance? While the agent would surely feel a strong desire to be with his loved one, he would not, if he is virtuous, act on this desire (he might rush to his spouse and say something to the effect that he will be with him soon). He would give the necessary help to the stranger, because a virtuous person is not blind to the immediate needs and suffering of others.

This is the right conclusion to reach because the stranger's needs are more urgent. Such conflict cases indicate that it is not always morally correct to act on one's desires to help and care for a loved one. Sometimes strangers have immediate needs that one is in a position to attend to and that one should attend to, even if this involves discomfort to the loved one.

In case 4, bribing a school official, the agent obviously violates just procedures. Given that the agent is being partial toward his child, would it be correct to say that his action is morally permissible? Surely not: even if the action is done out of care for the child, if Card's criticism that we need justice to ground our obligations to those we are not in caring relations with has any plausibility to it (and it has), then to argue that the agent's action in this case is permissible is to reject, in effect, the claims that justice has on us. Furthermore, a virtuous person would surely not act in this way, for she has the virtue of justice, a virtue that covers treating others fairly and according them their dues.

Now it is important to keep in mind that the virtuous person is just, since much of this discussion would be put in perspective. For an essential part of the story of what it means to be virtuous is that one has the virtues and that one has practical wisdom that allows the agent to decide on the correct exercise of the virtues given the context. It should then be realized that not every case of partial action is going to be morally permissible on VE. Whether it is will depend, partly, on whether it impermissibly violates the dictates of justice. And I am not here begging the question against proponents of CE, because if they claim that partial actions are morally permissible simply because they are partial, then they will be faced—again—with the objection that this neglects the important concept of justice. There is, therefore, the need for a way to reconcile the two, and VE can, in principle, do this.

To summarize the points about impartiality, I have argued that, typically, conflicts between the claims of strangers and those of cared-fors are rare. In cases in which there are conflicts, one would have to consider the factors involved in each case. Sometimes the claims of strangers are overridden when those near and dear to us require immediate attention. Sometimes the claims of strangers override those who are near and dear to us because the former's are pressing and humanly important, while the latter's can withstand delay of attention. When both are equally pressing and one can attend to only one, then the claims of loved ones take priority. And we morally cannot violate just procedures simply because this would help the ones that we love. While there are no neat formulas here, the point is that care considerations cannot simply trump other ones, even if we are in situations in which we are strongly desirous of attending to the cared-for. While care comprises an essential dimension of our ethical lives, strangers, acquaintances, colleagues, and others do have claims upon us, and these need to be balanced.

Second, we get to cases of irresolvable conflicts (the cases I have mentioned so far contain dilemmas, but they all seem to be resolvable). Consider the case—and others can be generated by following its basic recipe—in which the agent is the captain of a ship, the ship is sinking, and the only way to save the ship is for the agent to either throw out her spouse or the two other passengers (because the spouse weighs as much as the other two, and a certain amount of weight needs to be jettisoned). The agent, say, cannot commit suicide in this case because she is the only one who knows how to steer the ship to safety. In this case, the agent should, as captain, save the two other passengers, but should, as wife, save her spouse.[12] Either action is wrong from some point of view. Can VE still offer us an in-principle way of addressing such cases? And wouldn't CE have a clear answer to it and thus the upper hand?

First, while it might be true to claim that CE has a clear answer to this, it does not follow that its answer is correct, for the reason that the case is a dilemma. So it does not follow that we have a case in which VE cannot accommodate the claims of CE. For consider what CE is seen to be telling us: on the assumption that CE would indeed recommend that the agent save her spouse (and it is an assumption, because its claim need not command general assent from CE advocates), CE would give a controversial answer. Part of the case is that the agent is the captain of the ship, and captains have particular duties. The answer that the agent should save her spouse cannot, then, be uncontroversially the correct answer, and so CE does not obviously have the upper hand here.

Part of the difficulty has to do with the very idea of irresolvable conflicts, since the existence of these has been denied by quite a few philosophers. What is often involved in such denials is the attempt to resolve each case by stating what the agent ought to do and thus claiming that the case is not, after all, irresolvable. But that an answer can be given does not show that it is the right answer, but, rather, simply that, depending on one's theoretical commitments or intuitions, one can offer an answer. The points of this and the preceding paragraph are, of course, connected. An advocate of CE might offer an answer to the above case, but he will do so precisely because he is an advocate of CE, and this should indicate that the answer is controversial.

But what would VE tell us that the agent should do? I believe that cases such as that of the ship—and putting their suspicious fictitiousness aside—are irresolvable conflicts, and so I don't think that VE would—and should—claim that there is one correct answer to each. Either option is permissible, but on either one, the agent is going to emerge deeply shaken; whatever she does, her life is marred because of the serious wrongdoing that she could not avoid. To insist, moreover, that there should be one answer is to go against the fact that our lives are sometimes faced with situations from which the agent—barring suicide— emerges with her life deeply and irrevocably marred.

But we should keep in mind to what extent this discussion is relevant to the issue at hand. The issue is VE's ability to offer an in-principle method to justify partial and impartial actions when these are indeed justified, and surely the existence of irresolvable dilemmas does nothing to impugn the conclusion that VE is able to do this. The existence of such tragic cases would threaten this ability only on the assumptions that CE gives a clear and uncontroversial answer to the case and that VE's answer departs from CE's. But neither assumption is warranted. Some of the cases I mentioned earlier involve making decisions that leave the agent with unease and perhaps even with a good amount of pain, such as case (2), but the answer to the cases were clear, and so they did not constitute irresolvable dilemmas. In these cases, we can see how VE can balance care/partiality and other requirements. But that VE refuses to say that there is one right answer to cases of irresolvable dilemmas is not a strike against it (indeed, it is a point in its favor), nor is it a point against its ability to accommodate CE's concerns.

V. Care as a Primary Virtue

One might wonder whether there are independent reasons for thinking that care is a virtue; independent, that is, from those reasons that I have so far adduced, namely, that construing care as a virtue allows us to preserve what is important about CE while avoiding its problems. This issue becomes more pressing when we keep in mind that Noddings denies that care is a virtue, her reason being that if we claim that care or any other trait traditionally dubbed "virtue" is a virtue, then we somehow get saddled with paying too much attention to our own characters rather than displaying these traits in concrete relationships with others.[13] She instead gives care the status of a primary ethical concept, the concept which grounds our moral thinking, behavior, and emotion. Her two reasons for doing so seem to be that caring relationships are ethically basic, and in conjunction with the first reason, that caring is innate to human beings.[14] Noddings wants to carve out for caring an important and crucial place in moral discourse. If VE cannot offer care an important role to play in ethical life, then my thesis that VE can successfully incorporate CE becomes utterly implausible, since CE's main claim is that caring is an essential aspect of morality. VE cannot, then, treat care as simply one virtue among the others, but must give it an elevated status if it is to treat CE with the respect the latter deserves. So are there considerations that support the claim that care is indeed a virtue? And are there ones that support the claim that care is a primary and important virtue?

Yes there are, and the second type of consideration I will offer for the idea that care is a virtue also implies that it is a primary one, and that is why I chose to discuss the two issues of care being a virtue and of it being a primary one in one section (I should note that my remarks on this score will be brief and programmatic, due to space limitations). To show X as a virtue requires two crucial steps: 1) that it fits the definition of virtue, and 2) that it satisfies the criterion for a trait being a virtue. These two steps are programmatic and somewhat sketchy, but they do give some important and needed support to the claim that care is a virtue.

So, consider as a start Aristotle's definition of "virtue," namely, that it is a state involving choice and lying in a mean, with the mean relative to the individual.[15] There is no difficulty in thinking of care as an actual state that would dispose the agent to act given the right circumstances. It also involves choice: barring unusual circumstances, the agent is not coerced to care for others; it is ultimately up to the agent to decide whether to withhold or offer care on a particular occasion. Most importantly, caring can admit of a mean: caring can be done "at the right times, about the right things, toward the right people, for the right end and in the right way."[16] Exhibiting care can then be done wrongly (defectively, viciously): one can care for the wrong person (for example, a morally corrupt one); one can exhibit care at a wrong time (for example, attending to X whereas it is Y, a stranger, which needs attention at that time); one can exhibit care about the wrong thing (for example, supporting a project that should not be supported); one can care for the wrong reasons (for example, I give you chocolate because I want you to stop crying), and in the wrong way (for example, I calm your fears by lying to you)....

Consider next the second type of consideration: caring satisfies the criterion for being a virtue, namely, a trait one needs to flourish as a human being. It is, for example, an obvious point to make that without proper care human beings cannot generally grow up to lead mentally and emotionally healthy lives. This indicates strongly that proper care is generally necessary if one is to flourish. Furthermore, if intimate relationships are essentially characterized by caring, and if flourishing is constituted by intimate relationships (among other things), then the necessity of caring to a flourishing life stares us obviously in the face. Without giving and receiving care, the sociality and the rationality (mental health) of the agent is seriously endangered, and this strikes at the heart of the agent's flourishing qua human being (and it is from such facts that the plausibility of Noddings's claims about the importance of caring relationships is derived).

For this to imply that caring is a primary virtue, consider the suggestion that a glance at Aristotle's list of virtues yields the plausible idea that not all the virtues on the list deserve equal ranking. The virtue of wittiness, for example, cannot plausibly be placed on equal footing with that of truthfulness as far as the importance of these virtues for social life and for the agent's flourishing are concerned. Friendliness, to give another example, might be more important than wittiness, though it might not be more so than courage, and would certainly not be more so than justice. The point is that we need to be able to offer some sort of ranking of the virtues in terms of their importance. The ranking need not be precise and exact, and it need not be set in stone, either: we might want to leave the possibility open for cases in which, say, exercising wittiness is more important than being just, the difficulty of imagining such circumstances notwithstanding. Moreover, the ranking need not be rigid not just because of situations in which one generally less important virtue takes precedence over another, generally more important one. We should also keep in mind that sometimes a less generally important virtue might take precedence over a generally more important one in a person's life (as when people often need the virtue of tactfulness more so than honesty during times of oppression).

The above point tells us that VE is in principle perfectly hospitable to the idea that some virtues are more important than others. And this entails that, if care is a virtue, we are at liberty to give it a (rough) ranking among the virtues, provided we offer reasons to justify its assigned ranking. And the reasons for giving care a high ranking among the virtues are the ones offered above in the second type of considerations as to why care is a virtue, namely, that it is a trait one generally cannot do without to flourish qua human being. Thus not only is it plausible to construe care as a virtue, but it is plausible to think of it as a primary one. Alongside justice, honesty, and proper pride, care would take its deserved place as an essential virtue needed for living well.

VI. Conclusion

I have argued that CE should be incorporated within VE. This approach to the status of CE as a moral theory, in addition to its plausibility, avoids the shortcomings of other accounts that have been given regarding the relationship between care and justice reasoning....

Notes

1. Noddings, Nel. 1984. *Caring: A Feminine Approach to Ethics and Moral Education.* Berkeley: University of California Press. All page references to this book will be incorporated into the text.
2. Card, Claudia. 1990. "Caring and Evil." *Hypatia* 5, p. 107.
3. Davion, Victoria. 1993. "Autonomy, Integrity, and Care." *Social Theory and Practice* 19, p. 175.
4. Gilligan, Carol. 1982. *In a Different Voice.* Cambridge: Harvard University Press.
5. Sherman, Nancy. 1989. *The Fabric of Character: Aristotle's Theory of Virtue.* Oxford: Clarendon Press, p. 127.
6. Aristotle, *Nicomachean Ethics.* T. Irwin (trans.). Indianapolis: Hackett, 1170b 6–7.
7. Aristotle, *Eudemian Ethics.* J. Solomon (trans.). In *The Complete Works of Aristotle,* J. Barnes (ed.). Princeton: Princeton University Press, 1984, 1237b 10–17.
8. *The Fabric of Character,* p. 131.
9. *Nicomachean Ethics,* 1165b 12–36.
10. "Autonomy, Integrity, and Care," p. 179.
11. I borrow case (3) from Marcia Baron, *Kantian Ethics (almost) Without Apology.* Ithaca: Cornell University Press, 1995, p. 126 and case (4) from Lawrence Blum, "Gilligan and Kohlberg: Implications for Moral Theory." In *An Ethic of Care: Feminist and Interdisciplinary Perspectives,* M. J. Larrabee (ed.). New York: Routledge, 1993, p 55.
12. I borrow this case from Lynne McFall, "Integrity," *Ethics* 98, 1987.
13. *Caring,* pp. 96-7.
14. Ibid., pp. 3, 5, and 83.
15. *Nicomachean Ethics,* 1107a 1–4.
16. Ibid., 1106b 20–23.

CHAPTER 9

Pluralism and Particularism

MORAL CHOICE WITHOUT PRINCIPLES
Jean-Paul Sartre

Jean-Paul Sartre (1905–1980) was a leading figure in the existentialist movement in this century. His philosophical writings included Being and Nothingness *(1943) and his novels and plays included* The Age of Reason *(1945) and* No Exit *(1945). In the following selection, Sartre denies that there are moral principles of the sort sought by Aquinas, Bentham, and Kant that can provide guidance in a great many real-life situations. He illustrates this claim with his famous story about the young man torn between staying with his mother who needed him and joining the Free French Forces.*

I shall cite the case of one of my students who came to see me under the following circumstances: his father was on bad terms with his mother, and, moreover, was inclined to be a collaborationist; his older brother had been killed in the German offensive of 1940, and the young man, with somewhat immature but generous feelings, wanted to avenge him. His mother lived alone with him, very much upset by the half-treason of her husband and the death of her older son; the boy was her only consolation.

The boy was faced with the choice of leaving for England and joining the Free French Forces—that is, leaving his mother behind—or remaining with his mother and helping her to carry on. He was fully aware that the woman lived only for him and that his going-off—and perhaps his death—would plunge her into despair. He was also aware that every act that he did for his mother's sake was a sure thing, in the sense that it was helping her to carry on, whereas every effort he made toward going off and fighting was an uncertain move which might run aground and prove completely useless; for example, on his way to England he might, while passing through Spain, be detained indefinitely in a Spanish camp; he might reach England or Algiers and be stuck in an office at a desk job. As a result, he was faced

From *Essays in Existentialism* by Jean-Paul Sartre (New York: Philosophical Library, 1965). Reprinted with permission of the Philosophical Library, Inc., New York.

with two very different kinds of action: one, concrete, immediate, but concerning only one individual; the other concerned an incomparably vaster group, a national collectivity, but for that very reason was dubious, and might be interrupted en route. And, at the same time, he was wavering between two kinds of ethics. On the one hand, an ethics of sympathy, of personal devotion; on the other, a broader ethics, but one whose efficacy was more dubious. He had to choose between the two.

Who could help him choose? Christian doctrine? No. Christian doctrine says, "Be charitable, love your neighbor, take the more rugged path, etc., etc." But which is the more rugged path? Whom should he love as a brother? The fighting man or his mother? Which does the greater good, the vague act of fighting in a group, or the concrete one of helping a particular human being to go on living? Who can decide *a priori*? Nobody. No book of ethics can tell him. The Kantian ethics says, "Never treat any person as a means, but as an end." Very well, if I stay with mother, I'll treat her as an end and not as a means; but by virtue of this very fact, I'm running the risk of treating the people around me who are fighting, as means; and, conversely, if I go to join those who are fighting, I'll be treating them as an end, and, by doing that, I run the risk of treating my mother as a means.

If values are vague, and if they are always too broad for the concrete and specific case that we are considering, the only thing left for us is to trust our instincts. That's what this young man tried to do; and when I saw him, he said, "In the end, feeling is what counts. I ought to choose whichever pushes me in one direction. If I feel that I love my mother enough to sacrifice everything else for her—my desire for vengeance, for action, for adventure—then I'll stay with her. If, on the contrary, I feel that my love for my mother isn't enough, I'll leave."

But how is the value of a feeling determined? What gives his feeling for his mother value? Precisely the fact that he remained with her. I may say that I like so-and-so well enough to sacrifice a certain amount of money for him, but I may say so only if I've done it. I may say "I love my mother well enough to remain with her" if I have remained with her. The only way to determine the value of this affection is, precisely, to perform an act which confirms and defines it. But, since I require this affection to justify my act, I find myself caught in a vicious circle….

…In other words, the feeling is formed by the acts one performs; so, I can not refer to it in order to act upon it. Which means that I can neither seek within myself the true condition which will impel me to act, nor apply to a system of ethics for concepts which will permit me to act. You will say, "At least, he did go to a teacher for advice." But if you seek advice from a priest, for example, you have chosen this priest; you already knew, more or less, just about what advice he was going to give you. In other words, choosing your adviser is involving yourself. The proof of this is that if you are a Christian, you will say, "Consult a priest." But some priests are collaborating, some are just marking time, some are resisting. Which to choose? If the young man chooses a priest who is resisting or collaborating, he has already decided on the kind of advice he's going to get. Therefore, in coming to see me he knew the answer I was going to give him, and I had only one answer to give: "You're free, choose, that is, invent." No general ethics can show you what is to be done; there are no omens in the world….

... [The] objection: "You're able to do anything, no matter what" is not to the point. In one sense choice is possible, but what is not possible is not to choose. I can always choose, but I ought to know that if I do not choose, I am still choosing. Though this may seem purely formal, it is highly important for keeping fantasy and caprice within bounds. If it is true that in facing a situation, for example, one in which, as a person capable of having sexual relations, of having children, I am obliged to choose an attitude, and if I in any way assume responsibility for a choice which, in involving myself, also involves all mankind, this has nothing to do with caprice, even if no *a priori* value determines my choice....

... [M]an is in an organized situation in which he himself is involved. Through his choice, he involves all mankind, and he can not avoid making a choice: either he will remain chaste, or he will marry without having children, or he will marry and have children; anyhow, whatever he may do, it is impossible for him not to take full responsibility for the way he handles this problem. Doubtless, he chooses without referring to preestablished values, but it is unfair to accuse him of caprice. Instead, let us say that moral choice is to be compared to the making of a work of art. And before going any further, let it be said at once that we are not dealing here with an aesthetic ethics, because our opponents are so dishonest that they even accuse us of that. The example I've chosen is a comparison only.

Having said that, may I ask whether anyone has ever accused an artist who has painted a picture of not having drawn his inspiration from rules set up *a priori*? Has any one ever asked, "What painting ought he to make?" It is clearly understood that there is no definite painting to be made, that the artist is engaged in the making of his painting, and that the painting to be made is precisely the painting he will have made. It is clearly understood that there are no *a priori* aesthetic values, but that there are values which appear subsequently in the coherence of the painting, in the correspondence between what the artist intended and the result. Nobody can tell what the painting of tomorrow will be like. Painting can be judged only after it has once been made. What connection does that have with ethics? We are in the same creative situation. We never say that a work of art is arbitrary. When we speak of a canvas of Picasso, we never say that it is arbitrary; we understand quite well that he was making himself what he is at the very time he was painting, that the ensemble of his work is embodied in his life.

The same holds on the ethical plane. What art and ethics have in common is that we have creation and invention in both cases. We can not decide *a priori* what there is to be done. I think that I pointed that out quite sufficiently when I mentioned the case of the student who came to see me, and who might have applied to all the ethical systems, Kantian or otherwise, without getting any sort of guidance. He was obliged to devise his law himself. Never let it be said by us that this man—who, taking affection, individual action, and kind-heartedness toward a specific person as his ethical principle, chooses to remain with his mother, or who, preferring to make a sacrifice, chooses to go to England—has made an arbitrary choice. Man makes himself. He isn't ready made at the start. In choosing his ethics, he makes himself, and force of circumstances is such that he can not abstain from choosing one. We define man only in relationship to involvement. It is therefore absurd to charge us with arbitrariness of choice.

WHAT MAKES RIGHT ACTS RIGHT?
W. D. Ross

Sir William David Ross (1877–1971) was provost of Oriel College, Oxford University. His books include two important works in ethics, The Right and the Good *(1930) and* The Foundations of Ethics *(1939). Contrary to many moral theorists, Ross denies that there is some single moral principle that can be used to derive more specific moral obligations. Rather he defends a version of* ethical pluralism, *according to which there is a plurality of irreducible moral rules that are basic in moral thought. These rules express what Ross calls* prima facie duties—*duties such as keeping promises and avoiding injury to others—which may conflict in specific circumstances. When such duties do conflict, what is demanded is that we use moral judgment in order to determine which* prima facie *duty is (in that circumstance) weightiest and should be obeyed. Because he thought that the truth of the moral rules (he lists seven in all) could be grasped by intuition in the manner in which we grasp basic mathematical truths, Ross's view is sometimes called* intuitionism.

When a plain man fulfills a promise because he thinks he ought to do so, it seems clear that he does so with no thought of its total consequences, still less with any opinion that these are likely to be the best possible. He thinks in fact much more of the past than of the future. What makes him think it right to act in a certain way is that fact that he has promised to do so—that and, usually, nothing more. That his act will produce the best possible consequences is not his reason for calling it right. What lends color to the theory we are examining, then, is not the actions (which form probably a great majority of our actions) in which some such reflection as "I have promised" is the only reason we give ourselves for thinking a certain action right, but the exceptional cases in which the consequences of fulfilling a promise (for instance) would be so disastrous to others that we judge it right not to do so. It must of course be admitted that such cases exist. If I have promised to meet a friend at a particular time for some trivial purpose, I should certainly think myself justified in breaking my engagement if by doing so I could prevent a serious accident or bring relief to the victims of one. And the supporters of the view we are examining hold that my thinking so is due to my thinking that I shall bring more good into existence by the one action than by the other. A different account may, however, be given of the matter, an account which will, I believe, show itself to be the true one. It may be said that besides the duty of fulfilling promises I have and recognize a duty of relieving distress, and that when I think it right to do the latter at the cost of not doing the former, it is not because I think I shall produce more good thereby but because I think it the duty which is in the circumstances more of a duty. This account surely corresponds much more closely with what we really think in such a situation. If, so far as I can see, I could bring equal amounts of good into being by fulfilling my promise and

From *The Right and the Good* by W. D. Ross (Oxford: Oxford University Press, 1930). Reprinted by permission of the publisher.

by helping someone to whom I had made no promise, I should not hesitate to regard the former as my duty. Yet on the view that what is right is right because it is productive of the most good I should not so regard it....

In fact the theory of...utilitarianism...seems to simplify unduly our relations to our fellows. It says, in effect, that the only morally significant relation in which my neighbors stand to me is that of being possible beneficiaries by my action. They do stand in this relation to me, and this relation is morally significant. But they may also stand to me in the relation of promisee to promiser, of creditor to debtor, of wife to husband, of child to parent, of friend to friend, of fellow countryman to fellow countryman, and the like; and each of these relations is the foundation of a *prima facie* duty, which is more or less incumbent on me according to the circumstances of the case. When I am in a situation, as perhaps I always am, in which more than one of these *prima facie* duties is incumbent on me, what I have to do is to study the situation as fully as I can until I form the considered opinion (it is never more) that in the circumstances one of them is more incumbent than any other; then I am bound to think that to do this *prima facie* duty is my duty *sans phrase* in the situation.

I suggest "*prima facie* duty" or "conditional duty" as a brief way of referring to the characteristic (quite distinct from that of being a duty proper) which an act has, in virtue of being of a certain kind (e.g., the keeping of a promise), of being an act which would be a duty proper if it were not at the same time of another kind which is morally significant. Whether an act is a duty proper or actual duty depends on *all* the morally significant kinds it is an instance of....

There is nothing arbitrary about these *prima facie* duties. Each rests on a definite circumstance which cannot seriously be held to be without moral significance. Of *prima facie* duties I suggest, without claiming completeness or finality for it, the following division.

(1) Some duties rest on previous acts of my own. These duties seem to include two kinds, (*a*) those resting on a promise or what may fairly be called an implicit promise, such as the implicit undertaking not to tell lies which seems to be implied in the act of entering into conversation (at any rate by civilized men), or of writing books that purport to be history and not fiction. These may be called the duties of fidelity. (*b*) Those resting on a previous wrongful act. These may be called the duties of reparation. (2) Some rest on previous acts of other men, i.e., services done by them to me. These my be loosely described as the duties of gratitude. (3) Some rest on the fact or possibility of a distribution of pleasure or happiness (or of the means thereto) which is not in accordance with the merit of the persons concerned; in such cases there arises a duty to upset or prevent such a distribution. These are the duties of justice. (4) Some rest on the mere fact that there are other beings in the world whose condition we can make better in respect of virtue, or of intelligence, or of pleasure. These are the duties of beneficence. (5) Some rest on the fact that we can improve our own condition in respect of virtue or of intelligence. These are the duties of self-improvement. (6) I think that we should distinguish from (4) the duties that may be summed up under the title of "not injuring others." No doubt to injure others is incidentally to fail to do them good; but it seems to me clear that non-maleficence is apprehended as a duty distinct from

that of beneficence, and as a duty of a more stringent character. It will be noticed that this alone among the types of duty has been stated in a negative way. An attempt might no doubt be made to state this duty, like the others, in a positive way. It might be said that it is really the duty to prevent ourselves from acting either from an inclination to harm others or from an inclination to seek our own pleasure, in doing which we should incidentally harm them. But on reflection it seems clear that the primary duty here is the duty not to harm others, this being a duty whether or not we have an inclination that if followed would lead to our harming them; and that when we have such an inclination the primary duty not to harm others gives rise to a consequential duty to resist the inclination. The recognition of this duty of non-maleficence is the first step on the way to the recognition of the duty of beneficence; and that accounts for the prominence of the commands "thou shalt not kill," "thou shalt not commit adultery," "thou shalt not steal," "thou shalt not bear false witness," in so early a code as the Decalogue. But even when we have come to recognize the duty of beneficence, it appears to me that the duty of non-maleficence is recognized as a distinct one, and as *prima facie* more binding. We should not in general consider it justifiable to kill one person in order to keep another alive, or to steal from one in order to give alms to another....

The essential defect of the ... utilitarian theory is that it ignores, or at least does not do full justice to, the highly personal character of duty. If the only duty is to produce the maximum of good, the question who is to have the good—whether it is myself, or my benefactor, or a person to whom I have made a promise to confer that good on him, or a mere fellow man to whom I stand in no such special relation—should make no difference to my having a duty to produce that good. But we are all in fact sure that it makes a vast difference....

... That an act, *qua* fulfilling a promise, or *qua* effecting a just distribution of good, or *qua* returning services rendered, or *qua* promoting the good of others, or *qua* promoting the virtue or insight of the agent, is *prima facie* right, is self-evident; not in the sense that it is evident from the beginning of our lives, or as soon as we attend to the proposition for the first time, but in the sense that when we have reached sufficient mental maturity and have given sufficient attention to the proposition it is evident without any need of proof, or of evidence beyond itself. It is self-evident just as a mathematical axiom, or the validity of a form of inference, is evident. The moral order expressed in these propositions is just as much part of the fundamental nature of the universe (and, we may add, of any possible universe in which there were moral agents at all) as is the spatial or numerical structure expressed in the axioms of geometry or arithmetic. In our confidence that these propositions are true there is involved the same trust in our reason that is involved in our confidence in mathematics; and we should have no justification for trusting it in the latter sphere and distrusting it in the former. In both cases we are dealing with propositions that cannot be proved, but that just as certainly need no proof....

Our judgments about our actual duty in concrete situations have none of the certainty that attaches to our recognition of the general principles of duty. A statement is certain, i.e., is an expression of knowledge, only in one or other of two cases: when it is either self-evident, or a valid conclusion from self-evident premises.

And our judgments about our particular duties have neither of these characters. (1) They are not self-evident. Where a possible act is seen to have two characteristics, in virtue of one of which it is *prima facie* right, and in virtue of the other *prima facie* wrong, we are (I think) well aware that we are not certain whether we ought or ought not to do it; that whether we do it or not, we are taking a moral risk. We come in the long run, after consideration, to think one duty more pressing than the other, but we do not feel certain that it is so. And though we do not always recognize that a possible act has two such characteristics, and though there *may* be cases in which it has not, we are never certain that any particular possible act has not, and therefore never certain that it is right, nor certain that it is wrong. For, to go no further in the analysis, it is enough to point out that any particular act will in all probability in the course of time contribute to the bringing about of good or of evil for many human beings, and thus have a *prima facie* rightness or wrongness of which we know nothing. (2) Again, our judgments about our particular duties are not logical conclusions from self-evident premises. The only possible premises would be the general principles stating their *prima facie* rightness or wrongness *qua* having the different characteristics they do have; and even if we could (as we cannot) apprehend the extent to which an act will tend on the one hand, for example, to bring about advantages for our benefactors, and on the other hand to bring about disadvantages for fellow men who are not our benefactors, there is no principle by which we can draw the conclusion that it is on the whole right or on the whole wrong. In this respect the judgment as to the rightness of a particular act is just like the judgment as to the beauty of a particular natural object or work of art. A poem is, for instance, in respect of certain qualities beautiful and in respect of certain others not beautiful; and our judgment as to the degree of beauty it possesses on the whole is never reached by logical reasoning from the apprehension of its particular beauties or particular defects. Both in this and in the moral case we have more or less probable opinions which are not logically justified conclusions from the general principles that are recognized as self-evident.

There is therefore much truth in the description of the right act as a fortunate act. If we cannot be certain that it is right, it is our good fortune if the act we do is the right act. This consideration does not, however, make the doing of our duty a mere matter of chance. There is a parallel here between the doing of duty and the doing of what will be to our personal advantage. We never *know* what act will in the long run be to our advantage. Yet it is certain that we are more likely in general to secure our advantage if we estimate to the best of our ability the probable tendencies of our actions in this respect, than if we act on caprice. And similarly we are more likely to do our duty if we reflect to the best of our ability on the *prima facie* rightness or wrongness of various possible acts in virtue of the characteristics we perceive them to have, than if we act without reflection. With this greater likelihood we must be content....

In what has preceded, a good deal of use has been made of "what we really think" about moral questions....

...It might be said that this is in principle wrong; that we should not be content to expound what our present moral consciousness tells us but should aim at a criticism of our existing moral consciousness in the light of theory. Now I do not doubt that the moral consciousness of men has in detail undergone a good deal of modification as regards the things we think right, at the hands of moral theory. But … we have to ask ourselves whether we really, when we reflect, *are* convinced that this is self-evident, and whether we really *can* get rid of our view that promise-keeping has a bindingness independent of productiveness of maximum good. In my own experience I find that I cannot, in spite of a very genuine attempt to do so.…

I would maintain, in fact, that what we are apt to describe as "what we think" about moral questions contains a considerable amount that we do not think but know, and that this forms the standard by reference to which the truth of any moral theory has to be tested, instead of having itself to be tested by reference to any theory. I hope that I have in what precedes indicated what in my view these elements of knowledge are that are involved in our ordinary moral consciousness.

It would be a mistake to found a natural science on "what we really think," i.e., on what reasonably thoughtful and well-educated people think about the subjects of the science before they have studied them scientifically. For such opinions are interpretations, and often misinterpretations, of sense-experience; and the man of science must appeal from these to sense-experience itself, which furnishes his real data. In ethics no such appeal is possible. We have no more direct way of access to the facts about rightness and goodness and about what things are right or good, than by thinking about them; the moral convictions of thoughtful and well-educated people are the data of ethics just as sense-perceptions are the data of a natural science. Just as some of the latter have to be rejected as illusory, so have some of the former; but as the latter are rejected only when they are in conflict with other more accurate sense-perceptions, the former are rejected only when they are in conflict with other convictions which stand better the test of reflection. The existing body of moral convictions of the best people is the cumulative product of the moral reflection of many generations, which has developed an extremely delicate power of appreciation of moral distinctions; and this the theorist cannot afford to treat with anything other than the greatest respect. The verdicts of the moral consciousness of the best people are the foundation on which he must build; though he must first compare them with one another and eliminate any contradictions they may contain.

PRINCIPLES OR PARTICULARISM?
David McNaughton

David McNaughton is professor of philosophy at Florida State University and author of Moral Vision *(1988). Ethical particularism takes a skeptical view of the role and importance of moral principles in moral thinking. The particularist claims that we must judge each moral situation individually without the secure guidance of moral*

principles that many philosophers have sought. The particularist is united with the
pluralist in rejecting the claim (by monists) that there is some overarching single
moral principle that can effectively guide moral thinking and decision making. But the
particularist also rejects the pluralist's claim that certain features of actions and situ-
ations are always relevant to the moral assessment of actions. According to the par-
ticularist, then, making moral judgments about specific cases requires that we care-
fully examine the details of the situation and assess the various morally relevant fea-
tures of that situation in deciding what is right and wrong to do.

The Role of Moral Principles

... [T]he particularist is skeptical about the role of moral principles in moral reasoning....

... He believes that we have to judge each particular moral decision on its individual merits; we cannot appeal to general rules to make that decision for us. Moral particularism takes the view that moral principles are at best useless, and at worst a hindrance, in trying to find out which is the right action. What is required is the correct conception of the particular case in hand, with its unique set of properties. There is thus no substitute for a sensitive and detailed examination of each individual case.

Skepticism about the utility of moral principles may seem to strike at the very heart of our conception of morality. The concept of a moral principle appears to play a central, and apparently impregnable, role in our moral thought. To be virtuous is to have acquired, and to live by, a set of good moral principles. Moral education is viewed as the inculcation of the right principles in the young. The suggestion that we can do without moral principles is thus likely to appear unworthy of serious attention. This is certainly the opinion of most of the philosophers who have even bothered to consider the possibility of moral particularism.

The conviction that we cannot manage without moral principles finds its main expression in a concern about how we are to cope when we find ourselves in a new, and perhaps puzzling, situation. We require guidance to help us to do the right thing. What would meet that need for guidance would be a set of tried and tested rules that would enable us to apply what we have learned in the old familiar cases to the new and unfamiliar one. Moral principles appear to fit the bill; they tell us which of the nonmoral features of any situation are morally significant and so enable us to reach the right decision....

The ... source of this conviction ... is found in a strangely compelling picture of what it is to make a reasoned decision. In giving reasons for any decision, I am implicitly appealing to something general, to something that could be applied to other cases. If something is a reason in this case it cannot just be a reason in this case; it must be a reason elsewhere. Since we give reasons for our moral opinions we must, explicitly or implicitly, be appealing to general rules or moral principles. A moral principle is, if you like, a moral reason which has had its generality made explicit. Thus, if the reason this action is wrong is that it would involve telling a lie, then the wrongness of acting like that must somehow carry over into other cases which involve the telling of lies.

When I give reasons for my claim that an action is, say, morally wrong, I appeal to other properties of the action which make it wrong. I may appeal to some of its nonmoral properties—that it caused pain or that it involved the deliberate telling of an untruth—or to some of its "thick" moral properties—that it was ungenerous or cowardly. The latter kind of answer appears, however, only to offer a partial justification of my moral opinion. For I may properly be asked to give reasons for believing that it is ungenerous or cowardly and I shall then have to refer to the nonmoral properties which make it so. So, in giving the full reasons for my belief that the action was wrong, I shall have to give a list of the nonmoral properties that make it wrong. A full justification of my moral views as a whole would thus eventually involve the articulation of all my moral principles, that is, a list of all the nonmoral properties of actions which I believe to be generally morally relevant.

The search for the perfect moral theory might thus be seen as a quest for the best set of moral principles which, if followed, would enable the agent to reach the right decision in any case he may encounter. Such a system would provide a complete, finite, check-list of nonmoral properties which are morally relevant to the rightness or to the wrongness of an action. With the aid of such a check-list the agent could examine any actual or possible action and determine its rightness or wrongness by consulting his list. How long the list should be, just how many moral principles there are, is a matter for debate. The simplest system is, of course, a monistic one, in which only one property is morally relevant and all others may safely be ignored.

A PARTICULARIST RESPONSE

The particularist's objection to this conception of moral reasoning is that what we may want to say about the moral character of a particular action may always outrun any such attempt at codification. We have to be sensitive to the way the features of this individual case come together to determine its moral nature....

He also rejects the conception of reason to which the argument appealed. On that picture, whether or not some nonmoral feature of an action is a reason for its being morally wrong is quite unaffected by the presence or absence of other properties. If the presence of a nonmoral property is a reason for an action's being wrong then, since its being a reason will not be altered one whit by other properties the action may have, whenever an action has that property it will provide a reason for the action's being wrong. The particularist regards this account of reasons as unduly atomistic. It supposes that each reason is insulated from its surroundings so that the effect of each on the rightness or wrongness of the action as a whole can be judged separately. The particularist prefers a holistic account. We cannot judge the effect of the presence of any one feature in isolation from the effect of the others. Whether or not one particular property is morally relevant, and in what way, may depend on the precise nature of the other properties of the action.

To illustrate: I take my nephews and nieces to the circus for a treat. They enjoy it. I have done the right thing. Why? Because I succeeded in giving them pleasure. Because the fact that my action gave pleasure was here the reason for its being right, does it follow that, whenever an action gives pleasure, we shall have reason for thinking it right? No. Consider the following. A government is considering reintroducing hanging, drawing and quartering in public for terrorist murders. If reactions to public hangings in the past are anything to go by a lot of people may enjoy the spectacle. Does that constitute a reason in favor of reintroduction? Is the fact that people would enjoy it here a reason for its being right? It would be perfectly possible to take just the opposite view. The fact that spectators might get a sadistic thrill from the brutal spectacle could be thought to constitute an objection to reintroduction. Whether the fact that an action causes pleasure is a reason for or against doing it is not something that can be settled in isolation from other features of the action. It is only when we know the context in which the pleasure will occur that we are in a position to judge.

In short, the particularist claims that we cannot know, in advance, what contribution any particular nonmoral property will make to the moral nature of an action. We cannot know, in advance, whether it will be morally relevant at all and, if so, whether its presence will count for or against doing the action. The contribution that each property makes will depend on the other properties that go along with it in this case. It follows that there is no way of ruling out, in advance, some nonmoral properties as being morally irrelevant. Any property may be morally relevant. Whether it is so will depend, once again, on the surrounding properties.

Where does the particularist stand in the debate between monism and pluralism? Sometimes that debate is presented as being between those who hold that there is only one fundamental moral principle and those who hold that there is an irreducible plurality of principles....

... [T]he particularist rejects the terms of this debate. The issue is sometimes expressed in terms of morally relevant properties; is there one, or more than one, morally relevant property? In this debate the particularist takes an extreme pluralist position for no property can be ruled out, in advance, as never being relevant to the rightness or wrongness of an action....

... It would provide additional support for particularism if it could be shown that no ideal system of moral principles could deliver what it aspires to: a systematically organized set of moral principles that will tell the agent what to do in any particular case. The crucial test here is the problem of moral conflict.

Moral Conflict

... [O]ur ordinary moral thought appears to be pluralist rather than monist in character. We appeal to a variety of values and moral principles in our moral reasoning, and utilitarian attempts to show that there is just one ultimate value or one basic moral principle were unconvincing. The obvious difficulty facing a pluralist system is the problem of moral conflict. Where there is a plurality of moral principles there is the possibility that more than one might apply to a particular situation and suggest conflicting answers to the question: Which action is the right one?

In Sartre's famous example, a young man in occupied France during the Second World War was torn between loyalty to his sick and widowed mother and loyalty to his country. He felt that he ought to stay at home and look after her but he also believed that he should join the Free French Army. It is characteristic of such a painful conflict that the person facing it takes himself to be under two obligations, which conflict in this particular case, so that he cannot honor both. The problem that faces a pluralist moral theory is to find a method by which such conflicts can be resolved.

The problem of resolving moral conflicts is certainly a difficulty for a pluralist theory but it is not in itself an objection to pluralism. Indeed, since we do experience moral conflicts, it is a strength of pluralism that it makes room for them. For just that reason, a sophisticated monism will not rule them out either, for it will allow that there can be a plurality of subsidiary moral principles between which conflict can occur. It is a strength of monism that it offers a clear method of resolving such disputes; since there is one basic principle from which all the others derive it must be to it that appeal is made in such cases. The weakness of monism is that it cannot explain the anguish that such conflicts often cause. If the clashing principles are merely secondary ones then it is unclear why the agent should be torn between them. He must regard such a conflict as merely an indication that the system of secondary principles, which he has found it useful to construct, does not always deliver a decisive verdict so that he must resort to his basic principle. For him, conflicts should not even be a cause for unease, let alone anguish.

The pluralist, however, should be in a better position to account for that anguish. The agent is under two distinct obligations, each of which has its own claim on him and each of which, perhaps, represents a distinct value which he is called on to foster. In choosing between them he will necessarily fail to honor one moral claim on him and this is what makes the choice painful.

Stressing the difficulty of such choices on a pluralist view serves to emphasize the problem with which we started: How are such conflicts to be resolved? More particularly, what form will such a resolution take? If, in a particular case, there are two independent but conflicting obligations then one of them will have to give if the conflict is to be resolved. Yet how can one of them give if both genuinely apply in this situation?...

MORAL PRINCIPLES AND *PRIMA FACIE* DUTIES

Ross...distinguishes between a *prima facie* duty and a duty proper or an actual duty...An agent has a *prima facie* duty to do or to forbear doing x in a particular situation if a moral principle enjoining or forbidding x applies to that situation. Thus I have a *prima facie* duty not to tell my neighbor that I like her hat, since to do so would be to tell a lie, and there is a moral principle against lying. Where more than one moral principle applies then I will have more than one *prima facie* duty; in cases of moral conflict I will not be able to fulfill all my *prima facie* duties at once. In our example I also have a *prima facie* duty not to offend my neighbor, and I shall necessarily be in breach of one of these *prima facie* duties.

Where only one moral principle applies to my situation then my actual duty— the action that would be the right one in this particular case—is determined by that moral principle. In other words, where I only have one *prima facie* duty, that duty is also my actual duty. In cases where I am under conflicting *prima facie* duties then there is no set rule by which I can determine my actual duty. In each such case I have to examine that particular situation and determine which *prima facie* duty is the most stringent, or carries the greatest weight, in these circumstances. Deciding what to do in a moral conflict is a matter of judgment which cannot be codified. In wondering what to say in response to my neighbor's query I have to weigh the *prima facie* duty not to lie against the *prima facie* duty not to be rude....

... My mastery of a set of moral principles will serve to alert me to the fact that a moral conflict exists in cases such as that of my neighbor's hat, but that is as far as it will carry me. No appeal to moral principles can serve to resolve that conflict—at this point I am on my own.

Ross's theory also makes sense of the thought that, in a moral conflict, the agent is actually under two obligations both of which, in this case, he cannot fulfill. For both *prima facie* obligations do apply to the agent. Although he can fulfill only one of them, that does not make it any less true that the other applies to him. It can be a source of genuine regret that he has to breach one of them even if he knows his decision to be the correct one....

WEIGHING OBLIGATIONS

We saw that Ross did not believe that there was any set rule by which we could judge, where obligations conflict, which is the weightier. Attempts to codify such decisions only reveal the belief that there is some computational procedure by which competing obligations can be precisely weighed—but that is just what Ross and the particularist deny. Such decisions require judgment, and judgment is only possible for someone who has a real insight into the issues involved; it cannot be replicated by the use of a decision procedure which could be grasped by someone who had no appreciation of what was at stake. Yet that is what the original account of moral principles appeared to offer—a set of rules which could be applied by anyone, whatever their sensitivity or experience, to discover the right answer.

Moreover, it is absurd to suppose that there will be a determinate answer, in each particular case, to the question which of two obligations is the weightier. There may be cases where it is impossible to judge. This should not be taken to mean that, in such cases, the two obligations are of exactly equal weight. Nor should it be supposed that there must be an answer in principle but that it is difficult to arrive at it in practice. That would be to revert to the computational model. What it means is that there may be no correct answer or, perhaps better, that the correct answer is: there is no answer. But that does not mean that it does not matter what you do. That realization may increase rather than diminish the anguish of having to choose....

Particularism and Prima Facie Duties

Ross's understanding of the nature of moral principles is the only one that offers a satisfactory account of moral conflict. In such cases it accords well with what the particularist wishes to maintain. It insists that we can only reach a decision in such cases by looking at the features of the particular case in order to judge which *prima facie* duty is the weightier in these, and only in these, circumstances. It denies that moral conflicts can be settled by any mechanical decision procedure that could be applied by anyone whether or not he had insight into the moral issues. Such decisions require judgment and sensitivity.

What Ross offers is not, of course, particularism, since moral principles do play a role. First, we appeal to them in showing that there is a moral conflict to be resolved, and in determining which features are relevant to its resolution. Second, the appeal to them is decisive in cases where only one principle applies in that situation. How do I discover these principles?

According to Ross...we start with the particular case. We realize, say, that this action is wrong and then, perhaps, that it is so because of some particular feature—that it is a case, say, of telling a lie. Through our experience of particular cases of this kind we are enabled to grasp the *general* truth, that lying is what we might call a wrong-making characteristic. As we have already seen, that does not mean that any action which involves lying is actually wrong, for there may by other, right-making, characteristics of the action which outweigh this wrong-making characteristic on this occasion. Lying is a wrong-making characteristic in that the fact that something is a lie is—*always* a reason against doing it. The fact that some course of action involved telling a lie could never be a morally neutral characteristic of the action, still less a reason in favor of doing it.

The particularist denies that we can generalize from the particular case. We cannot know, in advance, that some nonmoral characteristic must be relevant in all cases and always in the same way. The particularist can learn from Ross's hostility to a computational approach to solving moral conflicts, but he is unconvinced by his generalism.

It is important to distinguish three different positions here. First, there is Ross's view that if a characteristic matters in one place it must matter everywhere. Second, there is the weaker view that there must be at least some characteristics which always matter, even if there are others which only matter sometimes. The particularist rejects these positions. Third, there is the much weaker view that there *may* be some characteristics which, as a matter of fact, always count in the same way. The particularist need have no quarrel with this position.

Moral Principles in Ordinary Life

At the beginning of this chapter I suggested that skepticism about the utility of moral principles not only undermined a certain kind of moral theory but also appeared at odds with our ordinary moral thinking. Since that skepticism turned out to be almost wholly justified it seems that the particularist has some explaining to do. He needs to show that his theory does not unduly distort our moral thinking.

It turned out, however, that the particularist's skepticism was not about anything that might be called a moral principle, but only about what we might call the check-list conception of what a moral principle is. There may, however, be kinds of moral principle to which the particularist would have no objection. If it turns out that it is to these kinds of principles that people appeal in ordinary life, then particularism can embrace them.

It is, in my view, quite difficult to determine just what moral principles are widely accepted in our society, since the role of moral principles is a good deal more talked about than illustrated. A number of the sayings to which people subscribe, some of them with a biblical basis, are quite general in their purport and themselves require interpretation and moral sensitivity to be applied: "honor your father and mother"; love your neighbor as yourself"; "be true to yourself." The purpose of such remarks appear to be to serve to indicate areas of general moral concern, leaving us to work out how, or if, they may have a bearing on any particular case.

In order to know, for example, whether a child's action is genuinely a case of honoring its parents we need to look at all the details of the case. Take the case of the Eskimos who, it is said, used to leave old people to die on the ice once they had become too old to hunt or to make a contribution to the welfare of the tribes in other ways. At first glance such an action appears callous and uncaring in the extreme. But more knowledge of the context can completely reverse that initial impression. When this practice flourished euthanasia was essential for the survival of the tribe as a whole. This was generally recognized and accepted by everyone, including the aged parents themselves, who would initiate the chain of events leading to their own death. I understand that a father would tell his son that he wished to go on one last hunting trip; they would go out together, kill a seal, and eat it. After they had talked for a while and said their farewells, the father would tell his son to go home, while he would stretch out on the ice and wait for death. The son's part in this ritual appears to be an example of honoring one's parents.

The particularist need find nothing objectionable in an appeal to such principles. In order to see whether they truly apply we have to look at each case in all its lived detail. Nor is appeal to such a principle decisive. For the principle only gestures toward one area of moral concern; there are others.

The need for precise moral principles is most clearly seen, it is said, in the teaching of children. Even this is doubtful. The role of moral principles in the proper education of the young can easily be exaggerated. Moral lessons are not usually taught by instilling a list of principles into the child's mind. Rather, when the child does something, or witnesses some action, the parent draws attention to the morally important features of this particular action. But let it be admitted that we do teach simple moral principles to children, such as "don't steal," and that we often pretend that they are exceptionless. Does this undermine the particularist case? Not in the least. It is often necessary, in matters of prudence as well as morality, to issue blanket rules for the good of the child—"*Never* talk to strangers." It does not follow that, when they grow up, they cannot throw away the leading strings of moral principles and learn to find their own way.

But why, it might be objected, teach them moral principles in the first place if it is better, in the end, if they dispense with them? Because they are useful at the time. When people are learning to write essays they are taught rudimentary rules of style. Later they come to realize that there is no rule of style that has not been broken by some writer to considerable effect. They could not have started without stylistic guidelines of any kind—rules which are, for the most part, acceptable. As their sense of prose rhythm develops they gradually dispense with them. In the end, if they are not discarded, they prove a hindrance to good writing. And so it may be with moral principles.

MORAL PARTICULARISM: WRONG AND BAD
Brad Hooker

Brad Hooker (see page 106 for biography) is critical of moral particularism—the view, as we saw in the previous selection, which claims that whether and how a property of an action is morally relevant depends on circumstances. Hooker argues that moral particularism is wrong because, contrary to what the moral particularist claims, there are general features of properties of actions that are always morally relevant and always count either in favor of or against the morality of an action. Second, he argues that moral particularism is bad because of the negative effects its acceptance would have on society.

In this paper, I focus on the view I think is most often meant by the title 'moral particularism'. This view is held by some of the most morally admirable people I know. Yet, as I shall explain, I think the view is wrong. I shall also argue that, whether or not it is wrong, the view would be a bad one for society to accept.

What Is Moral Particularism?

Particularism holds that whether any property of actions counts morally in favor of actions that have it depends always on the circumstances. Likewise, particularism holds that whether any property counts morally against actions that have it depends always on the circumstances. The moral polarity of any property depends on the circumstances, according to particularism. In other words, particularism holds that there are no properties that, whenever they occur, must always be moral pluses, and no properties that, whenever they occur, must always be moral minuses. On this view, any feature of an act that counts as a moral plus in one context may not count as a moral plus in another context.

Sometimes particularism is claimed to be the more modest view that at least some properties can have variant moral polarity depending on the circumstances. But if particularism is going to be worth discussing, it cannot be that modest view. Of course there are many features of actions whose moral polarity depends on the circumstances. That an act would help someone achieve her aims is a moral plus (or at least neutral) if her aims are neither immoral nor imprudent. But the fact

From Brad Hooker, "Moral Particularism: Wrong and Bad," *Moral Particularism*, Brad Hooker and Margaret Little, eds. (Oxford: Clarendon Press, 2000). Reprinted by permission of the publisher.

that an act would help someone achieve her aims would count as a moral minus if her aims were immoral. Let us then take particularism to be the radical and controversial view that there are no features of actions that always have invariant moral polarity.

What has come to be called moral generalism is simply the denial of particularism. So generalism holds that there is at least one feature or property of actions that always counts morally in favor of actions having that feature. Such properties are often featured in moral principles. Some versions of generalism are monistic. Monistic versions of generalism hold that there is only one property that is of fundamental moral relevance and always counts as a moral plus. One example of monistic moral generalism is the view that an act is morally permissible if and only if it is something the agent would want done to him. Another example is the view that an act is morally permissible if and only if it maximizes expected value, impartially considered. Another example is the view that an act is morally permissible if and only if it is allowed by rules that no one could reasonably reject as the basis for informed unforced general agreement. Yet another example is the view that an act is morally permissible if and only if it is allowed by the set of moral rules whose internalization by the overwhelming majority of everyone would produce the greatest expected benefit.

According to pluralistic forms of generalism, morality is composed of an irreducible plurality of principles that do not come in a *strict* order of priority.[1] (This form of generalism can, and should, hold that there are some rough priorities, on which I shall say more later.)

What general principles might be suggested here? One excellent candidate is a general principle against physically harming others except when necessary to defend either others or ourselves from physical harm. Another is a general principle against stealing or destroying others' property, breaking our promises, and lying. Yet another is a principle about giving special weight in our decisions (about the allocation of our own resources) to the welfare of those with whom we have special connections. Some principle about generally helping others also appears, as do principles about promoting justice, being grateful to one's benefactors, and making reparation to those whom one has wronged.[2]

Suppose we now have a list of such general principles. According to this version of pluralist generalism, whether an act is morally permissible depends on the interaction of all these principles.[3] Let me call this form of generalism *Rossian generalism*.

Rossian generalism maintains that these various principles about harming others, stealing or destroying others' property, breaking one's promises, and so on cannot themselves be usefully conjoined together to make one long principle. If all the various principles came in a strict order of priority, then really there would be just one multi-faceted, hierarchical principle. It could take the following general form.

Never do A; never do B unless necessary to avoid doing A; never do C unless necessary to avoid doing A or B; never do D unless necessary to avoid doing A, B, or C; never do E unless necessary to avoid doing A, B, C, or D; etc.

In holding that general moral considerations do not come in a strict order of priority, Rossian generalists hold that none is necessarily always overriding. Rather, each is capable of being overridden by the others. In just this sense, general moral duties (general moral considerations) are in Ross's terminology "prima facie".[4] Perhaps a better term is "pro tanto" (i.e., 'to that extent'). For example, a pro tanto duty to keep your promises is a duty to do certain things *to the extent that* they would constitute keeping your promises; the duty to keep your promises is not necessarily an 'all things considered duty'. The general idea is that a pro tanto duty or consideration is overridable in more or less extreme conditions.

Rossian generalists do subscribe to the general principle that one should always do what the balance or mix of moral considerations demands in the case. But such a general principle is hardly unique to the kind of generalism now under discussion. Nor is such a principle informative. A principle about which moral considerations override the others would be informative.

But Rossian generalism denies that any *general* consideration that is informative must always be overriding in determining right from wrong. This may need qualification. For perhaps we can think of some general moral reason that overrides whenever it appears. Consider, for example, the strength of the moral reason to refuse to do any act that would eliminate forever all consciousness in the universe (except where this really is the only way to prevent an eternity of universal misery). I cannot see what could outweigh this reason. But let me set aside this special case.

Rossian generalism implies agents will need to weigh moral reasons against one another. Rossian generalism thus maintains that there is an ineliminable role for *judgement* in order to resolve some conflicts between moral considerations. There will also of course be questions of *interpretation*. Interpretation is needed sometimes to ascertain whether an act would constitute breaking a promise, or whether an act would constitute destroying property, or stealing, or lying, or whether an event would make someone worse off, or whether someone's connection to you entitles her to special weight in your practical reasoning.

Rossian generalism hardly tells us that the details of cases are always unimportant. On the contrary, Rossian generalism holds that the details of the case can be crucial to the question of which generally important moral properties are instantiated. Furthermore, which of the instantiated properties is most important can depend on the details in the case. But, according to Rossian generalism, there are some properties that always count the same way whenever they occur.

Counterexamples to Particularism?

Is particularism refuted by counterexamples—that is, by general properties that always count morally in favour of an action, or by general properties that always count morally against? Consider the property of producing pleasure. One familiar idea is that the presence of this property counts in favour of any act that has it. If this idea is right, we have at least one counterexample to particularism.

However, particularists point out that, while the property of producing pleasure makes an act better in some circumstances, this property makes an act worse in other circumstances. That an act would give pleasure to the sadist is not merely an overridden positive feature of the act. Rather, sadistic pleasure actually makes the act morally worse than it would be if it didn't afford sadistic pleasure. As David McNaughton and Jonathan Dancy comment, the pleasure people get from watching executions makes letting them watch morally worse.[5]

I do not see how particularism can win on this battlefield. Rossian generalists try to ascertain a generally good-making property. Particularists then acknowledge that the property mentioned does often make acts morally better. But particularists go on to point to a context in which the property described counts against rather than for an action. At this point, Rossian generalists have two obvious options.

One is to stick to the line that (for example) producing pleasure is always a pro tanto moral plus, even if the pleasure comes to a wicked and undeserving person. Another is to start making distinctions. For example, there may be a distinction between *benefit to a person* and *moral value*. Thus sadistic pleasure might constitute some benefit to the sadist even if it has no *moral* value, indeed even if it has *moral disvalue*.

Many philosophers would say that not just the moral but also the self-interested benefit of pleasure depends on its source. Pleasure based on the truth might constitute a greater self-interested benefit than does pleasure based on illusion. And pleasures accompanying more complex true beliefs or more complex achievements might constitute greater self-interested benefits than pleasures derived from simpler beliefs and simpler achievements.

We might nevertheless hold that even the most base or vindictive pleasure constitutes *some* benefit to the agent. This is why we think that the pleasure that the wicked gets is an unjust benefit to him. Even the wrong kind of pleasure constitutes some benefit to the agent.

But the *moral* status of pleasure depends on, among other things, what kind of pleasure it is. Non-sadistic pleasure is always a moral plus. Sadistic pleasure, even where a *self-interested* plus, is always a *moral* minus. Moral pluses and minuses might be outweighed by other moral considerations. Thus, all things considered, an act can be impermissible although it gives someone non-sadistic pleasure. Likewise, all things considered, an act can be permissible although it gives someone sadistic pleasure. Nevertheless, the moral polarity of sadistic and of non-sadistic pleasures never changes.

If (but not only if) we can run the above line, particularism is in trouble. For if we can run this line, then we can point to at least one general property—i.e. 'would produce non-sadistic pleasure'—that always counts on the same moral side. When we point this out, we point to an informative general principle in normative ethics.

It is tempting to hold that sadistic pleasure is never a moral plus. But that tempting thought might be too hasty. I do not pretend to confidence about this matter. What I am confident of is that generalists are right to say that at least all non-sadistic pleasure is a moral plus.

Other Counterexamples to Particularism

As this discussion about benefiting others and promoting justice suggests, giving others non-sadistic pleasure is not the only thing that always counts as a moral plus. The fact that an act would benefit others, even if not by bringing them non-sadistic pleasure, always counts as a moral reason to do it. This reason can be overridden by other moral reasons. But it is a moral reason always anyway.

Likewise with promoting justice. How could the fact that an act would promote justice ever be anything less than a pro tanto moral plus? Again, justice may not be always overridingly important. But, where it is at stake, it always counts on the same side.

Now consider promise breaking. Does the fact that some act constitutes my breaking a promise count always on the same moral side? Perhaps centuries ago promise breaking was considered always a moral evil (even if sometimes less of an evil than the alternatives). Our modern understanding of promising, however, usually takes certain kinds of promises to carry no moral force. For example, morality exerts no pressure on agents to keep immoral promises. An immoral promise is a promise to offend against one's other obligations. So it would be a promise to physically harm someone, to steal, to destroy others' property, to break another promise to someone else, to promote injustice, or to ignore one's special responsibilities for those to whom one has special connections.

Our modern understanding of promising also dismisses promises that were made under certain conditions. Promises obtained under coercion or deception are without force. As Judith Jarvis Thomson writes, 'anyone who thinks a word-giving whose source is coercion or fraud does nevertheless give a claim [a claim right to the person who was promised] is excessively respectful of what goes on in a word-giving.'[6]

Let me summarize the main points about promise keeping. We have to be careful to state our principle about promise keeping. And we must admit that promises are not always the most important moral consideration in play, not even if they are important promises.[7] Still, we can state a general principle about promising: The fact that an act would involve keeping a morally permissible promise that was elicited from you without coercion or deception always counts morally in favour of your doing the act.

Now take stealing. Clearly, stealing is a moral minus. Yet there can be circumstances in which it is nevertheless justified. Suppose stealing someone's change is the only way I can call an ambulance. I'm stealing the change, not borrowing it, because I have no idea whose it is, and will never be able to find out. Although stealing in such circumstances is morally right, the stealing as such has not become morally neutral, much less morally positive. Rather, it is a moral minus, though heavily outweighed by the other considerations in play in this situation.

Breaking promises to others and stealing or destroying their property are normally harmful to them, but not always. Furthermore, of course there are many ways to harm others other than stealing from them or breaking promises to them. Hence the need for an independent principle against harming others. But is harming others always a moral minus? Is harming the guilty as part of justified punishment any moral minus at all? Is harming someone in self-defense any moral minus? What about in the defense of innocent others? What about harming someone even when this is not part of one's ends or means? What about harming others with their consent? What about harming their interests simply by outperforming them in some morally permissible competition?

As before, generalists have two obvious options here. One is to stick to the simpler line that, yes, harming others is always a pro tanto moral minus. In many cases, this minus is outweighted by opposing moral pluses. These might be the pluses of channeling disapproval of and deterring crime, or of protecting the innocent, or of respecting others' autonomy, or of fostering the goods that come out of competition.

The generalists' other option is to fine-tune their principle about harm. It might become 'there is a pro tanto duty not to harm others except in the course of justified punishment, or of protecting the innocent, or of respecting their informed wishes, or of pursuing morally legitimate competition.' Whichever option generalists take, they can think that their principle about harm gives them another weapon with which to beat particularism.

Particularism About the Content of Evaluative Concepts

Suppose generalists propose that the general property of producing *innocent* pleasure is always a moral plus. The particularist replies that we will not be able to set out in purely naturalistic terms what counts as innocent. Particularists could take the same line with respect to justice. They might say that we cannot specify in purely naturalistic terms what counts as just.

The first point I want to make about this line of thought is that there certainly are at least some principles linking entirely natural properties to pro tanto duties. For example, that an act would bring about the involuntary death of a self-conscious human being who is not threatening others' physical security is always a moral minus. Perhaps we do not even need the qualification 'who is not threatening others' physical security'. For perhaps bringing about the involuntary death of a self-conscious human *always* has something morally against it, though this consideration is often outweighed when that person threatens others' physical security.

Furthermore, I think we should hope to find some principles picking out natural properties. For to the extent that questions of justice and rights are not tied down by concrete terminology—indeed, by the use of terms with at least fairly clear naturalistic truth conditions—people can have difficulty forming stable expectations. I shall come back to this.

Even if naturalism loses out to a particularism about evaluative concepts like 'innocent' and 'just', the problem with defining particularism as the doctrine that these concepts cannot be naturalistically specified is that this definition classifies as particularist many who took themselves to be anti-particularists. Take, for example, those consequentialists who think the good is not just pleasure but also significant achievement, important knowledge, and the appreciation of true beauty, and who admit that we cannot naturalistically define significant achievement or important knowledge or true beauty. Although such consequentialists might tie the right directly or indirectly to the good, they do not think the good can be defined or described in purely naturalistic terms. Yet such consequentialists become particularists on the definition of particularism now on the table. It cannot be right to offer a definition of particularism that renders this sort of consequentialist as a particularist.

Particularism Versus the Value of Predictability

One of the things a shared commitment to morality needs to do is provide people with some assurance that others won't attack them, rob from them, break promises to them, or lie to them. Providing people with such assurance is of course one of law's most important functions. Ideally, perhaps, people's moral commitments would be adequate to provide this assurance, without the reinforcement of legal sanctions. But realistically we recognize the need for legal sanctions to protect persons and property from others, and to enforce contracts.[8] Yet there are some things which both (a) we want people's moral commitments to ensure that they do and (b) we do not want law to get involved with. An example may be that it is desirable for morality to pressure people to keep their spoken promises to their spouses, but we don't want the law to poke its big nose into such matters (though written contracts between spouses certainly should be legally enforceable). And even where law should and does stick in its nose, widespread internalization of moral restrictions is clearly needed. For knowing that others have certain firm moral dispositions can give us added assurance how they will behave.

Now if shared commitment to morality should, among other things, create settled expectations about how others will behave, how does particularism look? Imagine we knew of other people only that they were committed moral particularists. This is all we know of them—the particularist content of their moral view and their strong moral commitment to live by it. Would we have enough confidence that they'd virtually never attack us, rob from us, break their promises to us, etc.?

Some of my best friends think of themselves as moral particularists. These people are as dependable as anyone could reasonably desire. If one of them made a promise to me, I would certainly trust it. Experience has taught me these particular people are trustworthy. Is this empirical confirmation that moral particularism does provide enough assurance about how believers in it will behave?

But what morality people espouse and even think they follow might not be the morality they really follow. Think how common is the specter of someone who espouses kindness and sincerely thinks of himself as kind but is really uncaring, vindictive, ruthless, and so on. Since 'actions speak louder than words', if people who call themselves particularists act reliably and consistently in ways that accord with Rossian generalism, I may certainly have good reason to think they won't attack me, steal from me, break promises to me, or lie to me. My experience with them gives me good grounds for predicting their future behaviour. In fact, I may mostly ignore their own reports of their moral beliefs. I may think that these people are sincerely describing what they think they believe, but that they may be mistaken.

What we need to answer my question about particularism and reliable expectations is not merely someone who thinks of himself or herself as a particularist. What we need to consider is someone whom others think of as consistent with his or her particularist ethics. Suppose Patty is such a person. All you know of her is that she really does live by her particularist beliefs.

Now imagine that you can strike a deal with Patty. She asks you to help her get in her crop now in return for her promising to help you get yours in next month. Half her crop will spoil if you don't help her. This would drive her to bankruptcy. That is why she is willing to promise to help you later in return for your helping her now. Likewise, you must have help with your crop later if you are to avoid going bankrupt yourself. That is why she thinks you might be willing to accept the deal she proposes.

Suppose you have no direct or indirect experience of Patty. Nor do you have time to ask others how trustworthy she is. All you have to go on is her self-description as a particularist.

If you had some means of forcing her to keep her side of the deal, then you wouldn't need to rely on her moral attitudes to make her do it. You would have the means to force her to keep her side if you could bring in legal sanctions—e.g., by suing her if she doesn't keep her side. Or you might be able to prove to the world she is unreliable if she doesn't keep her side, and this would cost her more than would her keeping her side of her deal with you.

But suppose neither the threat of legal sanctions nor the threat of ruining her reputation would be enough next month to get her to keep her side of the deal. That is, suppose legal enforcement mechanisms and reputational effects are for some reason ineffective here. Assume that the only thing that could possibly make her keep her promise is her moral outlook. Assume there is no doubt about the strength of her moral motivation. She is completely committed to behaving morally, according to her moral outlook. The question is only whether her moral outlook, if consistently particularist, gives you enough assurance now.

As a particularist, Patty thinks that there are no considerations that always retain their moral polarity. She thinks a consideration (e.g., the fact that she promised to do something) might be a reason for keeping her side of the deal in one situation, but a reason against keeping it in another situation. So, will she think that having made a promise to you gives her any reason to do what she promised?

Not necessarily. As a particularist, she might attach no weight whatsoever to the promise when the time comes to keep it. And, as a particularist, she can't point to any general considerations that mark off the situations in which a promise would be morally binding from the situations in which it wouldn't. As a particularist, she also thinks that any fact can be morally relevant, depending on the circumstances. So she thinks any fact could conceivably interfere with the moral status and force of the promise. If Patty would really live by such beliefs, how much could you trust her?

We might think that someone would have to misunderstand the very nature of a promise in order to think that an informed uncoerced promise whose content is reasonable could lack moral force. We might also think that an ineliminable part of being trustworthy is being disposed to attach weight to every one of one's promises as long as they were informed, uncoerced, and had reasonable contents. If this claim about the concept 'trustworthy' is right, then a true particularist cannot meet the necessary conditions for being trustworthy.

Rather than rely on this conceptual argument against trusting the particularist, I want to point to a practical argument. How much trust would you put in the particularist Patty in my example? Would you trust her enough to make the deal with her? If the answer is no, then you would both be worse off than if you made the deal and then both kept their sides of it. But if you knew nothing of her except the information specified, you would have little assurance that you could predict how she would behave.

I myself think this is an extremely important argument against particularism. Of course, if the example about promise keeping is correct, the point generalizes to other moral considerations. If philosophers accept that there are general pro tanto duties, they are not particularists. If they are particularists, they think that the fact that some adult human beings have neither killed nor threatened others nor asked to be killed themselves need not be any moral reason to avoid killing them. Particularists will think that no moral reason for action always emerges from the fact that some property is owned by others, or from the fact that a statement would be a lie, or from the fact that some act would promote justice or relieve undeserved suffering. How safe would you feel in a society of people who lived by these beliefs?

Particularists might try to defend their view by pointing out that Rossian generalism is not absolutist. Absolutist generalism about promise breaking, in contrast, holds that promise breaking could absolutely never be morally permissible. Rossian generalism gives promises only pro tanto force. In other words, Rossian generalism holds that promise-breaking is always a moral minus but can sometimes be permissible, or even morally required, if there are important moral reasons on the side of breaking the promise. Then particularists might claim that, in order to trust Rossian generalists, we would need to trust their exercise of moral judgement about when to keep a promise. If we can rely on Rossian generalists to exercise good moral judgement about when to keep promises (particularists might retort) then we can likewise rely on particularists.

Let us compare our particularist Patty with a Rossian generalist, Gerry. Gerry believes that physically harming others is a serious moral minus, and that stealing or destroying others' property, promise breaking, and lying are moral minuses. He also believes that promoting justice, helping others, and expressing gratitude are moral pluses. But he believes each of these considerations can be overridden. Just like Patty, Gerry promises you that, if you help him get his crop in this week, he will help you with yours next month. You can make a deal either with Gerry or with Patty but not with both. As is the case with respect to Patty, you cannot depend on either law enforcement or concern about reputation to get Gerry to keep a promise to you. As with Patty, the only thing that might make him keep his promise is morality. You know what morality he is committed to, including which general principles he subscribes to, but you have not had experience with him before and can't ask others how he behaves. In sum, as is the case with respect to the particularist Patty, the moral convictions of our generalist Gerry are the only thing that could induce him to keep his promise, and his morality is the only thing you know about him.

You know Gerry subscribes to the general principle that promise-breaking is always a moral minus, unless the promise is extracted by means of coercion or deliberate deception, or is itself an immoral promise. None of these general defeating conditions obtains in the case at hand. So Gerry would hold that breaking his promise to you is a moral minus.

Admittedly, Gerry does not think that breaking his promise to you would necessarily be, all things considered, wrong. He is not an absolutist about the wrongness of promise breaking. He admits that, in certain circumstances, he should and would break his promise to you even though your financial ruin would result. In particular, he would break his promise if necessary to save the life or limb of anyone for whom he has special responsibility (because of some very special connection he has with this person). So Gerry would break his promise if necessary to save the life or limb of his parent, or family member, or friend. He would not break his promise to you, in order to work for Oxfam for the week (though this predictably would prevent more suffering and loss). For he believes the people whom Oxfam aims to rescue are not ones for which he has any special responsibility.

So, to decide whether you should depend upon Gerry, what you'd need to know is the probability of his deciding he has to break his promise in order to protect the life or limb of someone for whom he has special responsibility. Now we should admit, I think, that it isn't exactly clear for whom Gerry thinks he has special responsibility. And even with respect to someone who falls squarely within the circle, it isn't exactly clear how high the risk to that person's life or limb would have to be in order to induce Gerry to abandon his promise for the sake of protecting this person. A one-in-a-million risk is obviously too little. A one-in-two risk is obviously enough. But where is the threshold between too little risk to justify breaking the promise and enough risk to justify breaking it?

For all that, you have vastly less to worry about with the generalist Gerry than with the particularist Patty. First, Gerry necessarily attaches some moral weight to the promise; Patty does not necessarily attach any moral weight to the promise. Second, there are only a very limited number of facts that might interfere with Gerry's deciding to keep his promise. Admittedly, these facts may require interpretation and the exercise of judgement. Still, there are reasonably clear limits with Gerry. But with Patty, any fact can become pivotal to whether she will take her having promised as any moral reason at all for her to do what she promised. Given these points, and given the limited information you have about the Rossian generalist Gerry and the particularist Patty, clearly you should think Gerry would be more likely to keep his promise to you than Patty would.

Let me be clear that the argument above does not beg the question against particularism by assuming the particularist is going to make more moral mistakes than the Rossian generalist. My argument was that, whether or not particularism is likely to lead agents to make moral mistakes, the Rossian generalist seems in the circumstances more likely than the particularist to keep the promise.

I am not assuming that, because particularism is mistaken, someone trying to follow it will be less trustworthy than someone following some other theory. My argument that someone trying to follow particularism will be less trustworthy than someone following a different theory does not rely on the premise that particularism is mistaken. On the contrary, let us make the entirely non-question-begging assumption that Rossian generalism and particularism are initially equally plausible. My argument is that, given this non-question-begging assumption, particularism loses to Rossian generalism in that collective public commitment to Rossian generalism would lead to considerably more trust amongst strangers than would collective public commitment to particularism.

The example about promising generalizes. You know of generalists that they take certain general features to count morally in the same way every time they occur. You know of generalists that they point to a limited number of general features that can count as moral considerations, and thus can outweigh any one moral consideration. Neither of these things is true of particularists. By saying they reject general moral principles, particularists leave us unable to form confident expectations about what they will do. Here I am ignoring the special case where we observe some self-described particularist who is always behaving consistently and thus we discount this person's rejection of general principles.

Let me address one final possible objection to my argument. This is the objection that the truth about morality is one thing, and what would result from our believing that others believe that truth is another matter. According to this objection, a view such as particularism might be right—even if the consequences of its acceptance, and of public awareness of its acceptance, would be bad. This objection seems to me an overgeneralization.

True, belief in the best moral view could have bad consequences because of interference from some evil demon. To take a simple example, the demon might rain misery on the world if this moral view is believed. Concerning this sort of special case, we might reasonably hold the correctness of the moral view immune from contamination by the bad consequences of believing it.

But in the everyday world where demons aren't trying to bully people into rejecting some moral view, a moral view does seem unattractive if widespread awareness of its widespread acceptance would have very bad net effects on human well-being. And that is just what I think is the case with particularism.

Notes

This is an abridged version of a paper with the same title in *Moral Particularism*, Brad Hooker and Margaret Little (eds) (Oxford: Clarendon Press, 2000). Thanks go to Mark Timmons for help with the abridgement. I am also grateful to Jamie Ball, Emma Borg, John Broome, Roger Crisp, Jonathan Dancy, John Gardner, Berys Gaut, Peter Goldie, James Griffin, Dudley Knowles, Gerald Lang, Jimmy Lenman, Richard Norman, Derek Parfit, Philip Percival, John Preston, Geoffrey Sayre-McCord, John Skorupski, Tom Sorell, Philip Stratton-Lake, Elizabeth Tefler, Alan Thomas, Jay Wallace, Peter Vallentyne, James Williams, and Nick Zangwill.

1. See W. D. Ross, *The Right and the Good* (Oxford: Oxford University Press, 1930), ch. 2.
2. If a duty of self-improvement is added, this list looks much like Ross's (*The Right and the Good*, p. 21). I think a duty of self-improvement should not be added; there should instead be some qualification about how much one is required to sacrifice for others. See my 'Intuitions and Moral Theorizing', in P. Stratton-Lake (ed.), *Ethical Intuitionism: Re-evaluations* (Oxford: Clarendon Press, 2002, pp. 161–83).
3. For important complexities about how these principles interact, see Shelly Kagan, 'The Additive Fallacy', *Ethics* 99 (1988): 5–31.
4. Ross, *The Right and the Good*, pp. 22, 34–35; 1939, p. 79.
5. David McNaughton, *Moral Vision* (Blackwell, 1988), p. 193; Jonathan Dancy, *Moral Reasons* (Blackwell, 1993), p. 61.
6. Thomson, *The Realm of Rights* (Cambridge, MA: Harvard University Press, 1990), p. 311.
7. I will discuss a case in point later in this paper.
8. See H. L. A. Hart's classic discussion in his *The Concept of Law* (Oxford: Clarendon Press, 1961), pp. 189–95, esp. 193–5.